Roberto Esposito

Roberto Esposito: Law, Community and the Political provides a critical legal introduction to this increasingly influential Italian theorist's work, by focusing on Esposito's reconceptualisation of the relationship between law, community and the political. The analysis concentrates primarily on Esposito's *Catégories de l'Impolitique*, *Communitas*, *Immunitas* and *Bíos*, which, it is argued, are animated by an abiding concern with the position of critique in relation to the tradition of modern and contemporary legal and political philosophy.

Esposito's fundamental rethinking of these notions breaks with the existing framework of political and legal philosophy, through the critique of its underlying presuppositions. And, in the process, Esposito rethinks the very form of critique. As the first monograph-length study of Esposito in English, *Roberto Esposito: Law, Community and the Political* will be of considerable interest to those working in the areas of contemporary legal and political thought and philosophy.

Peter Langford is Senior Lecturer in Law at Edge Hill University, UK.

Nomikoi: Critical Legal Thinkers

Series editors:
Peter Goodrich
Cardozo School of Law, New York
David Seymour
School of Law, City University, UK

Nomikoi: Critical Legal Thinkers presents analyses of key critical theorists whose thinking on law has contributed significantly to the development of the new interdisciplinary legal studies. Addressing those who have most influenced legal thought and thought about law, the aim of the series is to bring legal scholarship, the social sciences and the humanities into closer dialogue.

Other titles in the series

Judith Butler: Ethics, Law, Politics
Elena Loizidou

Evgeny Pashukanis: A Critical Appraisal
Michael Head

Giorgio Agamben: Power, Law and the Uses of Criticism
Thanos Zartaloudis

Niklas Luhmann: Law, Justice, Society
Andreas Philippopoulos-Mihalopoulos

Henri Lefebvre: Critical Legal Studies and the Politics of Space
Chris Butler

Carl Schmitt: Law as Politics, Ideology and Strategic Myth
Michael Salter

Althusser and Law
Edited by Laurent de Sutter

Deleuze & Guattari: Emergent Law
Jamie Murray

Bruno Latour: The Normativity of Networks
Kyle McGee

Zizek and Law
Edited by Laurent de Sutter

Roberto Esposito: Law, Community and the Political
Peter Langford

Roberto Esposito

Law, Community and the Political

Peter Langford

a GlassHouse Book

First published 2015
by Routledge
2 Park Square, Milton Park, Abingdon, Oxon, OX14 4RN

and by Routledge
711 Third Avenue, New York, NY 10017

a GlassHouse Book

Routledge is an imprint of the Taylor & Francis Group, an informa business

© 2015 Peter Langford

The right of Peter Langford to be identified as author of this work has
been asserted by him in accordance with sections 77 and 78 of the
Copyright, Designs and Patents Act 1988.

All rights reserved. No part of this book may be reprinted or
reproduced or utilised in any form or by any electronic, mechanical, or
other means, now known or hereafter invented, including photocopying
and recording, or in any information storage or retrieval system, without
permission in writing from the publishers.

Trademark notice: Product or corporate names may be trademarks or
registered trademarks, and are used only for identification and
explanation without intent to infringe.

British Library Cataloguing in Publication Data
A catalogue record for this book is available from the British Library

Library of Congress Cataloging-in-Publication Data
A catalog record for this book has been requested

ISBN: 978-0-415-67351-8 (hbk)
ISBN: 978-0-203-79835-5 (ebk)

Typeset in Times New Roman by
Florence Production Ltd, Stoodleigh, Devon, UK

To my father
and
in memory of my mother

Contents

Acknowledgements	ix
Introduction	1
1 Rethinking community and law as genealogy: the mode of critique in *Catégories de l'Impolitique*	**10**

Genealogy and secularisation 11
Hobbes, Schmitt, Weber 14
The place of law 17
The question of the subject 18

2 *Catégories de l'Impolitique* **I: from the closure of political theology to the negativism of Canetti**	**20**

The unpolitical as political theology: Guardini
    and Schmitt 21
Beyond political theology: the unpolitical from
    Voegelin to Arendt 26
The unpolitical as the thinking of the negative: from Broch
    to Canetti 37

3 *Catégories de l'Impolitique* **II: from the negative anthropology of Canetti to the negative community of Bataille**	**46**

The other Canetti: beyond the confines of negative
    anthropology 47
Simone Weil: from negative anthropology to heterodox
    theology 48
Georges Bataille: the experience of the negative as the
    experience of community 56

viii Contents

4 From the unpolitical to *Communitas*   68

5 *Communitas*   78

The installation of the modern immunitary paradigm:
   Hobbes's fear 79
The questioning of the modern immunitary paradigm:
   Rousseau's guilt 84
The recognition of Communitas: Kant's law 87
Beyond law to coexistence: Heidegger's Communitas 93
The experience of non-knowledge: Bataille's Communitas 99

6 From *Communitas* to *Immunitas*   103

7 *Immunitas*   110

Law 110
Theology 118
Philosophical anthropology 126
Biopolitics 133
Common immunity 138

**8 From *Immunitas* to *Bíos*: the outline of an affirmative
biopolitics**   141

9 *Bíos* I: rethinking biopolitics – from Foucault to Nietzsche   148

The limits of Foucauldian biopolitics 148
Thinking with Foucault beyond Foucault: biopolitics and
   immunisation 156
The biopolitics of first modernity 160
The return to Nietzsche 166

10 *Bíos* II: towards an affirmative biopolitics   173

National Socialism: biopolitics as thanatopolitics 174
An affirmative biopolitics: the philosophy of Bíos 181

Conclusion   197

Bibliography   210
Index   229

Acknowledgements

I would like to thank the Commissioning Editor, Dr Colin Perrin, for his support for this contribution to the Nomikoi Critical Legal Thinkers Series, and my Editorial Assistant, Rebekah Jenkins, for all her assistance and help during the preparation and submission of the manuscript. I am very grateful to Professor Roberto Esposito, for his willingness, at a very busy period in his own schedule, at the Italian Institute for the Human Sciences, in Naples, to meet and discuss certain of the initial aspects of the project, and for his very generous provision of relevant materials. I would also like to acknowledge and thank all my friends for their interest and encouragement in this project. Finally, I would like to thank my father, to whom this book is dedicated, for his empathetic presence throughout this book project.

All translations from the French versions of Roberto Esposito's work in this text are my own, with acknowledgement to the original Italian editions. Many thanks to Il Mulino, Editions du Seuil, Polity Press, Einaudi and University of Minnesota Press for their kind permission for the use of material from *Catégories de l'Impolitique*, *Immunitas* and *Bíos* in this book.

Introduction

The pertinence, for critical legal thought,[1] of the work of Roberto Esposito arises from the distinctive reflection upon the notions of law, community and the political. The form of reflection is characterised by a critical distance and detachment from modern legal and political thought. From this initial position, a renewed engagement emerges with the notions of law, community and the political beyond this tradition of legal and political thought. The contours of this form of reflection, as critical legal thought, are rendered more concrete by tracing the notions of law, community and the political through four of Esposito's texts. These four texts – *Catégories de l'Impolitique*,[2] *Communitas: The Origin and Destiny of Community*,[3] *Immunitas: The Protection and Negation of Life*[4] and *Bíos: Biopolitics and Philosophy*[5] – form the essential corpus of the book's analysis. The conclusion then extends the final considerations of *Bíos* through certain aspects of *Third Person*[6] and *Living Thought*.[7]

The analysis commences with *Catégories de l'Impolitique*,[8] which marks both a break with Esposito's previous work and the determination of a 'non-place' from which reflection arises. The 'non-place' is the unpolitical; and the consideration of this 'non-place', as a thought of the negative, establishes an initial path for Esposito's further philosophical work. The increasing divergence from the unpolitical, in the three later texts, expresses the particular character of theoretical reflection in Esposito's work. Each text is both the determination of a critical apparatus and the openness of this apparatus to further reorientation. The circular

---

1 For alternative accounts of Esposito's work, see: Amendola (2012); Calabrò (2012); and Campbell (2011), ch. 2.
2 Esposito (2005).
3 Esposito (2010).
4 Esposito (2011).
5 Esposito (2008).
6 Esposito (2012b).
7 Esposito (2012c).
8 An English translation of this text is forthcoming from Fordham University Press. See Esposito (2009) for an English translation of the Preface. All translations from the French version are my own.

2 Roberto Esposito: Law, Community and the Political

pattern is essential to a form of reflection which understands itself to be situated historically. From this historical understanding, the relation between thinking, as reflection, and truth is then provided with its distinctive shape. The placing into question, effected by reflection, is both negation and affirmation, critique and reconstruction. Hence, truth is the revelation of a limit of thought and its attendant effects, and, in this revelation, the outline of a different path or possibility for thought.

The relation between thought and truth situates Esposito's form of reflection beyond the confines of the 'self-understanding of jurists',[9] as it is not prompted by an exclusive consideration of the relationship between law and morality. The juristic form of reflection, and, within it, the primacy accorded to either law (positivism) or morality (non-positivism), are displaced by interrogating the self-understanding from which it arises. The effect of the unpolitical is to comprehend the self-understanding of jurists as an aspect of a closed, fully determined tradition of political and legal thought.

The notion of the unpolitical opens thought to this 'non-place', an 'originary void', which is co-extensive with the political, as the origin of the concepts of politics and law. Reflection on the political 'does nothing but "remind" the political of its finitude': '[i]t postulates no coercive order capable of transposing that substantial negative into another, more powerful representative form'.[10] The insistence upon the finitude of the political is the coincidence of the political with 'its own bare being-such' – '[i]ts potential is only what it is'.[11] The site or position of the unpolitical, as one of critique, 'does not "critique" reality in the name of something other than reality – some different ideal, value, or interest'.[12] The unpolitical is 'the problem of origin – which the Modern neither discovers nor produces, but is limited to conceptualizing in an ever more conscious way'.[13] The problem remains constitutive of the unpolitical as 'the border of the political, that from which it springs and which it bears "eternally" within itself as its immanent transcendental'.[14] The unpolitical reveals the traditional space of critique, as one of closure, through its dissolution of the problem of origin into 'the pattern of contrastive succession that assigns either an emancipatory or a degenerative history to the political (or rather, gives each in compensation for the other)'.[15]

The 'return' to the concepts of political and legal thought, in *Catégories de l'Impolitique*, is made through recourse to the work of Simone Weil and Georges Bataille. The passage from Weil to Bataille relinquishes legal thought in order to conceive community as the being-in-common of human finitude. The notion of

---

9 Alexy (2008): 283.
10 Ibid., 104, 105.
11 Ibid., 104.
12 Ibid., 109.
13 Ibid., 110.
14 Ibid., 109.
15 Ibid., 109.

Introduction   3

community is essentially negative – a being-in-common which simply subsists as the experience of human finitude. In this experience, the notion of community 'is the truly extreme figure of the unpolitical: uncommunicable, irreducible to a common *site*'.[16] Community, as the exposure to this 'originary void', results in the shared experience of its formlessness, and the notion of community is transformed from one of representation to one of a 'destiny'.[17] Bataille's *Chronique nietzschéenne*,[18] in the figure of the tragedy of the mass suicide of the Numantines, exemplifies this destiny. The unpolitical, as the destiny of the category of community,[19] thereby excludes the notions of the political and law.

The position of *Catégories de l'Impolitique* is significantly modified in *Communitas*. The analytic of finitude which shapes the negative thought of *Catégories de l'Impolitique* is displaced by reflection upon the single notion of community within modern legal and political thought. The notion of community is interrogated by the tracing of its etymology to its Latin root, which reveals the 'origin' of community as a composite term, *communitas*, containing within it the term *munus*. The specific character of *communitas* shifts the 'origin' of community to a being-in-common which has the form of an originary exposure to that which is outside the individual: the shift from finitude to alterity.

The originary exposure, contained in the term *munus*, constitutes the being-in-common of *communitas*, through a notion of the gift, whose character is itself established in the contrast between *munus* and *donum*.[20]*Munus*, as the primary term, has the sense of an absolute obligation which precedes the individual. It is from this absolute obligation – 'the transitive act of giving' – that the secondary relationships of exchange, contained in the term *donum*, arise.[21] Being-in-common is determined, through etymological analysis, by a thought of the negative: the exposure to an absolute obligation is the experience of 'common non-belonging'.[22]

The 'origin' of community, as being-in-common, reveals the co-belonging of nihilism and community.[23] The deficient mode of comprehension of community, by both contemporary Anglo-American communitarianism and the work of Jürgen Habermas and Karl-Otto Apel,[24] then becomes evident in their opposition of nihilism and community. The opposition, in Anglo-American communitarianism, derives from the nihilistic drift of 'modernity's individualistic-universalistic model' which 'generates new communitarian forms as a posthumous reaction to

---

16   Esposito (2005): 238 (emphasis in original).
17   Ibid., 239.
18   Bataille (1970g).
19   For a similar position, though derived from Esposito's appropriation of Weil's critique of law, see Amendola (2012): 104–7.
20   Esposito (2010): 4–5.
21   Ibid., 5.
22   Ibid., 7.
23   Ibid., 139.
24   At present, Esposito's work contains no detailed, sustained engagement with either Anglo-American communitarianism or Habermas and Apel.

4 Roberto Esposito: Law, Community and the Political

its own entropy'.[25] This, in turn, creates the 'reciprocal exclusion that community enjoys with nihilism. The community advances or retreats; it expands or it contracts according to the space that the other has not yet "colonized"'.[26] The 'limitless communication community' of Habermas and Apel, contains the opposition as 'both the point of resistance and the reserve of meaning with respect to the progressive intrusiveness of technology'.[27] The 'limitless communication community' becomes 'the demarcating line and defence against the advance of nihilism; something replete (it could be a substance, a promise, a value) that does not allow itself to be emptied out by the vortex of nullity'.[28] The opposition between nihilism and community derives from a conception of community, as the extension and development of subjectivity,[29] which encompasses both the 'need to appropriate what is common to us' and the need to 'communicate what is most properly our own'.[30] The essential circularity and closure of subjectivity or inter-subjectivity within community represents the impasse of this thought of community.

Reflection upon the etymological 'origin' of community then proceeds to a genealogy of the destiny of this 'origin'. Modern political and legal thought is presented as the explicit thematisation and 'resolution' of the co-belonging of nihilism and community. Hobbes, through the nihilism of the state of nature,[31] is the exemplary 'resolution' of this 'origin', which 'establishes the erasure of *communitas* in favour of a political form [the Leviathan] founded on the voiding of every external relation in favour of a vertical one between individuals and sovereigns and therefore on their dissociation'.[32]

The 'nihilistic character' of the Hobbesian 'resolution' determines the further genealogical progression of reflection.[33] The work of Rousseau and Kant exemplifies the attempt by political philosophy, in Rousseau's semantics of 'guilt' and in the 'Kantian one of "law"', to reintroduce 'the question of community'.[34] The progression from 'the anthropological level of will [Rousseau] to that of the transcendental level of law [Kant]'[35] represents a certain return of the notion of law within Esposito's work. The law arises from the categorical imperative which contains the absolute character of obligation.[36] Yet, this thematisation of law, through the work of Kant, remains the limit, within political philosophy, of the thought of community.

25 Ibid., 136.
26 Ibid., 136.
27 Ibid., 136.
28 Ibid., 136.
29 Ibid., 2.
30 Ibid., 2.
31 Ibid., 13.
32 Ibid., 141.
33 Ibid., 14.
34 Ibid., 15.
35 Ibid., 17.
36 Ibid., 17.

Introduction 5

Heidegger displaces the absolute obligation of law by a more originary 'origin' which arises immediately from 'coexistence'. In this displacement, coexistence, as community, 'is neither promised nor to be disclosed beforehand, neither presupposed nor predetermined'.[37] The possibility that Heidegger opens for the exposition of *communitas* is, for Esposito, continually interrupted by 'a return to myth'.[38] This extends, beyond its most direct political expression in the identification of 'the *munus* within the horizon of the proper, and indeed of the property, of a single [German] people',[39] to the determination of the later interpretation of the common homelessness of Hölderlin.

These limits lead to the final genealogical stage centred upon Bataille's 'superimposition between anthropology and ontology'.[40] In this superimposition, being-in-common becomes 'the continuum into which every existence that has broken through its individual walls falls'.[41] The continuum expresses 'the common *munus*, in which the continuous is one with what is discontinuous, as is being with non-being'.[42] In relation to this thought of the *munus*, and of community, the concluding reflections of *Catégories de l'Impolitique*, on death and sacrifice, are now situated as the limit of Bataille's thought. The presentation of this final limit, in *Communitas*, becomes the impetus for further reflection.

Esposito is then led to reconsider the opposite Latin term to *communitas* of *immunitas*. The term *immunitas*, in *Communitas*, is the etymological origin of the exemption from the absolute obligation of *munus*. The 'sharing of a burden, office, task' is that from which *immunitas*, in the form of a specific dispensation, creates an individual 'who is instead "exempt" or "exempted"'.[43] This original sense of *immunitas* is rendered more complex, in *Immunitas: The Protection and Negation of Life*, by the inclusion of immunity in the biomedical sciences. The sense of immunity is transformed 'from natural to acquired immunity . . . from an essentially passive condition to one that it is actively induced'.[44] This is then the shift in the object of reflection to that of life and, within it, the antinomy of 'exclusionary inclusion'.[45]

The antinomy 'constitutes and reconstitutes community precisely by negating it';[46] and this framework of exclusionary inclusion is held to inhere in the modern disciplines of 'law, theology, anthropology, politics, and biology'.[47] Each discipline, through its framework of exclusionary inclusion, creates an increasing

37 Ibid., 18.
38 Ibid., 18.
39 Ibid., 18.
40 Ibid., 147.
41 Ibid., 147.
42 Ibid., 147.
43 Ibid., 6.
44 Esposito (2011): 7.
45 Ibid., 8.
46 Ibid., 9.
47 Ibid., 9.

6 Roberto Esposito: Law, Community and the Political

negative tendency which ends in its internal 'dissolution'.[48] The self-dissolution of an underlying framework, which 'juxtaposes and connects immunity and community', is presented genealogically, through 'a series of figures', until the presentation reaches the final 'figure' of biology.[49]

The genealogy presents law as the first 'figure' whose tendency towards self-dissolution is traced through the initial contours of legal exclusionary inclusion. This antinomic distinction between community and immunity creates a protected legal space from an outside which continually threatens it. The antinomy, between violence and law, emerges through 'immunizing the community from the violence that threatens it' and, thereby, incorporates and perpetuates violence in 'the immunitary procedures' of law.[50]

Within the system of legal relationships, the common is redefined as a 'claim to what is one's own'.[51] The 'inherently private, privative, nature of all law' has, as its necessary corollary, 'recourse to force, which constitutes both the transcendental precondition and the guarantee of its effectiveness'.[52] The reproduction of a 'shared life', through legal immunitary procedures,[53] is the exclusion of 'its free development'.[54] The protection of life, by law, through the prohibition of 'all acts that may contradict life' is an essentially 'anticipatory position, with the result that life is both protected and prejudged'.[55]

The self-dissolution of the 'figure' of legal exclusionary inclusion – the inherence of violence in law – appears to be overturned by the redefinition of immunity in Luhmann.[56] Law ceases to be traversed by this antinomy because, 'as a system of social communication that arose out of differentiation from a larger system', it 'can neither influence nor be influenced by society'.[57] Law, as a specific sub-system which expresses the relationship between system and environment, replaces the notions of order and conflict with communication and immunisation. Law facilitates communication with the environment, and this facilitation is immunisation: the creation of stability.

For Esposito, the passage to systems theory becomes the transition from the negative to the positive 'reappropriation of the common'.[58] The initial 'figure' of legal exclusionary inclusion had sought, in constant opposition to an outside, to create a space of 'common' legal relationships. This negative relationship to the common is replaced, in systems theory, with the effective self-dissolution of the

---

48 Ibid., 9.
49 Ibid., 9.
50 Ibid., 9–10.
51 Ibid., 10.
52 Ibid., 10.
53 Ibid., 10.
54 Ibid., 10.
55 Ibid., 10.
56 Ibid., 45.
57 Ibid., 45.
58 Ibid., 50.

Introduction   7

common into the relationship between communication and immunisation: social systems and their environments.

The self-dissolution of the 'figure' of legal exclusionary inclusion leaves the insistent question of the containment of the negative. This question animates the genealogical presentation of the 'figures' of theology and philosophical anthropology before reaching that of politics. Within the 'figure' of politics, the notion of the political, as the origin of politics and its associated institutional apparatuses, is situated in the 'absolute immediacy' of life.[59] The 'biopolitical apparatus', following the specific relation between life and politics of Foucauldian biopolitics, constitutes 'life as an object of direct intervention'; and, by reducing life to 'its nude biological content',[60] produces a form of exclusionary inclusion. Esposito, through the historical genesis and development of the 'metaphor of the body politic',[61] supplements the Foucauldian transition from the paradigm of sovereignty to that of biopolitical governance. The transition becomes the intersection of legal and biomedical discourse, and biopolitical governance is characterised by 'the passage from the sovereign order of the law to disciplinary order of the norm'.[62] The norm, however, maintains the immunitary form of exclusionary inclusion,[63] as it reproduces the 'negative connection . . . between the singularity of living being and the preservation of life: the conditions of preservation, or reproduction, of life are located outside and before the living being's natural line of development'.[64] The self-dissolution of this 'figure' of political exclusionary inclusion concludes the genealogical mode of presentation of immunity as 'a simple logic of negation'.[65]

The possibility of a different relationship between community and immunity centres on the shift to the biomedical 'figure' of immunity. In this analysis, immunity is 'a contradiction' in which 'identity is simultaneously affirmed and altered',[66] and is situated 'in a nonexcluding relation with its common opposite' – community.[67] The common, as the root of community, returns as 'a shared individuality or a sharing of individuality'.[68] The relationship between community and immunity, the inherence of community within immunity, is conceived as an originary bioethics. *Immunitas*, thus, indicates the outlines of an affirmative biopolitics whose further development will be undertaken in *Bíos*.

The prefiguration, in *Immunitas*, is significantly reworked and developed in *Bíos*. The notions of law, the political and community are reintroduced through

59   Ibid., 14.
60   Ibid., 14.
61   Ibid., 15.
62   Ibid., 141–2.
63   Ibid., 142.
64   Ibid., 142.
65   Ibid., 177.
66   Ibid., 177.
67   Ibid., 17.
68   Ibid., 17.

8   Roberto Esposito: Law, Community and the Political

a sustained critique of the theoretical framework of Foucauldian biopolitics. Esposito identifies two opposed logics – a politics of life and a politics of death – and an absence of the delineation of their relationship. These two logics are reconfigured by situating them within the immunitary paradigm of exclusionary inclusion. *Bíos*, therefore, introduces a 'structural connection between modernity and immunization'.[69]

The notions of law, the political and community re-emerge within biopolitics as the relationship between modernity and immunisation. The distinctiveness of modernity is that the 'question of immunity' is 'identified not only and simply as given, but as both a problem and a strategic option'.[70] The 'political categories of modernity' – sovereignty, property and liberty – create the conceptual and institutional framework for the mediation of politics and life. In first modernity, these categories function as an immunitary paradigm of exclusionary inclusion: the protection and preservation of life through 'the same powers that interdict its development'.[71] Law is present in a role which assists and reinforces the immunitary logic of each of these categories, which Esposito traces through the work of Hobbes (sovereignty), Locke (property) and Bentham (liberty). The immunitary purpose attributed to the political and law detaches the notion of community from that which is common, and reduces it to the effect of this immunitary purpose.

The transition from first to second modernity finds its exemplary reflection, for Esposito, in the work of Nietzsche, which occupies the contradictory middle-position between 'the exhaustion of modern political categories and the consequent disclosing of a new horizon of sense'.[72] In Nietzsche, there is an unstable combination of an affirmative biopolitics and a negative, immunitary biopolitics. Second modernity represents the extreme simplification of Nietzschean biopolitics as the wholly negative biopolitics – the thanatopolitics – of National Socialism.[73]

The collapse of National Socialism is, for Esposito, a fundamental break which cannot be adequately grasped, or responded to, by any simple return to modern political and legal thought. Rather, the originary bioethics, prefigured in *Immunitas*, becomes the alternative position from which to re-interrogate the three central elements of National Socialist biopolitics (the '*normativization of life*, the *double enclosure of the body* and the *preemptive suppression of birth*').[74] It is through this re-interrogation that the outlines of an affirmative biopolitics, and its associated notions of law, the political and community, are provided with their initial articulation.

---

69   Esposito (2008): 51.
70   Ibid., 54.
71   Ibid., 56.
72   Ibid., 78.
73   For Esposito, the transition is not to be understood through the category of totalitarianism. See Esposito (2013a).
74   Esposito (2008): 157.

The preliminary articulations of *Bíos* are then extended through the pertinent aspects of the later works of *Third Person*[75] and *Living Thought*.[76] In this presentation, Esposito's work is held to offer a distinct conception of juridical analysis beyond the parameters of the predominant self-understanding of jurists.

75 Esposito (2012b).
76 Esposito (2012c).

Chapter 1

Rethinking community and law as genealogy

The mode of critique in *Catégories de l'Impolitique*

The *Catégories de l'Impolitique*[1] undertakes a critique of political philosophy from a position which is explicitly characterised as that of the 'unpolitical'.[2] The text elucidates this position, and the categories through which it is to be grasped, by a critique of specific theories,[3] whose concepts articulate the political categories of modernity. Each of these theories is held to view these political categories as a language of representation, and the exposition of the critique demonstrates the failure of this language. From this demonstration, the critique proceeds to open onto the possibility of the 'unpolitical'.

The delimitation of the critique, by the political categories of modernity, indicates the explicitly historical position of this critique. The capacity to articulate itself is recognised to flow not from the strength and rigour of its methodological detachment from this history, but from a rethinking of its connection to this history. The rethinking involves the transformation of this history, through the reinterpretation of the notions of the limit and the end. The political categories of modernity are regarded as having achieved the fullest and final expression of the language of representation. It is at the point of this achievement – the limit and end of the language of representation – that the position of the 'unpolitical' is situated. This position, while acknowledging its origin within this history, differentiates itself from a simple determination by, or a continuation of, this history. It marks its definitive interruption – a boundary – whose demarcation differentiates the political categories of modernity from the categories of the 'unpolitical'.

---

1 Esposito (2005). This is an abridged French translation, of the Italian original, *Categorie dell' impolitico* (Bolognia : Il Mulino, 1988). All references are to the French version, and all translations from the French are mine.

2 The choice of 'unpolitical', rather than 'impolitical', as the English translation of the French '*impolitique*' and the Italian '*impolitico*', rests on the potential for 'impolitical' to gain its sense from 'impolitic'; and follows the decision of the English translation of Massimo Cacciari (Cacciari (2009a, 2009b)), whose essays share affinities with Esposito's book, to entitle the book, *The Unpolitical: On the Radical Critique of Political Reason*.

3 The term 'theories', rather than 'philosophies', reflects Esposito's lack of delimitation of philosophy from literature. Hence, the central place accorded to both the philosophical and literary work of Broch and Canetti.

The critique, in its demarcation of this boundary, proceeds by an engagement with these specific theories of the political categories of modernity. The exposition of each of these theories reveals the incapacity of their political categories of modernity to resolve the question of representation. It is their constitutive failure which marks the presence of this limit and end of the political categories of modernity. Each of these theories, apart from that of Bataille,[4] remains, as a theory of representation, located at this boundary.

Genealogy and secularisation

The form, through which *Catégories de l'Impolitique* constructs its critique, is a combination of a genealogy and a notion of secularisation. The association of these elements indicates that the influence of Nietzsche's thought[5] upon Esposito's mode of critique is tempered by its intertwining with a historical process of secularisation.

The Nietzschean notion of genealogy, as it is developed in the *Genealogy of Morality*,[6] seeks to produce a definitive break with all previous forms of genealogical analysis, which utilised this form of analysis to reaffirm contemporary ideals and values, through the revelation of an origin from which they arose and evolved. These ideals and values are, for Nietzsche, to be understood as appearances, whose genesis and truth is occluded by an analysis which strives to articulate their connection to an ultimate, stable foundation. A genealogy which does not have this effect of occlusion commences from a rethinking of this notion of origin and its relationship to ideals and appearances as values.

The origin, located in the subject, as a fundamentally mobile and complex assortment of drives and instincts, is profoundly unstable. It is characterised by an inexhaustible potentiality which renders any unification among these drives and instincts, such as that provided by the instincts for self-preservation and pleasure, one which simply furnishes a more distinct direction to the expression of these drives and instincts. The fluidity of this origin then renders its relation

---

4   For Esposito, Bataille's work constitutes a passage beyond the boundary: 'the final stage of our voyage and at the same time the final stage in the determination of category of the unpolitical' (Esposito (2005): 19).

5   The critical exposition, in *Catégories de l'Impolitique*, engages indirectly with Nietzsche, through his influence on the theories of Broch (from within 'this triangle of "strong" thought constituted by the three most terrible texts of contemporary political philosophy: Benjamin's *The Critique of Violence*, Freud's *Totem and Taboo* and the whole of the work of Nietzsche' (ibid., 15)); Canetti (from 'his predilection for the language of the "great enemies", these great "negative" thinkers – essentially Hobbes, de Maistre and Nietzsche – who *like* him, though, at the same time, *against* him, exclude all affirmative "flight" before the macabre visage of the analysed reality' (ibid., 128–9)) and Bataille (from 'a reading of Nietzsche which constitutes the line along which the unpolitical of Bataille simultaneously determines and reverses itself' (ibid., 20)). This marks a significant difference from the direct and explicit engagement with Nietzsche in *Communitas* and *Bíos*.

6   Nietzsche (2006a).

12   Roberto Esposito: Law, Community and the Political

with appearances, namely, the passage to its expression in the form of ideals and values, one which is characterised by its malleability. In place of the origin which confers stability and truth on the meaning of ideals and values, Nietzschean genealogy identifies a source from which ideals and values arise. The point at which these ideals and values arise, as appearances, initiates a history which can only be the expression of an origin which at once determines and exceeds them. Ideals and values are derived from this source, but can never represent the full and complete expression of this origin. However, these ideals and values, while necessarily partial expressions of this origin, are accorded the capacity to orientate human action.

Here, the notion of genealogy reveals its connectedness to the earlier writings of Nietzsche, in particular, *Truth and Lies in an Non-Moral Sense*,[7] in which a more general theory of language as metaphor is elaborated.[8] Language is, at root, a means of designating things with sounds. This capacity for designation, for Nietzsche, distinguishes man from animals, and, within man, enables an opening onto an active sharing of meaning. These designations are metaphorical, because they have no necessary connection to the things that they designate: they are an act of human will and not an ability of things to give expression to themselves in language. From this separation between sound and thing – the metaphorical character of language – arises the essentially arbitrary nature of designation. The arbitrary nature of this designation undergoes a historical transformation to the extent that language becomes systematised, and a particular set or combination of metaphors imposes itself as the accepted manner in which things are to be designated. The primary location of the arbitrariness of language passes from the individual human's capacity to designate things with sounds to the imposition of a particular manner of designating the totality of things in the world. This is the stage at which ideals and values, as appearances, emerge and attain the ability to direct and shape human action and understanding.

It is Nietzsche's earlier and more general theory of language which informs Esposito's genealogical approach in the *Catégories de l'Impolitique*. The political language of modernity is viewed as a language of representation, and representation is viewed as essentially metaphorical. It is the manner in which the community designates itself to itself by presenting, to the individuals who compose it, the value or ideal which it expresses. This process of representation designates the meaning of the community in a form in which its expression is intended to guide and regulate the interaction among the individuals who compose it.

The concentration upon the political categories of modernity displaces the particular position and description accorded by Nietzsche to Christianity in the *Genealogy of Morals* and, with this, Esposito disconnects this genealogical

---

7   Nietzsche (2006b): 116ff.

8   The presentation follows Vattimo (2002): 27–42. See also Stegmaier (2006), for the further periodisation of Nietzsche's thought from one of metaphors to that of signs.

approach from a theory of nihilism.[9] This displacement is accompanied by the incorporation of a history of secularisation which, in place of a theory of nihilism, involves the political categories of modernity in a process of disenchantment.

This process of disenchantment, for Esposito, arises at the moment of the separation of the political from politics,[10] and initiates a history of their differentiation into two distinct realms or fields. The moment of this separation is articulated in the political philosophy of Hobbes,[11] in particular, the *Leviathan*,[12] which Esposito views as marking the passage between two regimes of political representation. The passage is between that of the regime of the representation-image and the regime of the representation-mandate.

The regime of the representation-image, which characterises the political categories of the pre-modern period, takes the form of a hierarchical unity. Within this, the political and politics are elements held together by a vertical link, created by the representation-image, which ensures that politics is governed by the political.[13] The regime of the representation-mandate, which characterises the political categories of the modern period, severs this vertical link and, with it, initiates the '"de-formalisation" of the *ancient res publica Christiania*'.[14]

The 'de-formalisation' is the secularisation of the political categories and the regime of political representation of modernity. The relation between individuals is freed from 'the personal obligations and hierarchies of the pre-modern order',[15] and is transformed into one based upon 'multiple and diverse interests'.[16] The transformation expresses both the disconnection of the political from politics and the constitution of individual interest as the only basis upon which the possibility of community can arise. The political, if it is to exist, can only be derived from an essential relation to politics.

9   A connection developed further, by Nietzsche, in *Beyond Good and Evil*, *The Antichrist* and *Twilight of the Idols*. For an alternative articulation of the notions of critique, genealogy, secularisation and nihilism, see Vattimo (1988). For the influence of the concept of nihilism on contemporary Italian philosophy, see D'Agostino (2005), developed further in D'Agostino (2009).

10 These two terms translate the French terms *le politique* (the political) and *la politique* (politics), which express distinct understandings of, and rationales for, the relationships between individuals. The political (*le politique*) defines that which is common to individuals – their community. Politics (*la politique*) defines the relationship between individuals generated solely by the effects of interest, force and conflict.

11 Hobbes, in constrast to *Communitas*, receives no direct or explicit attention in *Catégories de l'Impolitique*.

12 Hobbes (1998).

13 For Esposito, the vertical link ensures that politics is constantly informed by 'reference to a transcendant alterity which was both the formative *virtus* of the political and its ultimate *telos*' (Esposito (2005): 7).

14 Ibid., 10.

15 Ibid., 11.

16 Ibid., 11.

14 Roberto Esposito: Law, Community and the Political

For Esposito, the 'solution' of the *Leviathan* is the social contract in which the political is introduced into politics through a new regime of representation. The political is constituted by the interest, immanent in each individual, in a community generated from a social contract. The social contract, however, cannot represent an image of the individuals who have become parties to it. Rather, it marks the passage to the internal differentiation of the community into the sovereign and the individuals subject to the sovereign's authority. It is this internal differentiation, between the representative (the sovereign) and the represented (the individuals as subjects), which now forms the new regime of representation (the representation-mandate).

The social contract is the constitution of a 'civil order' guaranteed by the authority of the sovereign. Its civil character is distinguished, by its 'civility', from both the perpetual conflict in the state of nature and the political – the realm of the sovereign's authority. The 'civil order' merely provides a framework through which these individual interests are regulated: the boundary between conflict and competition. The political, in the form of the social contract, can only guarantee a formal unity – the background conditions – through which individuals interact on the basis of interest: a set of techniques or organisational practices which maintain these background conditions of the 'civil order'.

Hobbes, Schmitt, Weber

Esposito's notion of secularisation involves a double displacement of the notion in the work of Max Weber. The first displacement is produced by commencing *Catégories de l'Impolitique* with the critique of the theory of Carl Schmitt. In this critique, Esposito, while rejecting the possibility of Schmitt's 'political theology', accepts Schmitt's characterisation of modernity to which this 'political theology' seeks to respond.

Esposito's critique, interlaced with that of a critique of Guardini, derives essentially from an engagement with Schmitt's *Political Romanticism*,[17] *Roman Catholicism and Political Form*,[18] *Political Theology. Four Chapters on the Concept of Sovereignty*[19] and *The Concept of the Political*.[20] From within these four texts, *Roman Catholicism and Political Form* is regarded as 'a type of pre-text [*pré-texte*] or key'[21] to Schmitt's thought. The designation of these texts' centrality is combined with an acceptance of their characterisation of modernity's intertwinement with a process of secularisation.

The presentation which *Roman Catholicism and Political Form* offers of this intertwinement is Schmitt's particular appropriation of Weber's notion of secular-

17 Schmitt (1986).
18 Schmitt (1996a).
19 Schmitt (2006).
20 Schmitt (2007).
21 Esposito (2005), 5.

isation. In this appropriation, Schmitt, who substitutes the term 'neutralisation' for 'secularisation', commences from Weber's sociology of action[22] – the combination of the predictability and the objectivisation of human action – to describe a process of historical evolution in which social institutions and realms of social action become dominated by an instrumental or purposive-rational form of rationality. This form of rationality, once embedded – objectivised – in social institutions, becomes a generalised technical rationality limited to the unending process of balancing the means and ends of particular realms of social action. Modernity is the development of this historical process which reaches its end or limit with the complete generalisation of this technical rationality over all realms of social action.

For Schmitt, this historical process results in the 'neutralisation' of the political by the dominance of purposive-rationality. The political becomes the objectivisation of purposive-rationality in the social institutions which form the background conditions for maintenance of the differentiated realms of politics, law and the economy.[23]

It is the question of these background conditions, however, which leads Esposito to effect a further displacement of Schmitt's position through a different characterisation of the position of Hobbes in this historical process of 'neutralisation' as 'secularisation'. For Esposito, in direct opposition to Schmitt,[24] regards Hobbes as the point at which the process of 'neutralisation-secularisation' arises. The separation of the political from politics, and their subsequent differentiation into separate realms, is that which organises and structures the text of Hobbes's *Leviathan*.

This further displacement produces a political origin, as a point of historical transition and development, for this process of 'neutralisation-secularisation', which is itself Schmitt's particular appropriation of Weber. This, in turn, enables Esposito to re-characterise or rethink the historical process of 'neutralisation-secularisation'.[25] The historical process of Weber and Schmitt is rendered more complex by the revelation of an internal contradiction or aporia within it.

---

22 See, Löwith, in *Max Weber and Karl Marx*, who emphasises that this sociology of action is itself guided by the aim of clarification of the present (Löwith (1993): 51–2).

23 For Esposito, '[i]t is this that Schmitt exposes in his essay [*Roman Catholicism and Political Form*], whose fundamental object is the institutional depoliticisation characteristic of modernity or, more exactly, the thesis according to which this depoliticisation is determined by the refusal of 'representation' in a form which connects the political decision to the 'idea' or, in other terms, as such which permits a passage between the Good and power' (Esposito (2005): 6).

24 This opposition only becomes explicit after *Roman Catholicism and Political Form*, namely, in *The Leviathan in the State Theory of Thomas Hobbes: Meaning and Failure of a Symbol* (German original 1938), and the article of 1965, 'Die vollendete Reformation' (Schmitt (1965, 1996b)). However, both Esposito, and Colliot-Thélène (1999), would argue for a fundamental continuity in Schmitt's position from *Roman Catholicism and Political Form* such that the later works are effectively the 'working through' of its essential problematic.

25 'My discourse commences, one could say, there where that of Schmitt finishes: at its exterior' (ibid., 5).

The unfolding of the process of 'neutralisation-secularisation' which, for Esposito, arises from the separation of the political and politics, while initiating the development of the autonomous realms of politics, law and economy, simultaneously creates the requirement for the representation of their unity. The plurality, resulting from these autonomous realms, is combined with the demand for its representation: the 'need of a determinate consciousness of its proper functioning'.[26] This combination creates the internal contradiction or aporia, which Esposito defines as the 'hyper-political'.[27]

The 'hyper-political' manifests itself distinctly in each of the differentiated realms of politics, law and the economy. In the realm of the economy, its autonomy arises from the separation of the political and politics, but it is not itself capable of maintaining and reproducing this autonomy. It needs both 'a force (political) capable of instituting and conserving the general conditions within which it can function',[28] and an objectivised knowledge which presents, in a unified form, the manner in which it functions. In the realm of law, the autonomy of law and the juridical apparatus, flowing from the separation of the political and politics, develops through a process of positivisation. This process, as the 'neutralisation-secularisation' of law, manifests this internal contradiction through law's detachment from a theological origin (natural law) which is combined with a demand that it 'must present itself, in order to have effective value, as universal, immutable and transcendent'.[29] In the realm of politics, the internal contradiction is contained in the regime of representation itself – the representation-mandate – and its expression of the relationship between the State (the political) and civil society (politics). The State, through the process of 'neutralisation-secularisation', is 'emptied of all political substance'[30] and, in parallel with this, the pre-modern political unity collapses 'into different powers and their contractual neutralisation'.[31] The level of contractual neutralisation is, at the level of civil society, incapable of generating and representing unity to the individuals within it. It requires a political form in which these individuals, and their interaction in the form of competition and 'contractual' negotiation, can be represented as a unity.[32]

---

26   Ibid., 11.
27   Ibid. The term is in italics in the original text.
28   Ibid.
29   Ibid.
30   Ibid., 12.
31   Ibid.
32   For Esposito: 'The very rupture of ancient representation produces a new representative demand. The interests present themselves [*se donnent*] as unrepresentable in a unitary manner, but once again this situation must itself be represented. It is, furthermore, the lack of foundation, the uprooting, which demands new roots. Similarly, it is precisely the technique which, although expressing the unlimited character of the will to power, "provokes" a new formal determination' (ibid.)

The limit and end of the political categories of modernity, arising from the 'Hobbesian paradigm of order',[33] is not, for Esposito, a simple unfolding of a process of 'neutralisation-secularisation'. It is a more complex process arising from the 'hyper-political' character of the separation of the political and politics. The essentially aporetic character is revealed as a process of differentiation, autonomisation and plurality which leads to a continuous and irreducible demand for unity. It is this aporia, or the essence of the political categories of modernity as this aporia, which modernity itself reveals in this process of 'neutralisation-secularisation'.

The place of law

The double displacement of Weber and Schmitt, through this notion of 'neutralisation-secularisation', is one which returns law and the juridical apparatus to its origin in the sociology of Weber. For the partial disqualification of Schmitt's appropriation of Weber retains certain of the essential traits of the Weberian characterisation of modernity.

Within the wider historical process of secularisation, the positivisation of law is retained. Weber's socio-historical account of positivisation[34] is, following Schmitt, reduced to the final stage of this account – the development of a modern, fully positivised law and juridical apparatus. In this development, modern law is characterised by a dual independence. It is distinguished from any stable, substantive origin and, on the basis of this distinction, generates the conditions for its legitimate enactment and application solely from its own legal criteria. In relation to the other realms of the economy and politics, a fully positivised law and juridical apparatus complements and reinforces these other domains, through the maintenance of certain of their background conditions and, more generally, through their contribution to the generalisation of instrumental or purposive-rational action within each of these realms.

In this process of positivisation, law, as positive law, is itself characterised by three main aspects, which are tied to the basic or essential element of positive law – the norm. Positive law, as an objectivised framework for the guidance of human action, is composed of norms which each define the boundary between an illegal and a legal form of human action. The norms within this framework are the product of legislation resulting from the formal procedure of politics – Esposito's regime of representation-mandate – and, as such, are situated within a framework which is open to the constant possibility of addition and/or revision. The fundamental mutability of this normative framework – its positivity – is accompanied by a form of guidance or direction of human behaviour which is limited to the conformity of the character and dynamics of human action to the requirements of this

---

33 Ibid., 8.
34 The essential elements of Weber's account are contained in Weber (1978): 865–900.

18   Roberto Esposito: Law, Community and the Political

framework. This form of guidance articulates the other two elements of legalism (guidance by a normative framework detached from any necessary connection with a moral or natural law) and formality (guidance by a normative framework in which the norms express themselves as the general, abstract boundaries of domains for the individual realisation of means-ends rationality).

Esposito, by the further displacement effected through the introduction of Hobbes, overlays the aporia of the 'hyper-political' on the realm of positive law. The tensions between law and morality, procedural and substantive law and the formalisation and materialisation of law, which Weber views as inhabiting the realm of positive law, are, for Esposito, a particular expression of the more foundational aporia arising from the separation between the political and politics. Hence, while Esposito's critique necessarily recognises, through its reliance upon this process of 'neutralisation-secularisation', a specific place for law and the juridical apparatus, the central focus of that critique is the more fundamental aporia which shapes each of the realms of the economy, law and politics. *Catégories de l'Impolitique*, therefore, is a critique which contains law as one of its essential elements, but the status it accords to law is that of a domain which arises from the more originary separation between the political and politics. The critique's concentration upon this separation entails an enduring connection with a critique of law, because the response to the separation between the political and politics necessarily involves a response to one of its effects or results – the positivisation of law and the juridical apparatus.

The question of the subject

The position of law within the theoretical framework of Esposito's critique entails that a similar position is accorded to a critique of the legal subject of positive law. The legal subject arises as one particular aspect of a wider modern subjectivity shaped by the process of 'neutralisation-secularisation'. The process results in the emergence of a number of domains of human interaction, of which law is one, which are each distinguished by a particular form of subject and interaction. Modern subjectivity is composed of each of these forms of subject, but is not founded upon one or more of them. It is characterised by a continuous circulation through each of these domains, and their respective forms of human interaction, in which it is simply the repository and expression of a particular point in this circulation.

It is this modern subjectivity, rather than any of the particular aspects which it contains, which Esposito views as the more fundamental effect of the separation between the political and politics. For each of the theories of representation, with which this critique engages, is held to commence from the limit or end of modernity as modern subjectivity. This subjectivity, and the plurality of domains of human interaction in which it is embedded, is accompanied, as part of Esposito's notion of the 'hyper-political', by an insistent demand for the representation of that plurality. With the notion of the 'hyper-political', the *Catégories de l'Impolitique* characterises each of these theories as united by their assumption that modernity is the 'hyper-political'.

The process and structure of exposition of the *Catégories de l'Impolitique* involves the presentation of the manner in which each theory responds to this initial characterisation of modernity. The position of each theory, and the passage from each theory to the other, marks the transformation in the understanding of the 'hyper-political', and the separation between the political and politics from which it arises. It traces the passage, within these theories, from determination by the subject to determination, beyond the subject, by a prior and more originary limit or relation. This transformation has, as its necessary corollary, a gradual passage to the interior of the subject.

In the final exposition of the theory of Georges Bataille, the understanding of the relation between the political and politics becomes the experience which arises, within the subject, of its internal differentiation. This withdrawal of the subject into itself reflects the recognition of the failure of a language of representation to articulate, beyond the 'hyper-political', another relation between the political and politics.

It is this experience of the negation of the language of representation with which the *Catégories de l'Impolitique* closes its critique. This is the demonstration of the impossibility of a solution to the aporia of the 'hyper-political' through all attempts based on a language of representation. The unpolitical, which commences from its 'constitutive opposition to modalities of representation',[35] leads not to the reconstitution or reinvigoration of modern subjectivity, but to its self-dissolution. In this self-dissolution, the separation between the political and politics has become the inner experience of subjectivity as a singularity in its relatedness to other singularities. Yet, this relatedness can only be experienced at the very limits of human experience – death – which Bataille characterises as the impossible experience of community. It is this very impossibility which, for Esposito, indicates its 'rigorously unpolitical destiny – removed from the grandiose ruins of the ancient communisms and from the painful misery of the new individualisms'.[36]

---

35 Esposito (2005): 6.
36 Ibid., 21.

Chapter 2

Catégories de l'Impolitique I
From the closure of political theology to the negativism of Canetti

The exposition of the unpolitical commences from the political theology of Romano Guardini and Carl Schmitt, and their fundamental convergence regarding the position and purpose of Christianity and, in particular, the Roman Catholic Church, within the plurality of spheres of value created by the process of secularisation. The position, as both in *and* outside these spheres of value, provides the possibility for the passage of the unpolitical into these spheres. This possibility rests upon the will – a decision – which secures the imposition of the unpolitical upon these spheres. It is an imposition which seeks to fundamentally reorder these spheres of value in accordance with the stability generated by the representational and juridical logic of the Roman Catholic Church.

The primacy which this political theology accords to the will, decision and the representation-image is the essential weakness of its conception of the unpolitical. This is revealed by Eric Voegelin's early critique of Schmitt's *Verfassungslehre*[1] in 1931.[2] This, in turn, becomes the point of transition to the unpolitical in the work of Hannah Arendt, which is traced through Arendt's *On Revolution*,[3] *The Life of the Mind*[4] and *Lectures on Kant's Political Philosophy*.[5] The exposition reveals a critique of the will, as a foundation for the modern political order, and the elaboration of a position for the unpolitical within a framework of reflective judgment. This is accompanied by the differentiation of the moments of decision, force and truth, and their re-articulation as the relationships between power, violence and law. In this re-articulation, the phenomenon of positive law is the middle term between power and violence – a theory of law as the mediation of power and violence – and never becomes a theory of positive law – a theory of law *as* law.

The fragility of this middle term is the limit of Arendt's conception of the unpolitical, and reveals a failure to conceive this more radically as the expression

---

1   Schmitt (2008a).
2   Voegelin (2001).
3   Arendt (1988).
4   Arendt (1978).
5   Arendt (1982).

of an absence. The philosophical anthropology of Hermann Broch is the transition to this thought of the unpolitical as situated without a direct and transparent relationship to the modern political order. The shift is itself expressed in Broch's reconstitution of the process of secularisation in which the phenomenon of positive law is merely an aspect of an existential-anthropological condition. The unpolitical, as the just, is external to this condition of a 'mass man', traversed by power and violence. In this position, the unpolitical is an essentially aporetic experience of the modern political order which acknowledges that the passage between the unpolitical and human existence has happened in the past, but that this contains no guarantee that it will or must continue to happen. All that can be articulated is this possibility itself: that the just remains able to be transposed into this existential-anthropological condition.

The representation of the aporetic experience of the unpolitical exceeds an exclusively theoretical framework, and encompasses the form of literature. The literary representation of this aporetic experience decentres the primacy of the will and reflective judgment, with the relationship between the imagination and literary production. This relationship, however, results in another type of aporia as the just cannot be represented other than in its possibility and, in this state or mode of its potentiality, it does not yet have actual definition. This aporetic experience becomes the impasse of the form of literature: the possibility and impossibility of the representation of the unpolitical.

It is Elias Canetti who, for Esposito, pushes beyond the aporia which shapes the unpolitical of Broch through the abandonment of the just. This abandonment replaces the aporetic experience of Broch with the thematisation of power. By thinking solely within the horizon of the existential-anthropological condition, by fully assuming and thinking through its negativity, the unpolitical re-emerges. The modernity of the political order, and its plurality of spheres of value, ceases to be the central question of this thematisation of power. In this 're-definition of the concrete',[6] the thematisation of power arises from a process of socialisation, detached from the question of secularisation, and in which legal norms, and their specifically legal validity, are peripheral. The resulting radical anthropological negativism of this aspect of Canetti's thought then determines the contours of the unpolitical.

The unpolitical as political theology: Guardini and Schmitt

The project of political theology – the initial manner in which the unpolitical arises – is a response, from within Catholic theology, to a particular conjuncture in European history. The project emerges, most forcefully, in the interwar period in Europe,[7] and, as such, marks an attempt to reorder the existing European order.

6 Kiss (2004): 725, 726–9.
7 For a sociological analysis of this movement of Roman Catholic renewal, during the German Weimar Republic (1919–33), see Bröckling (1993).

22 Roberto Esposito: Law, Community and the Political

This attempt is itself the acknowledgement that Catholic theology, and the Roman Catholic Church, resides within a European order traversed by secularisation, instrumental rationality, technology and atheism. It is the intertwining of the European order with these processes which animates the project of political theology.

The conception of law, within the project of political theology, is one which is resolutely anti-positivist. The positivisation of law, as the differentiation of a sphere of specifically legal norms, from both morality and other spheres, is a particular reflection of the effect of these processes which traverse the European order. The dissociation of law from morality is the dissociation of law from its true foundation. This foundation can only be one in which law, as a set of legal norms, is the expression, within the world, of God's will. The dissociation is not, however, final and irrevocable, as the continuing presence of the Roman Catholic Church and Roman law testify to the presence of the potential for a re-foundation of natural law.

The re-foundation is part of a wider re-theologisation of the European order in which only the elements of Catholic theology, the Roman Catholic Church and Roman law, through their lack of total dissolution by secularisation, contain the capacity for the restoration of its true foundation. This capacity constitutes the project of political theology as the initial characterisation of the unpolitical. In this characterisation, the thought of both Romano Guardini and Carl Schmitt are exemplary but distinct formulations of this project. For while both commence from the interpretative horizon of Catholic theology, their projects of re-theologisation involve divergent approaches to the particular manner in which the elements of Catholic theology, the Roman Catholic Church and Roman law continue to retain their capacity to project themselves into the European order.[8]

For Esposito, Guardini's political theology arises from the conceptualisation of Jesus Christ, as decision, in 1937, in Part Three of *The Lord*, entitled 'The Decision'.[9] Jesus Christ is decision in the double sense of the incarnation and the crucifixion. The incarnation – the creation of Christ as both God *and* man – is the decision of God. The crucifixion is the decision of Christ for his death by crucifixion – the freely willed acceptance of a destiny. It is also the decision of man – the 'no' which enables his crucifixion. The crucifixion – the cross of Christ – becomes the middle term between the original, absolute decision of God and the derivative and defective decision of man.[10] The relation between God, Christ and man is not one of necessity, but of freedom in which decision *and* opposition are contained.

---

8 Esposito is less concerned with the divergence between Schmitt's adherence to the National Socialist regime and Guardini's refusal to link his political theology to it. The central concern here is with the exposition of the limitations which are common to both formulations despite their overt differences. For Guardini's relation to National Socialism, see Krieg (2004).

9 Guardini (1996b): 177–254.

10 Esposito (2005): 25.

Catégories de l'Impolitique | **23**

Within this theological exposition of decision, there then arises the relation between theology and history. The emergence of Christianity in human history is the crucifixion of Christ: the decision which produces a conception of history, in Part Seven, as 'Time and Eternity'.[11] History is the presence not merely of God in history, but of the possibility of salvation. Salvation remains within the modality of possibility, because of its dependence on this freedom composed of both decision and opposition.

The theological primacy accorded to decision is as the continual site of passage between the religious and the secular. Decision derives its sense from an essential relation between the secular and the religious in which both the secular and the religious are contained in, and remain within, the decision. The theological foundation provides the force of the decision – its capacity to enter into and shape the secular. This force is not the product of cognition in which the decision is adjudged in conformity with an ideal.[12] It is immanent within it, as analogous to the figure of Jesus Christ *as* decision. Hence, decision, within the domain of theology, is one in which force is simultaneously authority. This, in turn, provides its immediate capacity to shape and order the secular.

In order for the authority and force of a decision to remain combined, it must attain the level of representation. This then introduces a further combination of 'history', 'visibility' and 'person' into the reordering of the secular.[13] It is at the level of representation that the political emerges most clearly in Guardini's theology. For the forms which are held to be integral to achieve this level of representation are the father and the State. These forms represent the religious in the secular: the combination of the personal and the divine. The relation between the father and his children and between the State and its citizens is that of an authority which is both personal and divine.[14]

At the level of the State, divine sovereignty is the origin of legal norms separating legal validity from both a mere psychology of effectiveness (obedience to legal norms) and Kelsen's legal positivism in which legal validity can only be generated from *within* the legal system itself.[15] For Esposito, it is this conception of representation which marks the strongest degree of affinity between the political theology of Guardini and of Carl Schmitt. The degree of affinity becomes evident from Schmitt's work of 1923, entitled *Roman Catholicism and Political Form*,[16] and, in particular, through Schmitt's presentation of the Roman Catholic Church

---

11 Guardini (1996b): 557–626.

12 Here, Esposito traces the origin of Guardini's position to a reply, in 1922, in *Die Schildgenossen*, to an article, in 1921, by Max Bondy, in the same journal. See: Guardini (1922): 96–100; and Bondy (1921): 44–56.

13 Esposito (2005): 30.

14 Ibid., 31. Here, Esposito refers to the later 1957 collection of Guardini's articles contained in Vol. I of *Sorge um den Menschen*.

15 Kelsen (1997). See also Kelsen's earlier article, of 1922/23, entitled 'God and State' (Kelsen (1973)).

16 For the development of Schmitt's political theology up to 1923, see Doremus (2004).

as a *complexio oppositorum*. This form of representative authority is generated by a combination of a descending and an ascending movement. In the descending movement:

> the power of the Roman *complexio* resides in the fact that its juridical and representative structure includes the 'a-rational' moment of *decision*, incarnated by the personal authority of the Pope, then descending until the singular person of each priest.[17]

In the ascending movement, this power resides in the intertwining of the decision with the idea: 'from the priest to Christ, from power to authority, from the decision to the *idea*'.[18] The Roman Catholic Church, as a foundation which is irreducible to a particular sphere of value, retains the capacity for direction of the whole. The foundation contains a mode of governance which is the sole possibility for this project of reordering.

This affinity is accompanied by the divergence in their respective thematisations of secularisation, and the potential for the realisation of this project of political theology. For Esposito, it is Schmitt's thematisation of the relationship between secularisation and technology which creates this divergence. Schmitt's essay of 1929, entitled 'The Age of Neutralizations and Depoliticizations',[19] redefines the specificity of the modern European order as that in which the necessity for a decision with regard to technology has arisen. Secularisation and modernity are, thereby, reconceived through a reflection upon technology. The character of this redefinition is also an acknowledgement of the essentially residual position of the political form of Roman Catholicism in this modern European order. Schmitt assumes the 'irreversibility of secularization as a general process',[20] and the extent and depth of secularisation has its corollary in the withdrawal of the religious into the Roman Catholic Church and Roman law. Hence, it becomes a political theology which commences from an essentially defensive posture. The project of re-theologisation rests entirely upon the reinvigoration of these surviving remnants.

In contrast, Guardini turns to a sustained reflection upon technology after World War II.[21] Prior to this, he remains within a theoretical framework in which theology understands itself as the comprehension of the world in thought, exemplified by *Der Gegensatz*[22] of 1925, which articulates the immersion of theology in the world. It is from the character of reality, understood through the category of polarity (*Der Gegensatz*), that the concepts of decision and representation gain their specifically theologico-political sense.[23]

---

17 Esposito (2005): 35 (emphasis in original).
18 Ibid., 35.
19 Schmitt (1993).
20 Esposito (2005): 43–4.
21 Guardini's *Letters from Lake Como*, of 1927, represent a prolegomenon to this later engagement.
22 Guardini (2010).
23 Esposito (2005): 38–42.

The later works of the 1950s, *The End of the Modern World*[24] and *Power*,[25] contain a greater recognition of the entwinement of modernity with technology, and the central challenge that it poses for the project of political theology. This recognition involves the comprehension, by theology, of the fundamental connection between science, technology and power.[26] The extensive apparatus of science and technology, while an instrument of control and domination, is orientated by a form of power which is, in itself, apolitical: 'it can be utilized for mutually contradictory ends'.[27] Hence, the project of political theology becomes the reordering and unified direction of the elements of science, technology and power.

In this reordering, theology introduces an internal differentiation into this concept of power. The entwinement of modernity and technology is the result of secularisation: the detachment of human action and decision from God. It is this which is at the origin of the apolitical, instrumental character of the power contained in science and technology. The reassertion of this relation is the introduction of this internal differentiation: the exercise of (divine) authority over the (secular) power contained in science and technology. The urgency of this reassertion, prescribed by this theological comprehension, is heightened by the context of the expansion of the domain of the science and technology, and the intensification of its power.

Guardini's earlier characterisation of the primacy of decision returns in a more intensified form. The figure of Jesus Christ retains its central position in this characterisation, not as a saviour,[28] but as the point of an *absolute* decision: the passage of the divine into the secular. It is only this form of decision which has the force to reorder the entwinement of technology and modernity: 'to know and to affirm that development does not move in the sense of well-being, but of sovereignty'.[29]

The assertion of sovereignty requires a locus or position from which sovereignty can be exercised; and marks the divergence between the later thought of Guardini and that of Schmitt. While Guardini views Europe as retaining this inherent possibility, Schmitt, from the *Nomos of the Earth in the International Law of the Jus Publicum Europaeum*,[30] of 1950 onwards, considers this a far more remote possibility. Here, the theologian, Guardini, is most strongly differentiated from the jurist,[31] Schmitt, within the project of political theology. For Schmitt, the

---

24 Guardini (1998).
25 Guardini (1954).
26 Esposito (2005): 46–8; Guardini (1954): 50.
27 Esposito (2005): 48; Guardini (1954): 15.
28 This characterisation of Jesus is, as Esposito underlines, rejected by Guardini in *Der Heilbringer in Mythos, Offenbarung und Politik*, of 1946 (Esposito (2005): 55–6).
29 Guardini (1954): 96. Quotation from Esposito (2005): 50.
30 Schmitt (2003). For the development of Schmitt's conception of international law, within the project of political theology, see Derman (2011). See also Marramao (2000).
31 This identity, and self-designation, of Schmitt is emphasised, in particular, through the analysis of Schmitt (1990) and by Carrino (1999).

26 Roberto Esposito: Law, Community and the Political

theological has now withdrawn far more radically from Europe, as it inhered in, and declined with, the history of the *Jus Publicum Europeaum*. This history is the history of Christian-European law as a *nomos* of the earth: a spatial division and ordering of the planet in which Europe is an element. As a spatial order founded upon the *Jus Publicum Europeaum*, Europe is a juridical space constituted by the neutralisation of religious conflict through the state, and the juridification of war between states. The distinctive character of the juridical structure of the *Jus Publicum*, elaborated on the basis of Roman law, ensures that this particular legal space is also a theological space. It is its weakening and collapse, initiated in the late nineteenth century, and accelerated by World Wars I and II, which informs Schmitt's uncertainty that the passage from the theological to the secular remains possible.[32]

The project of political theology, animated by the exemplary orientations of Guardini and Schmitt, determines a thinking of the unpolitical, in which each is 'an unfaithful echo'[33] of the other.

> One [Schmitt] strict, adhering to the reality of modernity, with its apparent eternity, the other [Guardini] stretching out towards its overcoming and, at the same time, attached to its ancient theological root. One [Schmitt] gripped by his desperate realism, the other [Guardini] suspended from his utopian hope.[34]

The thought of Guardini and Schmit reveals the oscillation between realism and utopianism as the limit of the project of political theology. The oscillation reflects the impasse of the conception of the unpolitical within the categories of political theology.[35] The impasse presents both the closure of political theology and the opening of the possibility for another thought of unpolitical.

Beyond political theology: the unpolitical from Voegelin to Arendt

The impasse of political theology is already evident to Voegelin, in 1931, in his extensive critical review[36] of Carl Schmitt's *Verfassungslehre*[37] of 1928. This seemingly marginal critical commentary is, for Esposito, a significant presentation of the limitations of the project of political theology. The significance of Schmitt's initial conception of the 'science of constitutional theory . . . within the horizon

---

32 Esposito (2005): 52–3.
33 Ibid., 57.
34 Ibid., 57.
35 In the case of the later Schmitt, in particular, Schmitt (2008b) and (2009), these categories become increasingly heterodox with regard to Roman Catholic theology. See Hohendahl (2008); Ifegan (2010); and Kervégan (2007).
36 Voegelin (2001).
37 Schmitt (2008a).

of a general political theory'[38] is combined with the limitations of Schmitt's theoretical position. The distinction between a constitution (*Verfassung*) and the set of legal norms of constitutional law (*Verfassungsgesetz*) displaces the question of validity from the level of legal norms to 'the act of a political decision'.[39] In this displacement, Schmitt confers an 'ontological status to validity':[40] '[t]he validity and unity of law ought not to be created by a synthesizing act of a transcendental subject of cognition, but rather by the syntheses of those who enact the reality of the state'.[41] The constitutional laws become the expression of this act of constitution and, as such, manifest its unity which is, in turn, the basis for Schmitt's presentation of the 'real unity of the state'.[42] The focus on the question of the 'real unity of the state' entails that:

> Schmitt does not approach the problems of the state as an external observer . . . His scientific judgments are not the statements of a neo-Kantian subject of cognition who objectively transcends his subject matter but rather are investigations of meaning from a perspective within political reality. Schmitt stands within the world of the constitutional-political ideas of the nineteenth century, just as the main object of his investigation, the Weimar constitution, stands within it as well . . . [He seeks] to order this conceptual world according to its *immanent* sense.[43]

For Voegelin, it is precisely Schmitt's situation on the plane of immanence which renders this presentation of 'real unity' essentially empty. The political will – Schmitt's 'ultimate unity'[44] – cannot present the unity of the state. It can merely show 'typical constituting moments of the reality of the state'[45] and that the 'actuality of the state, even in its constitution, simply is no unity'.[46] The question of unity must commence *transcendentally* in which unity, in a democratic state, can only be 'formed rationally by political ideas'.[47] These are 'concepts [which] correspond to no actual facts',[48] but 'are themselves contained as contents of belief and as political motifs within political reality. They themselves are constituent elements of the reality of the state'.[49] The unity of the state is, therefore, a *conceptual* unity in which 'there should be no doubt that political ideas are not

38 Voegelin (2001): 42.
39 Ibid., 43.
40 Ibid., 47.
41 Ibid., 47.
42 Ibid., 51.
43 Ibid., 63 (emphasis added).
44 Ibid., 52.
45 Ibid., 51.
46 Ibid., 51.
47 Ibid., 65.
48 Ibid., 65–6.
49 Ibid., 66.

28   Roberto Esposito: Law, Community and the Political

statements about reality so that (as Schmitt does) one might work through the constitutional world of ideas immanently'.[50]

The distinction between transcendence and immanence with which Voegelin concludes this review then becomes one of the essential elements of his later thought, commencing, in 1952, with *The New Science of Politics*.[51] The distinction now concerns the question of the foundation of theoretical reflection on politics, and is no longer to be sought within the boundaries of the juridico-political of the early work,[52] but is located in an 'anthropological structure'.[53] Within this structure, representation rests '(at the base) on the plurality of persons and on the other [level] (at the summit) on the transcendence of the foundation'.[54] Thus, representation, as a symbolic activity, can never fully represent this foundation which 'draws its roots from an experience of mystery'.[55] In this experience, the theological and the anthropological remain intimately entwined, but representation can no longer ensure the continuous reproduction of the theological in the secular.

This relation between the theological and the anthropological is one of a fundamental uncertainty. Christianity replaces polytheism, and the security created by a 'world full of gods',[56] with a 'world transcendent God'.[57] The connection between the world and God is confined to 'the tenuous bond of faith',[58] and the modern European order becomes a particular instance of an attempt to overcome this uncertainty. The origin of this attempt arises, prior to modernity, within Christianity,[59] in the form of Gnosticism. For Voegelin, modernity is a specific expression of this Gnostic consciousness[60] which accords itself the capacity to transform man and the world and, thereby, overcome this fundamental uncertainty.[61] This is the rejection of the mystery of transcendence for the certainty immanent within the world.[62]

---

50   Ibid., 66. This review was written at the same time as the unfinished work, entitled *The Theory of Governance*, of 1930–32. On the theory of the juridico-political developed in this work, see Sigwart (2006).
51   Voegelin (1987).
52   For an excellent analysis of Voegelin's early work, see Chignola (2001).
53   Esposito (2005): 61.
54   Esposito (2005): 61; Voegelin (1987): 18.
55   Esposito (2005): 61.
56   Voegelin (1987): 122.
57   Ibid., 122.
58   Ibid., 122.
59   The subsequent development of Voegelin's work, after the *New Science of Politics*, is marked by a continued reflection upon Christianity which increasingly situates the potential for the Gnostic deviation within Christianity itself. On this, see Jardine (1995).
60   On the subsequent development of Voegelin's concept of Gnosticism, see Wiser (1980).
61   Voegelin (1987): 152.
62   Wiser (1980): 94. In a letter of 1971, Voegelin refuses to characterise Schmitt as a Gnostic, and insists that this characterisation can only be the product of an investigation of specific propositions in Schmitt's work. See Voegelin (2007): 692.

The continued pertinence of theology to the analysis of the modern European order confronts the significant challenge of Hannah Arendt's *The Origins of Totalitarianism*. In Voegelin's review, the understanding of totalitarianism – 'the question of how to delimit and define phenomena of the class of political movements'[63] – remains at the level of purely phenomenal difference unless it applies 'the principles furnished by philosophical anthropology . . . to historical materials'.[64] Arendt's analysis remains at this purely phenomenal level, because it concentrates solely upon 'the factual level of history; arrives at well-distinguished complexes of phenomena of the type of "totalitarianism"; and is willing to accept such complexes as ultimate essential units'.[65] Hence, it develops an understanding of these historical phenomena as marking a fundamental change in history: a totalitarian revolution. For Voegelin, in contrast, this 'revolutionary outburst' is 'the climax of a secular evolution'[66] in which 'the spiritual disease of agnosticism'[67] has become 'the problem of the modern masses'.[68] This then renders Arendt's concentration on 'the institutional breakdown of national societies and the growth of social superfluous masses'[69] as purely phenomenal. They are the expression of this spiritual disease whose genesis is to be sought 'in the rise of immanentist sectarianism since the high Middle Ages'.[70] Hence, totalitarian movements are 'immanentist creed movements in which medieval heresies have come to their fruition'.[71] These movements, based on the simultaneous conversion and perversion of 'Christian faith in transcendental perfection through the grace of God',[72] enact 'a millennium in the eschatological sense through the transformation of human nature'.[73] This is, then, the expression of 'the idea of *immanent* perfection through an act of man'.[74]

Arendt's failure, for Voegelin, to extend this understanding of totalitarian movements to the theological level, entails that it too remains on the level of immanence. The demarcation and understanding of the phenomena, designated as totalitarian, rest on an acceptance of the secular foundation of law and history in human action; and is accompanied by a comprehension of human nature as essentially mutable. The very mutability which Arendt places at the centre of totalitarianism enables Voegelin to reveal that between liberals (Voegelin's designation of Arendt) and totalitarians there is an 'essential immanentism which

---

63 Voegelin (1953b): 84–5.
64 Ibid., 85.
65 Ibid., 84–5.
66 Voegelin (1953a): 69.
67 Ibid., 73.
68 Ibid., 73.
69 Ibid., 74.
70 Ibid., 74.
71 Ibid., 74.
72 Ibid., 74.
73 Ibid., 74.
74 Ibid., 74. Italics added.

30 Roberto Esposito: Law, Community and the Political

unites them'.[75] Therefore, '[t]he true dividing line in the contemporary crisis does not run between liberals and totalitarians, but between the religious and philosophical transcendentalists on the one side, and the liberal and totalitarian immanentist sectarians on the other side'.[76]

In her reply, Arendt rejects Voegelin's insistence on a philosophical anthropology and the theological framework which accompanies it. The rejection is predicated on an insistence on a reversal of Voegelin's relationship between essence and existence. For Arendt, the *Origins of Totalitarianism* only describes '"elements", which eventually crystallize into totalitarianism'.[77] The essence of totalitarianism 'did not exist before it had come into being'.[78] Its essence is not to be sought in 'intellectual affinities and influences',[79] but 'in the *event* of totalitarian domination itself'.[80] The essence of totalitarianism is in its existence as 'a much more radical liquidation of freedom as a political and a human reality than anything we have ever witnessed before'.[81] It is this which is obscured by Voegelin's understanding of the essence of totalitarian movements within a theological framework.

This, for Arendt, marks the limitation of Voegelin's reconfiguration of the relationship between theology and the secular. For it simply seeks to understand the phenomena of totalitarianism by clinging to:

> an unchangeable nature of man and to conclude that either man himself is being destroyed or that freedom does not belong to man's essential capabilities. Historically we know of man's nature only insofar as it has existence, and no realm of eternal essences will ever console us if man loses his essential capabilities.[82]

The theological which, for Voegelin, is the unpolitical divested of its connection to political theology is, for Arendt, an insufficient form of understanding. The theological is merely that which is free of the spiritual disease which invests the modern European order. A more radical, non-theological gesture is required which commences from *The Human Condition*;[83] and the unpolitical emerges through Arendt's critical reflection on human existence.

For Esposito, the connection between *The Human Condition* and Arendt's later texts concerns the possibility of a foundation for a realm of politics. In particular, it is in the subsection entitled 'The Traditional Substitution of Making for Acting',

---

75　Ibid., 75.
76　Ibid., 75.
77　Arendt (1953): 81.
78　Ibid., 81.
79　Ibid., 80.
80　Ibid., 80.
81　Ibid., 83.
82　Ibid., 84.
83　Arendt (1958).

in the chapter entitled 'Action', in *The Human Condition*[84] which provides this connection. For Arendt, the human condition of plurality is the essential condition 'for that space of appearance which is the public realm. Hence the attempt to do away with this plurality is always tantamount to the abolition of the public realm itself'.[85] This attempt, as the continual attempt to replace the limitations of action[86] 'with making',[87] is intimately associated with 'an argument against the essentials of politics'.[88] Arendt traces the origin of this attempt to replace action with rule, as the foundation for the realm of politics, to Ancient Greece.[89] Rule and rulership, which seek to transcend a public realm based on the plurality of human action, are contained in Plato's distinction, in *The Statesman*,[90] between 'two modes of action, *archein* and *prattein* ("beginning" and "achieving")'.[91] It is this 'logical and semantic separation'[92] which accords primacy to commencement or beginning – 'the task of directing without action' – and confines achieving 'to act without directing, namely, to execute'.[93] From this Platonic origin, for Arendt, there develops an enduring tradition which expresses the 'transformation of action into a mode of making'.[94]

For Esposito, it is with and against this tradition that Arendt's later work develops. In *On Revolution*,[95] Arendt explores the distinction between beginning and achieving through the 'relevance of the problem of beginning to the phenomenon of revolution'.[96] The distinction becomes one between revolution and foundation; and involves the connection between concepts which the traditions of political theory and philosophy have distinguished by their 'reciprocal opposition': 'revolution and constitution, uprooting and foundation, freedom and power'.[97] The reflection on this connection, through the events of the American and French Revolutions, introduces both the specifically modern concept of revolution and the aporetic character of modern politics.

In this interpretation[98] of Arendt, *On Revolution* becomes a stage on the path towards *The Life of the Mind*, and the central interpretative focus rests on the essential condition of modern politics: freedom as plurality. It is this condition

---

84   Arendt (1958): 220–30; Esposito (2005): 67.
85   Arendt (1958): 220–30.
86   For Arendt, these are 'the unpredictability of its outcome, the irreversibility of the process, and the anonymity of its authors' (Ibid., 220).
87   Ibid., 220.
88   Ibid., 220.
89   Ibid., 221–5.
90   Plato (2000): 76 (305d).
91   Arendt (1958): 222.
92   Esposito (2005): 67.
93   Ibid., 67.
94   Arendt (1958): 229.
95   Arendt (1988).
96   Ibid., 20.
97   Esposito (2005): 70.
98   For Esposito's further consideration of Arendt in relation to Simone Weil, see Esposito (1996a).

32　Roberto Esposito: Law, Community and the Political

which the events of the American and French Revolutions reveal in their failure[99] to overcome the 'reciprocal opposition' of the traditional concepts of political theory and philosophy. The revelation then remains as one which all post-revolutionary politics, as a specifically modern politics, has to confront.

Arendt reveals the failure of the American Revolution through its incapacity to represent the plurality of this freedom within its normative and institutional structures. The event of the revolution creates the necessity for a connection between freedom and power: 'the contradictory necessity of a normative principle – a source of authority – to which political action as such would be subordinated'.[100] This, in turn, requires the connection between revolution and constitution in which power and freedom are mediated by a normative and institutional framework created by a constitution. The introduction of mediation is, however, the failure of the revolution to represent this freedom as plurality.

> The representative institution transcends in all cases the will of the represented subjects. The will – the decision – of these subjects is subordinated to the transcendence of representation. One cannot decide freely because representation breaks the immediate relation between will and freedom, because it interposes between them an absolute mediating filter. In the final analysis, it is mediation which blocks political action, which translates it – betrays it – in administrative technique.[101]

The failure of the American Revolution, as a failure of representation,[102] leads to the attempt, by the French Revolution, to formulate a theory of the will to establish the essential unity of this plurality. The link between the will and freedom, which is broken by representation, is to be restored by the articulation of a will which transforms the 'many into one'.[103] The transformation of the plurality of distinct, particular wills into a general, unified will is, however, produced through the maintenance of permanent conflict.

The condition of conflict derives from the definition of the particular will as an entity whose internal unity, and its unity with other wills, can only be generated by, and through, exclusion. The particular will becomes, for Arendt, 'the two-in-one of the soul' in conflict.[104] The interiorisation of conflict is that which engenders the 'the general will, and thus he will become a true citizen of the national body

---

99　For an alternative conception of this failure, and its place within Arendt's thought, see Tassin (2007).

100　Esposito (2005): 71.

101　Ibid., 74.

102　For Arendt (1988): 75, this failure is equally a product of the development of the French Revolution itself, in which 'the Girondans had failed to produce a constitution and to establish a republican government'.

103　Ibid., 77.

104　Ibid., 80.

politic'.[105] The conflictual passage from the particular will to the general will, at the national level, is then reinforced, at the international level, for Arendt by the national will's conflict with the common national enemy.

Arendt's reflection reveals the failure of the French Revolution in the attempt to connect the will and freedom which creates a fundamental simplification of politics: the process of the generation of the general will through conflict. The French Revolution is the failed response of 'hyper-politicisation' to the preceding failure of 'depoliticisation' exemplified by the American Revolution.[106] Both of these failures – 'the failure of the revolutionary will'[107] – become the framework for Arendt's later work shaped by the 'more complex task'[108] of a genealogical investigation of the relationship between concept of the will and politics. The unpolitical, in the form of Arendt's later work, thus becomes the reflection upon the aporia of the will in relation to political freedom.

The initial parameters of this aporia are elaborated in Arendt's essay entitled, 'What Is Freedom?',[109] in which the distortion of freedom arises from its transposition from the realm of politics to that of the will. The aporia of the will is the expression of a confinement of the question of freedom 'to an inward domain, the will, where it would be open to self-inspection'.[110] The transformation of freedom, as 'acting and associating with others',[111] into the question of freedom of the will introduces a division within the will itself. This is experienced in the division between 'to will and not to will at the same time',[112] in which freedom is then reduced to those instances where 'the I-will and the I-can coincide'.[113] The essential impotence of the will is thereby expressed which, in turn, involves a further distortion of freedom. For the I-will, in contrast to the I-think, remains secured to the self; and, in this, 'the will and the will-to-power have become practically identical'.[114] This leads to the identification of the free will with sovereignty, and the further aporia of:

> either a denial of human freedom – namely, if it is realised that whatever men may be, they are never sovereign – or to the insight that the freedom of one man, or a group, or a body politic can be purchased only at the price of the freedom, i.e., the sovereignty, of all others.[115]

---

105 Ibid., 78.
106 Esposito (2005): 76.
107 Ibid., 78.
108 Ibid., 78.
109 Arendt (1963).
110 Ibid., 145.
111 Ibid., 163.
112 Ibid., 158.
113 Ibid., 160.
114 Ibid., 163.
115 Ibid., 164.

34 Roberto Esposito: Law, Community and the Political

The essay concludes with the attempt to restore the primacy of a political freedom by identifying 'a freedom which is not an attribute of the will but an accessory of doing and acting'.[116] The search for this notion of freedom, and the interpretative horizon of the political which accompanies it, initially opens onto the 'pre-philosophical' tradition of antiquity.

In the second part of Arendt's final, unfinished work, *The Life of the Mind*,[117] entitled 'Willing', the preliminary approach of 'What Is Freedom?' is modified. The return to the structure of the will proceeds from the search for a notion of freedom which is unaffected by 'the perplexities' of 'the reflexivity of mental activities'[118] revealed in the first part, entitled 'Thinking'. However, this reflection reveals the will to have an aporetic structure which is of a far more enduring and fundamental character than the earlier essay. The aporia is redrawn as that of the aporia of beginning which is held to be analogous to the 'task of *foundation*' of a political order.[119] The aporetic structure becomes an existential condition which cannot be resolved within the faculty of the will itself. It can only be 'covered up' through 'understanding the *new* as an improved restatement of the old'.[120]

For Esposito, the further development of Arendt's reflection has then to be traced from the tentative indications, in the conclusion to 'Willing', in which the aporia of the will has to be rethought within the faculty of judgment. This was to form the final part of *The Life of the Mind*, but only the initial sketches were finished at the time of Arendt's death. The theory of judgment, in Arendt, has then to be reconstructed from these few sketches and the lecture course on Kant, entitled *Lectures on Kant's Political Philosophy*,[121] which was posthumously assembled for publication.

From this reconstruction, Arendt's transition to the faculty of judgment is no longer the resolution of the aporia of the will, but its displacement,[122] through the interpretation and appropriation of Kant's faculty of reflective judgment, in the 'Analytic of the Beautiful', in the first part of *The Critique of Judgment*.[123] The elements of 'taste', 'imagination' and '*sensus communis*', appropriated from Kant's faculty of reflective judgment, are utilised to articulate this faculty as a faculty of political judgment.[124] The aporia of the will is displaced by the distinction between actor and spectator-narrator. The displacement of the aporetic structure of the will is also the displacement of the primacy of the relationship between the plural political order and the unity created by the will. The primacy

---

116 Ibid., 165.
117 Arendt (1978).
118 Ibid., 216.
119 Ibid., 211.
120 Ibid., 216.
121 Arendt (1982). On Arendt's theory of judgment, see: Taylor (2001); Yar (2000); and Zerilli (2005).
122 Esposito (2005): 82–4.
123 Kant (2007).
124 Esposito (2005): 85–6.

accorded to the exercise of the faculty of reflective judgment creates a conception of political judgment centred on the weaker unity of the *sensus communis*.

The origin of the political order in the plurality of human existence is thereby actively preserved by a faculty which originates from, and remains shaped by, this plurality. The faculty of reflective judgment, and not the will, is the essential expression of human freedom as political freedom. Judgment, as an opinion, is, however, not simply the reflection of a plurality of opinion. It contains the possibility, which arises from the particular form of universalisation, inherent in reflective judgment, of the enlargement of opinion.

The enlargement initially arises from the position of judgment in relation to both the past and the future. Judgment preserves the primacy of the present over both the subordination of the present to the past (tradition) and the subordination of the present to the future (progress). It asserts the present as an 'empty place'[125] from which the sense of the past and the future is open to determination. The unpolitical then lodges in the faculty of judgment as '[t]his absence *in* the present, this division of the present, separating itself from itself, this gap within this which however exists and which is *all* that exists, can take the name of the unpolitical'.[126]

The temporal and historical openness of judgment is the passage from the particular to the universal. Universalisation of a particular opinion, formulated as a judgment, commences from the acknowledgement, by its holder, of its particularity in relation to a plurality of other opinions. The recognition of an opinion, within a plurality of opinion, reveals this plurality as the world of the *sensus communis*. The further universalisation of a particular opinion then involves an exchange – the communicability of opinion – in which the limits of the *sensus communis* are established.

The *sensus communis*, as the realm of political freedom within human existence, provides a space for deliberation and persuasion in which a specifically political truth is generated. The multiplicity of opinions from which it arises remains reflected in the weaker unity which it creates: unity conceived 'as plurality but *not as conflict*'.[127] A separation is thereby created between violence and this peaceful plurality; and, with this separation, a difficulty emerges within Arendt's thinking, which, for Esposito, ultimately leads to the generation of new aporias.

These new aporias, expressed in the specific form of legal aporias, become evident in Arendt's essays, *Civil Disobedience*[128] and *On Violence*.[129] Law, for Arendt, is situated as the necessary limit or boundary between this space of political freedom and its dissolution or obstruction. *On Violence* introduces the aporia of constitution – the formation of a new political community – as the aporetic relation between violence and power.[130] For Arendt:

125 Ibid., 91.
126 Ibid., 92.
127 Ibid., 93.
128 Arendt (1972a).
129 Arendt (1972b).
130 Ibid., 155.

> Power springs up whenever people get together and act in concert, but it derives its legitimacy from the initial getting together rather than from any action that may then follow. Legitimacy, when challenged, bases itself on an appeal to the past, while justification relates to an end that lies in the future. Violence can be justifiable, but it never will be legitimate. Its justification loses plausibility the farther its intended end recedes into the future.[131]

The distinction becomes aporetic, for Esposito, once one recognises that the origin of a new political community can be created by violence. The 'getting together', as the product of the violent overthrow of the previous regime, then becomes far less clearly one of power.[132]

The aporia then requires the introduction of law – the 'getting together' as a legally formalised constitution – as the creation of a legal origin for this legitimacy. Although this is alluded to in *On Violence*,[133] it receives its fullest development in *Civil Disobedience*. Here, Arendt complicates the original separation of power and violence by interposing between them the open, non-violent phenomenon of civil disobedience.[134] It is civil disobedience which raises the question of law or, rather, 'with what *concept* of law it is compatible'.[135]

The concept of law which Arendt then elaborates is predicated on finding a 'constitutional niche for civil disobedience'.[136] The niche emerges from a conception of law based on its capacity to 'regulate our life in the world and our daily affairs with each other'.[137] The capacity of law is also its specific limitation: the 'law can indeed stabilize and legalize change once it has occurred, but the change itself is always the result of extra-legal action'.[138] The common capacity of all legal systems is then differentiated, and rendered particular, by 'the *spirit* of its laws'.[139]

In this manner, Montesquieu's differentiation of legal systems is appropriated, and combined with Locke's notion of *societas* – 'the horizontal version of the social contract'[140] – to identify the exemplary character of the Constitution of the United States of America. Its particularity is simultaneously one which contains a universal significance, because it is the 'only government having at least a chance to cope'[141] with the phenomenon of civil disobedience. This chance, contained in the spirit of its Constitution, concerns its origin in consent as voluntary

---

131   Ibid., 151.
132   Esposito (2005): 92.
133   Arendt (1972b): 140.
134   Arendt (1972a): 74–7.
135   Ibid., 83.
136   Ibid., 83.
137   Ibid., 79.
138   Ibid., 84.
139   Ibid., 83.
140   Ibid., 86.
141   Ibid., 83.

membership. The particular origin of consent, in which dissent is an equally integral component, creates two distinct forms of consent. A tacit, general consent to the Constitution is distinguished from a specific consent to particular laws or policies created within the Constitutional framework.[142]

From this spirit, however, a further legal aporia arises. The essential function accorded to law of stability immediately confines change to the realm of politics – the extra-judicial. Civil disobedience is, therefore, placed uncertainly between the realm of politics and the realm of law. It is law, in its Constitutional origin, which effectively circumscribes, or juridifies, the 'operational space' of political power.[143] Stability manifests itself as institutionalisation and regulation which then confronts an extra-juridical realm which alone contains the potential for change. For Esposito, the aporia is revealed by the position accorded by Arendt to civil disobedience.

> Civil disobedience responds to the law through the language of politics, namely, by the projection into the future which is at the same time a call to this beginning henceforth stifled by the law. This beginning carries within it, as we have seen, a germ of necessary violence. However, political language, to remain as such, must necessarily be non-violent, and non-violence is in fact civil disobedience. We are at the crux [*l'apex*] of the contradiction. In order to combat the latent violence of the law, politics must have recourse in a non-violent manner to this origin which is always violence: combat the violence of a non-violent law through the non-violence of a violent origin.[144]

The particular categories with which Arendt seeks to articulate the unpolitical confront the difficulty of the perpetual generation of aporias. The presence of these aporias, within Arendt's thought, expresses the limitation of her thought, and its associated conceptual framework, as a thought of the unpolitical.

The unpolitical as the thinking of the negative: from Broch to Canetti

The passage beyond Arendt is unable to be achieved through the resolution of Arendt's aporetic categories of the unpolitical. For Arendt's categories of the unpolitical cannot provide the theoretical resources which would enable the elaboration of a thought beyond the limits of these categories. These Arendtian categories are thus relinquished for a consideration of the unpolitical in the thought of Hermann Broch.[145]

142　Ibid., 88.
143　Esposito (2005): 98.
144　Ibid., 99.
145　Ibid., 99. For an overview of Broch's early writings, see Cassier (1960).

38 Roberto Esposito: Law, Community and the Political

In the passage beyond Arendt, the Arendtian interpretation[146] of Broch is itself modified. This involves Esposito in the reconstruction of Broch's thought as a conscious and overt engagement with the relationship between the unpolitical and the political. For Esposito, this relationship is to be understood as one in which law, as the Arendtian mediation between the political and the unpolitical, has been displaced by the separation of the unpolitical, as the realm of the ethical, from the political, as the realm of modern, mass democratic politics.

The form in which Broch considers this relationship commences, for Esposito, from a philosophy of history which is then effectively replaced by that of literature. The displacement marks Broch's recognition of the incapacity of a philosophy of history to overcome the separation between the ethical (unpolitical) and modern, mass democratic politics (the political). The separation has to be considered as fundamentally irresolvable; and it is then *The Sleepwalkers*[147] and *The Death of Virgil*[148] which undertake the task of literary presentation of this separation.

The turn to the form of literature is the expression of Broch's reconsideration of the possibility of the political to represent the unpolitical. In this reconsideration, the possibility is acknowledged, but the representation will always result in the degradation and dogmatic simplification of the ethical.[149] The passage through representation always produces an essentially negative relationship between the unpolitical and the political: modernity as both the differentiation of value spheres and the phenomenon of revolution.

For Esposito, Broch's review essay of 1922, 'Die erkenntnis – theoretische Bedeutung des Begriffes "Revolution" und die Wiederbelebung der Hegelschen Dialektik',[150] through the reinterpretation of the notion of revolution, marks the point of transition to literature in *The Sleepwalkers*. In this essay, the separation between the ethical and the politics of modern mass democracy is that between 'the ahistorical absolute' and 'historical becoming'.[151] Within this temporal framework, revolution is the essential expression of the original separation, because it holds within itself both the absolutely unconditioned and an absolutely historical content.[152]

The Sleepwalkers is the further deepening and radicalisation of the separation between the realm of 'historical becoming' and the ethical. For Esposito, this emerges, in particular, in the final section, entitled 'The Realist', in which the narrative is interspersed with a number of sections devoted to a consideration of the disintegration of values (*Zerfall der Wertes*).[153] In these sections, the specificity

---

146 Arendt (1995); (2007a); (2007b).
147 Broch (1986).
148 Broch (1995a).
149 Esposito (2005): 108–11.
150 Broch (1977).
151 Esposito (2005): 113.
152 Ibid., 114.
153 Broch (1986): 343–648.

of the notion of revolution, as political change, of the 1922 review essay, is generalised as modernity's form of change and development. The realm of 'historical becoming' dissolves into a plurality of value spheres which develops without regulation or conciliation. The 'polytheism of values' is the expression of the essential antagonism resulting from the existence of a plurality of value spheres: the 'absolutisation of the relative'.[154]

It is this absolutisation which is articulated in the final consideration of the disintegration of values, entitled 'Epilogue'.[155] In this section, the central protagonist of the last epoch of the novel – Huguenau The Realist – exemplifies the final unfolding of the disintegration of values. He embodies a value-system which, as the mere reflection of 'the individual and his irrational impulses', 'remains the point of absolute degeneracy; the point, so to speak, of an invariant absolute zero that is common to all scales of value and all-value systems without reference to their mutual relativity'.[156] It is, however, at this 'zero-point of atomic dissolution'[157] that the possibility for the apprehension of the unpolitical, as the ethical, emerges. However, this possibility remains divided between a dim inner awareness, at the level of the figure of Huguenau, and the more expansive reflection offered by the 'Epilogue'. The division attests to the essential indeterminacy of this possibility: the passage between the ethical and the historical is, as yet, unrealised.

The state of abeyance with which *The Sleepwalkers* concludes is then reconceived in Broch's later novel, *The Death of Virgil*. In this reconception, the relationship between the unpolitical and the political is transposed into the dialogue between the Emperor Augustus and the poet Virgil in the third section of the novel, entitled 'Earth – The Expectation'.[158] For Esposito, the eventual decision, by Virgil, at the conclusion of the dialogue, to give Augustus his final poem, 'The Aeneid', continues to mark the separation between the unpolitical and the political. It maintains the divergent conceptions, clearly manifest throughout the dialogue, of the relationship between the State and its representation in the poetic form of 'The Aeneid'.

The divergence contained within the dialogue centres on the ambivalence of the State as the form of passage between the unpolitical and the political. Virgil's dialogic position reveals this ambivalence as one contained within the new, imperial Augustan State. The installation of Octavian, as Emperor Augustus, defines the end of the political system of the Roman Republic, and inaugurates a new imperial system. Virgil does not contest this termination of the Roman Republic, and holds Augustus to have restored order.[159] The point of contestation

---

154 Esposito (2005): 115. This is also an expression of Broch's critical engagement with Weber: see Harrington (2006).
155 Broch (1986): 625–48.
156 Ibid., 645.
157 Ibid., 645.
158 Broch (1995a): 303–98. For an alternative to Esposito's approach, see Eiden (2006).
159 Broch (1995a): 337; Esposito (2005): 118–19.

40　Roberto Esposito: Law, Community and the Political

centres on whether, and in what manner, this event is also the passage between the unpolitical and the political.

From Augustus's dialogic position, the passage takes place with his installation as emperor. The restoration of order is the realisation of the unpolitical – the ethical – in the form of the Roman imperial state. This state form is simultaneously divine and profane; and this simultaneity ensures the conformity between the gods and the Roman people.[160] It is this which ensures that the restoration of order, which originates in Octavian's military victory at Actium, 'has the force to transform evil into good'.[161] Within this understanding, Virgil's 'Aeneid' is sought as a poetic representation of this character of the state form. Augustus regards Virgil's 'Aeneid' as that from which 'emanates the spirit of Rome':[162] the divine and the profane. As a Roman, formed within the state, Virgil owes a 'reasonable duty and service' to place his poetic work within the 'more comprehensive' work of this state.[163]

Virgil resists this appropriation of 'The Aeneid' by insisting upon a distinction between the 'standards of the state' and those of 'artistic perfection'.[164] The distinction flows from an alternative understanding of metaphor and, with this, of the limits of poetic representation. For Virgil, poetic representation, through metaphor, is a necessarily deficient form of representation. Hence, it cannot ensure the direct presentation of the divine in the reality of the new Augustan state. Rather, it interrupts the attempt, by Augustus, to present ruling as an art which has an analogical relationship with poetry.[165]

The interruption represents the continued divergence between Virgil and Augustus over the meaning of 'the Empire'. In particular, it centres on the status of the new Roman state which Augustus has inaugurated. The divergence marks a profound disagreement regarding poetry as a representation-image of the Empire. It is a divergence in which Virgil and Augustus express the difference between the unpolitical and the political. Augustus, as the expression of the political, understands the new Roman state as a real, concrete entity which shapes a 'disciplined humanity' in which '[s]tate and spirit are one and the same'.[166] This disciplined humanity is that of a people within a *Roman* Empire whose 'highest duty' is to shape time within this political order.[167] Virgil's poetry, for Augustus, cannot be anything other than a representation-image of this Empire. It can only be the representation of the reality of the new Roman state as poetry.

Virgil's response to this characterisation of his poetry, which is also at the root of Augustus's request to be given 'The Aeneid', is to deny that it can have this

160　Esposito (2005): 120.
161　Ibid., 121.
162　Broch (1995a): 314.
163　Ibid., 333.
164　Ibid., 312.
165　Ibid., 327.
166　Ibid., 366, 365.
167　Ibid., 352.

character. The denial is also a denial of the new Roman state as the form which achieves this fusion of state and spirit. In these denials, Virgil reiterates the limits of the political in relation to the more originary ground of the unpolitical. The ground of the unpolitical cannot be grasped directly through either the form of poetry or the form of the new Roman state. These forms can never represent this originary ground transparently and directly, but can, in Virgil's sense, only be metaphors. For Virgil, metaphor is a form of representation which, while real, can only suggest the ideal as that which is beyond this form. Poetry, as metaphor, is not perception: 'the ground of perception may be divined from art, but its creation, its re-creation lies beyond the power of art'.[168]

This division between perception and metaphor extends beyond poetry to Virgil's conception of the new Roman state. The primary duty is to perception and not to any of the metaphorical forms which have sought to represent it. The new Roman state is, apart from its poetic representation, a form which is a deficient representation of the 'kingdom of perception'.[169] The state inaugurated by Augustus remains, for Virgil, the expression of the 'expansion of government power over militarily protected territory'.[170] In this limited form, the political, as the new Roman state, can only indicate the potential for its representation of the unpolitical as this kingdom of perception. It has established peace, but this is merely the preparatory condition for the emergence of this kingdom.

It is Virgil's revelation of the fundamental divergence between the political and the unpolitical that Augustus cannot accept. The new Roman state – the reality of the work of Augustus – 'must be more than a mere metaphor'.[171] For Augustus, to accept that one's duty relates to a ground outside the state results in a 'shattering of the structure of the state'.[172] The all-embracing Roman state, at the centre of the Empire, in which 'the state personifies the people' and 'the people personify the state', is the full realisation of the unpolitical in the political.[173] There can be no residue or remainder of the unpolitical outside the 'all-commanding state'.[174]

Augustus's incomprehension of Virgil's position becomes increasingly violent during the dialogue. Immediately prior to Virgil's statement that he will give 'The Aeneid' to Augustus, Virgil's position is characterised as a direct challenge to Augustus. Virgil's position can only be comprehended, by Augustus, through the ascription of a merely political motivation. For Augustus, Virgil's position as a poet, and the poetry which he has produced, is one which flows from '[your] thoughts of being king but [you] were too weak to make the slightest effort to become one'.[175] Hence, this position is one of envy and hatred:

168 Ibid., 349.
169 Ibid., 367.
170 Ibid., 360.
171 Ibid., 359.
172 Ibid., 376–7.
173 Ibid., 368.
174 Ibid., 368.
175 Ibid., 387.

42   Roberto Esposito: Law, Community and the Political

> . . . you hate me [Augustus] because you had no other choice than to put your cravings into your poem, by which you show yourself, here at least, as mightier than kings; you hate me because I was able to work for all that you desired for yourself . . . you hate me because you hold me responsible for your own impotence.[176]

Virgil's decision to give the poem to Augustus seems, from the violent exchange which precedes it, to erase the divergence between the political and the unpolitical. However, it does not erase this divergence, because Virgil will die leaving the poem unfinished. 'The Aeneid' will never be completed and Augustus will never receive the representation-image of the new Roman state. Virgil knows that when Augustus receives 'The Aeneid' it will remain, in its incompletion, a deficient metaphor of the originary ground of perception.

> At the end of *The [Death of] Virgil*, the unpolitical voyage of Broch seems to have attained its end. The ethico-political project, which he still described affirmatively in terms of philosophy of history in his youthful works, appears henceforth as torn apart, emptied from the inside by a *force of negation* which drives back the 'positive pole' of the political beyond the margins of the representable.[177]

The divergence between the unpolitical and the political with which *The Death of Virgil* concludes is also the subject of Broch's final, unfinished work on mass psychology.[178] Here, the divergence between the unpolitical and the political becomes, in Chapter 4 of the third section – entitled 'Jurisdiction and the New Type of Human' – that between meta-law and law.[179] Meta-law, as the realm of the ethical and the just, is held to be fundamentally distinct from the framework of norms of positive law realised within the institutions of modern, mass democracy.

The unfinished character of this work on mass psychology indicates the limit of Broch's categories of the unpolitical. The development of his thought, and the turn to literature as the favoured mode of exposition, concludes with the presentation of the impossible relation between the unpolitical and the political. The impossible relationship is presented as a 'double postulate: the impracticability of a politics in ethical terms and of an ethics as unthinkable in political terms'.[180] The experience of this impossible relationship, in both fictional and non-fictional forms, is the impasse produced by Broch's categories of the unpolitical.

---

176   Ibid., 387.
177   Esposito (2005): 125 (emphasis in original).
178   Broch (1995b). All references are to the French translation, Broch (2008).
179   Broch (2008): 420–70.
180   Esposito (2005): 106.

Catégories de l'Impolitique | 43

For Esposito, the passage beyond this impasse is to be sought in the work of Elias Canetti; and involves the repudiation rather than the reworking of Broch's categories of the unpolitical. The relationship between the unpolitical and the political in Canetti is distinguished by the fundamental difference in its conception of negativity and its presentation through the categories of the unpolitical.

The fundamental difference is explicitly acknowledged in an exchange which Canetti records, in the third volume of his autobiography, entitled *The Play of the Eyes*,[181] regarding the purpose of the literary form. In this exchange, in which the subject is the literary form of Canetti's *The Wedding* and *Auto-da-Fé* and of Broch's *The Sleepwalkers*,[182] their differences centre upon the presentation of the negative. In contrast to Broch, Canetti's mode is one in which the negative is unflinchingly portrayed, and consists of the explicit generation of tension between the characters. The effect of this tension is to present an experience of fear which the audience or reader will recognise as their own: '[t]hey help us *rehearse* our fear'.[183] Through this rehearsal, the experience of fear becomes intelligible and comprehensible.

However, for Broch, the effect of this intelligibility is not to diminish, but rather, to '*heighten* fear'.[184] The positive pole of the unpolitical, for Broch, finds no specific inherence in Canetti's work: 'in both *The Wedding* and the novel [*Auto-da-Fé*], you end cruelly, mercilessly, with destruction'.[185] Yet, it is this conception of negativity which remains after the impasse of Broch's categories of the unpolitical. The unrepresentable positive pole of the unpolitical, in Broch, becomes, with Canetti, the absence of a positive pole distinguishable from that of the negative.

> In relation to the conception of Broch, it is a question here both of a completion and of a reversal. If only the negative is representable – evil in the language of Broch and power in that of Canetti – , therefore it is from this alone, of its meticulous and persistent analysis, that can emerge, indirectly, as through a *reflection* or a reversed echo, the silence of the *positive*.[186]

The completion and reversal produced by Canetti's thought entails that Broch's initial distinction between a realm of the ethical (the just) and a framework of norms of positive law disappears. A negative anthropology, in which law *as law* is not fundamentally distinct from power, dissolves Broch's increasingly weak differentiation of the unpolitical from the political.

---

181   Canetti (1991a).
182   Canetti (1986b); Canetti (2005); Broch (1986).
183   Canetti (1991a): 38.
184   Ibid., 38.
185   Ibid., 39.
186   Esposito (2005): 128 (emphasis in original).

44 Roberto Esposito: Law, Community and the Political

The anthropology is negative because the process by which a human being becomes a subject, prior to the existence of any legal subject within a framework of legal norms, is indissociable from power and its exercise. For Esposito, this negative anthropology can be traced from Canetti's novel, *Auto-da-Fé*, to his later work, *Crowds and Power*,[187] and remains a constant theme in his notes between 1942 and 1972 contained in *The Human Province*.[188] The essential motif which Esposito considers to unite these works is 'the exclusion of every historical alternative to the language of power'.[189] Power is an integral component of human life and, as such, the basic reproduction of human life – continuing to live – involves the forcible imposition of the human being on the natural and human world. The character of this imposition, at the individual and collective level, becomes Canetti's descriptive task. The imposition is an anthropological invariant, but the form in which this invariant is expressed contains the variation of Canetti's descriptive task.

The variation within invariance, which Canetti describes, is underlain by the notion of metamorphosis (*Verwandlung*). The notion contains the essential ambivalence of this negative anthropology which is 'vital, liberating, but *at the same time* mortal, destructive'.[190] The notion of metamorphosis determines the relationship between concept of the crowd and the concept of power in Canetti's *Crowds and Power* as one marked by their capacity for reciprocal transformation.

> This appears from the opening pages, while the crowd takes *all* the attributes of power – growth, duration, instinct for destruction –, which makes it – *simultaneously*: 1) enemy of power; 2) instrument of power; 3) object of power; 4) power itself. Opposed [to] and at the same time realisation *en masse* of this One, of this Subject which power incarnates, even through the crowd. A new unity which ensues from the One, tends towards the One and wants the One as leader and victim simultaneously. For the oscillatory movements . . . are two: that which transforms power into its contrary, which dissipates it as power – as continually recounted, and for this even without possibility of safety, in the epilogue entitled 'The End of the Survivor' –, and that which transforms the anti-power, the metamorphosis, the crowd, into a new power, always more powerful.[191]

The radical reduction of the relationship between the political and the unpolitical to that of metamorphosis is accompanied, in the epilogue, with a task. It is this task which represents what remains of the juridico-political in Canetti's thought.

---

187 Canetti (2005); Canetti (1981). On Canetti's further reflections on the composition of *Auto-da-Fé*, see Canetti (1989).
188 Canetti (1986a); Esposito (2005): 129–39. For an overview of Canetti, as a social theorist, see Elbaz (2003).
189 Esposito (2005): 130.
190 Ibid., 136.
191 Ibid., 138 (emphasis in original).

The juridico-political is reduced to the notion of command and, in this reduction, a command is never sought to be provided with a specifically legal character. For Canetti, the command is tied to a philosophical anthropology of power which is incapable of recognising a separation between the factual existence of a command and the particular nature of the obligation which it imposes. The notion of command is a type of power which is exercised by the survivor over the crowd; and it is the survivor's potential to use commands which is 'the most unquestioned and therefore the most dangerous thing he does'.[192]

The danger arises not from the assertion of the primacy of force over legitimacy, but from the anxiety which is concentrated in the position of the survivor as the origin of commands. The very uniqueness of the survivor who 'seizes control of such a system [of commands]' is accompanied by 'an abnormal measure of the anxiety of command and [he] will inevitably try to get rid of it'.[193] The anxiety at the origin of command exacerbates the character of the command which, for Canetti, is 'no less than a suspended death sentence'.[194] Hence, the juridico-political becomes co-extensive with a pathology of power which has the continuous potential to unleash a 'catastrophe'.[195]

The unpolitical emerges as the response, or task, in relation to this connection between the survivor and a system of commands; and entails separating a command from the effect on the recipient or addressee of the command. This involves both a separation of the command from its sting and to effectively 'search for a means to deprive it of its sting'.[196] However, this task is continually in opposition to the invariant negative anthropology from which the relationship between crowds and power is developed. The task of separating the notion of a command from its sting has to confront the more originary character of survival which inheres in this negative anthropology.

This is the impasse with which Canetti's theory appears to conclude. The essential negativity of the relationship between the political and the unpolitical confines thought to the continual process of metamorphosis – the 'fundamental triad' of 'producing-outdoing-surviving'.[197] Canetti's categories of the unpolitical remain in a state of a permanent lack of concretion as they circle around a basic anthropological aporia: 'How to eat without killing? How to grow without eating? How to live without growing? Simply, how to live without surviving? Is a subject in opposition to power conceivable? Or rather is power the *absolute* verb of the subject?'[198]

---

192 Canetti (1981): 469.
193 Ibid.
194 Ibid.
195 Ibid., 470.
196 Ibid. Canetti (1996) elaborates further on this task in his discussion with Adorno. See especially 14–15.
197 Cacciari (2009b): 162.
198 Esposito (2005): 139.

Chapter 3

Catégories de l'Impolitique II
From the negative anthropology of Canetti to the negative community of Bataille

The impasse of Canetti – the lack of distinction of the categories of the unpolitical from a social reality permeated by the dynamics of negative anthropology – forms the basis for the subsequent development of *Catégories de l'Impolitique*. The reflection involves thinking both with and beyond Canetti and Simone Weil to the categories of the unpolitical in the work of Georges Bataille. The approach to their work is accompanied by a progressive displacement of the juridico-political, as the primary form of relationship between the political and the unpolitical, by a notion of community as the final exposition of the categories of the unpolitical.

In the transition to the notion of community, the categories of the unpolitical continue their movement away from the domain of political philosophy to a more heterodox theoretical framework. The move to encompass literature, presented in the discussion of the categories of the unpolitical in Broch and Canetti, is further radicalised to place into question the very tradition of political philosophy. The questioning involves the search for a form of experience which is prior to, and other than, that of the tradition of political philosophy. For Esposito, the initial indications of this experience are to be found, despite the dominance of a negative anthropology, in Canetti's attempt to detach the subject from power. The notions of passive force and a free-floating imagination suggest the possibility of think- ing beyond the limits of metamorphosis. These initial indications in Canetti are only fully conceived in the work of Simone Weil. Here, the relationship between the subject and power commences from a meta-physical origin which fuses together elements of philosophy and theology in a heterodox combination. In this combination, the juridico-political is subjected to significant reflection and critique as an integral part of an experience of necessity. The experience of necessity – a mixture of theology and philosophy – contains Weil's categories of the unpolitical.

These categories, while developing the initial indications of Canetti, place the unpolitical in an ambivalent relationship to the political. The experience of necessity, when characterised as an experience of justice, opens the question of whether this constitutes an alternative foundation for the political. For Esposito, it is Bataille who assumes and reflects upon the ambivalence of the experience which Weil delineates. Bataille, through the interrogation of Weil's philosophical and theological elements, relinquishes the juridico-political and re-centres reflection upon the question and experience of community.

The other Canetti: beyond the confines of negative anthropology

The passage beyond the limits imposed by Canetti's negative anthropology is already present within those other elements of Canetti which demonstrate the potential separation of the subject and power. The separation is introduced through Canetti's indication of the subject's capacity for passivity in its relationship to power. Passivity, for Canetti, marks the subject's preservation of a source of thought and action by relinquishing its connection to power. It is a stance which is *actively* adopted by the subject, and it implies not the creation of a point of opposition to power, but 'an escape from the mechanism of power'.[1]

The forms of escape are identified and reconstructed from their fragmentary presence in Canetti's *The Human Province, Kafka's Other Trial: The Letters to Felice*[2] and *The Play of the Eyes*;[3] and Esposito reconstructs them to indicate Canetti's concept of passivity. The reconstruction is initiated from certain aphorisms contained in *The Human Province* which present action, which is the product of the interweaving of the subject and power, as synonymous with violence. The dominant negative anthropology, through the inextricability of action and violence in the paired terms of action-violation, violation-eating and eating-killing, renders passivity the only source of action whose potential is not inherently violent.[4]

Canetti's literary texts then provide figures who express a mode of action detached from power and violence. The first of these figures is that of Kafka, as revealed in Canetti's *Kafka's Other Trial: The Letters to Felice*, which locates this passivity in Kafka's self-ascription of the motifs of smallness, dwindling and disappearance.[5] In these motifs, Esposito identifies a type of metamorphosis which is distinct from that developed by Canetti's negative anthropology.

> In escaping from his proper body, in sliding thus towards bodily emptiness, Kafka experiments with perhaps the sole metamorphosis which does not produce an increase, the sole transformation which is not subjected to a return of 'form'; which moreover does not reflect any action, any act, not even the 'intransitive' one of the *escape* from action . . .[6]

1 Esposito (2005): 142.
2 Canetti (2012).
3 Canetti (1991a).
4 Esposito (2005): 143–4.
5 Ibid., 145. For an alternative reading of these motifs, see Gilman (1995).
6 Esposito (2005): 146 (emphasis in original).

48   Roberto Esposito: Law, Community and the Political

To this figure of Kafka, Esposito appends the figure of Sonne in Canetti's *The Play of the Eyes*. Sonne is himself an admixture and reversal of characteristics which Canetti defines as originally belonging to Karl Kraus and Robert Musil: the 'unheard part of Kraus, his *silence*'[7] and the spoken descriptive transparency which Musil only achieved in written form. Both of these reversals create an 'I' that has detached itself from language and thought as instruments of action.

> A refusal – a dispossession – which concerns not only the will, the faculty of reasoning towards an end, the dimension of the expansion and of the project of the self, but also the body itself; reduced – as with Kafka –, diminished to the point of liberating pure thought, the *thought of thought* . . . Once again returns the unpolitical theme of non-action, rather, of a non-active action, 'potential', halted in its actual 'power', rendered inapt to discharge itself in activity, to make itself 'act'. An action all the more 'decided', all the more responsible as it is deprived of the effects of imposition and of appropriation; a *non-appetitive* action.[8]

In this refusal, passivity manifests itself, for Esposito, as the interruption of the legal subject which:

> accomplishes itself within the trajectory of two interrelated operations: the dissolution of all freedom of action, of every willed action; and correlatively the concentration of the faculty of thinking in a reflection methodologically deprived of all finality, in an attention freed from the subjective dross of perception and imagination.[9]

The self-dispossession of the subject – the rendering of itself passive – reconstructed from these elements of Canetti indicates the possibility for another conception of the categories of the unpolitical. However, it is the work of Simone Weil which, for Esposito, through its considered reflection on 'the metaphysical relationship between subjectivity and power',[10] develops the potential of these initial indications of Canetti.

Simone Weil: from negative anthropology to heterodox theology

The interruption of the connection between the subject and power, indicated in Canetti's work, is re-thematised by Weil's notion of action. The appetitive intention, as the intertwining of the subject and power, is distinguished from a

---

7   Ibid., 147.
8   Ibid., 149–50 (emphasis in original).
9   Ibid., 151–2.
10 Ibid., 152.

non-appetitive intention which acknowledges and preserves the existence of a world containing other subjects.[11] These two intentions coexist within the subject, and create an internally differentiated notion of action. The predominance of one form of intention over the other determines the degree of connection between the subject and power.

Appetitive intention is an expansive power in which the subject reduces external reality to the domain of the satisfaction and representation of this intention. Other subjects, and the wider world in which they are situated, have no essential identity except as a limit or threat to the realisation of this appetitive intention. The origin of non-appetitive intention is in the relationship between the subject and other subjects created through the gaze. The vision or perception of the other subjects, produced by the subject's gaze, is non-appetitive, as it is a letting-be of these other subjects. They are not grasped as limits or threats to the subject, but as *other* subjects to whom the subject is related.

Each intention contains a form of understanding of the distinction between freedom of the will and necessity. For appetitive intention, the origin of freedom of the will is in the subject and necessity is contained in the constraints imposed, by other subjects and the wider world, upon the full expression of this will. Non-appetitive intention, in contrast, acknowledges the necessary existence of other subjects and the wider world as the condition and possibility of its freedom. Action in conformity with non-appetitive intention is action based upon necessity as it exists outside the voluntarism which directs appetitive intention towards its object.[12]

The opposition between appetitive and non-appetitive intention contains the foundation for Weil's categories of the unpolitical. Non-appetitive intention, through its particular understanding of necessity, indicates an understanding of justice situated beyond the existing concepts of political philosophy and law generated, for Esposito, through three political essays[13] of the early 1930s, culminating in the extended essay *Oppression and Liberty*[14] of 1934. These essays develop a critical examination of the concept of social and political revolution, as the passage between the political and the unpolitical. The condition of the working class in Europe, created and reproduced by the existing political system, is the origin of the unpolitical. The injustice of this condition cannot be changed other than through the supplanting of the existing political system by revolution. The validity of the concept of revolution, for Weil, depends on the identification of the potential for the revolutionary transformation of the existing political system.

---

11   Ibid., 153; Weil (1997): 454; (2002): 368; and (1994): 295.
12   Esposito (2005): 161; and Weil (1997): 123.
13   'L'Allemagne en attente' (Weil (1999)); 'Perspectives. Allons-nous vers la révolution prolétarienne?' (Weil (2001a)); 'Réflexions sur la guerre' (Weil (1987a)).
14   Weil (2001b).

The first essay, confined to an analysis of the situation in Germany in 1932, demonstrates that, despite the effects of the economic crisis, the existing Left political parties (social democrats and communists), in place of the possibility of radical social transformation, produce a situation of inertia and paralysis. This, in turn, indicates, for Weil, that neither is capable of providing significant resistance to the pseudo-revolutionary National Socialist movement.[15]

The insights and mode of critical examination are then extended, in the second essay, to encompass the potential, within Europe, for proletarian revolution. The expansion of the purview of the analysis is accompanied by a broader critical examination of the 'categories of classical Marxism'.[16] The potential for proletarian revolution – 'the struggle of the oppressed would now lead to a true emancipation, not a new oppression'[17] – identified by Marx, animates Weil's consideration of the continued pertinence of classical Marxism. For Weil, the categories of classical Marxism are placed into question by the character of the development of capitalism and the emergence of both the Soviet Union, in Russia, and the National Socialist regime, in Germany. The continued expansion of capitalism confronts the 'actual limits of the earth's surface',[18] but these limits have failed to generate any substantial 'premonitory signs of the advent of socialism'.[19] Rather, they have been accompanied by the emergence of the Soviet Union and the National Socialist regime, neither of which can 'find a place within the traditional picture of the class struggle'.[20]

This, in turn, leads Weil to formulate the 'hypothesis' that:

> up to the present mankind has known two principal forms of oppression, the one (slavery or serfdom) exercised in the name of armed force, the other in the name of wealth thus transformed into capital; what we have to determine is whether these are not now being succeeded by a new species of oppression, oppression exercised in the name of management.[21]

The transition to a new form of oppression originates, for Weil, in the displacement of the primacy of the labour contract (subordination of labour to capital) by the primacy of the rationalised organisation of the factory (subordination of labour to the machine). The organisation of the factory, based on the separation 'between those who have the machine at their disposal and those who are at the disposal of the machine',[22] is accompanied by a separation between management and ownership. The separation enables the emergence of the bureaucratic element in

15 Weil (1999): 231–4.
16 Weil (2001a): 6.
17 Ibid., 2.
18 Ibid., 1.
19 Ibid.
20 Ibid., 8.
21 Ibid., 9.
22 Ibid., 10.

industry – the managing personnel who administer the factory – which constitutes 'an order of problems independent of the order of problems presented by the operation of the capitalist economy so called'.[23] For it reveals that whether or not capitalist property relations are retained, the 'whole evolution of present-day society tends to develop various forms of bureaucratic oppression and to give them a sort of autonomy in regard to capitalism as such'.[24] Hence, the rationalised factory, for Weil, becomes the representation of the political, in its transition from capitalism to bureaucratic dictatorship.[25]

The 'potential threat' of this transition – the 'hypothesis' of a new form of oppression – is indicated, beyond the new regimes in Russia and Germany, by the increased presence of bureaucracy in the remaining European democracies. The bureaucratisation originates in the period of increased State intervention in the economy during World War I, and has extended 'in monstrous fashion' into 'all spheres'.[26] Within the remaining European democracies, the further process of bureaucratisation is limited by the internally differentiated forms of trade-union, industrial and State bureaucracy.

The three forms of bureaucracy are 'diffused, [and] scattered about in a host of administrative organs which the free play itself of the capitalist system prevents from crystallizing around some central nucleus'.[27] However, this free play is itself increasingly undermined by the combination of the economic crisis, created by the Wall Street Crash of 1929, and the 'systematic preparation for war'.[28] The goal of preparation for war – 'superiority in the armed struggle'[29] – is intimately intertwined with 'superiority in production itself';[30] and necessarily involves both the 'regimentation of the economy'[31] and its implementation by 'technicians organized into a State bureaucracy'.[32] The 'hypothesis' is of a general transition towards an essentially uniform social system in which 'neither war nor production is any longer possible without a total subordination of the individual to the collective industrial machine'.[33]

The 'hypothesis' presents a transformation of the political which simultaneously affects the unpolitical as proletarian revolution. The potential for proletarian revolution finds only a weak and sporadic inherence in the transition to this new form of oppression,[34] and indicates an initial separation of the unpolitical from

23 Ibid., 10.
24 Ibid., 10.
25 Ibid., 13; 15.
26 Ibid., 16.
27 Ibid., 16.
28 Ibid., 16.
29 Ibid., 15.
30 Ibid., 15.
31 Ibid., 16.
32 Ibid., 15.
33 Ibid., 19.
34 Ibid., 19–22.

the political, but confines this to a differentiation between the 'task of theoretical elucidation and the tasks set by the actual struggle'.[35]

The separation is reinforced by the final essay, entitled 'Reflections on War',[36] which extends the central motif of the rationalised factory of the second essay to the incorporation of war within the bureaucratised state. The distinctiveness of modern war is the 'inextricable mixture of the military and the economic, where arms are put at the service of competition and production at the service of war'.[37] The mixture results in the 'subordination of the combatants to the instruments of combat, and the armaments, the real heroes of modern wars, are, just like the men dedicated to their service, controlled by those who do not fight'.[38] The modern war is, therefore, 'a war of the state and military apparatus against its own army'.[39]

The unpolitical, as proletarian revolution, confronts the inherent difficulty of 'how, in the very act of producing or fighting, it is possible to avoid this hold of the apparatus on the masses'.[40] Once a revolution becomes 'involved in a war [it only has] the choice of succumbing to the deadly blows of the counterrevolution or of transforming itself into a counterrevolution through the very mechanism of the military struggle'.[41] The task, for Weil, is to understand modern war as an essential expression not of foreign policy, but of the 'domestic policy' of an 'administrative, police, and military apparatus'.[42] Hence, the preservation of this apparatus, 'even if led by revolutionaries' will be a 'reactionary factor'.[43]

The development of Weil's position, over the course of these three essays, leads to the more substantial reorientation of *Oppression and Liberty*. In this extended essay, Weil passes from a critique to a meta-critique of Marxism in which the categories of classical Marxism are effectively relinquished. For Esposito, the meta-critique is a transition towards 'the roots of political anthropology'[44] which reconfigures the understanding of the connection between the unpolitical and the political.[45]

In this reconfiguration, the conception of oppression is held to be far more fundamentally embedded in human existence. The history of human existence described by Weil traces an inextricable connection between force and oppression;[46] and enables Weil to develop a history of oppression in which forces interpose themselves between 'ordinary man and his own conditions of existence

35 Ibid., 22.
36 Weil (1987a).
37 Ibid., 241.
38 Ibid., 241.
39 Ibid., 241.
40 Ibid., 247.
41 Ibid., 243.
42 Ibid., 242.
43 Ibid., 242.
44 Esposito (2005): 168.
45 Ibid., 168.
46 Weil (2001b): 60.

Categories de l'Impolitique II 53

. . . which are, inherently the monopoly of a few'.[47] This monopoly has, however, to be actively reproduced, and it requires the maintenance of a stable division between 'those who command and those who obey'.[48] The capacity to maintain a stable division is continually undermined by a 'fundamental contradiction':[49] the opposition between the material limits of the exercise of power and the 'unlimited character of the race for power'.[50]

The history of oppression, considered in terms of the 'problem of power',[51] becomes the recognition of the 'necessity of power'[52] in social existence. With this recognition, the revolution becomes 'literally inconceivable'[53] because 'it would be a victory of weakness over force'.[54] The 'problem of power' transforms social reality into one which holds no intrinsic potential for liberation.[55] The real, as the political, is the history of oppression, and the unpolitical becomes the 'drawing up of an inventory of modern civilization'.[56] The preparation of this inventory is, beyond any future effect it might have upon social existence, the unpolitical: the experience of the 'original pact between mind and universe'.[57]

Commencing with Weil's essay, *War and the Illiad*,[58] the 'original pact', announced at the end of *Oppression and Liberty*, and comprehended through a form of science of history,[59] becomes one which is part of a heterodox Christian theology. The separation of the real and the ideal is progressively transformed into a metaphysical experience. The detached observer of the science of history is displaced by the experience of a reciprocal relationship between necessity and the soul.[60] In this relationship, 'one cannot know the soul itself without its relation to necessity, but conversely the study of its effects upon the soul (including and even above all in misery) *alone*, can enable us to know the true nature of necessity'.[61] The reconfiguration originates in Weil's turn to a heterodox form of Christian theology in which the relationship between necessity and the soul opens onto the experience of God.[62]

47 Ibid., 61.
48 Ibid., 63.
49 Ibid., 64.
50 Ibid., 72.
51 Ibid., 68.
52 Worms (2007): 227.
53 Weil (2001b): 74.
54 Ibid., 74. See also the later reiteration at 110.
55 Esposito (2005): 173.
56 Weil (2001b): 116.
57 Ibid., 117.
58 Weil (2005a).
59 Weil (2001b): 69.
60 Or, as Weil will express it, '[s]cientific investigation is simply a form of religious contemplation' (Weil (2002c): 259).
61 Worms (2007): 229.
62 For a discussion of the character of this heterodox theology, compare Vetö (1997) and Waterlot (2010).

54   Roberto Esposito: Law, Community and the Political

For Esposito, the final works transform Weil's conception of the political and the unpolitical. Social existence – the political – remains Weil's central concern, but it is now differentiated from a notion of the unpolitical which is essentially theological. The position of the unpolitical, as the origin of the critique of the political, is in a supernatural realm distinguished from social existence marked by 'God's absence and non-activity'.[63] The critique of the political becomes the revelation of the covering over of its primordial relationship to the eternal realm of the unpolitical. It is a critique which extends equally to Roman Catholicism and to the juridico-political concepts of modern politics.

The primordial relationship between God and the world is intimated by Greek philosophy and literature.[64] The covering over arises, for Weil, through a combination of the effects of Judaism, early Christianity and Roman law. These effects remain imprinted upon modern, secular juridico-political concepts and theories of history.[65] The occlusion of the supernatural position of the unpolitical is accompanied by the rise of idolatry. For Weil, the notion of idolatry describes a representation-image of social existence which substitutes itself for the experience of God by the soul. This notion extends beyond a critique of religion to encompass all representation-images of social existence as a social order.[66] The critique is an examination of secularisation in which the 'poisons' of Christianity, as an institutionalised religion, are reproduced in all attributions of 'a sacred character to the collectivity'.[67]

The critique of idolatry is combined with a critique of the fundamental concepts of the political. The notions of rights, personality and democracy are to be understood as notions which are 'entirely alien to the supernatural but nevertheless a little superior to brute force'.[68] They retain only a limited validity for the 'middle region . . . of ordinary institutions',[69] which interposes itself between the individual and God. The circumscription of these concepts is the corollary of the re-expression of the relations between 'the collectivity and the person . . . with the sole purpose of removing whatever is detrimental to the growth and mysterious germination of the impersonal element of the soul'.[70] In this process, the notion of rights is a central focus of Weil's critique, as it seen to express the continuing presence of 'pagan and unbaptizable' Ancient Rome within Christianity.[71]

For Weil, the attribution and assertion of rights is the corollary of a particular form of subjectivity. This form – human personality – is the deficient and limited

---

63   Weil (2002a): 159.
64   Weil (1987b). See, on the question of Weil's interpretation of the Greeks, Meaney (2007).
65   Weil (2002a): 162–3. Compare also Weil (2002b): 29 and the account in Weil (2002c): 293–5.
66   Ibid., 60–1.
67   Weil (2005b): 76.
68   Ibid., 81.
69   Ibid., 97.
70   Ibid., 79.
71   Ibid., 81.

Catégories de l'Impolitique II   55

expression of appetitive desire.[72] The human personality, set within a framework of rights, relates to others solely through force and contention. The assertion of a rights-claim or the exercise of an existing legal right becomes an intrinsic property of the human personality.[73] The juridification of the middle region, whether through a theory of natural or positive law,[74] is the creation of a framework of legal rights which can only 'evoke a latent war and awaken the spirit of contention'.[75] It is juridification as idolatry – the 'double illusion' of the sacredness of the human personality.[76]

The connection between this critique and the unpolitical rests upon another experience of the self in its relation to others. Sacredness is within the world, but this 'presence for which God needs the cooperation of the creature is the presence of God, not as Creator but as Spirit'.[77] God as Spirit, the presence of the supernatural in social existence, concerns the recovery of the sacredness of man in contrast to the 'false divinity' of the human personality.[78] Sacredness, as the true presence of God, in social existence, originates in the supernatural and is, therefore, essentially unconditioned. Hence, it can only be articulated in the language of obligations.[79]

The language of obligations, in contrast to that of rights, expresses respect for the human being through 'the medium of Man's earthly needs'.[80] It is a language through which an inventory of 'eternal duties towards each human being' is formulated.[81] The language of obligation is the sole language which is attentive to the insuppressible expectation lodged within 'every human being . . . that good not evil will be done to him'.[82] The object of this language is justice which contains the possibility to 'touch and awaken the spirit of attention and love'.[83] Through this language, subjectivity is divested of the shape of human personality animated by appetitive desire.

The opposition between rights and justice, as the differentiation between two levels of injury, reflects the distinction between human personality and man. However, this distinction retains the question of the relation between the unpolitical and the political, because, for Weil, the relationship is that of an impersonal Providence – 'the non-intervention of God in the operation of grace'.[84] Impersonal,

---

72   Weil (2002a): 33.
73   Weil (2005b): 84; and Esposito (2005): 181.
74   Weil's critique of rights involves the natural rights of the French Revolution of 1789 together with the neo-Thomist natural law theory of Maritain.
75   Weil (2005b): 83.
76   Ibid., 78.
77   Weil (2002a): 38.
78   Ibid., 34.
79   Weil (2002c): 4–5.
80   Ibid., 6.
81   Ibid., 6. See 10–39 for the specification of the inventory.
82   Ibid., 71.
83   Weil (2005b): 83.
84   Weil (2002c): 260.

56 Roberto Esposito: Law, Community and the Political

divine Providence 'is itself the order of the world; or rather it is the regulating principle of the universe'.[85] The regulation is the limitation of force itself, or, rather, the understanding of force as *intrinsically* limited. The divesting, or 'decreation', of the human personality becomes the comprehension of a divine mechanics;[86] and it is this divine mechanics which is both the limit and the possibility of force. The dualism of the unpolitical and the political, and its repetition at the level of the political between rights and obligations, are then set within this framework of a divine mechanics.

Reality, as a divine mechanics, is the creation of God, but from which God has withdrawn. This is expressed as a heterodox theology predicated on the fundamental dualism of the supernatural and the natural or the real. In this dualism, there is both distinction and connection between the two spheres through the notion of relation. The notion of relation indicates the limit of Weil's conception of the unpolitical, which is simultaneously that of an impasse.[87] For as an experience of the negative, in the form of a dualism of necessity, it articulates a (meta-)physics of power continually seeking its self-limitation in a mechanics which must simultaneously be an ethics.

Georges Bataille: the experience of the negative as the experience of community

The impasse of Weil's final rethinking of the unpolitical, as the dualism of necessity, leads to the thought of Georges Bataille, and the direct engagement with Weil's *The Need for Roots*, in Bataille's article, 'La victoire militaire et la banqueroute de la morale qui maudit'.[88] Here, Bataille's critique of Weil is held to mark a double movement of both appropriation and rejection which flows from Bataille's reconception of Weil's notion of relation, which displaces Weil's opposition between rights and obligations by a notion of community as immanence.

The transition to Bataille also marks an alteration in Esposito's interpretative approach. The more directly chronological ordering and interpretation of texts is replaced with a freer interpretative position. By this alteration, Esposito seeks to emphasise, in Bataille, the dissolution of all thought of a simple opposition or dualism between the political and the unpolitical. With this dissolution, there is a reformulation of the experience and character of the negative which becomes, in the *Catéories de l'Impolitique*, 'the conclusion not only of this chapter, but of the entire book'.[89]

---

85 Ibid., 280.
86 Ibid., 282–8; and Esposito (2005): 182–5.
87 Esposito (2005): 172.
88 Bataille (1988a).
89 Esposito (2005): 239.

Catégories de l'Impolitique II   57

The double movement of Bataille, contained in 'La victoire militaire et la banqueroute de la morale qui maudit', is shaped by Weil's failure to fully experience the negative. The limitations of this experience are embedded in Weil's conception of mysticism: the access to, and experience of, the supernatural. The realm of the supernatural, in Weil, is that 'which connects existence to an element outside it';[90] but it is a form of connection which renders mysticism as a self-contained knowledge merely replicating the traditional model of cognition. The supernatural, and its mystical experience, remain within the traditional separation between subject and object, as it is always generated by its connection to a realm of the supernatural as object. Hence, the 'mystic project is always a method of salvation, and not of perdition, where one loses oneself to save oneself, according to the intention of the ascetic, which is inevitably [a] project'.[91] The rigorously dualist perspective, which Weil seeks to express through mystical experience, rather than holding apart the terms of the dualism, envisages 'the direct contact of politics and the sacred'.[92] The realm of the supernatural establishes a connection with social reality through mystical experience which, in *The Need for Roots*, as the realm of the unpolitical, becomes a 'new political project'.[93]

This, however, is not the central concern of Bataille's engagement with Weil, but rather, and here is the simultaneous character of rejection and appropriation, the purpose of morality. Weil's notion of obligation, which manifests 'a boundless faith in the absolutely eternal character of obligation',[94] is, for Bataille, to be re-thematised as the demand 'that we create a relation of life between these [human] beings, we can tentatively say: *communication is the good*'.[95] Yet, it is a good in which communication is not a relation between human beings who confront each other as fully formed entities 'as with the stone or the tool, but as an intimacy, a *sovereign presence*, deserving of infinite respect and upholding its sovereignty on the basis of a characteristic that the name *extravagant* evokes'.[96] These human beings, in their 'perishable and particular intimacy',[97] are not dependent on the existence of a formal notion of the good. Hence, 'this *good* is exactly this which the transparent consciousness cannot reduce to its norms and which it only apprehends as exceeded, sensing its limits outstripped'.[98]

It is at this juncture in Bataille's text that Esposito detaches his exposition from the text's development, and concentrates on the philosophical influences shaping Bataille's critique of Weil. The change in the manner of exposition also involves Esposito in an interpretation which searches for these influences in both the

---

90   Ibid., 196.
91   Ibid., 196.
92   Ibid., 194.
93   Ibid., 195; and Bataille (1988a): 536–7.
94   Bataille (1988a): 534.
95   Ibid., 541.
96   Ibid., 541.
97   Ibid., 541.
98   Ibid., 541.

58   Roberto Esposito: Law, Community and the Political

earlier and later texts of Bataille. In this search, Esposito traces a thinking of the negative which is that of an 'alterity in common'.[99] Beyond all notions of right and obligation, even in their previous unpolitical reformulation in Weil, this alterity becomes Esposito's re-articulation of the good which Bataille distinguishes in the critique of *The Need for Roots*.

For Esposito, the philosophical influences which animate Bataille's critique of Weil consist of an orientation to Hegel and Nietzsche which is initially provided by Kojève's lectures on Hegel's *Phenomenology of Spirit*, and the combination of Chestov and Jaspers' work on Nietzsche. These interpretations form an initial interpretative horizon[100] from which Bataille, by thinking beyond its parameters, simultaneously re-conceives the relationship between the political and the unpolitical.

The differentiation of Bataille's thought from that of Kojève's interpretation of Hegel's *Phenomenology of Spirit* begins in the *Lettre à X., chargé d'un cours de Hegel . . .*, of 1937.[101] In this letter, Bataille accepts Kojève's interpretation of the conclusion of *The Phenomenology of Spirit* as the end of history, but the notion of this end is to be understood differently. This understanding emerges from Bataille's inability to completely resign himself to the end of history as an experience of inactivity:

> If action (the 'doing') is – as Hegel states – negativity, therefore the question poses itself of knowing if negativity which has 'nothing more to do' disappears or subsists in a state of 'unemployed negativity': personally, I can only decide in one sense, being myself exactly this 'unemployed negativity' ['*négativité sans emploi*'].[102]

The sense of this 'unemployed negativity', as the experience of the negative at the end of history, is not of passivity, but of immanence. It is an experience of negativity which cannot become 'the object of a contemplation'[103] in the form of either art or religion. The two later articles of Bataille on Hegel, entitled *Hegel, la mort et le sacrifice*[104] and *Hegel, l'homme et l'histoire*,[105] are then deployed by Esposito to emphasise the more specific differentiation from Kojève's interpretation of Hegel. For Esposito, Bataille accepts Kojève's presentation of Hegel's relationship between action and negativity; and its attendant understanding of philosophy as a 'philosophy of death and of atheism'.[106] The human being, as

---

99   Esposito (2005): 236.
100   Chestov (1925); Chestov (1926); Jaspers (1997); and Kojève (1980).
101   Bataille (1973).
102   Ibid., 369.
103   Ibid., 371.
104   Bataille (1988b).
105   Bataille (1988c).
106   Esposito (2005): 202 ; Bataille (1988b): 328–9.

'temporal and finite',[107] is part of nature, but in its action upon it, nature is negated. Death becomes the negation of nature, through human action; and atheism – the displacement of God by man – as the rendering co-terminus of the spiritual and the human.

The end of history, which, in the earlier letter, Bataille articulates as an experience of negativity analogous to 'facing a wall',[108] becomes, in the later articles, an experience of negativity flowing from 'man's transition to a homogeneous society'.[109] Homogeneity is to be understood as the fundamental historical condition, which is to be distinguished from neutralisation, and Carl Schmitt's assertion of neutralisation as the repression of the more fundamental friend/enemy distinction.[110] It is in relation to this potential slippage of homogeneity into neutralisation – here the repression of the man/animal distinction – that Bataille insists that the experience of negativity subsists within this 'fundamental homogeneity'.[111]

For Esposito, this insistence is also Bataille's delimitation of his thought from that of both Kojève and Weil.

> The first is that of the Weilian Presupposition, there where the Other, the Different is saved in the form of silence. It is to this which belongs the very essence of the unpolitical, its irreducibility to the existant. The second is that of the Accomplishment of Hegel and Kojève. This which accomplishes itself in the master-slave dialectic, is nevertheless the principle of the political: absolute knowledge such that it excludes from the field of the possible – makes impossible – every element external to it; and for this very reason will to power taken to its highest degree.[112]

The delimitation is effected through the influence of Chestov and Jaspers' interpretations of Nietzsche. Chestov is the intial influence offering Bataille, as the co-translator, in 1925, of Chestov's *L'ideé de bien chez Tolstoï et Nietzsche*, and reader of the later *La Philosophie de la tragédie. Nietzsche et Dostoïevski*, 'a "depoetised" reading of Nietzsche, namely, a reading of Nietzsche as philosopher belonging to this history of philosophy'.[113] This is then supplemented by the later engagement with Jaspers' 1936 work on Nietzsche, entitled *Nietzsche: An Introduction to the Understanding of his Philosophical Activity*.[114]

For Bataille, Jaspers' work is that of a 'philosopher of tragedy', offering an interpretation which 'enters into the philosophy of Nietzsche, follows its

---

107 Esposito (2005): 202.
108 Bataille (1973): 371.
109 Bataille (1988c): 363.
110 Schmitt (1993). See Geroulanos (2011) for Kojève and Bataille's engagement with Schmitt.
111 Bataille (1988c): 364.
112 Esposito (2005): 221–2.
113 Surya (1995): 216.
114 Jaspers (1997).

contradictory movement without ever reducing it to ready-made conceptions'.[115] In particular, for Bataille, it detaches '"nietzschean" politics' from 'the fascist interpretation';[116] and, in this detachment, provides the impetus for Bataille's rethinking of the relationship between the political and the unpolitical.[117] This, in turn, enables Bataille to install Nietzsche's thought in the 'clearing' left by Kojève's interpretation of Hegel. Nietzsche's thought becomes not a foundation, but rather the possibility to effect a reversal of 'the discourse of Accomplishment in order to revive and to reopen it to the future'.[118] The notion of the instant becomes the beginning or commencement after the end of history. This notion 'must not be thought as a type of abandon to the insignificance and to the transience of the moment',[119] but, rather, in its relation with the Eternal which is to be grasped as that which comes after the end of history. The relationship between the instant and the Eternal is the temporal expression of a human existence '*as the life of "unmotivated" celebration*', which reflects the unresolved difficulty of Nietzsche: 'an absence of causes' which 'pushes us into solitude'.[120] Bataille assumes this difficulty and, through it, effects a reversal of Nietzsche's notion of the eternal return.

> The understanding I encourage involves a similar absence of outcome and takes a similar enthusiasm for torment for granted. In this sense, I think the idea of the eternal return should be reversed. It is not what makes moments caught up in the immanence of return suddenly appear as ends. In every system, do not forget, these moments are viewed and given as means: Every moral system proclaims that 'each moment of life ought to be *motivated*'. Return *unmotivates* the moment and frees the life of ends – thus first of all destroys it. Return is the mode of drama, the mask of human entirety, a human desert wherein each moment is unmotivated.[121]

In this reversal, Esposito understands a relationship between 'immanence and transcendence' which cannot be reconstructed as a 'bipolar opposition'.[122] From this perspective, Bataille's *L'Expérience intérieur* (1943) and *Sur Nietzsche* (1945) are the reworking of a relationship between two central aspects of his contributions to the Collège de Sociologie between 1937 and 1939. For Esposito, Bataille's articulation of the relationship between both the sacred and the profane, and the will to power and the will to tragedy are the prefiguration of this subsequent concentration on immanence and transcendence.

115   Bataille (1970f): 474.
116   Ibid., 475.
117   Esposito (2005): 216–7.
118   Ibid., 222.
119   Ibid., 223.
120   Bataille (1994): xxxii (italics in the original).
121   Ibid., xxxiii (emphasis in the original).
122   Esposito (2005): 224.

The process of articulation is developed through a critical engagement with two other founders of the Collège, Michel Leiris and Roger Caillois. The distinction between the sacred and the profane, as one which is sociological, differentiates Leiris from Bataille.[123] In his letter to Bataille,[124] commenting on Bataille's summary of the Collège's activities and its dissolution,[125] Leiris indicates this divergence from Bataille over the very definition of the sociological and its study of the sacred. The object of sociology, for Leiris, is 'the study of "social structures"',[126] and it is only within this framework that the sacred can be comprehended sociologically. The sociology which the Collège has sought, in Bataille's summary, to elaborate fails to attain the sociological level of Durkheim; and – in its sole concern with a sacred sociology 'as the unique principle of explanation – [it] is in contradiction with the contributions of modern sociology and, notably, with the maussian notion of [the] "total phenomenon"'.[127] The methodological distance from the object studied, and the constitution of the sacred as one particular field, is not at the centre of Bataille's 'interrogation of the sociological sphinx'.[128] The interrogation is, rather, for Bataille, one which has 'singularly increased the precision and the brutality of the metaphysical interrogation . . . this bottomless interrogation'.[129] The meta-physical interrogation is the interrogation of subjective experience conceived as an affective condition of the subject of which the sacred is an integral part. Hence, the sacred, as subjective experience, regards methodological distance, resulting from the construction of the sacred as an object for sociological study, as an obstacle which limits comprehension of this subjective experience. The sacred, and its subjective experience, are, for Bataille, to be sought within and between subjects, and sociology merely radicalises the interrogation: the 'bottomless interrogation' becomes the attempt to comprehend the contours of this subjective experience.

In this interrogation, the relationship between the sacred and the profane occurs on the plane of immanence. The distinction between the sacred and the profane is the product of 'a movement translating *la mise en jeu* of an intense repulsive force';[130] and the methodological 'detour' of psychoanalysis and French sociology[131] enables the recognition of this movement within subjective experience. A fundamental identity is, thereby, experienced 'between the taboo which strikes impure things and the sacred in its purest forms'.[132] From this experience, there

---

123 See Louette (2008) for the divergences between Leiris and Bataille prior to their collaboration in the Collège.
124 Leiris (1979).
125 Bataille (1979d).
126 Leiris (1979): 548.
127 Ibid., 549.
128 Bataille (1979d): 535.
129 Ibid., 535.
130 Bataille (1979b): 222.
131 Ibid., 224.
132 Ibid., 224.

62   Roberto Esposito: Law, Community and the Political

then arises 'the violent repulsions which constitute the specificity of the movements of the [social] whole [as] creators of a human community'.[133] It is a conception of the sacred in which society is 'a field of forces ... external to the needs and to the conscious will of each individual'.[134] The description of the dynamics of this field of forces becomes 'the law of historical and social development, constituted precisely by the transformation of the original sacred node, of the impure heterogeneity into pure heterogeneity'.[135]

The law of socio-historical development described by Bataille is one in which the phenomenon of positive law is not specifically delineated. The experience of the subject is of a law which precedes and exceeds it – the sacred – which generates a form of social cohesion which is irreducible to the obedience to norms of positive law. Within the sacred, as a law of socio-historical development, however, there is lodged the phenomenon of crime – the tragic act which transgresses the sacred – as an integral aspect of its development.[136] The relation between the sacred and crime is of a process of sacralisation in which crime operates as a 'mechanism of sacred reinvigoration'.[137] The reinvigoration, for Bataille, is one which, from the event of the crucifixion of Christ, experiences a progressive decline. Christianity, as the re-sacralisation of the crime of the crucifixion, involves the 'propensity to identification, no longer with the criminal, but with the victim of the crime – this which already constitutes the first erosion of the original "spirit of tragedy"'.[138] The progressive decline is accompanied by the emergence of power: the 'institutional combination of sacred force and of military force in a sole person utilising them for his individual benefit and through this solely for the benefit of the institution'.[139] Power is the interruption of the sacred by an attempt to direct and utilise it. The attempt at instrumental direction of the sacred involves a 'force which searches blindly to eliminate the crime from the earth while all the religious forms are in a way saturated with it'.[140] The continued interruption of the sacred by the intrusion of power contributes to, and accelerates, the progressive decline of sacred reinvigoration.[141]

The socio-historical account of the sacred and power forms the basis for the more profound divergence, in the Collège, between Bataille and Caillois concerning the question of community. The divergence emerges from their respective approaches to the possibility of the subjective experience of community

---

133   Bataille and Caillois (1979): 293. On the wider question of the relationship, in Bataille, between a notion of the death of God and anthropology, see Goddard (2010).

134   Ibid., 293.

135   Esposito (2005): 226. On the question of history in Bataille, see Ferri and Gauthier (2006).

136   In order to comprehend the degree of divergence of Bataille's approach from that of Durkheim, see the account of Durkheim's sociology of law in Schluchter (2002).

137   Esposito (2005): 227.

138   Ibid., 227.

139   Bataille (1979c): 246.

140   Ibid., 252.

141   Ibid., 252–3.

Catégories de l'Impolitique II 63

in a context of generalised de-sacralisation. For Caillois, in *Le Vent d'Hiver*,[142] the possibility is contained in the individual's detachment and self-assertion within the formation of a group. The reinvigoration of the sacred is installed by the process of '*sursocialisation*'[143] in which the group's singularity and capacity for action are enhanced to the greatest possible extent. The experience of community, presented by Caillois as the transcendence of the limits of modern individualism, through the reorientation of the will, is at variance with the parameters of subjective experience presented by Bataille in *L'apprenti sorcier*.[144] The experience of community is not one which results from a transformation of the will, but, rather, from the revelation of all forms of conscious human transcendence – science, art and politics – as partial and deficient modes of an experience of the common. This experience is that of the essential finitude of the subject, and the encounter with 'the figure of destiny fixed by the whim of *fate*'.[145] Beyond the encounter between lovers described by Bataille,[146] this destiny is that of death.

For Esposito, this destiny, which becomes an integral aspect of *L'Expérience intérieur* (1943) and *Sur Nietzsche* (1945),[147] is an experience of finitude as a loss of the subject's certainty and centrality. The loss is that which is common to each subjective experience, but 'it is a sharing which does not bring together nor create identity between the parties; [but] which on the contrary separates them infinitely'.[148] Death is an essentially unappropriable experience to both the observer and the one who dies. It is an

> intermediary as a result of which this finitude is capable of constituting the beings of whose differences it is composed; and which compose it therefore not through the modality of relation (as Caillois conceived it), but through the modality of *alterity in common*, of a *shared* alterity. It is not a presence but an absence which one shares.[149]

The experience of finitude is the 'interiorization of alterity'[150] which 'does not bring together nor create identity between the parties'.[151] The alterity in common is a community of shared separation which, through the intermediary of death,

---

142 Caillois (1979). See also Bridet (2007).
143 Caillois (1979): 83.
144 Bataille (1979a).
145 Ibid., 57.
146 See the critical caution which Jean-Luc Nancy expresses with regard to the potential in Bataille to reduce the relation between lovers to that of community (Nancy (1991): 36–40).
147 See Bataille (1988d): 69–74; and Bataille (1994): 20–21, 47–8.
148 Esposito (2005): 237.
149 Ibid., 236 (emphasis in original).
150 Ibid., 237.
151 Ibid., 237.

64 Roberto Esposito: Law, Community and the Political

'separates them infinitely'.[152] The community, as this intermediary, remains immanent and is experienced as the exposure to finitude.

Finitude, as the shared limit between singular subjectivities, is an integral aspect of singular subjectivity. The exposure to these limits of singular existence, for Esposito, renders representation of this community impossible.

> Nothing is representable of this community, nothing of it can be taken to the level of a presence – not even its separation, the fact that it is a separation. If it was not thus, if one could represent something of the community, if the community would cede only one of its parts to representation, it would disappear (in absolute immanence or in absolute transcendence). In this sense, the community is the truly extreme figure of the unpolitical: uncommunicable, irreducible to a common *site*.[153]

The interruption of the representation of community, which Esposito traces in the work of Bataille, is the exposure to the formlessness of this shared alterity. The impossibility of representation arises from this formlessness itself; and finitude, as the exposure to this formlessness,[154] is the experience of the loss of the certainty and centrality of the subject: the loss of its operations of thought and action upon the world and others.

For Esposito, Bataille's presentation of this experience of finitude involves an affirmation of this loss, as absolute radicalism, which is that of 'the destiny – *not* the work – of the community'.[155] Hence, representation becomes the representation of this formlessness, namely, a representation which leaves it unshaped and unmastered. The categories of the unpolitical, as the representation of this formlessness, find their exemplary expression, for Esposito, in Bataille's *Chronique nietzschéenne*, which is the continuation of *Propositions sur le fascisme*.[156]

In the conferral of an exemplary status upon this text, Esposito's interpretation of Bataille detaches itself most clearly from an exposition guided by a chronological approach to, or periodisation of, Bataille's work. It also marks the divergence from Jean-Luc Nancy's critical engagement with Bataille in *The Inoperative Community*.[157] The situation of the *Chronique nietzschéenne*, as the conclusion to *Catégories de l'Impolitique*, closes the consideration of Bataille's categories of the unpolitical upon a text which presents the affirmation of this

---

152 Ibid., 237.
153 Ibid., 238 (emphasis in original).
154 See also in this regard Bataille's earlier contributions, in 1929 and 1930, entitled 'Materialisme', 'L'Informe' and 'La Base Materalisme et la Gnose' to the review *Documents*. Bataille (1970a); (1970b); and (1970c). For a discussion of Bataille's materialism, see Hollier (1990).
155 Esposito (2005); 239 (emphasis in original).
156 Bataille (1970g); (1970d).
157 See Esposito (2005): 234 fn. 3, where the influence and pertinence of Nancy's *The Inoperative Community* is specifically acknowledged.

Catégories de l'Impolitique II   65

formlessness as a response to Fascism. Through this approach, a double exclusion is effected with regard to both Bataille and Nancy. The post World War II work of Bataille, in particular, *La Part Maudite*, and its reinterpretation of the categories of the unpolitical through the Marshall Plan, are absent from Esposito's considerations. This absence is combined with a silence regarding Nancy's notion of 'literary communism' as a writing to and after Bataille which is 'an *inscription* of communitarian exposition, and . . . this exposition, as such, can *only* be inscribed, or can be offered only by way of an inscription'.[158] The double exclusion enables Bataille's text to effect an exemplary intensification of this formlessness as the affirmation of the unpolitical.

The exemplarity of this intensification is, however, one which emerges from a characterisation of the political as Fascism and the unpolitical as a form of remembrance. The intensification of the unpolitical, through remembrance or anamnesis, is undertaken, by Bataille, in the presentation of the Numantines as tragedy.[159] The text of *Chronique nietzschéenne* presents the tragedy as a manner of restaging the question of the opposition to Fascism, the internal dynamics of which had previously been presented in the earlier *Propositions sur le fascisme*.[160] The text is also the continuation of *Nietzsche et les Fascistes*,[161] in which Bataille extricates Nietzsche from his appropriation by the Fascists and National Socialists. Esposito, however, is less interested in the textual history of *Chronique nietzschéenne* than in the figure of the tragedy of the Numantines. The interest in this figure is also marked by a concern to expose its essential relation to the unpolitical which is other than the reaffirmation of its location, by Bataille, 'in the region of the Night and of the Earth, in the region haunted by the phantoms of the Tragedy-Mother'.[162]

For Esposito, this figure – or, rather, sign – is an object which signifies the absence of an image of community other than in the 'free decision' for death in common in the face of a choice between surrender or death. It is a sign of 'the limit – and in this manner at the origin – of the unpolitical'.[163] The remembrance of the Numantines is the sign, for Esposito, not merely of the absence of the Numantines – 'the lack of reality of a pure *name*'[164] – but of categories of the

---

158 Nancy (1991): 39 (emphasis in original).
159 An Iberio-Celtic people referred to by their fortification on the River Duero in Spain. They were part of the 20-year conflict between the Roman Republic and Iberio-Celtic peoples, from 154 BC to the final siege of the Numantines' fortification. This ended in 133 BC, with the decision by the remaining Numantines to commit mass suicide rather than surrender to Rome.
160 Bataille (1970d).
161 Bataille (1970e).
162 Bataille (1970g). It should also be stressed that contemporary archaeological research on funerary images, among the Hispanco-Celtic peoples of the Iberian Peninsula, emphasises that it is Air and Water which are the predominant representative images for the relationship between life and death. See Simón (2008).
163 Esposito (2005): 239.
164 Ibid., 240 (emphasis in original).

66   Roberto Esposito: Law, Community and the Political

unpolitical which are other than a simple opposition to, or reversal of, the categories of the political. It is an experience of negativity, as remembrance, which understands this limit as the opportunity to '"listen", politically, to this which is beyond political opposition (of the political), beyond the conflict between opposed parties'.[165] Through this exposition of the tragedy of the Numantines, Esposito detaches its sense from the original parameters of Bataille's presentation in which '[l]ife demands that men gather together, and men are only gathered together by a leader or by a tragedy':[166] the opposition of Caesarian unity to headless community.

In this interpretation, the tragedy of the Numantines ceases to be centred on its operation as a response to Carl Schmitt's distinction between friend and enemy, in the *Concept of the Political*,[167] and its associated conceptual framework.[168] The experience, as remembrance, of this tragedy, is a refusal which is situated outside the friend and enemy distinction, or, which reveals that which is prior to this distinction. For Esposito: 'Beyond this refusal the space of *affirmation* opens itself. Uninhabited and even, as such, uninhabitable. However, to this space – this extreme Yes – is connected, by an invisible thread, this which *cannot* yet be said of the unpolitical.'[169] The exemplarity of Bataille's text becomes, through the interpretation of the tragedy of the Numantines, a radical critique of the political and its modes of representation (representation-image and representation-mandate), in its position as a pure name without a material referent. The radicalism of this critique is contained in its rendering impossible all attempts to reanimate the relationship between the political and the unpolitical. The categories of the unpolitical are now to be sought exclusively within the space opened by the experience of this tragedy. The space is then also one in which legal or juridical categories are an essentially secondary or a derivative product of the categories of the unpolitical which may emerge from this space. It is a space whose possibility arises from a bracketing of all attempts to dissolve the political and the unpolitical into categories of the juridical.

The relationship between law, community and the political is thereby transformed by according a primacy to community, as an experience of negativity, in which both law and the political have been displaced. The final exposition of

---

165   Ibid., 241 (emphasis in original).

166   Bataille (1970g): 489.

167   Schmitt (2007). Carl Schmitt is the subject of specific attention in the preceding text, *Nietzsche et les Fascistes*, as a National Socialist jurist who 'has always been alien to the influence of Nietzsche' (Bataille (1970e): 458).

168   It should be emphasised that, on the basis of contemporary archaeological research, and re-excavation of the site at Numantia, the effect on the Roman army of the protracted conflict and siege was to produce a profound transformation in its military organisation. Hence, the eventual mass suicide coincided with a strengthening of the military organisation and force of the Roman army. Rather than undermining Rome's capacity to install the friend/enemy distinction, it essentially enhanced it. See Dobson (2007).

169   Esposito (2005): 241 (emphasis in original).

the possibility of categories of the unpolitical leaves open the question of the manner in which these categories can be accorded a determinate and, hence, positive content. It is this question which Esposito will confront and rework in *Communitas: The Origin and Destiny of Community*[170] and *Immunitas: The Protection and Negation of Life*.[171]

---

170 Esposito (2010).
171 Esposito (2011).

Chapter 4

From the unpolitical to *Communitas*

Communitas: The Origin and Destiny of Community[1] combines a development and modification of the theoretical framework of the *Catégories de l'Impolitique*. In its further development, the critique of the presuppositions of modern political philosophy is retained, but is modified to concentrate on a single category of modern political philosophy: community.

Communitas situates the category of community as an exemplary expression of the presuppositions of this tradition of modern political philosophy. The exemplary status of community is, however, detached from its exclusive association, in *Catégories de l'Impolitique*, with the questions of finitude and death. The centrality of questions of finitude and death are displaced by the question of alterity. This displacement is itself an aspect of the rethinking of both the form and purpose of the critical reflection upon the tradition of modern political philosophy.

The *Catégories de l'Impolitique* approaches the question of the presuppositions of modern political philosophy against the alternatives of political theology and the secular politics of administrative technique. The unpolitical is revealed only negatively as that which remains unthematised or obscured by these two alternatives. The progression of the reflection leads, in the final section of the text, in the work of Bataille of the 1920s and 1930s, to the unpolitical, as the negativity of finitude and death, which is accompanied by the outlines of a notion of community: a community of death.

Bataille's presentation of the collective suicide of the Numantines is the limit of the unpolitical. It is a community of death, formed by a decision for collective suicide, in which the affirmation of finitude and death is the disappearance of the community. As an event, it is, for Esposito, the limit of the representation of the unpolitical: the simultaneous presence and absence of that which modern political philosophy obscures.

The unpolitical, in its exclusive concern with, and attunement to, the negative entails placing modern political philosophy perpetually into question. The capacity of the thought of the unpolitical to maintain this external relationship to modern

---

1 Esposito (2010).

political philosophy rests upon its own negative self-presentation. It defines itself by what it is not and, hence, by the impossibility of the generation or development of an alternative transparency and certainty attributable to politics.

The negative self-presentation reveals a distinctive aporia within modern political philosophy, which relates to Esposito's particular understanding of political conflict. In this understanding, political conflict is the negative origin from which all politics arises. This negative origin is designated as the political in relation to which politics is always the second, derivative term of the distinction. The distinction between the political and politics expresses the primacy of the political over politics. The thought of the unpolitical, as this distinction between the political and politics, reveals an aporia which modern political philosophy seeks to dissolve in the ever-renewed attempt to assert the primacy of politics over the political.

The revelation and insistence upon this aporia situates the thought of the unpolitical as the negative corollary of the positive content of the concepts of modern political philosophy. The path beyond the conceptual framework of modern political philosophy, in the text's progression from Weil to Bataille, involves the disappearance of law – the mere expression of the intersection of force, violence and property – as a derivative form through which the primacy of politics is asserted over the political. The disappearance of law, as an intrinsic component of modern political philosophy, orients the further thought of the unpolitical to the notions of the political and community. The relationship between the aporia and community becomes, through the thought of Bataille, the impossibility of community as other than a fragile and tentative bond constituted by the essentially negative being-in-common of finitude and death.

The modification introduced by *Communitas* results from a re-conception of the origin of the gift, which shifts from an earlier appropriation of the relationship between Heidegger and the Greeks[2] to the etymological analysis of Latin. The decision to place Latin at the origin of the etymological analysis is to insist upon the importance of a language which, for Heidegger, was always considered to be essentially deficient and derivative, as the pre-figurative horizon from which meta-physics arose.[3] The Latin term *communitas* is held, through etymological analysis, to reveal a non-meta-physical sense at the origin of a thought of community. This term indicates both a sense and an experience of community which is rendered unthinkable by both modern and contemporary political

---

2 Esposito (1995); and Esposito (1996b).
3 On this, see Volpi (2001). This characterisation of Latin, is for Volpi, exemplified in Heidegger's *The Origin of the Work of Art*, *Parmenides* and *The Letter on Humanism*. It is possible to consider Esposito's choice of the concept of *communitas* as an assertion, following Volpi, of the distinctive importance of this Latin term. This assertion is, however, accompanied by the further assertion, against Volpi, that this importance is exactly the independence of this Latin term from any association with Volpi's list of Latin juridical and political concepts as integral elements of a positive European culture.

70   Roberto Esposito: Law, Community and the Political

philosophy.[4] The experience, revealed by the presence of the further Latin term *munus* within *communitas*, is that of an aporia. The aporetic experience, arising from the term *munus*, becomes the re-conception of the notion of the gift.

The origin of the gift in the term *munus* establishes its primacy in relation to the other Latin term for gift, *donum*. The term *donum* is, for Esposito, a derivative category which is conditioned by the more fundamental term *munus*. *Donum* expresses the conventional structure of gift exchange in which reciprocal relations of giving and receiving are created, maintained or extinguished. The conventional structure of the *donum* rests upon an absolute gift – *munus* – which precedes, and can never be exhausted by, this conventional structure.[5] The effect of the absolute gift of *munus* is that of the primacy of ethics over a theoretical or practical reason centred on the subject. The primacy installed by this ethics is not in the form of a positive ethics – a theory of virtue – but in the form of a negative ethics – an experience of aporia.

The aporetic experience is of a 'common non-belonging' in which the common is distinguished and detached from modern and contemporary political and social theory. This experience is one of an exposure to an obligation which attests to the subject's fundamental lack of substance and, with this, its insubstantial connection with others: they share nothing in common beyond their finitude. The experience reveals that the subject is not contained within, nor attached to, a community as another subject or subject-like entity. Hence, the common, as the *munus* within *commnunitas*, is the openness or exposure of the community to alterity.

The exposure to alterity is simultaneously 'the most extreme of its possibilities' and 'the riskiest of threats': 'the constitutive danger *of* our co-living'.[6] For the *munus* within *communitas* generates

> the unreachable Object into which our subjectivity risks falling and being lost. Here then is the blinding truth that is kept within the etymological folds of *communitas*; the public thing [*res publica*] is inseparable from the no-thing. It is precisely the no-thing of the thing that is our common ground.[7]

In this experience of the absence of a positive, independent foundation, the subject becomes aware of its being conditioned by the *munus*. The sense of the withdrawal of this foundation becomes the recognition that the *munus* 'constitutes us and makes us destitute in our moral finiteness'.[8]

---

4   The distinction between modern and contemporary political philosophy, for Esposito, in *Communitas*, is that between the modern political philosophy of Hobbes, Rousseau and Kant and the contemporary Anglo-American political philosophy (liberals and communitarians) and German social theory (Habermas and Apel).

5   See Weir (2013) for a critique of Esposito's conception of *munus*.

6   Esposito (2010): 8.

7   Ibid., 8.

8   Ibid., 8.

From the unpolitical to *Communitas* 71

The originary character of community is then situated within a genealogy of the common, which describes the initial erasure of this origin and the subsequent traces of its reappearance. Esposito re-interrogates modern political philosophy and reconfigures, through a distinct analysis of Heidegger and Bataille, the presentation of the common with which *Catégories de l'Impolitique* was concluded. The re-interrogation, proceeding from the inherent alterity of *communitas*, as a negative concept, is orientated to the critical reflection on the genealogical recovery of this originary character of the community.

The genealogy commences with the particular interpretative transformation of *munus* and *communitas* within Christianity. The Christian community, as a '*res publica christiana*', is the effect of the articulation of *communitas* with the Christian notion of *koinonia*.[9] In this articulation are contained a juridico-political and a theological notion of community. For Esposito, the theological notion entails the more complex combination of *munus* and *koinonia*, and this is the aspect of Christianity which retains the traces of the originary character of community.

These traces are present in Saint Paul, the 'Patristic literature' and Saint Augustine and, for Esposito, centre on the relationship between man and God as one of unity and separation.[10] In Saint Paul, the community, as a *koinonia*, is one in which the horizontal common bond is dependent on 'the gift (here surfaces again the *munus*) that God, through the sacrifice of Christ, makes to him'.[11] This originary gift is that 'from which we come and toward which we are called'.[12] The unconditional gift from God creates an obligation to respond, but the response is necessarily 'inadequate, wanting, purely reactive'.[13] Participation in the common bond of the Christian *koinonia* entails 'not the glory of the Resurrection but the suffering and the blood of the Cross'.[14] For 'the gift is withdrawn from us in the precise moment when it is given to us; or that it is given to us in the form of its withdrawal'.[15]

The 'void of subject' revealed by Saint Paul, through this originary and unconditional gift from God, is conferred with a more negative status by Saint Augustine.[16] The unity and separation of man and God is shaped by original sin.[17] Community 'coincides with the complicity established initially by Adam and

9   Ibid., 9.
10   Ibid., 10.
11   Ibid., 10. Esposito relies on Saint Paul's *Letter to the Corinthians*. In particular: 1 Cor. 1:9; 1 Cor. 4:7; 1 Cor. 10:16; and 2 Cor. 9:15.
12   Ibid., 10.
13   Ibid., 10.
14   Ibid., 11.
15   Ibid., 10–11. See, however, Agamben (2005b) and Badiou (2003).
16   Here, Esposito refers to Augustine's *City of God against the Pagans*, *Confessions*, *Answer to Julian* and *Commentary on the Epistle to the Galatians*. He also acknowledges the pertinence of Arendt's interpretation in *Love and St Augustine*, in particular, the notion of the 'community of guilt'.
17   Esposito's interpretation of Augustine is modified in *Immunitas*.

72 Roberto Esposito: Law, Community and the Political

fixed by Cain even before the moment when Abel constituted the city of God'.[18] The Creation is the first origin from which the second origin, the fact of human birth and the existence of a human community, shaped by original sin, is 'a kind of thorn or poisoned gift in the first origin'.[19] The human community, as a community of sin, is traversed by:

> ... fear, no one can be secure in this life, which is literally besieged by death; but also the *communitas fidei*, which, structured so as to be the salvific compensation of the first, inevitably remains prey to the fear no less acute of another, and even more definitive, death.[20]

The community of sin, for Esposito, represents the point of transition between the Augustinian relationship between man and God and the origin of modern political philosophy in *The Leviathan* of Hobbes. The community on earth, which contains both Christian good and evil, in the form of sin, becomes the state of nature.[21] The origin of modern political philosophy, in Hobbes, is the transformation of the relationship between death and community into the fundamental question of human coexistence.

The notions of the political, community and the law arise in Hobbes, for Esposito, as a response, which in its radical character marks this political philosophy as distinctively modern. Hobbes renders the first modern political philosophy a response to an ontological question – 'the absence of the *origin* ... of *communitas*'[22] – through its suppression by an anthropological question. The exposure of the subject to the originary *munus*, within *communitas*, becomes an exposure, within a state of nature, to the threat of death from others. In this displacement, the state of nature, as the original absence of community, contains, through the perpetual threat of death, the necessity for the preservation of life.

This earthly resolution of the state of nature becomes the origin of the political. The notions of community and law arise from the introduction, through the agreement of a contract, of an external mechanism or apparatus – the Leviathan state. The Leviathan state delineates a form of community based on an exclusive site of personalised authority – the sovereign – and the constitution of peaceful coexistence: the vertical relationship between the sovereign and individuals subject to the absolute authority and commands of that sovereign.

For Esposito, the radicalism of the Hobbesian transformation of the relationship between death and community is to be understood as a specifically modern form of nihilism. The notions of modern political philosophy express a 'more powerful

---

18 Esposito (2010), 11.
19 Ibid., 11.
20 Ibid., 12.
21 Ibid., 13. Here, Hobbes' theological transformation of Christianity and its connection to his political philosophy is largely unexamined. On this, see Crignon (2007) and Weber (2009).
22 Ibid., 140 (emphasis in original).

From the unpolitical to *Communitas* 73

nothing[ness] that has the function of cancelling the potentially disruptive effects of the first [nothingness]'.[23] The genealogy presents the work of Hobbes as a resolution which is accompanied by 'the tragic knowledge of the nihilistic character of this decision'[24]: 'a sense of "guilt" with respect to a community, both whose absence and necessity one recognizes'.[25] This 'guilt', as the trace of the experience of the originary character of community, remains within, and shapes, the subsequent development of modern political philosophy.

The unpolitical of *Catégories de l'Impolitique*, as a position for reflection external to political philosophy, is thereby relinquished, in *Communitas*, for a genealogical reflection on the expression of this 'guilt' in the work of Rousseau and Kant. The initial Hobbesian definition of the notions of the political, community and law are reworked, thereby reintroducing 'the question of community' Hobbes had sought to forcibly suppress.[26] The question of community, beyond Hobbes, is, however, subject to 'a mythic drift',[27] the temptation to overcome the bare, negative terrain of the state of nature through the attribution of a positive content to 'the void . . . constituted by the originary *munus*'.[28]

In Rousseau, the question of community occurs as a direct confrontation with the Hobbesian state of nature. This is a false origin, because it 'is nameable only beginning from the perspective of history that negates it':[29] community is 'nothing other than what history has negated, the nonhistoric backdrop from which history originates in the form of a necessary betrayal'.[30] The history of betrayal is the historical reduction of the origin of community to 'shared fear' from which the Leviathan becomes 'shared servitude'.[31] While the Hobbesian state of nature is rendered a historical and defective origin, predicated upon self-preservation, the logical origin of Rousseau remains dependent, despite its more complex composition, on the will of a self-sufficient subject. The mythic drift appears in the attempt to conceive community outside the history of its betrayal. For the history of this betrayal is the history of the divergence from this logical origin through the introduction of forms of mediation between the originally self-contained individuals. The limit of the break with Hobbes is the continued potential for the logical origin to dissolve into 'the myth of a naturally incorrupt dimension'.[32]

23 Ibid., 140.
24 Ibid., 14.
25 Ibid., 14.
26 Ibid., 15.
27 Ibid., 15.
28 Ibid., 142.
29 Ibid., 45.
30 Ibid., 16.
31 Ibid., 50.
32 Ibid., 17.

74   Roberto Esposito: Law, Community and the Political

The question of community is reposed by Kant, who breaks definitively with both Hobbes and Rousseau. The thought of community is presented in the form of an antinomy, as 'the conjunction of freedom with evil'.[33] The origin 'cannot be defined except by the otherness that separates itself from itself'.[34] From this 'destructuring of the philosophy of origin', human nature becomes 'irremediably unsocial [in] character'; and the notion of a positive content for a 'law of community is not feasible as a matter of principle'.[35]

The notion of law, which had been marginalised, through the presentation of Weil's critique of law and the juridical character of social relations, in the *Catégories de l'Impolitique*, reappears as an integral aspect of the thought of the question of community.[36] In this analysis, Esposito's reflection detaches itself from Weil's critique to accord the notion of law its first distinct thematisation. The analysis of Kant confines the notion of law, at the transcendental level, to a moral law without positive content – the categorical imperative – which contains the traces of the originary character of *communitas* in its transcendental position in relation to the self-certainty of the subject.[37] The categorical imperative is understood as analogous to 'a gift that does not belong to the subject, indeed that weakens the subject and hollows him out through a never-ending obligation'.[38] The obligation is without determinate content, as it subsists simply as pure obligation or prescription.[39]

The shift to the transcendental level of the moral law introduces, beyond Rousseau, a new and potentially 'radical language of community', which remains underdeveloped, because the moral law, despite its 'reduction of community to its unattainable law discloses a residue of teleology'.[40] The moral law, in its transcendental position prior to the subject, expresses the existence of community as one without relation to the present other than in the form of 'its destination-presupposition'.[41] The genealogical presentation, acknowledging the limit of the Kantian response, passes beyond the tradition of modern political philosophy to the thought of Heidegger and Bataille.

33   Ibid., 17.
34   Ibid., 17..
35   Ibid., 17.
36   The analysis of Kant and, in particular, the Kantian relationship between law and the question of community, is confined to *Communitas*. Kant has only a residual presence in *Immunitas*, and is effectively absent from *Bíos* and *Third Person*. In these later works, either the analysis of law returns to Weil's thematisation of the juridical (*Immunitas* and *The Third Person*) or the mode of analysis is entirely different (*Bíos*).
37   Here, Esposito situates the categorical imperative within an interpretative framework which is composed predominantly of the *Conjectures on the Beginning of Human History*, *Groundwork of the Metaphysics of Morals* and *Religion with the Limits of Reason Alone*. The Kantian consideration of law in the *Metaphysics of Morals*, with its Doctrine of Right and Virtue, is effectively absent from this analysis in *Communitas*.
38   Esposito (2010), 17.
39   Ibid., 17.
40   Ibid., 17.
41   Ibid., 92.

From the unpolitical to *Communitas* 75

The genealogical presentation in *Communitas* attributes to Heidegger and Bataille a fundamental critique of the subject which creates the potential receptiveness of their work to the question of community. The enhanced receptiveness of their thought to thematise the originary character of community is accompanied by enduring limitations. The orientation of the genealogy, which places Heidegger prior to Bataille, indicates the limits of Heidegger's potential receptiveness to the originary character of community.

The Heideggerian critique of Kant's philosophy reveals the Kantian moral law to be only a partial thought of the negative character of community, because it derives from an essential relationship to the subject. The transcendental origin of the moral law introduces, despite its negative form as pure obligation or prescription without positive content, a presupposition which obscures the origin of community in '*coexistence*'.[42] The Heideggerian critique, prepared by the lecture course *Phenomenological Interpretation of Kant's Critique of Pure Reason*,[43] and re-expressed in *Kant and the Problem of Metaphysics*,[44] shifts the consideration of community from the Kantian subject of theoretical and practical reason to the Heideggerian notion of *Dasein*, which exists as a being-in-the-world. The notion of being-in-the-world, as the immediate relationship between existence and coexistence, is the introduction of the question of community as coexistence.

Esposito insists on the specificity of Heidegger's terminology, in the corpus of work in the decade of the 1920s, because it delineates a thought of community which entails the interrelationship between fundamental ontology and an ethics. Coexistence commences from nothing other than the coincidence of our existence;[45] and the '*singularly plural* constitution'[46] coexistence becomes an ethics which is without a striving for a 'historical-empirical actualisation' of community.

The potential for a thought of community, in Heidegger's work of the 1920s, is recaptured by a mythic drift in the 1930s, in which the notion of destiny introduces an originary essence or origin which precedes coexistence; and transforms ethics into a decision, by *Dasein*, to strive towards 'its own future by rediscovering its own purest origin'.[47] The origin, which precedes coexistence, installs the 'reproductive mimesis of an originary model'.[48]

Beyond the association of destiny with that of the German people and National Socialism, the limits of Heidegger's thought of community encompass the later thought of the origin in its withdrawal. The 'impossibility of every return to an origin' introduces a distinction between mortals and poets, and, in particular, the

---

42 Ibid., 18.
43 Heidegger (1997a).
44 Heidegger (1997b).
45 Esposito (2010): 95.
46 Ibid., 92 (emphasis in original).
47 Ibid., 100.
48 Ibid., 100.

76 Roberto Esposito: Law, Community and the Political

exemplary position accorded to Hölderlin's poetry as a response to the withdrawal of the Greek origin.[49] However, for Esposito, the negative experience, in Hölderlin's poetry, of being cast adrift from this origin is confined, by Heidegger's interpretation, to the initial stage of a movement of experience which involves a return or an arrival: a recuperation of the proper. The 'homelessness', the negative experience expressed in Hölderlin's poetry, alludes to the originary character of the *munus* of community, which eludes Heidegger's later thought.

The critique of Heidegger is accompanied by a reworking of the interpretation of Bataille in *Catégories de l'Impolitique* which displaces the collective suicide of the Numantines by consideration of Bataille's *Accursed Share*,[50] *Theory of Religion*[51] and writings on prehistoric art and culture.[52] Bataille's work becomes only the intuition of a thought of community outside the parameters of modern political philosophy; and is the expression of the limit of this further development of 'post-philosophical' reflection beyond Heidegger.

Bataille's divergence from Heidegger arises from a notion of experience which is subjective destitution: 'being exposed to what denies and negates it'.[53] Experience – 'without destination and with no return'[54] – is severed from notions of resoluteness, decision or recuperative return. It is the exposure to 'our other and the other from us'[55] – and indicates the originary character of community in Bataille's thought: the common condition of life as 'the impulse of desire and the vertigo of risk'.[56] The exposure to this common condition is a fundamentally aporetic experience in which the subject's separation from 'the continuity of non-being from which he originates' introduces the desire for community.[57] Here, for Esposito, are the rudiments of the distinction between *communitas* and *immunitas* as 'life is nothing other than desire (for community), but the desire (for community) is necessarily configured as the negation of life'.[58] This insight remains rudimentary, as the aporia is accompanied by a 'sacrificial logic':[59] the simultaneous intensification and reduction of experience to 'the "joyous" condition of being in direct contact with death'.[60]

In *Communitas*, sacrifice as the residue of subjectivity – inner experience – which strives, beyond the condition of a common finitude, for direct experience of the negative redefines the mass suicide of the Numantines as a figure of

49 Esposito (2010): 102.
50 Bataille (1991).
51 Bataille (2012).
52 Bataille (2005a).
53 Esposito (2010): 119.
54 Ibid., 117.
55 Ibid., 117.
56 Ibid., 124.
57 Ibid., 124.
58 Ibid., 121.
59 Ibid., 19.
60 Ibid., 126.

nihilism: the putting to death, through mass suicide, of common finitude. The limit which this sacrificial logic imposes on Bataille's reflection is qualified by the later *Theory of Religion* and writings on prehistoric art and culture. In these works, another intimation of the originary character of community emerges from a common origin of life in which a '*communitas* that constitutes us without belonging to us' is revealed in an 'unbreakable interweaving of humanity and animality'.[61]

The work of Bataille reveals the site of closest proximity between thought and the originary character of community. Yet, these intimations, for Esposito, marked either by the limits of a logic of sacrifice or by the essentially allusive indications derived from the writings on prehistoric art and culture. The genealogical path of *Communitas* concludes with a conception of community whose elaboration requires that a 'post-philosophical' thought proceed, in a renewed questioning, beyond the limits of Bataille. The reorientation provides the impetus for the renewed reflection, in *Immunitas* and *Bíos*, on the notions of community, law and the political.[62]

---

61 Ibid., 134. See Ungar (1990) for an alternative approach to Bataille's writings on prehistoric art and culture.
62 Ibid., 19.

Chapter 5

Communitas

The community, or being-in-common, presented by the text involves the simultaneous disengagement from contemporary political philosophy and the revalorisation, within modern philosophy, of a certain 'self-problematisation' of the question of community. The disengagement, elaborated in the Introduction, arises from the reduction, by contemporary political philosophy, of the notion of community to an object, which is conceived as a 'wider subjectivity'.[1] It is this operation which, for Esposito, impoverishes the conception of community and, in this impoverishment, renders it unthinkable.[2] The impoverishment results from the underlying presupposition that 'community is a "property" belonging to subjects that join them together',[3] and is maintained and reproduced by three central elements: the community as a fullness/whole; the community as a good/value/essence; and the community as 'that which is most properly our "own"'.[4] The three central elements create a 'semantics of *proprium*';[5] and in relation to this semantic closure, Esposito traces, through 'the etymology of the Latin term *communitas*',[6] a radically distinct notion of community. The etymology reveals, through the presence of the term *munus*, within *communitas*, a notion characterised by its fundamental impropriety. The relationship between subject and community – being-in-common – is one of finitude constituted by 'a limit that cannot be interiorized because it constitutes precisely their "outside"; the exteriority that they overlook and that enters into them in their common non-belonging'.[7] The common non-belonging is 'the originary *munus* that constitutes us and makes us destitute in our moral finiteness'.[8] Destitution, as the decentring of 'the proprietary subject',[9] is also the continuous potential for the internal

1 Esposito (2010): 2.
2 Ibid., 2.
3 Ibid., 2.
4 Ibid., 2.
5 Ibid., 3.
6 Ibid., 3.
7 Ibid., 7.
8 Ibid., 8.
9 Ibid., 7.

Communitas   79

decomposition of *communitas*, as the exposure to 'the breach, the trauma, the lacuna out of which we originate'.[10] The etymological derivation of this notion of community is accompanied by a re-conceptualisation of the history of political philosophy.

In this re-conceptualisation, modern political philosophy commences with Hobbes, for whom the destitution and decomposition of *communitas* is explicitly recognised as that which must be expelled. This institutes an occupation of 'the void of the *munus*, the originary fault line, with an even more radical void; eliminate the danger of the *cum* by utterly eradicating it'.[11] The occupation is undertaken by 'the juridically "privatistic" and logically "privative" figure of the contract' and the Leviathan-State.[12] Hence, modern political philosophy arises, for Esposito, as a framework of *immunisation* against the intertwining of death and community of *communitas*. The expulsion of *communitas*, by this framework, is, however, accompanied by 'the tragic knowledge of the nihilistic character of this decision' for immunisation.[13] The presence of this tragic knowledge, in the emergence of modern political philosophy, becomes the point of transition to Esposito's reconstruction and re-valorisation of a fragile tradition which both reintroduces and radically transforms the question of community.[14]

The fragile tradition is presented through the work of Rousseau, Kant, Heidegger and Bataille; and is centred less upon textual chronology and internal coherence than upon 'the difficulty of taking on and supporting the void of the *munus* as the object of philosophical reflection'.[15] From this enduring difficulty, Esposito situates Rousseau, Kant, Heidegger and Bataille as a sequence of responses which each reconsider the limits of the preceding conception of the void of the *munus*. Within this re-construction and re-valorisation, law and the political are recognised as central, but limited, forms of reflection on this void. These limitations result, in the final chapter on Bataille, in a response to the void of *munus* in which reflection has relinquished the centrality of both law and the political.

The installation of the modern immunitary paradigm: Hobbes's fear

The break which Hobbes effects, for Esposito, in relation to the Roman and Christian conceptions of *communitas*, concerns an initial simplification of the connection between death and community through its explicit thematisation as a philosophy of human nature.[16] Within this philosophy of human nature, it is the experience or sensation of fear which expresses Hobbes's simplification

---

10   Ibid., 8.
11   Ibid., 14.
12   Ibid., 14.
13   Ibid., 14.
14   Ibid., 15.
15   Ibid., 15.
16   This commences from Hobbes (1999).

of the connection between death and community. The sensation or experience of fear is, for Esposito, 'not only at the origin of the political, but fear is *its* origin in the literal sense that there would not be politics without fear'.[17]

Fear is to be specifically distinguished from the 'negative semantics of terror'[18] because it is an experience or sensation which 'does not only cause flight and isolation, but also causes relation and union'.[19] Fear, as the foundation of Hobbes's 'entire political anthropology',[20] is never extinguished, but rather 'transformed from "reciprocal", anarchic fear, such as that which determines the state of nature (*mutuus metus*), to "common", institutional fear, [which] characterizes the civil state (*metus potentiae communis*)'.[21] In this transition, Esposito emphasises the passage from the state of nature to the civil state as a mere clarification – a rendering certain – of the objects and limits of fear.[22] The transition, marked by 'an indelible imprint of conflict and violence',[23] enables Esposito to identify the presence of the 'modern archaic'[24] in Hobbes's political anthropology. It is a transition in which 'the political-civil state is not born against or after the natural one but through its reversed inclusion in terms of an emptiness rather than a fullness'.[25]

The modern archaic emerges through the reduction of the initial character of being-in-common to 'a capacity for killing generalized to such a degree as to become the sole link that joins individuals who would otherwise be divided and independent'.[26] Being-in-common is then traversed and shaped solely by 'changing and uncontrollable relations of force'.[27] Hence, the temporary and contingent 'ordering' of this initial being-in-common is the expression of the intertwining of 'power and survival'.[28]

> One can ensure life, which is the first necessity, only by accumulating power, which is the first passion. Yet one can accumulate power only at the expense of others, at the cost of *their* life; living in their place, at the loss of their death . . . This means that the relation that unites men does not pass between friend and enemy and not even between enemy and friend, but between enemy and enemy, given that every temporary friendship is instrumental . . . with regard to managing the only social bond possible, namely, enmity.[29]

17 Ibid., 22 (emphasis in original).
18 Ibid., 23.
19 Ibid., 23.
20 Ibid., 23.
21 Ibid., 23.
22 Ibid., 25.
23 Ibid., 25.
24 Ibid., 25.
25 Ibid., 25.
26 Ibid., 26, citing Hobbes (1991): 113–114.
27 Esposito (2010): 26.
28 Ibid., 26.
29 Ibid., 27 (emphasis in original).

Being-in-common is essentially destructive – the constant elimination of 'every kind of social bond'.[30] The only community that exists is that of a community of crime: 'there does not remain anything except the crime of the community'.[31] *Communitas* is reduced to 'a gift of death'.[32]

The fear of the gift of death contains an 'instinct for self-preservation'[33] from which the transition to the civil state is realised. In this transition, however, the instinct for self-preservation appears to effect an 'absolute dissociation' from generalised 'lethal contact'[34] through the form of a contract. Here, the legal form of the contract is at the foundation of the Leviathan-State, and, upon its foundation, the contractual relationship becomes the predominant form of being-in-common for those individuals within the Leviathan-State. The contractual form, through its avowedly artificial, constructed character, presents itself as the absolute dissociation from the 'archaic paradigm of the gift'.[35]

For Esposito, this absolute dissociation is only apparent because the contract – the covenant – at the origin of the Leviathan-State merely absorbs and repositions the gift of death in the exceptional place of the sovereign. In the transition to the civil state, 'the state of fear' becomes 'the fear of the state'.[36] The covenant creates the Leviathan-State, but this creation is simultaneously the authorisation of its absolute sovereignty over the subjects whose covenant is its foundation. The instinct for self-preservation, through the covenant, institutes an entity 'with whom all relate without any further need of relating among them'.[37] Being-in-common, within the Leviathan-State, is an artificial unity created by an exclusively vertical union between the subjects and the sovereign of the Leviathan-State. The subjects of the sovereign 'are those that have nothing in common since everything is divided between "mine" and "yours": division without sharing'.[38] This essential lack of anything more enduring between the subjects than the contractual form is the counterpart of the particular position of sovereignty within the Leviathan-State.

Sovereignty, although originating in the covenant, and, therefore, seeming to establish its juridical foundation, necessarily 'subordinates and then exceeds the juridical',[39] thereby reinstalling the primacy of the political. For the covenant remains 'ineffectual without a sword to enforce it'.[40] The underlying logic of the subordination of the juridical to the political is accompanied by a series of

---

30 Ibid., 27.
31 Ibid., 27.
32 Ibid., 13.
33 Ibid., 21.
34 Ibid., 27.
35 Ibid., 29.
36 Ibid., 29.
37 Ibid., 29.
38 Esposito (2010): 28, citing Hobbes (1999): 84.
39 Ibid., 30.
40 Ibid., 30.

82 Roberto Esposito: Law, Community and the Political

other subordinations. The notions of 'order and decision, norm and exception, universality and contingency' are all subject to the same logic of 'the superimposition of the two terms and the surplus of the second with regard to the first'.[41] The primacy of the political inheres in the relation between subjects and the sovereign of the Leviathan-State generated by the covenant's linkage between authorisation, representation and identification.[42] Once authorisation situates the sovereign as the subjects' representative, it detaches the sovereign from control by the subjects of the original covenant. In the position of representative, the subjects identify with the sovereign, but it is a total identification in which they 'renounce any margin of autonomy with respect to his actions, precisely because they are considered as one's own'.[43] The Leviathan-State is, for Esposito, the installation of a sacrificial apparatus: the institutional expression of the modern archaic.

The transition to the civil state, and the vertical union of the Leviathan-State which underpins it, breaks with the gift of death. The dissociation of life from death can, however, only be achieved 'by entrusting it to the one who has the right to take it away [the sovereign], based upon the terrible conjunction that gives him the power "of life *and* death"'.[44] The conjunction establishes the space of the Leviathan-State as one traversed by the reversibility of protection and persecution: 'the coincidence of the preservation of life and the capacity to sacrifice it in a framework predefined by the primary relation of enmity'.[45]It is this enmity which also renders the distinction between punishment and persecution relative to the position of the individual subject with regard to the covenant. Punishment is exercised by the sovereign in relation to those who were party to the original covenant, but who have strayed from obedience to the sovereign. Hence, their original authorisation of the sovereign, as the covenanting party's representative, furnishes the sovereign with the power to compel their obedience: the actions of their will have authorised their own punishment.[46] In contrast, persecution relates to individuals designated as 'enemies of the commonwealth' and, therefore, outside the boundaries of the Leviathan-State. Once defined as outside the commonwealth, the sovereign's actions are no longer classifiable as those of punishment, but of persecution. The relative distinction between punishment and persecution is the reflection of the Leviathan-State as a 'victimising mechanism' which maintains community.[47] The community or commonwealth, bound by the Leviathan-State, is reproduced through 'an absolute exteriorization that subtracts community from itself: the "common" now describes

---

41 Ibid., 30.
42 Here, Esposito draws upon Zarka (1987).
43 Esposito (2010): 31.
44 Ibid., 32.
45 Ibid., 33.
46 For Zarka (2001): 228–50, this represents Hobbes's substitution of an *a posteriori* for an unattainable *a priori* foundation for punishment in the form of the modalities of its exercise by the sovereign.
47 Esposito (2010): 33.

Communitas 83

in fact the enemy that attacks it and the power that keeps it united against the enemy'.[48] The power perpetually reproduces unity, because this very unity cannot be produced other than 'by dividing it, eliminating it as community. This is how the community of sacrifice is turned inside out or doubled in the sacrifice of community.'[49] The endless cycle of fear and sacrifice – life 'sacrificed to the preservation of life'[50] – defines Hobbes's political anthropology as one structured by 'the opposition between *immunitas* and *communitas*'.[51]

The intensity and virulence of this opposition is, for Esposito, a symptom of the presence of a more fundamental origin which precedes the transition from the state of nature to the civil state. In order to reconstruct, or render visible, this more fundamental origin, Esposito situates his interpretative position beyond 'Hobbes's explicit theorization'.[52] The combination of Freud's *Totem and Taboo*,[53] *Civilization and Its Discontents*[54] and *Moses and Monotheism*[55] enables the transition to be understood as the consequence of a preceding origin in which sacrifice is logically prior to fear. The 'structural logic of the sacrificial paradigm'[56] arises from the killing of the father by the sons: 'the principle and primal crime of both the individual and humanity'.[57] From this interpretative position, the character of the fear embedded in the being-in-common of the state of nature is transformed into the experience of the modern archaic. It is a fear which expresses the ineradicable memory of this primal crime. The transition to the civil state, situated in relation to this more fundamental origin, becomes the reincorporation, by the sons, of the dead father as a mytho-totemic figure.[58] The covenant, as the installation of the Leviathan-State and its sovereignty, reveals the linkage of authorisation, representation and identification as the expression of guilt for this primal crime. The agreement of the covenant is an act of self-sacrifice in which the emergence of law and morality corresponds to an 'absolute reciprocity'.[59] It is an absolute reciprocity in which the 'incorporation of the father on the part of the sons corresponds to the incorporation of the sons of the part which, upon the death of the father, substitutes for him'.[60] The absolute reciprocity of incorporation, which this interpretative position reveals, is, for Esposito, represented in the engraving on the frontispiece of the first English edition of the *Leviathan* of 1651. The image is that of the 'uncanny' – the return of the most familiar – in which:

48   Ibid., 33.
49   Ibid., 33.
50   Ibid., 14.
51   Ibid., 28.
52   Ibid., 34.
53   Freud (1955).
54   Freud (1961a).
55   Freud (1964).
56   Esposito (2010): 35.
57   Ibid., 35–6, citing Freud (1961b): 183.
58   Ibid., 37.
59   Ibid., 39.
60   Ibid., 39–40.

84   Roberto Esposito: Law, Community and the Political

the many small human forms wedged in together one against the other in the shape of a scale of impenetrable armour ... [represent] the inclusion again of the murderous sons on the part of the 'second' father *in one's own body*.[61]

The modern archaic, which Esposito reveals through Freud, renders Hobbes's political anthropology a far more complex and enduring immunitary paradigm. This theoretical construction creates a being-in-common marked by the 'nihilistic character of this decision': the sole relation of a 'vertical exchange of protection-obedience'. [62]

The questioning of the modern immunitary paradigm: Rousseau's guilt

Rousseau's thought marks the first articulation of the question of community through the critical reflection upon the Hobbesian framework. The critical potential which inheres in Rousseau's reflection will then become the interpretative horizon from which Esposito will reconstruct 'a line of thought, which ... reintroduces the question of community'.[63] The presentation of Rousseau ranges over the whole corpus of his work, in both its literary and philosophical modes of expression, as this corpus is held to be organised by a common philosophical anthropology. For Esposito, Rousseau's thought, while relinquishing the Hobbesian categories, remains a philosophical anthropology centred on 'the individual fully and perfectly closed'.[64] The philosophical anthropology of the will, which Rousseau elaborates, introduces a break in the Hobbesian framework which is qualified by the limitations revealed by Esposito's analysis.

The presentation of Rousseau, as a thinker of community, animated by a rejection of the Hobbesian immunitary paradigm, focuses on the philosophical character of this critique.[65] The Hobbesian categories are relinquished through the re-conception of the transition from the state of nature to the civil state which contests Hobbes's 'internal logic, the productive relation between preservation and sacrifice: a community preserved by sacrifice is for that reason promised to death'.[66] The contestation involves a rethinking of the definition and character of guilt, crime and sacrifice. In this rethinking, a redefinition of negativity renders fear, and the potential Freudian supplement of guilt to Hobbesian fear, flowing from the 'primal crime', inoperative. The crime becomes that which transcends the presupposition of fear or a 'primal crime': it becomes 'the antecedent that

61   Ibid., 39–40 (emphasis in original).
62   Ibid., 14.
63   Ibid., 17.
64   Ibid., 50.
65   Hence, the question of Rousseau's relationship to political economy, and to the French Revolution, is not central to Esposito's philosophical reconstruction.
66   Ibid., 43. Citing Rousseau (1992).

withdraws the possibility of community's own realization from itself'.[67] Hence, it posits a 'transcendental criterion of the negativity of history and indeed of history insofar as it is negative, this then means that guilt cannot be atoned for through any kind of sacrifice'.[68]

The intertwining of guilt and sacrifice is interrupted through the positing of a non-historical origin which is 'not temporally definable because it is not inclusive of time, or at least of that linear and progressive time of history that articulates the different phases of human civilization'.[69] The conception of a non-historical origin, for Esposito, contains both the potential radicalism and the actual limitation of Rousseau's philosophical reflection on community. The potential radicalism is embedded in

> the hypothesis of an unsociability even more extreme than that of Hobbes. For Rousseau, men in the state of nature are not *even* united by war with each other, even if they are otherwise amoral and potentially given to conflict like the Hobbesian wolf-man.[70]

The extreme character of this hypothesis reveals the origin as fundamentally *negative*, a condition of 'non-society, non-state, non-history',[71] in which man is beyond 'any moral qualification'.[72] The origin indicates that 'there is nothing to be found where the origin is except the trace of its withdrawal.[73] It is exactly this indication which Rousseau will not explicitly thematise, but will, instead, accord the origin a positive presence 'from the perspective of the history which negates it':[74] a constant 'lamenting [of] the disappearance of the origin'.[75] The limitation which this imposes on the rethinking of the question of community is reflected in a series of aporias or antinomies in its exposition.

By situating the origin non-historically, the question of the presentation or representation of that negative origin returns insistently in Rousseau. The fundamental lack of relation between men posited at this non-historical origin constitutes it as one of 'immediacy, transparency, and innocence'.[76] With regard to this origin, history can only be linked to it as that which comes after: 'in the form of a necessary degradation'.[77] Hence, history, and more broadly civilisation, is degradation through mediation – the development and insertion of 'language,

---

67 Ibid., 42.
68 Ibid., 42.
69 Ibid., 44.
70 Ibid., 51.
71 Ibid., 51.
72 Ibid., 45.
73 Ibid., 46.
74 Ibid., 45.
75 Ibid., 46.
76 Ibid., 46.
77 Ibid., 47.

86   Roberto Esposito: Law, Community and the Political

power, money, writing, laws'[78] – between the men posited at the origin. The counterpart of this characterisation is that the man at the origin, formed without prior mediation, already exists in a pure, fully formed condition.[79] Beyond the difficulties sustained in the coherent presentation of the anthropo-genesis of man,[80] a more fundamental difficulty arises from the distinction between man and animal which it entails. The human is distinguished from the animal by the freedom of the will, and this freedom of the will contains the possibility for the forms of mediation associated with the degradation of history. The potential of this freedom, located within the man who arises at the origin, renders the origin co-extensive with its denaturalisation. The origin already contains 'difference from itself',[81] and is constituted by an essential impurity.

> It [is not] by accident that the natural features in all the examples Rousseau cites are always introduced by an 'almost' (as 'almost naked'), by an 'only' ('armed only with a bow and arrow'), by a 'like' or by a conditional verb: zero [is not] representable except as an 'almost one', one as 'almost two', and so forth because of the inexpressible limit that separates as well as unites 'already' with 'not yet': already *and* not yet history, still *and* no longer nature . . .[82]

The interpenetration, while sundering the Hobbesian link 'between individualism and absolutism',[83] creates an irresolvable antinomy: 'the community is both impossible and necessary'.[84] The antinomy is reflected in the unbridgeable passage between Rousseau's experience of solitude and his constitution of community as the object of philosophical consideration.

For Esposito, the antinomy presents a limit which reveals that Rousseau was 'the first to think community together with and within its myth'.[85] The opening onto and the limits of the consideration of community flow from the primacy accorded to 'the subject in its existence and not in thought'.[86] It is a consideration of community which results from the primacy accorded to sensation over ideation, and the further assertion of existence as sensation: '[e]xisting is a truth of the heart, of feeling, of passion, of suffering more than it is of the mind . . .'.[87] The subject's sentiment of its existence is the indication of a being-in-common – existence as

---

78   Ibid., 47.
79   Ibid., 47. Citing Rousseau (1992): 18–19.
80   Esposito acknowledges the pertinence of the critiques of this anthropo-genesis by Leroi-Gourhan (1993) and Stiegler (1998).
81   Esposito (2010): 49.
82   Ibid., 49.
83   Ibid., 50.
84   Ibid., 53.
85   Ibid., 54.
86   Ibid., 55.
87   Ibid., 55.

Communitas 87

a 'common, shared feeling'.[88] Being-in-common, as sentiment, is an experience of community which is only experienced actively, through 'its intensity'.[89] Intensity, while rendering the subject 'a substance that continually exceeds its proper site',[90] is always a return to the self and its essential unity.

> Existence, as such, is shared in common, but this 'common' is also always ownership, what is most *properly* owned by him who experiences his own existence: the *subiectum* as what cannot allow anything in that is not properly of the substance that substantiates it.[91]

The circular movement of this experience of intensity, as being-in-common, engenders a thinking of community which is always centred on the expansion and contraction of the existence of the subject. The subject remains 'the subject of its own loss'.[92]

For Esposito, Rousseau's conception of pity is the exemplary circularity of the experience of intensity. While man at the origin already has a sensation of pity,[93] the projected linear development and expansion of this sensation into a refined civic sentiment is closed in upon itself. The suffering and vulnerability of others is grasped and fully graspable only through the subject's identification with that suffering and vulnerability. The subject's sensation of pity is the effect of its expansion into the other's existence and the concomitant desire not to be situated in an existence which suffers.[94] The circularity of the sensation of pity reveals that Rousseau's 'thought of community is born within the terms of its closure'.[95]

The recognition of *Communitas*: Kant's law

The difficulty in which Rousseau's philosophy is enmeshed is, for Esposito, that which Kant expressly confronts and seeks to transform. However, the particular distinctiveness of Kant's approach to the question of community remains occluded, for Esposito, if one seeks to place Kant within a history of political philosophy which either retains the assumption of a common philosophical framework between Rousseau and Kant[96] or which seeks to marginalise the connection, in

88 Ibid., 56.
89 Ibid., 56.
90 Ibid., 56.
91 Ibid., 57 (emphasis in original).
92 Ibid., 60.
93 Rorty (1991): 416, defines Rousseau's pity as 'a sympathetic responsive awareness of the vulnerability and suffering of other creatures'.
94 Here, Esposito considers Rousseau's *Emile* (Rousseau (1979)) to present this essential circularity.
95 Esposito (2010): 61.
96 Ibid., 62–4. Here, Esposito considers the presumption of a common philosophical framework, although the position of ascendancy is different, to be shared by both the immediately post-Kantian philosophers of German Idealism (in particular, Hegel), and the later Neo-Kantian philosophy of Ernst Cassirer.

88   Roberto Esposito: Law, Community and the Political

Kant's philosophy, between the notion of the limit and the question of community.[97] These two forms of engagement with Kant's approach to the question of community, despite their differences, both cover over Kant's distinctiveness as the point of transition from, rather than the continuation of, a history of political philosophy. Esposito seeks to extract Kant from this understanding within political philosophy, by insisting upon Kant's reworking of Rousseau as a rethinking of community which intimates a thinking of *communitas*. The presence of this thought of *communitas* is contained in the particular conception of law in Kant's work; and Esposito's interpretation of Kant is developed, through this conception of law, against both existing traditions of Kant interpretation and a strictly chronological approach to Kant's work.

The parameters of Esposito's engagement with Kant, and the accompanying elaboration of Kant's conception of law, are initially shaped by centring and developing the distinction between Rousseau and Kant regarding the question of community upon the nature of theodicy.[98] The initial focus is then supplemented by an examination of the internal structure of, and relationship between, the works within Kant's corpus; and this is overlain by an emphasis on the presence within them of a 'correspondence between the semantics of community and the crises of subjectivity'.[99] The approach effectively displaces the conventional designation and division of Kant's corpus between major or marginal texts and, within a text, between a major or marginal part. In this displacement, the conception of law is held to contain a recognition of *communitas*, but one which has yet to break more radically with the modern tradition of political philosophy.

The conception of law and its recognition of *communitas*, which Esposito reveals in Kant's work, involves an almost exclusive concentration on the relation between the subject and the law as one which renders the subject finite. The rendering finite of the subject, by the law, is simultaneously the recognition of community 'within the limits of the law'.[100] The recognition, in the form of a paradox or contradiction, detaches Kant from the modern tradition of political philosophy 'divided between those who deny even the question of community, as Hobbes does, and those who attempt to resolve the question through myth, as Rousseau does'.[101] The paradox expresses the finite subject's relation to community as 'the impossible that is their common *munus* . . . This is the very object

---

97   Ibid., 77–8. Here, Esposito considers the approaches to Kant of Lucien Goldmann, Karl-Otto Apel and Jürgen Habermas, beyond their differences, to be united by the definition of Kant's notion of the limit as that which is to be discarded in order to respond to the question of community.

98   See Steinbrecher (2007) for an alternative reading of the centrality of theodicy for Kant's philosophy centred on Kant's 'On the Miscarriage of All Philosophical Trials in Theodicy' of 1791. In contrast, this essay is accorded a central position in Esposito's chapter devoted to theology in *Immunitas*.

99   Esposito (2010): 75.

100   Ibid., 76.

101   Ibid., 76.

of the law of community: this nothing-in-common cannot be destroyed.'[102] The nothing-in-common subsists, however, as lack: it can neither be 'reduced to a simple nothing' nor can it be 'made substantial'.[103] The law which Eposito reveals in Kant's work has the status of a limit which, in rendering the subject finite, exposes this finite subject to an aporetic experience of community as this nothing-in-common.

The presence of this conception of the law in Kant is established, for Esposito, by acknowledging a fundamental divergence between Rousseau and Kant concerning the notion of freedom in its relationship to the will and the law. It is initially situated in Kant's *Conjectures on the Beginning of Human History*[104] and *Religion within the Boundaries of Mere Reason*,[105] in which the will, through the recognition of 'the presence of evil',[106] ceases to be coextensive with the subject and its freedom. For Esposito:

> This is the decisive line which separates Kant from Rousseau: the law does not dictate a return to nature because human nature contains within it a seed that is the exact opposite of the law . . . [the] essence [of man] is configured from the outset as a debt, as lack, as a *negativum* not produced by history and which therefore it cannot somehow remedy.[107]

The initial presence of this conception of the law emerges in Kant's engagement with the question of theodicy. The *Conjectures on the Beginning of Human History* insert, within the historical record, a 'historical account of the first development of freedom from its original predisposition in human nature', which is to be distinguished from 'an account of the progression of freedom' formed entirely from the historical record.[108] These conjectures, which are neither pure fiction nor the actually recorded occurrences of the historical record, remain, for Kant, close to the biblical account offered in *Genesis*. From these conjectures, Kant introduces a distinction between the realm of nature and its history – the creation of God and, hence, that which originates in goodness – and the realm of freedom – the creation of man, and, hence, that which originates in evil.

Esposito then views Kant's *Religion within the Boundaries of Mere Reason* as replacing the conjectural status of this division with a distinction between an origin in reason and an origin in time. This distinction provides a philosophical formulation of the compatibility of 'the principle of the naturalness of evil with that of absolute freedom'.[109] In this philosophical formulation, evil and freedom

---

102   Ibid., 77.
103   Ibid., 77.
104   Kant (2003).
105   Kant (2004).
106   Esposito (2010): 65.
107   Ibid., 65–6.
108   Kant (2003): 221.
109   Esposito (2010): 67.

90 Roberto Esposito: Law, Community and the Political

are co-originary, for good and evil are now situated as 'the ground antecedent to every use of freedom in experience'.[110] The maxim adopted by the will – the use of freedom in experience – can be either good or evil. The relationship between freedom and evil, articulated by *Religion within the Boundaries of Mere Reason*, in which freedom is to be defined through 'the possibility of evil that is present in it',[111] then accords to a law, not freedom, the recognition and opposition to evil.[112] Yet, this law, in order to delimit and oppose evil, has to be situated, 'as an arch-origin',[113] prior to evil which itself has already been accorded the 'quality of being original'.[114]

The paradox which *Religion within the Boundaries of Mere Reason* expresses is understood, by Esposito, to enable one to discern the distinctiveness of Kant's *Critique of Practical Reason*[115] in contrast to the *Groundwork of the Metaphysics of Morals*.[116] For, the *Critique of Practical Reason* reflects this paradox, as opposed to the *Groundwork*, which seeks to resolve this paradox, in its formulation of the law. In place of the transcendental deduction of 'the ethical principle from the freedom of the will',[117] in the *Groundwork*, the *Critique of Practical Reason* detaches the law from the freedom of the will and situates it prior to the will as 'the primary "fact" of the law'.[118] This 'fact' of the law, which the *Critique of Practical Reason* establishes, presents law as a *moral* law determining the shape and character of the freedom of the will. The relationship between law and freedom of the will opens onto a further distinction, within man's existence, between that of 'the intelligible order of ends and the sensible order of productive causes'.[119] Freedom and the moral law are, thus, situated on two levels of existence marked by a simultaneous coincidence (the intelligible order of ends containing a 'shared principle of reason'[120]) and divergence (the sensible order of productive causes) of freedom and the moral law. The recognition, within the structure of the *Critique of Practical Reason*, of the potential for divergence between freedom and the moral law – 'the dark side of freedom'[121] – then orientates Kant's thought of the political to the regulation of this inherently destructive capacity of freedom.

For Esposito, if one seeks Kant's thought of community as one which is co-extensive with his 'political writings', then both the social contract and the project

---

110 Kant (2004): 47.
111 Esposito (2010): 68.
112 Ibid., 68.
113 Ibid., 68.
114 Ibid., 68–9.
115 Kant (1997).
116 Kant (1998).
117 Esposito (2010): 69.
118 Ibid., 69.
119 Ibid., 70.
120 Ibid., 70.
121 Ibid., 70.

Communitas 91

of perpetual peace are intimately shaped by this structure of the *Critique of Practical Reason*. The social contract becomes 'the result of an interplay of forces that power limits itself to legitimating a posteriori';[122] and the project of perpetual peace confronts a 'sociability [that] is balanced and contradicted by an overpowering unsociability'.[123] This creates a 'purely analogic' relation between the moral law and the political, and, within this relationship, the political is detached 'from that "being-in-common" that the political is not and can never hope to be'.[124] Kant's thought of 'being-in-common' – the presence of *communitas* in his work – has then to be sought beyond these 'political writings'.

It is in the specific character of the moral law itself that Esposito reveals a thought of 'being-in-common'. The Kantian categorical imperative produces both the experience of the subject's own finitude and a 'being-in-common' which is confined to a common subjection to this law. 'Being-in-common' is merely the sharing of an obligation to obey a law which designates no content. The form of a categorical imperative, in 'its absolute, unconditional, and irrevocable sovereignty', is accompanied by 'its aporetic withdrawal from any attempt at performing the law'.[125] Esposito's insistence upon the 'negative power'[126] of this form of law is the insistence upon Kant's transitional position in relation to a thought of community as a thought of *communitas*. The *Critique of Practical Reason*, through the form of the categorical imperative, installs a direct correspondence between 'being-in-common' and 'the nonsubjective character of the law'.[127] The presence of this conception of law is the presence of a law of community as *communitas* in Kant's work.

The law of community, as *communitas*, is one of circumscription and circumspection: the imposition of a limit as 'Non-Accomplishment or Non-Actualization itself'.[128] It interrupts any recourse to Kant's structure of aesthetic judgment, in the first part of the *Critique of Judgment*,[129] as the potential source of a '"humanistic" layering of intersubjectivity and community'.[130] The structure of aesthetic judgment as community would be the link between the subjective universality of the reflective judgment of taste and the presupposition of a *sensus communis*.

---

122 Ibid., 70.
123 Ibid., 71.
124 Ibid., 71.
125 Ibid., 75. This is predicated on marginalising Kant's *The Metaphysics of Morals* (Kant (1996)), in which the categorical imperative of the *Critique of Practical Reason* is developed into a Doctrine of Right and a Doctrine of Virtue.
126 Ibid., 71.
127 Ibid., 74.
128 Ibid., 75.
129 Kant (2007).
130 Esposito (2010): 72. It is Arendt's interpretation of Kant, in her *Lectures on Kant* (Arendt (1982)) that is, here, the focus of Esposito's critical concern.

The community would correspond in this case to the multiplication of subjectivity for an indeterminate number of individuals, just as the individual would constitute a fragment of community that is simply waiting to have a relation with others so as to completely come into its own ... In order for the community to be realized, there would not even be the need for law that for no good reason complicates matters ...[131]

The pertinence of the *Critique of Judgment* to a law of community as *communitas* is, in contrast, to be sought not in the text's Analytic of the Beautiful, but in the Analytic of the Sublime.

For Esposito, the essentially negative law of community prevents its articulation as a reflective judgment of taste predicated on 'the absolute separation between ethics and aesthetics'.[132] The 'antinomical superimposition between community and law' is only to be grasped in the passage which the sublime provides 'between the felt area of aesthetic judgment and the ethical-rational of the law'.[133] The shift to the sublime is the transition from the Kantian faculties of the understanding and the imagination to those of the imagination and reason. The sublime expresses the forcible limitation of the imagination by reason which reflects, for Esposito, 'the empty space in which the enigmatic shadow of the Thing becomes visible. Not the thing (*die Sache*) but the Thing (*das Ding*) that fascinates us and paralyses us like the face of the Medusa'.[134] The Thing to which the imagination is drawn, and from which reason restrains it, is the experience of the infinite as an 'experiencing [of] community on one's own flesh, taking pleasure in the Real beyond the imaginary and the symbolic'.[135]

The presence of *communitas* in Kant's concept of law – the negative community composed of the subject's finitude and the 'being-in-common' of the categorical imperative – marks the point of transition from the comprehension of the question of community within the 'individualistic-subjective paradigm'[136] of modern political philosophy. Yet, the precariousness of this transition, predicated on the primacy of law to achieve the passage to the conception of community as *communitas*, is evident in the fragile status of law as the limit which separates the empty space of a 'being-in-common' from disappearance into 'a world without limits'.[137]

131 Ibid., 72–3.
132 Ibid., 83.
133 Ibid., 82.
134 Ibid., 85.
135 Ibid., 85.
136 Ibid., 73.
137 Ibid., 84.

Beyond law to coexistence: Heidegger's *Communitas*

Kant reaches, but does not cross, a boundary or border pointing beyond the tradition of modern political philosophy. Kant's radical gesture of the displacement of the primacy of the subject by the primacy of law, creating an 'abyss in or *of* subjectivity',[138] prevents the determination of the subject 'according to ontic categories but never arrives at its ontological determination'.[139] The transition which Kant's thought merely indicates is undertaken by Heidegger – 'the only philosopher who took up Kant's question on the community'.[140] It is this ontological determination which Heidegger's initial encounter with Kant reveals in the Lecture Course of 1927 to 1928, entitled, *Phenomenological Interpretation of Kant's Critique of Pure Reason*,[141] and the later book of 1929, *Kant and the Problem of Metaphysics*.[142] For Esposito, the Davos Lecture Series of 1929, in which Heidegger and Cassirer engaged in a debate over Kant, is the site for the clear emergence of the central position of Kant's categorical imperative – the moral law – in Heidegger's philosophical transition beyond Kant.[143]

For Heidegger, the interpretation of the categorical imperative begins not with 'that to which ethical action conforms', but with 'the inner function of the law itself for *Dasein*': 'We cannot discuss the problem of the finitude of the ethical creature if we do not pose the question what does law mean here, and how is the lawfulness itself constitutive for *Dasein* and for the personality?'.[144] This orientation to Kant denies that the categorical imperative opens onto 'something eternal or absolute, but which also cannot escape into the world of things'.[145] The character of the law is thereby altered from one which connotes 'a sense of *having to be*' to one of 'a *being* that is required' – it is this alteration which provides the 'absolute identity of ethics and ontology'.[146] The categorical imperative is itself preceded by something more primary:

> by *an other* law, which is outside the law to the degree in which it places law in *being*. This is what Heidegger means when he writes that the 'originary ethics' is always ontology. It does not furnish moral, theological, or juridical commands inasmuch as these are derived from and secondary to a more originary instance that coincides with the being-law of every law, which is to say coincides with the same possibility of the law.[147]

---

138 Ibid., 87.
139 Ibid., 88.
140 Ibid., 86.
141 Heidegger (1997a).
142 Heidegger (1997b).
143 On the importance of this encounter, see Gordon (2010) and Poirier (1999).
144 Heidegger (1997b): 196–7.
145 Ibid., 196.
146 Esposito (2010): 90.
147 Ibid., 89.

94 Roberto Esposito: Law, Community and the Political

The revelation of this identity allows the rethinking of the abyss 'from which Kant retreated with the installation of the law as barrier or limit'.[148] The abyss becomes the very site of the common in the sense of 'the fundamental question of "dwelling in" for Heidegger',[149] which is that of a being-with: 'an "inter-being", as a "being between" in the in-between of a common place'.[150] The abyss, for Heidegger, has become the place of a gathering which is 'nothing other than the infinite *cum* of our finiteness'.[151]

For Esposito, the being of community is exactly this *cum* which, for Heidegger, escapes Kant, and it is to be understood as 'that very being there in its *singularly plural* constitution'.[152] With the transition beyond Kant, the thought of the being of community emerges out of the structure of finitude relinquishing any philosophical framework predicated on a theory of intersubjectivity or intentionality. In the 'originally singular and plural character of a shared existence, which is properly ecstatic: each opens to all, not despite but inasmuch as single, contrary to the individual'.[153] The coexistence which Heidegger's philosophy articulates is then 'the deconstruction of a political philosophy in the thought of community'.[154] On this interpretation, a central position is accorded to paragraphs 25 and 26 of *Being and Time*[155] both within the structure of this text and as an integral element of 'a philosophy of the community elaborated especially in the second half of the 1920s, from the *History of the Concept of Time: Prolegomena* until *The Fundamental Concepts of Metaphysics*'.[156] This, in turn, renders the elements of *Dasein* of mineness and existence, distinguished by the analytic of *Dasein*, in section 9 of *Being and Time*, of less importance than those of being-in-the-world and care.

These elements, as a singular and plural coexistence, are a thought of community in an essentially negative form. The coherence of Heidegger's position is, for Esposito, unaffected by the absence of either a 'fully elaborated theory of sociality'[157] or the 'incompleteness of communitarian conception'.[158]

> ... the community needs to be understood literally as 'coincidence', as a falling *together* with the warning that such a fall, the 'being thrown', is ...

---

148 Ibid., 90.
149 Ibid., 90.
150 Ibid., 91.
151 Ibid., 91.
152 Ibid., 92 (emphasis in original).
153 Ibid., 94.
154 Ibid., 92.
155 Heidegger (1962).
156 Heidegger (2008a); Heidegger (2008b). Esposito's engagement with Heidegger derives a fundamental orientation from Jean-Luc Nancy's *Being Singular Plural*, but its divergence from Nancy's subsequent interpretative trajectory is evident once one refers to Nancy (1992) and (2008a).
157 Esposito (2010): 94.
158 Ibid., 95.

the sole and original condition of our existence. *Dasein* is neither the result nor the subject of the fall but the fall itself, the 'there' of being thrown there . . . [T]his defective condition . . . [is] the insurmountable incompleteness of an entity characterized by the nothingness of its own foundation. Our action, or better, the acting that we are, emerges as completely invested by this nothingness as well when the making constitutive sense of, which is expressed in action, is nothing other than the projected side of an underlying lack of sense.[159]

Being-in-the-world, as coexistence with others, is a fundamentally negative mode of existence. Each 'anonymous and impersonal "one"',[160] within their singular and plural existence, coexists in a relationship of 'care'. For Esposito, the associated Heideggerian notions of authenticity and inauthenticity do not transpose 'care' into a dynamic orientated to 'the impossible unmaking of the "inauthentic"'.[161] Authenticity is the assumption of a fundamentally negative mode of existence, as coexistence, and 'the "task" of the community is not that of freeing us from care but of looking after care as that alone that makes community possible'.[162]

This 'task' is expressed, by Heidegger, in a combination of two divergent forms which, for Esposito, reveals care as a 'caring-in-common':

. . . on the one hand, 'taking care' of the other with whom we share existence, substituting ourselves for the other, taking the other's place, so as to free the other from care; on the other hand, that of soliciting care of the other, of freeing him not *from* but *for* care.[163]

The co-belonging of these 'two different and opposed modalities'[164] describes a fundamental condition of coexistence which 'constitutes – that deconstructs – subjectivity in the form of its alteration'.[165] Hence, the community, as coexistence, detaches itself from an origin in the subject, and 'from every demand for historical-empirical actualization'.[166] It is this which marks both its distance from the modern tradition of political philosophy and its passage beyond Kant. For coexistence entails that the 'community is not before or after society' – 'there are no individuals outside their being-in-a-common-world'.[167] Coexistence is not that of 'elements that at a certain point come together, nor in the mode of a totality

159 Ibid., 95 (emphasis in original).
160 Ibid., 96.
161 Ibid., 96.
162 Ibid., 96.
163 Ibid., 96 (emphasis in original). The reference, here, is to Heidegger (1962): 115.
164 Ibid., 96.
165 Ibid., 97.
166 Ibid., 97.
167 Ibid., 92.

96   Roberto Esposito: Law, Community and the Political

that is subdivided, but . . . [as] that of always being the ones-with-others and the ones-of-the-others'.[168]

The appearance and exposition, in Heidegger, of this thought of community, is one which, for Esposito, is compromised by a regression behind this initial breakthrough beyond Kant. This prevents the simple attribution to Heidegger's work of the 1920s of the pertinent philosophical expression of a thought of community. The regression reveals a philosophical failure, and requires an interrogation of the potential for this failure in which 'the most discerning thinking of community could slip into its most devastating negation'.[169]

The intimation of this regression is, for Esposito, to be found in the thought of destiny, in the final section of *Being and Time*,[170] which is introduced into the thought of community. The presence of this notion of destiny, and its potential to facilitate a certain form of affinity between Heidegger's philosophy and National Socialism, animates this interrogation. The notion of destiny is traced, within *Being and Time*, through two levels. The first 'philological' level identifies, in the analytic of *Dasein*, the absence of the Heideggerian notion of coexistence – *Mitsein* – and, hence, that *Mitsein* is 'always derived from and a supplement to *Dasein*'.[171] The 'a posteriori'[172] convergence of *Dasein* and *Mitsein*, rather than the constitution of *Dasein* by *Mitsein*, facilitates the capacity to superimpose *Mitsein* over *Dasein*. The 'belatedness'[173] of the introduction of the thought of community into the analytic of *Dasein* opens onto the second level, which is the re-marking of the notions of authenticity and inauthenticity in which coexistence becomes a process of 'loss and discovery'.[174] The re-marking reactivates the dynamic of actualisation, by transposing the position and experience of community 'as part of our destiny'.[175] The differentiation of the authentic from the inauthentic, through the 'presupposition and destination'[176] of community, is, for Esposito, Heidegger's affinity with National Socialism:

> the attempt to address directly the proper, to separate it from what is improper, and to make the improper speak affirmatively the primigenial voice; to confer upon it a subject, a social, and a history, as well as a genealogy and a teleology. A teleology through *its* genealogy.[177]

---

168 Ibid., 94.
169 Ibid., 98.
170 Heidegger (1962): 352.
171 Esposito (2010): 98.
172 Ibid., 98.
173 Ibid., 98.
174 Ibid., 99.
175 Ibid., 99.
176 Ibid., 99.
177 Ibid., 100 (emphasis in original).

Communitas 97

The regression, and its affinity with the 'destructive potential' contained within a 'destinal origin',[178] leads Esposito to focus on the presence of another thought of the origin in Heidegger. This, rather than either a return to Kant and the primacy of law or a rethinking of the analytic of *Dasein*, of *Being and Time*, is the path towards a reopening of the thought of community. The reopening is sought, beyond the indications in the *Introduction to Metaphysics*,[179] of 1935, and *Contributions to Philosophy (from Enowing)*[180] of 1936 to 1938, in Heidegger's subsequent engagement with the poetry of Hölderlin.

In this manner, Esposito implicitly accepts the 'historical' designation that Heidegger ascribes to this bringing into relation of philosophy and poetry. The bringing into relation expresses the continued possibility for thought at the end of the history of philosophy as the history of meta-physics. Poetry, here, is that of Hölderlin,[181] whose 'poetry is sustained by his whole poetic mission: to make poems solely about the essence of poetry'.[182] Esposito shares Heidegger's presentation of the thought of the essence of poetry, in Hölderlin, as non-dialectical, and, thereby, firmly demarcated from Hegel and, in particular, the Hegelian thought of community in its relation to Greece and the Greeks. However, Esposito seeks to rethink the character of this demarcation by interrupting Heidegger's insistence upon Hölderlin's relationship to Nietzsche. This is initiated by reaffirming the importance of Kant for Hölderlin's thought of community.[183]

The importance of Kant[184] is also the importance of the law in the specific sense which Hölderlin attributes to it in a letter to his brother. Here, Kant assumes the role of Moses in relation to 'our nation' and, therefore, 'leads it out of the Egyptian apathy into the free, solitary desert of his speculation and who brings the rigorous law from the sacred mountain'.[185] The rigorous law is, for Esposito, the expression of an essential 'fracturing of the subject', commencing from its 'temporal constitution', and presented in the form of a 'caesura that blocks any form of knowing beforehand or a repetition between what was and that which can no longer be'.[186] This 'originary splitting', or '*Ur-Teilung*', entails that the split cannot relate to the origin as 'rebirth and return, since there is nothing from which

---

178 Ibid., 100.
179 Heidegger (2000a); Esposito (2010): 101.
180 Heidegger (2000b); Esposito (2010): 101–2.
181 Esposito, through Heidegger's relation to Hölderlin, effectively asserts the primacy of this relationship for the thought of community in regard to Heidegger's engagement with the poetry of George and Trakl. This indicates a degree of agreement with Lacoue-Labarthe (2007).
182 Heidegger (2000c): 52.
183 Esposito (2010): 104. See also Heidegger (2011): 6–14.
184 One should note here that there is also, in Hölderlin, the question of Rousseau, and all that this would require of Esposito's interpretation of Hölderlin. See Hölderlin's poem, 'Rousseau', in Hölderlin (1998): 49–51; and Link (1995).
185 Hölderlin (1988): 137. One should also note, here, that the nation to which Hölderlin refers, in this letter of 1799, is a moral-cultural idea of common identity.
186 Esposito (2010): 104.

98 Roberto Esposito: Law, Community and the Political

to start again or to which to return'.[187] The caesura, created by this originary splitting, then determines the thought of Greece and the Greeks.

The guiding elements of this thought are articulated in the letter to Böhlendorff,[188] which centres on the question of the relation to Greece and the Greeks through the use of the originally Greek dramatic form of tragedy – here, Böhlendorff's *Fernando*. For Hölderlin, Böhlendorff's decision to utilise this dramatic form raises the difficult question of learning 'to freely use the national'.[189] This free use can only be learnt if one understands the appropriate interpretative relationship to Greece and the Greeks. Hölderlin insists that 'in the progress of education the truly national will become the ever less attractive', which manifests itself, in the Greeks, in displacement of inborn and, hence, 'national' sacred pathos by 'their talent for presentation'.[190] In relation to this Greece, the mere repetition of Greek presentation – the deduction of 'the rules of art for oneself exclusively from Greek excellence' – is 'so dangerous'.[191] For what is lost in repetition is exactly the ability to 'veritably appropriate what is foreign': 'the *free* use of *what is one's own*'.[192] This free use is the non-dialectical relation to Greece and the Greeks: 'Greece is a lacuna, a caesura, a vertigo, rather than a site, a fatherland, a rootedness'.[193] In this relationship, free use cannot be imitation, other than as the reproduction of 'otherness within oneself or through a withdrawal from a land . . . In the withdrawal it rediscovers something that is not an essence, or a destiny, let alone a fulfilment'.[194]

The constitutive limitation of Heidegger's orientation to Hölderlin is the intertwining of this free use with the relationship between the proper and the improper. Heidegger appropriates the foreign in a manner which inscribes it within an 'understanding of homelessness as that which permits, precisely because of the "journeying in the foreign", the attainment of the proper'.[195] This intertwining, for Esposito, continually manifests itself in Heidegger's approach to Hölderlin and, thereby, limits the 'tragic and anti-dialectic Hölderlin'.[196] The thought of community, beyond the analytic of *Dasein*, remains unable to assume 'the finitude of our existence'[197] in this bringing together of thinking and poetising. The new

187 Ibid., 105.
188 Hölderlin (1988): 149–51.
189 Ibid., 149.
190 Ibid., 149.
191 Ibid., 150.
192 Ibid., 150 (emphasis in original). On this, see also Dastur (1992).
193 Esposito (2010): 106.
194 Ibid., 106.
195 Esposito (2010): 106. One could also indicate here, as a supplement to Esposito's quotation from Heidegger's *Lecture Course on Hölderlin's Hymn 'The Ister'*, Heidegger's particular interpretation of the letter to Böhlendorff in the final pages of the earlier course on *Hölderlin's Hymns 'Germanien' and 'The Rhine'* (see Heidegger (1988): 266–9).
196 Esposito (2010): 110.
197 Ibid., 109.

Communitas   99

task of thinking,[198] which Heidegger articulates at the end of philosophy, is limited by its continued dialectical association 'with that Greek beginning that it both surpasses and reactivates. It is its *beyond* rather than its *other*'.[199]

The experience of non-knowledge: Bataille's *Communitas*

The tragic and non-dialectic thought of finitude, whose outline Esposito reveals in the poetry of Hölderlin, is to be located in the thought of Bataille, which seeks to break with all forms of recommencement, repetition and mimesis.[200] For Bataille, the 'end of philosophy is not the epochal task that opens a virginal space for new knowledge but precisely a "non-knowledge", which from the beginning destines thought to a chronic "unfulfillment"'.[201] Non-knowledge, as a form of thinking, recognises the fundamental incompleteness of thought as thought. The experience of non-knowledge 'carries the subject outside itself and, for which reason, therefore, there cannot be a subject of experience. The only subject is experience but it is an experience of that lack of every subjectivity.'[202]

For Esposito, non-knowledge, as the experience of a lack within every subjectivity, thereby, opens this form of thinking to a 'conception of community'.[203] The opening is constituted by the experience of non-knowledge as 'being exposed to what denies or negates it . . . [N]on-knowledge consists in holding open the opening that we already are; not in blocking but rather of displaying the wound *in* and *of* our existence'.[204] This wound is, therefore, the experience of the 'unpresentability of the subject to itself',[205] which simultaneously places 'us in communication with what we are not: with our other and the other from us'.[206] The experience of non-knowledge displaces the initial '"idealistic" conception of the relation of subject and object'[207] by the superimposition of a truth held in common and a punctual truth manifested in the passage between – the communication of – isolated experiences of this originary lack.

The superimposition of these truths is the experience of 'the perennial contradiction between desire and life . . . [L]ife is nothing other than desire (for community), but the desire (for community) is necessarily configured as the negation of life'.[208] The perennial contradiction then shapes the character of the

198   Heidegger (2010).
199   Esposito (2010), 114 (emphasis in original).
200   Ibid., 115.
201   Ibid., 115.
202   Ibid., 117.
203   Ibid., 118.
204   Ibid., 118.
205   Ibid., 118.
206   Ibid., 118.
207   Esposito (2010): 120. Here, Esposito draws on Bataille's texts from the early 1940s, *Inner Experience, On Nietzsche* and *Guilty*.
208   Ibid., 121.

100   Roberto Esposito: Law, Community and the Political

relationship of 'subjects' – as points of isolated experience – to each other. Here, the *cum*, as the relation to these others, is not confined to the loss of one point of isolated experience in the other, but extends to all other points of isolated experience 'through a metonymical contagion that is spread to all members of the community and to the community as a whole'.[209] In this contagion, both the life and the death of a 'subject', as a particular point of isolated experience, are incapable of furnishing a passage to community in which this 'subject' would be positively absorbed or contained. The 'subject' is abandoned[210] to a common lack of identity in which even death – 'the extreme limit of our experience'[211] – is merely the sharing of a common lack: 'death is neither "mine" nor " his" because it is a taking away of what is properly one's own, expropriation itself'.[212]

The experience of non-knowledge, as the experience of abandonment, expresses the particular form of relationship which Bataille's thinking enters into with that of Nietzsche. Bataille's interpretative stance in relation to Nietzsche considers thinking 'is placed under the same conditions as was his [Nietzsche's]'.[213] For Esposito, it is these conditions – Bataille's perception of 'a basis for starting anew'[214] – which open onto an experience of the intertwining of nihilism and community whose contours Bataille cannot adequately articulate. The limits derive not from Bataille's refusal of 'the reign of things' and the 'mind's subordination to science' as 'mankind's limit and end',[215] but, rather, from the insistence upon 'the theme of sacrifice and in general of the "sacred"'.[216] The nothingness embedded in the experience of non-knowledge is merely rearticulated by sacrifice in a manner which divests it of any capacity for compensation or redemption.[217] Sacrifice is 'the cruel proof' of the finitude of existence, and becomes 'the sacrifice of loss, which loses and is lost without gaining anything'.[218]

Here, the figure of the Numantines' collective suicide, with which the *Catègories de l'Impolitique* concluded, is itself subjected to an implicit critique, as it is now considered to reproduce, rather than to escape, the limitations accompanying Bataille's thought of sacrifice.[219] For Esposito, the limitations of sacrifice and the sacred originate in the unacknowledged residue of the Hobbesian structure of sacrifice in Bataille's thought. The fear of death in a state of nature,

---

209   Esposito (2010): 122.
210   Bataille (2011): 58.
211   Esposito (2010): 123.
212   Ibid., 123.
213   Bataille (1993): 367.
214   Ibid., 367.
215   Ibid., 367.
216   Esposito (2010): 126.
217   Ibid., 126.
218   Ibid., 126.
219   As Esposito (2010): 127 now asks, 'What do we have in common beneath the "heaven" of sacrifice if not sacrifice itself? What is a community built around the sacrifice of its members as happens at Numantia in front of the Roman legions?'

Communitas 101

which is sacrificed for 'an order governed by the law of necessity and the rule of fear',[220] finds no inherence in the heterodox materialism of 'a theory of a super-abundance of energy'.[221] Yet, it is, for Esposito, 'as if, once this Hobbesian sacrificial paradigm has been reversed, he wound up somehow enmeshed in it; or as if the circumference of his "community of death" emerged in turn as circumscribed by a larger and more ancient circle such as that of sacrifice'.[222] Bataille's determination to 'pledge men to something other than a constant increase in production' is accompanied by the requirement to confront the history of the 'enigmatic act' of sacrifice: the recognition of 'a link with death, tragic horror, and sacred ecstasy; [one] must admit that for want of an answer, men have remained ignorant of *what they are*'.[223] This inclination to link the experience of existence to sacrifice – to entangle finitude with sacrifice – is the enduring 'Hobbesian moment' in Bataille's thought: 'the shadow that covers his clearest perspective on community, when he refused to see in existence exactly that which cannot be sacrificed'.[224]

Esposito's critique of Bataille, initially guided by Jean-Luc Nancy's critical engagement with Bataille and the wider question of the West's relation to sacrifice,[225] indicates the passage beyond the Hobbesian residue in Bataille's thought. Esposito follows Nancy's detachment of finite existence from sacrifice – the constitution of existence as unsacrificable – but diverges from Nancy in revealing it to have a stronger initial presence *within* Bataille's work. The outline is contained in Bataille's consideration of the intimate relationship between animal and man – the particular anti-humanism of his work on prehistoric art and culture and the *Theory of Religion*.[226]

Against every originary logos, what the grottos of Lascaux reveal is the unbreakable interweaving of humanity and animality produced precisely by the civilizing hand of man. In the design in which the superiority of the human species takes form, 'man ceases to be animal giving to the animal (and not to himself) a poetic image', and indeed depicting himself with an animal mask. What comes to light in this text is certainly another and extreme mode for breaking the identity of the subject through its violent rootedness in that animal that at one time men 'loved and killed'; something as well in close proximity of friendship and death refers to that same *communitas* that constitutes us without belonging to us.[227]

---

220 Ibid., 124.
221 Ibid., 124.
222 Esposito (2010): 127.
223 Bataille (1986): 61 (emphasis in original).
224 Eposito (2010): 128.
225 Nancy (1991); Nancy (2003).
226 Bataille (2005a); and (2012).
227 Esposito (2010): 134. The quotations are from Bataille (2005b).

In the intimate relation between the human and the animal, Bataille's work suggests a thought of community in the passage between two forms of finite existence. The passage from animal to man approaches a thought of *communitas* as the relation between community and nihilism. This thought of *communitas* remains, for Esposito, that of an intimation as, in 'the final decades of the last century',[228] the 'extreme realization of nihilism',[229] has placed into question the very notion of a world. This requires a reorientation of 'our thinking of community in a direction that Heidegger and Bataille were only able to intuit but not to thematize'.[230]

228 Ibid., 148.
229 Ibid., 149.
230 Esposito (2010): 148.

Chapter 6

From *Communitas*
to *Immunitas*

The notion of *communitas*, analysed from the etymological derivation of the origin of community, undergoes displacement in Esposito's subsequent book *Immunitas: The Protection and Negation of Life*.[1] The path of thinking in *Communitas* is not rejected, but becomes a form of preparation and facilitation for the subsequent mode of theoretical reflection undertaken in *Immunitas*. In this transformation, the tradition of modern political philosophy is replaced with the phenomenon of life as the framework from which to engage in a renewed questioning of the concepts of law, community and the political.

The transition from *Communitas* to *Immunitas* is explicitly presented in the Introduction to *Immunitas*. The initial reflection upon immunity remains an etymological approach. The previous etymological derivation of the origin of community, in the Latin term *communitas*, becomes the privileged semantic field from which to identify the presence of a Latin notion of immunity. The 'semantic origins' of the 'interpretative category'[2] of immunity can only be adequately considered 'against the backdrop of meaning created by community'.[3] The Latin noun *immunitas*, and the Latin adjective *immunis*, both function as a 'negative or privative term whose meaning derives from what it negates or lacks, namely, the *munus*'.[4] The essential meaning underlying both noun and adjective is 'an exemption from the obligation of a *munus*, be it personal, fiscal, or civil'.[5] It denotes a combination of an exemption and a privilege: an 'exception to a rule that everyone else must follow'.[6] However, this semantic relationship becomes more complex, for Esposito, once one considers that *immunitas* functions in a broader comparative capacity. The sense of *immuntias* is not confined to designating isolated instances of 'dispensation from an office or an exemption from a tribute', but indicates 'something that interrupts the social circuit of reciprocal gift-giving, which is what the earliest and most binding meaning of the term

---

1 Esposito (2011).
2 Ibid., 1.
3 Ibid., 5.
4 Ibid., 5.
5 Ibid., 5.
6 Ibid., 6.

104   Roberto Esposito: Law, Community and the Political

communitas referred to'.[7] The ascription or assumption of a position of *immunitas* releases the individual from their embeddedness within *communitas*.

While the origin of this relationship in the discourse of Roman law expresses the relationship between immunity and community as one of 'primal juxtaposition',[8] the full comprehension of immunity as an interpretative category requires the introduction of 'another semantic trajectory' constituted by its 'biomedical aspect'.[9] The further semantic trajectory shifts from the initial etymological sense to the sense of immunity in biomedical discourse and, in particular, the specific field of immunology. In this transition, the primary interpretative horizon for the comprehension of the category of immunity is displaced from the framework of legal identity to that of biological identity. The shift marks the preliminary passage beyond the indications of a thought of *communitas* in the work of Heidegger and Bataille.

The reorientation concerns, in particular, the notion of the end of philosophy, in Heidegger and Bataille, situated, in *Communitas*, as the site for the initiation of the task of theoretical reflection upon community. *Immunitas* maintains this understanding of its position; however, reflection on this position is now directed towards an engagement with the sciences and especially the natural sciences. The reorientation retains an emphasis on the consideration of the question of community, but this is now one which is posed through the more fundamental question of immunity.

Immunity becomes, in the transition from its legal antecedents in Roman Law to its articulation in biomedial discourse, a phenomenon of life determined by the operation of an immune mechanism. The prefiguration of the simultaneous identity and difference of the 'lexical fields, one legal and political, and the other bio-medical' is to 'be found in the right to immunity granted [to] practicing physicians in Imperial Rome'.[10] The position of a private Roman physician contains a permanent contradiction between 'a highly remunerative but socially unimportant position . . . [T]hey were remunerated, but they were immune from the obligations and honours that were common to the rest of the free citizens'.[11] The private Roman physician protects life, but this protection is undertaken from a position which is outside, and, therefore, effectively the negation of the '*munus*, which, together with the weight of the *onus*, also includes the dignity of an *officium* that is prestigious because it participates in the public sphere'.[12]

The indicative presence of the 'immunitary paradigm',[13] in this specific position of the private Roman physician, assumes a general significance with the central

---

7   Ibid., 6.
8   Ibid., 7.
9   Ibid., 7.
10   Ibid., 18.
11   Ibid., 20.
12   Ibid., 20.
13   Ibid., 7.

From *Communitas* to *Immunitas*   105

position accorded to it in the field of biomedical knowledge 'between the eighteenth and nineteenth centuries'.[14] The development of this knowledge entails that the phenomenon of life is conceived as intimately intertwined with that of immunity. The intimacy of this connection arises because immunity is now conceived as a 'mechanism [which] functions precisely through the use of what it opposes. It reproduces in a controlled form exactly what it is meant to protect us from.'[15] This, in turn, reconfigures the 'relationship between the protection and negation of life' in which 'life combats what negates it through immunitary protection, not a strategy of frontal opposition but of outflanking and neutralizing'.[16]

For Esposito, theoretical reflection identifies the immunitary paradigm, in biomedical discourse, as one of 'exclusionary inclusion or exclusion by inclusion'.[17] The guiding figure is one in which life:

> must incorporate a fragment of the nothingness that it seeks to prevent, simply by deferring it. This is where the structurally aporetic character of the immunitary process is to be located: unable to directly achieve its objective, it is forced to pursue it from the inside out. In doing so, it retains its objective in the horizon of meaning of its opposite: it can prolong life, but only by continually giving it a taste of death.[18]

The figure of exclusionary inclusion, as an immunitary paradigm, is one which contains two mutually contradictory elements – the preservation and the negation of life. The structure in which they are contained is that of antinomy, but one which cannot be resolved within this structure by elaborating a different, non-contradictory form of understanding of the relationship between these elements. Hence, the antinomy describes a far more intractable aporia which requires that the task of thinking be orientated to the question of whether 'life can be preserved in some other form than that of its negative protection'.[19]

The task determined, in *Immunitas*, for a thought which remains after the end of philosophy involves a far more extensive questioning of the domains of knowledge than had previously been undertaken in *Communitas*. The modern tradition of political philosophy and its critique, in *Communitas*, is replaced with the identification of the presence of this figure of exclusionary inclusion in the disciplines of 'law, theology, anthropology, politics and biology'.[20] These disciplines are themselves examples of the existence of an aporetic figure which

14   Ibid., 7.
15   Ibid., 8.
16   Ibid., 8.
17   Ibid., 8.
18   Ibid., 8–9.
19   Ibid., 16.
20   Ibid., 9.

106   Roberto Esposito: Law, Community and the Political

'traverses all the languages of modernity, leading them to their outcome in dissolution'.[21] This more extensive questioning is also one which breaks with both the earlier approach of the Marburg school of Neo-Kantianism, exemplified in the work of Hermann Cohen and the early work of Ernst Cassirer,[22] and the later approach of Jürgen Habermas to the relationship between philosophy and the sciences. The identification of the presence of the aporetic figure of exclusionary inclusion undermines the Neo-Kantian conception of Cohen of the sciences as a factum, encompassing a wholly positive body of knowledge, in relation to which theoretical philosophy engages in a task of ground-laying. It also undermines Cohen's attempt to situate the discipline of law in an analogous relationship to ethics in the domain of practical philosophy.[23]

The later conception of Habermas, while distant from the earlier critical idealism of Marburg Neo-Kantianism, involves a conception of the relationship between a post-metaphysical philosophy and the sciences in which philosophy 'can and ought to retain its claim to reason, provided it is content to play the more modest roles of stand-in and interpreter'.[24] This modest conception is the corollary of an acceptance of the implausibility of 'a foundationalist theory of knowledge' combined with the attempt to retain a conception of modernity as:

> a formal, differentiated reason ... characterized by the rejection of the substantive rationality of inherited religious and metaphysical worldviews and by a belief in procedural rationality and its ability to give credence to our views in the three areas of objective knowledge, moral-practical insight, and aesthetic judgment.[25]

It is this characterisation of modernity that is equally undermined by Esposito's approach, as the internal differentiation of modernity is formal in the far weaker sense of domains which furnish particular examples of the general paradigm of immunity: exclusionary inclusion. In relation to this figure, the thinking which remains after the end of philosophy provides a description which can adhere to neither the role of stand-in nor the role of interpreter. For Esposito, it is only by a further 'deepening of the internal contradiction' of the immunitary paradigm that the task of thinking opens the possibility of a different philosophy of immunity.[26]

The particular designation of the relationship between the task of thought and the sciences is a reflection of a more general development of Esposito's thought from *Communitas* to *Immunitas*. In this development, the structure of the gift is

---

21 Ibid., 9.
22 E.g., Cohen (1978); and Cassirer (1953).
23 See Gibbs (2005).
24 Habermas (1990): 4.
25 Ibid., 3–4.
26 Esposito (2011): 18.

From *Communitas* to *Immunitas* 107

displaced by the paradigm of immunity, which involves a reconsideration of the critique of the subject underlying the presentation of the tradition of modern political philosophy in *Communitas*. The critique of the subject in *Communitas* emerges from the presence of the term *munus* within the term *communitas*. The effect of the presence of the term *munus* – an obligation to give which is other than a structure of gift and counter-gift – in the term *communitas* articulates a being-in-common constituted by a lack. The term *communitas* defines the common as that which divests the subject of its self-sufficiency, and, thereby, reveals to the subject its essential finitude.[27] The etymological inquiry reveals an originary relationship between *munus* and *communitas* constituted by a double negation of both subjectivity and origin. It is this 'unacceptable *munus*',[28] and the proximity of death and community that accompanies it, that Esposito's *Communitas* then situates in a history of modernity. This history, which originates with Hobbes, is the suppression of *communitas* by *immunitas* together with the 'tragic knowledge of the nihilistic character of this decision'.[29] The subsequent responses of Rousseau, Kant, Heidegger and Bataille represent a series of attempts to grasp the originary character of *communitas*.

The distance from this approach becomes evident, in *Immunitas*, as the reference to this originary *munus* has been relinquished for a more radical critique of the sciences. It is the figure of exclusionary inclusion – the paradigm of immunity or immunisation – which, when subjected to this critique, reveals or opens onto another thought of immunity as 'something more complex that implicates and stimulates the common'.[30] The figure of exclusionary inclusion is one which:

> occurs along the *clivage* that at the same time juxtaposes and connects immunity and community, making one not only the contrasting background of the other, but also the object and content of the other. From this point of view, it is important . . . that immunity, as a privative category, only takes on relief as a negative mode of community. Similarly, when viewed in a mirror image, community appears to be entirely immunized, attracted and swallowed up in the form of its opposite. Immunity, in short, is the internal limit which cuts across community, folding it back on itself in a form that is both constitutive and deprivative: immunity constitutes and reconstitutes community precisely by negating it.[31]

The paradigm of immunisation, as exclusionary inclusion, rather than the sciences which are merely its reflection, becomes the object of sustained critical reflection. The critique articulates the outline of an alternative relationship between

27 Esposito (2010): 8.
28 Ibid., 12.
29 Ibid., 14.
30 Esposito (2011): 18.
31 Esposito (2010): 9.

immunity and community beyond the essentially negative figure of exclusionary inclusion.

The alternative understanding rejoins an etymological approach, but one now shaped by the question of the relationship between immunisation and subjectivity. The common has ceased to be sought in the etymology of *munus/communitas*, and has become, instead, that which inheres in the immunological self. The focus is shifted from an initial etymological investigation of the semantic complexity of *munus/communitas*, in *Communitas*, to the subsequent application, in *Immunitas*, of the etymological roots of the grammar of the subject to the outlines of an immunological self.

The shift marks a transformation in Esposito's conception of the task of thinking or recognition of the notion of the negative or negativity in the concepts of law, community and the political. In *Communitas*, the etymological task of identifying the *munus/communitas* relationship reveals a notion of community which is to be thematised in the negative. It precedes all legal and political representations of community, and its precedence rests on its incapacity to be represented in modern political philosophy. In *Immunitas*, the outlines of an immunological self, which the critique of immunisation as exclusionary inclusion reveals, becomes a figure in which the negative now refers to alteration. Alteration is not the modification or overcoming of an originally fully formed state or stage, but a fundamental condition which originates from the inception of the immunological self. It is not the personality, but, rather, the impersonality of the immunological self which the grammatical etymology seeks to grasp. Latin remains a privileged source of this etymology; however, attention has turned to the grammar of pronouns rather than nouns. The negativity of *communitas*, which flows from the instability created by the presence of the term *munus* within it, is reconceived in the understanding of the immunological self. The grammar of pronouns enables negativity to be the expression of a chiasmus: a figure which has an inherent negativity within it.

Immunitas has then proceeded beyond the opening which Bataille and Heidegger gestured towards at the conclusion of the development of *Communitas*. In this movement, *Immunitas* has also rearticulated a position in relation to law, community and the political. The concepts of law, community and the political elaborated by the sciences are, despite their significant divergences, underlain and limited by the reproduction of the figure of exclusionary inclusion. The sciences, apart from those of biomedicine, offer a conceptually limited semantic field which furnishes no possibility for critical transformation. It is only with biomedicine, and the biomedical paradigm of immunisation, that the conceptual field provides the possibility for transformative critique. At the conclusion of this critique, the figure of immunisation as chiasmus is outlined, and any thought of law, community and the political can now only be undertaken in relation to this figure.[32]

---

32 It is in Esposito's subsequent texts, *Bios* and *Third Person*, that this task begins to be undertaken.

The position that law is accorded in *Communitas* compared with that in *Immunitas* is exemplary in this regard. The third chapter of *Communitas*, entitled 'Law', fulfils a central role in the text, through the critical discussion of Kant, as the moment, in the history of modern political philosophy, where the Kantian conception of law indicates a potential transition to a thought of community beyond the limits inscribed in this history. The law, in the form of the Kantian moral law, dispossesses the subject of the sense of its own origin. The subject is constituted by something prior to it – the moral law – which indicates that community has an origin and sense which is prior to the subject. The exposure of the subject to this moral law is the dispossession of the subject by an obligation which specifies no particular duty or set of duties. It thereby establishes that the law exposes the subject, by its dispossession, to an obligation-in-common. Yet, this common obligation is itself without content and, hence, the community constituted by the moral law can only be thematised in the negative. Law, in Esposito's particular interpretation and exposition of Kant, introduces a distinction or difference within the subject of modern political philosophy, but, due to the constraints of law as moral law, remains within the boundaries of modern political philosophy. It indicates a possibility for thought whose further determination emerges, beyond the form of law, in Heidegger and Bataille.

In *Immunitas*, Kant has ceased to be accorded the pivotal, transitional position in Esposito's exposition. Kant has only a minimal presence, and this occurs not in the discussion of law, but in the discussion of theodicy in the chapter devoted to the figure of exclusionary inclusion in theology: theological or religious immunity. With this absence, law has been detached from its formulation as the Kantian moral law, and its form is considered through its presentation in the social sciences. This alteration in the mode of presentation of law is not a denial of the importance of law. Rather, it is a redefinition of its importance as an exemplary expression of this immunitary figure. The variants of law, as a figure of exclusionary exclusion, are then described culminating in the place accorded to law in the social systems theory of Niklas Luhmann. The thought of Luhmann has no transitional purpose in the development of *Immunitas* because, for Esposito, it is the culmination of a logic of dissolution, namely, the 'preventive immunisation' of community.[33] It is a logic whose function can only generate an initial textual development based on analogy: the description of the paradigm of immunity as the overlap of vectors of meaning between the particular sciences.[34]

---

33 Esposito (2011): 50.
34 Ibid., 11.

Chapter 7

Immunitas

The question of immunity and immunisation arises in the contemporary phenomena of epidemics, computer viruses, 'illegal' immigration and heads of state involved in human rights abuses. The disciplines of 'medicine, law, social politics, and information technology',[1] limited by their concentration upon, and response to, a single phenomenon lack the potential to recognise an identity between these seemingly diverse phenomena. This potential arises, for Esposito, with the introduction of the category of immunisation.

The category of immunisation, as a figure of exclusionary inclusion, is initially analysed through a genealogy of its self-dissolution in the disciplines of law, theology and philosophical anthropology. The discipline of politics, in the transformation of politics into biopolitics, presents the figure of exclusionary inclusion at 'its point of extreme radicality':[2] the 'reproductive protection' of life as 'the ultimate criterion for legitimizing power'.[3] The self-dissolution of this figure, as the 'hypertrophy' of life, arises from adapting 'the perception of risk to the growing need for protection – making protection itself one of the major risks'.[4] This marks the point of transition from geneaolgy to another thinking of immunisation, elaborated through a critical reflection upon the concept of the immune system, which 'situates immunity in a non-excluding relation with its common opposite [community]'.[5] The new comprehension of immunity, as immunisation, enables Esposito to outline an originary bioethics beyond the figure of exclusionary inclusion present in the text's preceding presentation.

Law

The figure of exclusionary inclusion in law, determined by the relationship between law and violence, initiates a logic of the 'reappropriation of the common'.[6]

1 Esposito (2011): 1.
2 Ibid., 15.
3 Ibid., 15.
4 Ibid., 16.
5 Ibid., 17.
6 Ibid., 50.

The 'Hobbesian moment',[7] which *Communitas* acknowledges as an enduring limitation upon the thought of community, is transformed, in *Immunitas*, into the paradigmatic expression of law. In this exposition, the specifically Hobbesian genesis of law has been replaced with a purely conceptual exposition centred on the immunitary function of law.

Law, as the figure of exclusionary inclusion which simultaneously dissolves and reconstitutes the character of being-in-common, enables the preservation of 'peaceful cohabitation among people naturally exposed to the risk of destructive conflict'.[8] The risk within being-in-common is the presence of the 'connective power of the *munus*'[9] which, as an essential exposure to openness and alteration, is always a source of potential instability. *Munus* as '[c]ommon life is what breaks the identity-making boundaries of individuals', and creates 'a common relationship that is necessarily one of reciprocity, [which] tends to confuse the boundaries between what is proper to each individual and what belongs to everybody and nobody'.[10] The specifically legal figure of exclusionary inclusion is the reappropriation of the common, the redefinition of the limits of being-in-common:[11] the installation of the proper in place of the common – the protection of the community 'from the risk of expropriation – expropriation being community's most intrinsic, natural inclination'.[12]

The legal figure of exclusionary inclusion, through the relationship between law and violence in the work of Weil, Benjamin and Girard, is then revealed to contain a negative logic of self-dissolution. The logic arises, for Esposito, with Simone Weil's critique of law[13] and the notion of the legal person which enables the introduction of the difference between the common and the proper. The difference is the expression of 'legal immunisation':[14] the reversal of the 'primacy of obligation [as *munus*] over rights'[15] and the assertion of the centrality of 'the person as the sole bearer of rights'.[16] The legal person, whether public or private, is the point of attribution for a variety of rights which become the property of that legal person. The existence of the legal person marks the transition from the infiniteness of obligation to the particularity of right in which legal persons are related by the 'immunitary sense of privilege or privation'.[17] The particularity of

---

7 Ibid., 128.
8 Ibid., 21.
9 Ibid., 22.
10 Ibid., 22.
11 Ibid., 22.
12 Ibid., 22.
13 Weil (2005b). Here, Weil's work is far less central, and the interpretation is far less extensive, than in *Categories de l'Impolitique*.
14 Esposito (2011): 23.
15 Ibid., 23.
16 Ibid., 23.
17 Ibid., 24–5.

112   Roberto Esposito: Law, Community and the Political

right situates each legal person within a wider legal form constituted by 'comparison, negotiation and contention'.[18]

> The legal form [in] safeguard[ing] the community from the risk of conflict ... reverses the affirmative bond of common obligation into the purely negative right of each individual to exclude all others from using what is proper to him or her. This means that society is legally governed and unified by the principle of common separation: the only thing that is common is the claim to whatever is individual, just as the object of public law is precisely the safeguarding of that which is private.[19]

The exclusion, by legal personality, of the risk of obligation reveals its more significant negative potential in the necessity for legal rights to be enforced. For Esposito, Weil identifies something more originary than the order of constraint which Hans Kelsen considers the inevitable development of positive law.[20] The origin of the positive legal order is, for Weil, derived from an etymological analogy or concordance in Roman Law between '*ius*, property, and violence'.[21] This, in turn, displaces Kelsen's periodisation of a break between the natural law tradition and the science of law of the nineteenth and twentieth centuries with an essential continuity with the categories of Roman Law. These categories are held to be permeated with a violence which arises from the intertwining of legal personality and personal force: 'right is rooted in the original form of *ownership*'.[22]

For Esposito, Weil's critique indicates an affinity with the nineteenth-century legal theory of Rudolf von Jhering and, in particular, Jhering's *Geist des römischen Rechts*.[23] The interpretation of Roman Law offered by Jhering is one of the genesis of an autonomous legal form which derives solely from 'its own founding force'.[24] The force impresses itself into the legal categories of Roman Law, and constitutes the origin of a 'metaphysics of appropriation'.[25] This is expressed in 'the primary meanings of three verbs *capere*, *emere*, and *rapere*: the fact that plundering is not a crime means that taking, grabbing and tearing away are at the root of legal ownership, or what is legally proper'.[26] The essential connection between property and plunder extends, for Jhering, beyond the dynamics of individual acquisition and possession to 'territorial land'.[27] The negative logic of

---

18   Ibid., 24.
19   Ibid., 25.
20   See Kelsen (1997).
21   Esposito (2011): 27.
22   Ibid., 27.
23   Jhering (1993). See also, in the contemporary tradition of classical scholarship, Schiavone (2012).
24   Esposito (2011): 27.
25   Ibid., 26.
26   Ibid., 28.
27   Ibid., 28. Citing Jhering (1993): 112–13.

Immunitas 113

this particular figure of exclusionary inclusion entails that 'the subordination of law to force is joined to the subordination of individuals to the collective to which they belong'.[28]

The negative immunitary logic of law – the entwining of law and force – is developed further in the thought of Walter Benjamin, and centres on *The Critique of Violence*.[29] Esposito presents *The Critique of Violence* as the transposition of the figure of exclusionary inclusion into a 'repetitive, cyclical pattern',[30] through the notion of *Gewalt*, which constitutes law and violence 'as modes, or figures, of the same substance'.[31] The thought of law is situated prior to the distinction between natural or positive law 'in myth and destiny'.[32] This is 'the point where history is seized once again by its previous natural origin and forced to perpetually retrace its contours'.[33] Benjamin reveals a 'mythical core of law' which 'consists in violently retracing any moment in historical development back to its initial stage, in crushing the entire history into the tracing of its nonhistoric origin'.[34] The perception of 'a dialectical rising and falling in the lawmaking and law-preserving formations of violence' is replaced with the idea of a cyclical law 'governing their oscillation'.[35]

> [A]ll law-preserving violence, in its duration, indirectly weakens the lawmaking violence represented by it, through the suppression of hostile counterviolence ... This lasts until either new forces or those earlier suppressed triumph over the hitherto lawmaking violence and thus found a new law, destined in its turn to decay.[36]

For Esposito, Benjamin's critique of violence, as 'the philosophy of its history',[37] describes the history of law as the aporetic interiorisation of exteriority.[38] This aporia re-expresses and intensifies the negative logic of exclusionary inclusion, as it situates human life at the centre of the relationship between law and violence. Law functions to interrupt and, thereby, immunise, 'life from its irresistible

---

28 Esposito (2011): 26.
29 Benjamin (1989).
30 Esposito (2011): 31.
31 Esposito (2011): 29.
32 Ibid., 29.
33 Ibid., 29.
34 Ibid., 29.
35 Benjamin (1989): 300.
36 Ibid., 300.
37 Ibid., 299.
38 For Esposito, in contrast to Carl Schmitt and Giorgio Agamben, this aporia determines the general character of law. It is neither rendered visible nor provided with exemplary intelligibility in the specific situation of a state of exception or emergency. However, this presupposes a clear separation between Benjamin and Schmitt (for a contrasting position, see Bredekamp (1999)); and does not consider the presence of the notion of divine violence in Benjamin's text.

114   Roberto Esposito: Law, Community and the Political

impulse to overcome itself . . . so as to take on a "form of life" such as "right life" or "common life"'.[39] The interruption involves a combination of anticipation – 'making becoming into a "state" a "given", and "already-become"'[40] – and 'a logical reversal between guilt and condemnation'.[41] The presentation of the myth of Niobe in *The Critique of Violence* is the exemplary description of this function of law: 'the revelation of its specific immunitary significance'.[42] Niobe's comparison of herself to the gods – the assertion of her transcendence of the merely human – initiates a mythical violence whose object is not punishment, but the reassertion of a boundary between gods and men. The mythical violence reasserts the guilt of the human who seeks self-transcendence and symbolises, in the transformation of Niobe, 'the boundary stone on the frontier between gods and men'.[43] It reveals power as 'the principle of all lawmaking'.[44] For Esposito, 'it is the line that both separates and unites life and death. Life is preserved by its proximity to death, with death settled on the horizon of life'.[45]

The negative logic of exclusionary inclusion, as 'cyclical-fate',[46] is displaced in the thought of René Girard. Law no longer receives its intelligibility from myth, but from its relation to sacrifice; and Benjamin's position of critique has been supplanted by a theory of mimetic desire and rivalry. The notion of mimetic desire distinguishes between appetite and desire; and mimetic desire is a genuinely free and non-appetitive desire based on the imitation of models. The process of imitation involves a choice of models and, thereby, introduces the potential for mimetic rivalry which, in turn, 'stores up conflictual energy'.[47] Sacrifice becomes the manner in which to channel and expend this conflictual energy in 'the sacrificial victim in a form that diverts its natural course, and in such a way as to separate the situation of the victim from that of the aggressors'.[48] The victim, as the Girardian scapegoat, is a point of separation and concentration within the community 'on which all collective evil will converge in order to distance it from the rest of the body'.[49] The relation of law to sacrifice becomes the 'evolution from preventative to curative procedures . . . and the recognition of a judicial system's superior efficacy'.[50]

The distinction between sacrifice and the legal system is one based on a 'fundamental identity':[51] 'to achieve a radically new type of violence, truly

---

39   Esposito (2011): 31.
40   Ibid., 31.
41   Ibid., 32.
42   Ibid., 32.
43   Benjamin (1989): 295.
44   Ibid., 295.
45   Esposito (2011): 34–5.
46   Ibid., 36.
47   Girard (2008): 64.
48   Esposito (2011): 39.
49   Ibid., 39.
50   Girard (2005): 21.
51   Ibid., 25.

decisive and self-contained, a form of violence that will put an end once and for all to violence itself'.[52] The passage to 'an independent legal authority' marks the installation of a non-religious form of transcendent authority through which the law is simultaneously concealed and revealed as violence.[53] The increased effectiveness of the legal system is accompanied by the transfer of the origin of this transcendental authority to the legal system itself. The legal system assumes 'a monopoly on the means of revenge';[54] and, in contrast to sacrifice, 'the violence does indeed fall on the "right" victim; but it falls with such resounding authority, that no retort is possible'.[55] The functional superiority of law is relative, rather than absolute, as its development entails the loss of the obscurity of religion and ritual which surrounds sacrifice.[56] The interdependence of religion, ritual and sacrifice is simplified into an origin which, as law, is both violence and transcendent origin. This simplification is the rationalisation of the authority of the violence which immunises the community against its potential for generalised violence. It is a rationalisation which, through the increased transparency of its transcendent origin, contains the continuous possibility of the return of the 'spectre of reciprocal reprisal'.[57] The transfer of transcendent authority from religion to 'the machinery of law'[58] contains the risk of the reduction of this authority to tautology: the law is the law.

> The dynamic that Girard reconstructs is thus twofold: first, the law internalises violence; second, and at the same time, the law moves to a theatre external to the one where it will actually perform. Rather than simply incorporate what lies outside itself (namely violence), the law places itself in a different dimension from the social body onto which it perpetuates the violence. From this perspective, the judicial 'cure' – the sentence and the penalty – appear both immanent and transcendent: the transcendence of an immanence.[59]

However, this dynamic is beset, due to the threat of the reduction of its authority to tautology, with the capacity to intensify the crisis into which sacrifice and religion always risk relapsing. The sacrificial crisis, for Girard, arises when there is a 'complete separation of the sacrificed victim from those beings for whom the victim is a substitute but also a similarity between both parties'.[60] The legal system intensifies this crisis when, in place of the sacrificial victim, the separation between illegal and legal has become indistinguishable: its external, autonomous position

52 Ibid., 28.
53 Ibid., 22.
54 Ibid., 23.
55 Ibid., 22.
56 Ibid., 24.
57 Ibid., 24.
58 Ibid., 22.
59 Esposito (2011): 41.
60 Girard (2005): 41.

116   Roberto Esposito: Law, Community and the Political

can no longer 'define the legitimate form of violence and [. . .] recognize it among the multitude of illicit forms'.[61] The figure of exclusionary inclusion, as the machinery of the legal system, becomes the 'transformation of violence into violence against violence until this violence ricochets back on itself, threatening to unloose onto the community the same forces it was intended to save it from'.[62] The crisis, beyond the original sacrificial crisis, is one in which the figure of exclusionary inclusion, as law, has dissolved the tangible distinction between law and violence. The negative logic has thereby become, for Esposito, a 'catastrophic outcome that Girard envisages for an entire cycle of civilization [which] radically questions the immunitary logic that characterizes it'.[63]

The interruption of this negative logic appears to be present in the fundamental re-description and reworking of 'the relationship between law and community'[64] in the social systems theory of Niklas Luhmann.[65] The theory of social systems[66] transforms the immunitary paradigm of exclusionary inclusion into a description of the system's coincidence with its environment. The relationship between law and community is replaced with that between legal system and environment in which the environment is situated 'as non-system, as other-than-system'.[67] The intelligibility of the environment becomes the presence of the environment within the system which is to be understood through the concept of autopoiesis.

Autopoiesis, for Luhmann, is the concept which enables a functional comparison[68] between organic and social systems, but it is a comparison in which autopoiesis – 'the system's closed self-reproduction'[69] – 'secures not the continuity of life [organic systems] but the connective capacity of actions'.[70] This capacity is comprehensible once it is acknowledged that contradiction cannot be held to exist at the level of structure or of event, but presupposes 'a relationship between structure and element (event)'.[71] Contradictions, therefore, are simultaneously

---

61   Ibid., 25.
62   Esposito (2011): 42.
63   Ibid., 45. Esposito, while briefly indicating that Girard's later work has developed an 'evangelical solution', considers that this still leaves unaffected the initial, problematic radicalisation of the relationship between law and violence in Girard (2005). However, the presence of the figure of the *katechon* (the title of Chapter 2 of *Immunitas*) in Girard (2001), together with the conversations with Benoît Chantre (Girard (2010)), would suggest that Girard's position has developed beyond that of Girard (2005).
64   Esposito (2011): 45.
65   Luhmann's explicit self-understanding of his social systems theory is of a response to a crisis within sociology which involves a break with an Old European mode of thinking. See Luhmann (2013).
66   It should be noted here that Esposito concentrates on the description of law contained in Luhmann (1995a). There is no reference to Luhmann's later, specific concentration on law itself in Luhmann (2008).
67   Esposito (2011): 48.
68   Luhmann (1995a): 372.
69   Ibid., 372.
70   Ibid., 372.
71   Ibid., 372.

destructive and productive. For, while their emergence undermines 'the system's total pretension to being ordered, reduced complexity', they 'possess enough form to guarantee the connectivity of communicative processing via meaning. The system's reproduction is merely directed to different paths.'[72] Hence:

> contradictions enable but do not compel the elimination of deviations, they have qualities that promote the development of an *immune system*. An immune system must be compatible with self-reproduction under changing conditions. It is not simply a mechanism for correcting deviations and re-establishing the *status quo ante*; it must manage this function selectively, namely, must be able also to accept useful changes. It also does not serve to preserve unconditionally structures under attack, but also presupposes structures and limits of possibility for its own functioning and especially for recognizing contradictions.[73]

Law, understood as a distinct legal system, is attributed with the central function of operating as a mechanism of social immunisation, through 'the use of the schematism of legal and illegal, which is available only to it'.[74] The schematism enables the legal system to transform conflict into legal communication, and to pursue its resolution through this schematism.[75] The operation of this schematism, while specific to the legal system, 'must also secure the autopoeisis of society's communication system as much as possible against as many disturbances produced by this system as possible'.[76] Hence, law, as a legal system, is 'formed in anticipation of possible conflict'.[77] The 'highly abstract and unaccustomed concept of mechanisms of social immunization'[78] is formulated as a response to a reconception of the relationship between conflict and the social system. For Luhmann, 'we ask, not for a "solution" or even a "good ending" to conflict, but rather to what degree conflict can be *conditioned*'.[79] Therefore, the 'goal is not the "solution of conflict" but rather a by-product of the reproduction of conflict'.[80]

For Esposito, the generalisation of the mechanisms of social immunisation reverses the preceding functional primacy of law with regard to immunity. Law, as the legal system, 'is a function of the immune system'.[81] Law, as a particular mechanism of social immunisation:

---

72 Ibid., 369.
73 Ibid., 369 (emphasis in original).
74 Ibid., 375.
75 From this perspective, legal argumentation is also reconceived within the theory of social systems. See Luhmann (1995b).
76 Luhmann (2013): 376.
77 Ibid., 374.
78 Ibid., 373.
79 Ibid., 393 (emphasis in original).
80 Ibid., 394.
81 Esposito (2010): 51.

118 Roberto Esposito: Law, Community and the Political

does not imply violent repression of the community as Benjamin viewed it, or the sacrifice of the victim, as in Girard's model. It does not spill blood and is no longer covered in blood because there is nothing and no one outside it to which it can apply itself: the system cannot communicate, immunizing with its own components, except by immunizing them. From Luhmann's perspective, then, the outside is the inside, conflict is order, and the community is immunity. Hence, immunization is not only a protective shield of something that precedes it, but the object itself of protection: self-protection. It is at once subject and object, form and content, part and whole of itself.[82]

The transformation of the relationship between conflict and social system overturns the 'need of violence to pacify violence, because in this generalized immunization, extended to all communication and coinciding with it, there is no place left for violence'.[83]

The apparent reconstitution of the immunitary paradigm, by this theory decision,[84] is however, one which exacerbates the logic of the self-dissolution of the immunitary paradigm. Social systems theory, in its break from the Old European thought, becomes the functional description of the mechanism of social immunisation, predicated on the articulation of options and choice, and the identification of an 'exit point'.[85] This break, however, reveals an essential continuity and intensification of the logic of the Hobbesian paradigm of order. The generalisation of immunisation 'seeks to eliminate community's violence by eliminating community itself, by identifying it with its preventative immunization'.[86] The break with the Old European thought overturns the limitations of the conception of the relationship between law and community, but it is one which enables the appropriation of the common. Legal immunisation, as a mechanism of social immunisation, operates within a general theory of social systems in which community 'no longer exists, or never has existed as such'.[87] The re-articulation, by social systems theory, of the immunitary paradigm of exclusionary inclusion coincides with the disappearance of community, without remainder, into the difference between legal system and environment.

Theology

The passage from law, and its figure of exclusionary inclusion, to that of theology rests on the analogous orientation of law and religion to the containment of the negative. The immunitary figure of religious exclusionary inclusion is composed

---

82 Ibid., 50.
83 Ibid., 51.
84 Luhmann (2013): 254.
85 Ibid., 254.
86 Esposito (2011): 51.
87 Ibid., 51.

of the relationship between a vital, biological element and a restraining juridical element. Theology, in its specifically Christian version, then becomes the more comprehensive theory and doctrine of this originary immunitary structure at the origin of religion. The difficulties encountered by theology in elaborating an immunitary figure reach their moment of greatest intensity with the emergence of the question of theodicy. It is the impossibility of theodicy which, for Esposito, represents the failed attempt to transform theology into a presentation of religion which is itself immune from contestation. The failure of theodicy, as the projected auto-immunity of theology, results in the self-dissolution of theology.

The analysis commences from Derrida's essay, 'Faith and Knowledge: The Two Sources of "Religion" at the Limits of Reason Alone'.[88] Derrida's exposition is, however, confined to initiating, rather than fundamentally shaping, Esposito's analysis. For Esposito, against the 'methodological' cautions of Derrida,[89] retains the etymological approach of Benveniste, in *Indo-European Languages and Society*,[90] as the indication of the originary immunitary structure – exclusionary inclusion – of all religion. Esposito thereby denies or minimises the distinction which Derrida seeks to introduce, in response to the two 'temptations' of Hegel and Heidegger, between 'theo-*logy* (the discourse on God, faith and revelation) and theio-*logy* (discourse on being-divine, on the essence and the divinity of the divine). The experience of the sacred, the holy or the saved (*heilig*) would have to be reawakened unscathed'.[91] This distinction is the aporetic experience of the question: 'is revealability (*Offenbarkeit*) more originary than revelation (*Offenbarung*), and hence independent of all religion?'[92]

In this manner, Esposito presents the notion of the sacred as the fundamental framework for the comprehension of religion. The etymological approach of Benveniste indicates 'the intrinsically immunitary character of religion'[93] through the presence, within the sacred, of both an organic, biomedical meaning and a juridical meaning. This indication requires, for its full comprehension, that Latin is attributed with the status of the origin of this immunitary paradigm. The overlapping of the Latin terms *relegere* ('to collect again to reunite') and *religare* ('to bind, to reunite') in the Latin term *religio* reflects the immunitary paradigm of religion.

> The positive significance of salvation is not diminished, but it remains within a framework that makes it dependent upon the presence of a restraint, a block, a closure: an opening that is maintained through the incorporation of a closure or an immanence bound by a transcendence . . . Religion, we might say, is

---

88 Derrida (1998).
89 Derrida (1998): 67, fn. 2; 71–2, fn. 22.
90 Benveniste (1973).
91 Ibid., 15 (emphasis in original).
92 Ibid., 16.
93 Esposito (2011): 55.

120   Roberto Esposito: Law, Community and the Political

the impracticability of the *novum*, the impossibility of man to be a beginning for himself, his continual reinscription within a predefined framework that makes every beginning a re-beginning, a taking up again of something that is always already taken up in what precedes and predetermines it.[94]

The basic figure of immunity enables one to comprehend Benveniste's indication of the connection between the sacred and sacrifice. Sacrifice is the simultaneous preservation of life through the production of death[95] and, therefore, the exemplary expression of a fundamental aporia: '[t]he aporetic node of life and death, of momentum and restraint, of opening and binding, is inherent to all religions. It actually constitutes the precondition for religion'.[96] The fundamental aporia extends the divergence between Esposito and Derrida by displacing the aporia of revealability (*Offenbarkeit*) and revelation (*Offenbarung*) by the immunitary paradigm of life and death.

For Esposito, religion 'does not exist, or at least it is unthinkable, outside of its dual source: dynamic and static, universal and particular, communitary and immunitary. It is always both things at once; indeed, one is always inside and through the other.'[97] Christianity then becomes intelligible as a specific development or instance of this immunitary structure. The 'event' of Jesus Christ's life, death and resurrection[98] is to be comprehended in relation to this immunitary origin of religion. The religion which emerges from this 'event' develops from the reconstruction of the immunitary paradigm in the transformation of the 'open and fluid formulation of the evangelic message'[99] into its 'dogmatic institutionalization'.[100] Within this process, Paul, in propounding the 'analogy between the individual body and the body of Christianity',[101] is the exemplary repetition of the contradiction opened by the incarnation of Christ.[102] The analogy enables the reconstruction of the immunitary paradigm in which the social body of Christian believers, as a congregation, becomes the 'body of Christ'. For Esposito, 'the organismic metaphor of the body and corporation . . . destines it for the language of immunity. In other words, he [Paul] submits it to the logic of its preservation through biological and legal rules that protect us from evil by incorporating the same principle'.[103]

---

94   Ibid., 56–7.
95   Ibid., 57.
96   Ibid., 57.
97   Ibid., 59.
98   Here, one should note both the affinity and difference between this treatment of Jesus Christ and that of the opening part of Esposito's earlier *Catégoires de l'Impolitique*.
99   Ibid., 60.
100   Ibid., 61.
101   Ibid., 62.
102   Ibid., 65.
103   Ibid., 62.

The presentation of Paul, as this inaugural figure in the history of the immunitary paradigm of Christianity, involves a complex interpretative analysis through which Esposito traces the self-dissolution of this theological paradigm. Paul is accorded the position of the first elaboration of a specifically Christian immunitary paradigm in order to become the authoritative source for the further development of the paradigm under Origen and Augustine. The further development is itself the response to the challenge of heresy and, in particular, that of Marcion, for whom the 'event' of Jesus Christ, through its exacerbation of the contradiction of the incarnation, places the immunitary paradigm into question.[104] Marcion undermines Jesus Christ as the representative of the passage between creation and salvation,[105] by emphasising the delay or deferral of the second coming (*parousia*). This gap opens the question of the possibility of a 'community afflicted with evil'[106] despite the 'event' of Jesus Christ. The response to this question extends, through the explanation of the cause or origin of this delay and affliction, to the placing into question of God as the Creator of the world. Human salvation is then sought 'from the evil world . . . by an entirely different, unworldly redeemer god, a god who, battling with the world's evil creator, destroys it in a redeeming eschatology'.[107]

The response of Origen and Augustine to the challenge of Marcion is to reassert the Christian immunitary paradigm which, for Esposito and Marquard, involves a double gesture claiming the authority of Paul while engaging in a reinterpretation of Paul. The central aspect of this double gesture is the detachment of the affliction of evil from the act of Creation. God the Creator cannot be situated at the origin of this delay or affliction, because the origin of this affliction is the free will of the human being.[108] The notion of sin becomes the doctrine of the human being's original sin; and is accompanied by the marginalisation of Paul's notion of the *katechon* which, for Augustine, is unintelligible.[109] The *katechon*, in Paul's *Second Letter to the Thessalonians*,[110] which maintains the Christian community by restraining evil, ceases to be accorded a central place in the

---

104 Here, Esposito follows the interpretation of Marquard (1991). This is the development of Marquard's earlier essay in Taubes, 1984, which acknowledges the important influence of both Blumenberg (1999) and the earlier seminal 1921 study of Harnack (1996). However, see Tyson (2006) and Moll (2009).

105 Esposito (2011): 60–1, 76–7.

106 Ibid., 76.

107 Marquard (1991): 12.

108 This characterisation, by Esposito and Marquard, of Origen and Augustine, as the 'first response' to Marcion, necessarily simplifies the interpretations of Origen and Augustine. On Origen, see Tzamalikos (2007) and Nordgaard (2012). On the relationship between Augustine and Origen, as part of the wider Origenist controversy, see Clark (1992). On Augustine's notion of original sin, see Keech (2012).

109 See Augustine (1998): Book XX, Chapter 19.

110 See Paul (2 Thess. 2: 6–7). Esposito (2011): 62–3. On the interpretation of this notion, see Peerbolte (1997).

122   Roberto Esposito: Law, Community and the Political

reassertion of the Christian immunity paradigm. The *katechon* is displaced by the question of 'the religious foundation of sovereignty'[111] and, from this foundation, the associated question of the division of competences between the Christian Church and the Christian Monarch. The religious foundation of the sovereignty and authority of the Christian Church rests on the re-articulation, as a *corpus mysticum*, of the original Pauline notion of the body.[112] The initial meaning of the *corpus mysticum*, as 'the consecrated host', is displaced by 'the Church, or Christianity as a whole'.[113] Hence, the Church is situated as the sole possibility for 'the flesh of Christ, after his resurrection', to take the 'form of a collective body that could gather into it all the members of Christianity'.[114] The sovereignty of the Christian Monarch develops from an analogous religious foundation:[115]

> . . . through a complex process of incorporating a sacred core, conducted in parallel with the incarnation of Christ. According to the original Pauline formula, later transferred to the entire Paristic and Scholastic tradition of the *corpus mysticum*, just as Christ unites all Christians who identify in him thanks to his dual nature, similarly, the physical and institutional person of the monarch concentrates the unifying principle of the body politic, thereby preventing its fragmentation and disintegration.[116]

The division of the body of the Christian Monarch constitutes the domain of royal authority as 'the organic form of the body' by 'normatively subjugating it to a transcendental principle in order to guarantee its survival over time'.[117] The transcendental principle, as 'the dual nature (human and divine) of Christ in his own flesh',[118] creates the distinctive authority of the Christian Monarch, 'both personal and impersonal, of *universitas*',[119] which ensures that the death of the Monarch reproduces the 'permanence of order'.[120]

> A relationship of mutual functionality is established between the two bodies of the king: the individual body gives his mystical body its fleshy consistency, while the mystical body ensures stability and durability to the individual body. It makes his mortality immortal through the hereditary chain that plays the

---

111   Esposito (2011): 67.
112   Here, Esposito follows the reconstruction and analyses of Henri de Lubac (2006).
113   Esposito (2011): 67–8.
114   Ibid., 68.
115   Here, Esposito follows Kantorowicz (1997), who utilises the analyses of de Lubac. See, however, Bourreau (2000) and (2006). Also, for the variations in the sacralisation of the Medieval Monarch, see Bourreau and Ingerflom (1992).
116   Esposito (2011): 67.
117   Ibid., 68.
118   Ibid., 69.
119   Ibid., 69.
120   Ibid., 71.

same role as the resurrection: it immunises him through a separation from himself that makes his natural death the vehicle for his institutional survival.[121]

The Christian Church and the Christian Monarch form two complementary immunitary paradigms of the body which maintain and reproduce the Christian community. Within this process of immunitary reproduction, the Pauline figure of the *katechon* has simply been absorbed into the operation of each paradigm. The question of the personification of the *katechon* has been replaced by 'introducing the principle of exclusion or by normalizing the exception'[122] within each of these paradigms of immunity.

The advent of the Reformation renders the immunitary paradigms of Christian Church and Christian Monarch unstable, in particular, for Esposito and Marquard, by Luther's reconception of the will, in his dispute with Erasmus,[123] as a doctrine of the will as *servum arbitrium*.

> In this way, the creator god is again burdened with the world's evils. He evades this burden, in the role of the alien and hidden redeemer God who at the same time no longer orders anything intelligibly in the world, so that human beings have to dispute – ultimately in a bloody manner – about questions of salvation. The religious civil wars make manifest the terrifying side of the world's end that is supposed to end in salvation; here, delivery from evil presents itself as itself an evil, which – as, for example, the reason for permanent civil war – has to be put out of operation: The eschatology of redemption has to be neutralized. This neutralization of the eschatology of redemption is the modern age.[124]

The neutralisation requires a theologico-philosophical explanation which, while excluding the possibility of redemption, renders human existence in the world created by God comprehensible. This then confronts, after the collapse of the 'first response' originating in Origen and Augustine, the renewed question of the evil of God the creator and the evil of the created world. The second, though unacknowledged, response to the re-emergence of a potential Marcionism is that of theodicy.

The central text for this 'second response' is Leibniz's *Theodicy*,[125] which, for Esposito, is the attempt to furnish Christianity with an auto-immunitary paradigm. The theologico-philosophical argumentation of Leibniz, in the form of a theodicy,

---

121 Ibid., 70.
122 Ibid., 71.
123 See Rupp and Watson (1999).
124 Marquard (1991): 13.
125 Leibniz (1990). On the composition of the *Theodicy*, as the effect of the engagement between Leibniz, Antoine Arnauld and Nicolas de Malebranche, see Nadler (2010). For detailed studies of Leibniz's *Theodicy*, see Poma (2012) and Rateau (2012).

124   Roberto Esposito: Law, Community and the Political

presents 'the defence of God from the accusation of having created, or at least having allowed, evil in the world'.[126] Auto-immunity is conferred through the refutation of these accusations, by the demonstration, in 'the ontotheological language of the double principle of non-contradiction and sufficient reason',[127] of 'God as the best possible Creator of the best possible world'.[128]

> God is not wicked, but neither is he a merely 'principled' Creator who – in an unworldly way, disregarding detrimental side effects – only *means* well; rather, he is a worldly-wise 'responsible' Creator who endeavours, paying heed to compossibilities, to 'make the best of it'. On the basis of an optimizing calculation that is aware of marginal utility (the kind of calculation that might come naturally to a thinker in the age of mercantilism), God permits those evils in the world that – as *conditiones sine quibus non* – increase the overall goodness of his creation, making it indeed the 'good' world, but the 'best possible' world, at any rate. Creation is the art of the best possible.[129]

The 'second response', as a theologico-philosophical explanation is, however, one which leaves unresolved or unanswered the following question: 'If the best possible creation is only the best possible, and inevitably includes evils, why then did God not refrain from creating it?'[130] It is this difficulty which, for Marquard and Esposito, confronts Kant and post-Kantian philosophy; and it requires, as a response, the reconception of the relationship between theology and philosophy. In the process of reconception, initiated by Kant's essay of 1791, 'On the Miscarriage of All Philosophical Trials in Theodicy',[131] the relationship can no longer rest on a simple repetition of the Leibnizian form of theodicy. The essay marks the dissolution of all attempts of a positive theodicy to provide a distinct paradigm of auto-immunity for Christianity.[132]

The dissolution, initiated by Kant, involves the limitation of the thought of the connection between human and divine wisdom to an essentially 'negative wisdom': 'insight into the necessary limitation of what we may presume with respect to that which is too high for us [divine wisdom]'.[133] The continued underlying presence of this Kantian position shapes the further development of a post-Kantian philosophy: the inability 'to entirely escape the lexicon of theodicy'.[134] The incapacity rests, for Esposito, on an attempt to contest the

---

126   Esposito (2011): 74.
127   Ibid., 75.
128   Marquard (1991): 14.
129   Ibid., 14 (emphasis in original).
130   Ibid., 14.
131   Kant (2001).
132   Ibid., 30.
133   Ibid., 30.
134   Esposito (2011): 78.

legitimacy of the limitation of 'negative wisdom' which reintroduces certain elements of a positive theodicy.

The revelation, following Marquard, of the 'theodicy motive of modern philosophy',[135] entails that post-Kantian philosophy reflects a failed attempt to overcome the essential Kantian presupposition of human finitude. This failure, in removing the final traces of theodicy, radicalises the understanding of human finitude to encompass existence within a finite human world. The process of radicalisation 'is the crucial transition from theodicy to anthropodicy . . . [in which] the immune function assigned until then to religion can now be assigned directly to man'.[136] The development which Esposito traces enables theodicy, and its failure, to perform a parallel critical operation. The thought of religion, or theology, in Derrida, Agamben[137] and Schmitt,[138] becomes a necessarily problematic endeavour. For it seeks to reanimate a thought of religion after its dissolution by the failure of theodicy.

The different understanding of this dissolution marks the point of divergence between the scepticism of Marquard and 'the negative identity of the immunological self'[139] of Esposito. The most immediate consequence is the divergence regarding the position accorded to philosophical anthropology. For Marquard, philosophical anthropology is simply the continuation of the theodicy motive:

> Contemporary anthropology defines man centrally as one who seeks refuge from his imperfections, and can only exist by means of compensations, as homo compensator. The modern and contemporary boom in philosophical anthropology takes place, representatively, under the sign of the idea of compensation, which is a theodicy motive in modern philosophy.[140]

In this essentially compensatory role, philosophical anthropology, for Marquard, is the articulation of a philosophical scepticism which navigates between theoretical abstinence and theoretical monism.[141] For Esposito, the underlying compensatory dynamic has its origin in theodicy, but this does not delimit the importance of, and response to, philosophical anthropology. The tradition of philosophical anthropology establishes a distinct immunitary paradigm of exclusionary inclusion. The understanding of this paradigm, in the work of Scheler, Plessner and Gehlen, requires a comprehension of the specifically 'nihilistic aspect of philosophical anthropology'.[142]

---

135 Marquard (1991): 15.
136 Esposito (2011): 79.
137 Agamben (2005b); and Esposito (2011): 64–6.
138 Schmitt (2003); and Esposito (2011): 63–4.
139 Esposito (2011): 176.
140 Marquard (1991): 23.
141 Ibid., 24–5. The contours of this scepticism are more fully articulated in Marquard (1989).
142 Esposito (2011): 85.

126   Roberto Esposito: Law, Community and the Political

Philosophical anthropology

The dissolution of the religious auto-immunitary paradigm of theodicy leaves only the human being, and the comprehension of its exclusively human limitations, to be thematised by the philosophical anthropology of Scheler, Plessner and Gehlen. For Esposito, the thematisation involves the elaboration of an immunitary paradigm of exclusionary inclusion which is, from the outset, accompanied by the spectre of nihilism. The spectre becomes progressively more manifest, as its presence is traced through the work of Scheler, Plessner and Gehlen. In this increasingly overt manifestation, the spectre of nihilism reveals itself as 'an entropic drift'[143] in which the immunitary paradigm, 'in the attempt to immunize itself from its own effect',[144] 'slips into the vortex of infinite duplication'.[145]

The spectre of nihilism emerges, in philosophical anthropology, from the distinct consideration of the human being through a broader and more fundamental notion of life. The notion arises as a relationship between organism and environment[146] in which the human is distinguished by the 'break in the "biocycle of life" . . . in the sense of a rupture in instinct, impulse, sensory organs, movement (everything that is characteristic of living beings)'.[147]

> Man finds himself in his (objective) body, in the living thing as body, and from within, as a living subject in the world and confronted with the world (the subject-object relation), without ever feeling at one with the internal perspective. For man exists in this double-aspect. From within, he feels like and as a centred living subject, but at the same time, by observing himself out of the corner of his eye, at a distance, he finds himself a body among material bodies, marginalized, de-centred, objectified, like a 'mere animal' (Plessner), a thing among things.[148]

Human life, a form of life marked by its continued embeddedness in, and attachment to, organic life, constitutes the foundation for the development of a distinct immunitary paradigm of exclusionary inclusion.

The distinctiveness of the immunitary paradigm emerges from the essentially negative condition of human life, resulting from the differentiation from other forms of organic life, which can only be ameliorated or rendered benign by 'embracing the negative as the only form that can save humankind from its own negativity'.[149] The active embrace of this negative condition is regulated by the mechanisms and functions of an external framework which effectively

143   Ibid., 89.
144   Ibid., 109.
145   Ibid., 109.
146   Fischer (2009): 157.
147   Ibid., 157.
148   Ibid., 158.
149   Esposito (2011): 84.

Immunitas 127

absorbs and, therefore, reduces, the intensity of the experience of this negative condition.

The outlines of this immunitary paradigm are present, for Esposito, in the final philosophical anthropology of Max Scheler,[150] in the ambivalent role accorded to the place of human life. For, in the differentiation from other forms of organic life, there emerges the question of the designation of that which is specific to human life. Philosophical anthropology, as the response to this question, offers a 'description of man's relationship to the world'[151] which expands to become 'the consideration of the extent to which a "foundation of the world" is at all attainable'.[152] In this description:

> The human living being's 'openness to the world' – as a transformation of the animal's *Umweltgebundenheit* [state of being bound to the environment] – is neither a defining feature of the mind nor a defining feature of the vital, but is the result of a genuine wedding of 'urge' (resistance) and 'mind' (negation) in the human living being.[153]

Human life, as this specific 'openness to the world', must simultaneously 'anchor his very own centre of being somehow *outside* and *away from* the cosmos'.[154] The 'openness to the world' is accompanied by an experience of 'the contingency of the world and of the curious accident of his *place outside the world* [or cosmos]'.[155] The response to this contingency introduces 'a history of man's consciousness of self',[156] which, while marking 'the *growth* of human consciousness of self',[157] is, at its origin, 'on the brink of falling into nothingness'.[158] It is this origin of the 'openness to the world' – the self and self-consciousness as the creation of an 'alienation from nature and the objectification of nature'[159] – from which emerges the outlines of a paradigm of exclusionary inclusion.

The paradigm is merely prefigured, in Scheler, because the question of the 'essence and origin of man'[160] is presented as the 'meeting-place of spirit and impulsion'.[161] The human being is, as this meeting place, a site of creation and action, but one in which the fall into nothingness – 'nihilism' – is 'overcome'[162] by a 'metaphysics of action' in which 'the *being of man as microtheos is also the*

---

150 Scheler (1958b); (2009).
151 Fischer (2009): 164.
152 Ibid., 165.
153 Ibid., 160.
154 Scheler (2009): 64.
155 Ibid., 64.
156 Scheler (1958b): 66.
157 Ibid., 66 (emphasis in original).
158 Scheler (2009): 64. For a slightly different, interrogative articulation of this position, see Scheler (1958b): 68.
159 Scheler (2009): 64.
160 Scheler (1958b): 65.
161 Scheler (2009): 66.
162 Ibid., 64.

128   Roberto Esposito: Law, Community and the Political

primary access to God.[163] The notion of God, however, for Scheler, is 'not an object',[164] 'an insurance company for weak people in need of protection'.[165] The notion of God is situated after Kant's critique of theodicy: it 'is not there to support and complement us on our weaknesses and needs'.[166] The primacy of creation recognises only a reciprocal relationship between 'the human being and God-in-becoming'[167] which reveal themselves in the 'spirit's historical manifestation *and* in the evolution of life in the world'.[168]

However, the 'semantics'[169] of spirit and God-in-becoming are unable, for Esposito, to effect the overcoming of nihilism. Scheler's philosophical anthropology, despite its description of 'the *relationship to self* as a living "centre of action"',[170] remains circumscribed by the nothingness which it seeks to definitively overcome. The dynamics of the relationship between human being and God-in-becoming reveal the essential dependence of God-in-becoming on human action. God-in-becoming or 'spirit' is 'powerless with respect to the impulsive and instinctual sphere it is supposed to dominate'.[171] The powerlessness reveals, for Esposito, the outlines of the paradigm of exclusionary inclusion. The realm of God-in-becoming 'is forced to feed on the same vital power that it seeks to neutralize': 'Spirit, the principle of health and safety, can exonerate itself from the material forces that bear down on it and oppress it only through a regular intake of the same forces.'[172] The evolution of life in the world is, therefore, equally affected by this powerlessness, reflected in the indeterminacy of the freedom of the human being. The 'history of man's consciousness of self' is continually haunted by the capacity to become the expression of contingency and impermanence: 'an inverse proportion between natural power and the capacity of artificial mediation – or, in more general terms, between intensity and duration'.[173]

The work of Plessner[174] assumes, and seeks to prevent, the entropic drift which underlies Scheler's philosophical anthropology.[175] The relationship between human action and God-in-becoming is despiritualised and reconceived as a

---

163   Scheler (1958a): 11 (emphasis in original).
164   Scheler (2009): 66.
165   Ibid., 66.
166   Ibid., 66.
167   Ibid., 66.
168   Ibid., 66 (emphasis in original).
169   Esposito (2011): 91.
170   Fischer (2009): 166 (emphasis in original).
171   Esposito (2011): 91.
172   Ibid., 91.
173   Ibid., 89.
174   Esposito bases his analysis, in particular, on Plessner (1966); (1975); (1999); (2003a); (2003b); (2003c); and (2003d).
175   The discussion, by Esposito, of Günther Anders' early, critical approach to philosophical anthropology is unexamined here – in particular, because Esposito leaves unemphasised that the further development of Anders' work involves a shift from the relationship between man and animal to that between man and technology. See David (2011).

Immunitas 129

relationship of identity and difference within the unity of the human body. The concept with which Plessner describes this relationship is that of ex-centric positionality (*exzentrische Positionalität*). This specific position of the human being introduces an internal difference in the human body between the lived body (*Leib*) and the physical body (*Körper*) which differentiates it from all other organic forms of life. The negative, or nothingness, re-emerges in the 'ontological gap'[176] between these two forms of body.

> Plessner therefore proceeds from the sensory-appearance relationship to a description of the relationship to self as a *Futteralsituation*; the self that can feel the living body that is itself, and can at the same time observe that living body from an excentric position, behind the casing (*Futteral*) of which it remains forever hidden to itself, only experiences itself – mediated – as an actor, who gives a sentient/meaningful 'embodiment' to this fractured situation. In this displayed embodiment the self is made manifest, but at the same time it remains veiled to itself during this display.[177]

The relationship between lived body (*Leib*) and physical body (*Körper*) is predicated upon the fundamental lack of coincidence of the relationship to self. The lack of coincidence, as an experience of the 'inner world of the person',[178] is 'not formed from the standpoint of the organism but, rather, from that of its shared world (*Mitwelt*)'.[179] The distinctive 'relation between persons rather than organisms'[180] is that of mediated immediacy (*vermittelte Unmittlebarkeit*): 'It concerns an ambivalent, in itself fragmentary, structure (a "hiatus-lawfulness"), which, consequently, can only be lived in a historical process. It continually poses the task of integrating body (*Körper*) and lived body (*Leib*) anew.'[181]

For Esposito, the description of the historical development of this shared world of human beings is Plessner's explicit presentation of a structure of exclusionary inclusion. This is 'a compensatory artificial equilibrium able to balance the natural imbalance that places man beyond himself'.[182] The further passage from philosophical anthropology to politics arises from the immunitary redefinition of the 'antithesis', established by Tönnies,[183] 'between community [*Gemeinshaft*] and society [*Gesellschaft*]'.[184] In this process, society is ascribed the function of an exclusionary inclusion of community: Plessner commences from immunisation

---

176 Esposito (2011): 95.
177 Fischer (2009): 166.
178 Krüger (2010): 268.
179 Ibid., 268.
180 Ibid., 268.
181 Ibid., 270.
182 Esposito (2011): 96.
183 Tönnies (2001).
184 Plessner (1999): 41.

130   Roberto Esposito: Law, Community and the Political

'in order to define *communitas*'.[185] The redefinition, based on 'the possibility of a spiritualization and refinement of the use of force', articulates a 'certain harmony'.[186] From this flows the further 'possibility for a societal culture in the narrowest boundaries of a personal lifestyle and in the widest politico-diplomatic forms of interaction between nations'.[187]

This possibility, at the level of both the individual and the nation, is, for Esposito, an essentially ephemeral one. The structure of exclusionary inclusion intensifies, rather than resolves, the original 'antithesis' between community and society. The intensification derives from Plessner's demonstration of both the impossibility of community as a self-sufficient form of social life and the presentation of society as a public sphere (*Öffentlichkeit*) of mediated immediacy. The public sphere is justified as a 'system of hygiene for the soul',[188] which installs a range of forms of human public behaviour (ceremony, prestige, tact), each one operating as 'preventative immunization'.[189] Each form functions to exclude the immediacy of communal forms of human behaviour, while retaining the capacity for a 'mediated' type of common social interaction. Relations of mediated immediacy constrain the 'excess of community'[190] – the potential dissolution of social life contained in 'indiscretion, indecency, excessive closeness, or even lack of distinction'.[191] These relations of mediated immediacy involve a preventive immunisation predicted on a division or splitting of human beings 'into the polarity between inner and outer, private and public, invisible and visible, and by arranging each pole to safeguard the other'.[192]

Mediated immediacy – the system of hygiene for the soul – reveals the underlying paradigm of exclusionary inclusion in Plessner's philosophical anthropology. For Esposito, Plessner

> is a theoretician of the preventative immunization of all social forms, which are thereby desocialized at the level of the individual atoms that compose and simultaneously decompose it as such. He does not commit the mistake of abstracting individuals from the community, which he presupposes as their condition of existence, but according to a relation that unites them in separation and connects them in estrangement.[193]

---

185   Esposito (2011): 101. Esposito leaves unexamined the relationship between *The Limits of Community: A Critique of Social Radicalism* and Plessner's later work contained, in particular, in Plessner (2003c).
186   Plessner (1999): 62.
187   Ibid., 62.
188   Plessner (1999): 194.
189   Esposito (2011): 99.
190   Ibid., 97.
191   Ibid., 101.
192   Ibid., 97.
193   Ibid., 99.

The presentation of the public sphere, as the exclusionary inclusion of the community, is one determined by the requirement to resist the potential resurgence of the common and its associated violence. The preventative immunisation of the community creates a negative unity 'governed by this need to build a compensatory artificial equilibrium able to balance the natural imbalance that places man beyond himself'.[194] The negative unity is reflected in the relation of mediated immediacy, which contains 'a fragment of the very violence it is meant to restrain'.[195] The 'possibility of a spiritualization and refinement of the means of force'[196] becomes, for Esposito, the logic of a continuous intensification of the forms of preventative immunisation utilised to 'contain the nothing that presses around [human beings] from all sides'.[197]

The underlying nihilism of Plessner is brought 'to its final completion' in the work of Arnold Gehlen.[198] The paradigm of exclusionary inclusion is situated,[199] beyond the philosophical anthropology of Scheler and Plessner, in the inherent deficiency (*Mänglewesen*) of the human being. The human being, exposed to 'the undirected complexity of external stimuli and drives', experiences an intrinsic insecurity 'between perception and behaviour'.[200] From this insecurity derives the necessity for survival which is initially achieved, at the individual level, through the formation of 'character' which introduces 'a process of selection and distancing [*Distanzierung*]'[201] and, hence, discipline over the 'inner world'[202] of the human being. The formation of character 'as immunization remains [insufficient] at an individual level, and [if it] is not incorporated into a wider social mechanism, it remains exposed to the risk of rapid dissolution'.[203] The immunitary purpose of character is, therefore, complemented, at the societal level, by that of the institution. The immunitary purpose of institutions derives from the 're-utilization of behavioural modes, and has a vitally stabilizing function, providing the framework for the formulation of life-style goals'.[204] The institution, therefore, creates 'a "background" of routinized activity'[205] (*Hintergrundserfuellung*), which produces the stability to enable 'a "foreground" for deliberate, reflective, purposeful actions'.[206]

---

194 Ibid., 96.
195 Ibid., 98.
196 Plessner (1999): 62.
197 Esposito (2011): 100.
198 Ibid., 103. Esposito bases his analyses, in particular, upon Gehlen (1993); (1957); (1961a); (1961b); (1980); and (1988).
199 Gehlen (1993); and (1988). It should be noted that the English translation is not of the original 1940 edition, but of a later edition, in which the positive thematisation of, and references to, the National Socialist regime were removed.
200 Fischer (2009): 162.
201 Esposito (2011): 105.
202 Fischer (2009): 167.
203 Esposito (2011): 106.
204 Fischer (2009): 163.
205 Berger and Kellner (1965): 112.
206 Ibid., 112.

132 Roberto Esposito: Law, Community and the Political

The relationship between human being and institution is one which, for Esposito, contains a 'heteronomous tendency'.[207] For 'freedom expands in proportion to the growth of an institutional apparatus' and emerges 'from the same necessity that holds it in check, and which only in this fashion makes it compensatorily possible'.[208] The heteronomous tendency becomes explicit in the work of the 1950s and 1960s;[209] and situates a critique of 'industrial society' within a historical account of the emergence and development of institutions. The developmental history of institutions, as an anthropological process of institutionalisation, traces a phenomenon of 'negative self-identification': 'the institution associates those who recognize themselves in it through the sharing of the same alienation'.[210] The preservation of life, enabled by the institutional framework, installs 'immunization [as] our only common behaviour, and the common [as] the very object of immunization'.[211] The entropic stability generated by this process, condensed in Gehlen's own concepts of *posthistoire* and *crystallisation*, becomes manifest in the phenomena and tendencies of 'industrial society'.

The entropic stability of 'industrial society' is fragile, as a number of 'countereffects'[212] arise from the expansion of the 'subjective hypertrophy' of human existence.[213] The inner discipline of character is undermined by the 'excess of subjectivity' facilitated by the expansion of this foreground.[214] The 'background' framework of institutions is then itself affected by this 'subjective hypertrophy' in the form of 'a flood of demands with which they are unable to cope'.[215] The response which Gehlen articulates – the reinforcement of character and institutional effectiveness – involves the exacerbation, rather than the regulation, of these counter-effects.

The self-dissolution of the paradigm of exclusionary inclusion of philosophical anthropology is, for Esposito, thereby revealed. The projected reinforcement of character, initially through the emergence of an ascetic elite which breaks with the general demand for increased consumption; and then becomes an ethos of 'moral obligation to the preservation of the state',[216] is 'simply ineffectual'.[217] The central dynamic of dissolution is located in the parallel project of an intensified institutionalism. For Esposito, the 'reinforcement of institutional barriers' accelerates 'the irresistible tendency toward overdetermination that counterfactually

---

207 Esposito (2011): 106.
208 Ibid., 106.
209 Gehlen (1957); (1961a); (1961b); (1969); and (1980).
210 Esposito (2011): 107.
211 Ibid., 107.
212 Ibid., 108.
213 Ibid., 108.
214 Ibid., 108.
215 Ibid., 108.
216 Honneth (2009): 190, referring to Gehlen (1969), chs 7 and 8.
217 Esposito (2011): 108.

gives rise to renewed indeterminacy, just as the reinforcement of norms creates increasing abnormality'.[218]

The dissolution of this paradigm of exclusionary inclusion is, therefore, the logic of the self-dissolution of philosophical anthropology. The 'self-destructive power' derives from 'the immune apparatus that turns the negative into a positive': the institution becomes 'a machine that has to produce more and more order, it loses contact with the disorder that establishes its confines and provides its material'.[219] The paradigm of exclusionary inclusion, in the final form of Gehlen's philosophical anthropology, dissolves 'into the vortex of infinite duplication'.[220]

Biopolitics

The question of compensation, embedded in the paradigms of exclusionary inclusion of Scheler, Plessner and Gehlen, remains the exclusive purview of philosophical anthropology. The dissolution of this immunitary paradigm, through the self-destructive power of its compensatory logic, reveals the impasse of these paradigms of exclusionary inclusion. The impasse is the failure of the underlying conception of the form in which the 'immunitary paradigm relates to the collective dimension of life'.[221] The failure exacerbates, rather than ameliorates, the internal division of the human being, through 'the excess of institutional mediation'.[222]

The impasse is displaced by the final immunitary paradigm of biopolitics. The question of philosophical anthropology is transformed by the specific relationship between immunisation and life developed in the work of Michel Foucault. The question of human finitude, in Foucault, is posed differently from that of philosophical anthropology, because the response to Kant, as a response to the question of finitude, cannot be the formulation of a theory of the human being. The response can only be the insistence upon the human being as an entity which is permanently in question, and this questioning extends to the presentation of the formation of this human being. The permanence of this questioning involves a critique of the status of the social and natural sciences as a framework of theoretical synthesis for the derivation of a theory of the human being and society. The questioning presents the social and natural sciences as historical discourses on the human subject; and Foucault's biopolitics thus emerges from

> an analysis having for its central theme the problem of the deconstruction and the reconstruction of the subject, more precisely of the deconstruction

218 Ibid., 108.
219 Ibid., 108–9.
220 Ibid., 109.
221 Ibid., 14.
222 Ibid., 14.

134   Roberto Esposito: Law, Community and the Political

of the subject as *arché* (cause, principle, origin) and of the reconstruction of subjectivity as effect.[223]

The orientation of Esposito to Foucault's project, and the historical analysis of this process of deconstruction and reconstruction, is to emphasise the relationship between immunisation and life. The emphasis traces the continued presence of a paradigm of exclusionary inclusion within this theory of biopolitics.

The analysis represents Esposito's initial engagement with Foucault,[224] and centres on the emergence of biopolitics in the historical analysis of medical discourse and practice. In this analysis, Foucault's texts are situated within a framework which accords primacy to the body in its focus upon the connection between politics and life. The body is, for Esposito, the dimension in which 'life lends itself to being preserved, as such by political immunization'.[225] The dynamics of political immunisation are traced through the relationship between the natural body and the 'metaphor of the body politic'.[226]

The analysis of Foucault's texts is, therefore, preceded by a presentation of the continued centrality of the metaphor of the body politic in the passage from the thought of Hobbes to that of Rousseau and Sièyes.[227] The metaphor, while 'adapted to the changed historical and conceptual context',[228] in each of these thinkers, continues to demarcate an 'irresistible tendency of political philosophy (and political practice) to incorporate social plurality'.[229] The many natural bodies of human individuals continue to be incorporated by the operation of a metaphor of the body politic.

The process of incorporation, effected by the metaphor of the body politic, is, for Esposito, reanimated, rather than relinquished, by the French Revolution. The work of Sièyes,[230] in combination with the vast semantic field of other texts and images of the French Revolution,[231] is the emergence of a modern politics which reproduces the metaphorical process of incorporation. The third estate – represented through the National Assembly – is situated in this metaphorical role as the simultaneous representation of the 'unity of the body politic' and 'the point of rupture with the theory of anatomical distinction between classes, organs, and functions of monarchy'.[232]

---

223   Nigro (2012/13): 61.
224   The engagement with Foucault is deepened and extended in Eposito's *Bíos*.
225   Esposito (2011): 113.
226   Ibid., 113.
227   Ibid., 114–18.
228   Ibid., 114.
229   Ibid., 118.
230   It is the figure of Sièyes as the proponent of the National Assembly, rather than that of Sièyes who, with Bonaparte, participates in the 'termination' of the Revolution in 1799, that is the exclusive focus of Esposito's attention. See, however, the important work by Quiviger (2008).
231   Here, Esposito draws on the analyses of de Baecque (1997).
232   Ibid., 134.

The French Revolution marks the transition from sovereign rule to biopolitical governance. For Esposito, biopolitical governance, as the coincidence of the nation with the individuals who form its population, is the 'effective realization of the body-politic metaphor in the material body of the individuals who constitute a population'.[233] The transformation of the relationship between the natural bodies of citizens and the nation is the corollary of a transformation of medical knowledge. The two central aspects of 'the location of disease' and 'its relation to health'[234] are reconceived within a medical knowledge of the body in which death is the 'essential structure of medical perception'.[235] For Esposito, these two transformations indicate a homology between the new, unified metaphorical body of the National Assembly and the 'new anatomical pathology that culminated in the teaching of Xavier Bichat'.[236]

Foucault's *The Birth of the Clinic* and, in particular, the presentation of the transformation of French medical knowledge from Valsalva to Bichat,[237] is, therefore, accorded a central position in this analysis. The transformation involves a re-conception of 'the origin and cause of disease' from 'a specific area of the body' to 'the vital relationship that connects the various parts of the body to the inseparable unity of a single organism'.[238] The organism, as the underlying unity of the different bodily organs, then becomes the life whose intelligibility is to be grasped by 'the knowledge of death'.[239] The individual, as organism, is rendered comprehensible against the common horizon of death: '*embodied* in the *living bodies* of individuals'.[240]

The medical knowledge of the body, articulated from this 'stable, visible, legible basis of death',[241] introduces a modern individual whose body, as organism, exists together with all those other human bodies, situated within the territory of a nation-state. The emergence of biopolitics originates in the distinction between 'the spheres of the individual and the species'.[242]

> Foucault identifies the object of biopower as the population, he does not refer to individual holders of certain rights, nor to their confluence in a people defined as the collective subject of a nation, but rather to the living being in the *specificity* of its constitution. In other words, he is referring to the only element that groups all individuals into the same species: the fact that they each have a body. Biopolitics addresses itself to this body – an individual

233 Ibid., 137.
234 Ibid., 122.
235 Ibid., 135.
236 Ibid., 134.
237 Foucault (2003): 152–82.
238 Esposito (2011): 134.
239 Ibid., 135.
240 Foucault (2003): 243 (emphasis in original).
241 Ibid., 243.
242 Esposito (2011): 136.

136 Roberto Esposito: Law, Community and the Political

one because it belongs to each person, and, at the same time, a general one because it relates to an entire genus – with the aim of protecting it, strengthening it, and reproducing it, in line with an objective that goes beyond the old disciplinary apparatus because it concerns the very existence of the State in its economic, legal, and political 'interests'.[243]

The historical development of the biopolitical governance of the modern nation-state involves the reproduction of an immunitary paradigm of exclusionary inclusion, through the medium of the body.

It is from this perspective that Esposito then presents Foucault's other texts on the history of medicine as a history which, following the distinct trajectories of the nation-states of Europe, from the end of the eighteenth century to the twentieth century, describes the installation of this immunitary paradigm. The relationship between the body and medical knowledge becomes a 'nosopolitics':[244]

> ... meaning not so much mandatory State intervention in the domain of medical knowledge as the emergence of health care and related practices on the scene of every public sector ... in a growing interplay between the biological, legal, and political.[245]

The history of a 'generalized, undefined medicalization',[246] in Foucault's later texts on medicine, also describe 'the passage from the sovereign order of the law to the disciplinary order of the norm'.[247] The practices of biopolitical governance institute a form of regulation, through the norm, between the body and politics, which is 'repressive but also productive'.[248] The life of the population, through the bodies of the individuals which compose it, becomes the object of this normative framework of regulation.

The historical transition, which these texts of Foucault reconstruct, to the disciplinary order of the norm, remains an immunitary paradigm of exclusionary inclusion in which 'the subjects are preconstituted by something that both exceeds them and precedes them'.[249] Hence, for Esposito, biopolitics, within the parameters of this historical reconstruction, is merely a differentiation of the relationship between 'the singularity of the living being and the preservation of life'.[250] The preservation and reproduction of life, through the form of the norm, is merely

---

243 Ibid., 136 (emphasis in original).
244 It should be noted that Foucault also uses the term 'somatocracy' to describe 'the care of the body, corporal health, the relation between illness and health etc. As appropriate areas of State intervention' (Foucault (2004b): 7).
245 Esposito (2011), 138.
246 Ibid., 139.
247 Ibid., 141–2.
248 Ibid., 142.
249 Ibid., 142.
250 Ibid., 142.

Immunitas 137

the proliferation and intensification of the primary relationship of 'presupposed anticipation'.[251] There remains a fundamental 'structural homology' which 'maintains the disciplinary norm in the immunitary cycle of the law';[252] and the homology defines the limits of Foucault's historical reconstruction of a modern, European biopolitics. The description of the transformation from the sovereign order of the law to the disciplinary order of the norm retains the 'transcendental presupposition of the law'.[253]

The presence of this presupposition, for Esposito, opens the question of the critical potential of this historical reconstruction in relation to the immunitary paradigms which it describes. The historical reconstruction, centred on the transformation of the immunitary paradigm of exclusionary inclusion into biopolitics, represents the 'point of extreme radicality' of this immunitary paradigm. For it describes the reversal of the relationship between power and life: 'life – its reproductive protection – became the ultimate criterion for the legitimizing power'.[254] In this reversal arises the history of the contemporary immunitary paradigm of exclusionary inclusion.

The essentially descriptive, historical approach to the presentation of the contemporary biopolitical form of the immunitary paradigm reveals the antinomy of the contemporary immunitary paradigm in the dynamics of the relationship between power and life. The antinomy, for Esposito, is contained in the immunitary paradigm's dynamics of reproductive protection. It is a

> self-protective syndrome [which] ends up relegating all other interests to the background, including 'interest' itself as a form of life-in-common; the effect it creates is actually the opposite of what is desired. Instead of adapting the protection to the actual level of risk, it tends to adapt the perception of risk to the growing need for protection – making protection itself one of the major risks.[255]

The revelation of this antinomy becomes the limit of the critical potential of Foucault's historical reconstruction and the contemporary biopolitical paradigm.[256] The critical potential derives exclusively from the presupposition of an external relationship between the application of techniques, practices and technologies and the formation of the body into a subject: a process of both individuation and integration. The description of the transformation of human beings into subjects – the direct relationship between power and life – operates through the prior

---

251 Ibid., 142.
252 Ibid., 142.
253 Ibid., 142.
254 Ibid., 15.
255 Esposito (2011): 15–16.
256 The limits of Foucault's analysis are reconsidered in *Bíos*.

138   Roberto Esposito: Law, Community and the Political

separation of 'technique and body: as if the body, although historically determined, ontologically preceded the technical practice destined to transform it'.[257]

The underlying relationship between technique and body indicates that Foucault remains at the level of descriptive presentation of the contemporary immunitary paradigm. The delineation of the antinomy – the potential for the self-dissolution of the paradigm through the pathology of protection – is the limit of Foucault's critique. For Esposito, one has to think beyond Foucault's relationship between technique and body in order to avoid the repetition of the impasse of the level of descriptive presentation.

Common immunity

The final section of *Immunitas* commences from the inseparability of the concept of immunity from that of community: 'there is no community without some kind of immunitary apparatus'.[258] The concept of immunity cannot be rejected or eliminated. Rejection would result in a conception of life 'radically external' to both immunity and community; and active elimination would be to dissolve the concept of immunity through the constitution of another paradigm of exclusionary inclusion.[259] The thought of immunity is reconceived, displacing the distinction between technique and body by a process of differentiation, within the body, of an immune system. This displacement involves a return to the 'biological plane' – 'the safeguarding of life in the body of each individual' – as the site for the articulation of 'a different philosophy of immunity'.[260]

The alternative philosophy of immunity commences, on the biological plane, by re-conceiving the subject, through its relationship with the immune system, as the generation of subjectivity. In this re-conception, Donna Haraway's *Simians, Cyborgs, and Women. The Reinvention of Nature*,[261] and, in particular, the chapter entitled, 'The Biopolitics of Postmodern Bodies: Constitutions of Self in Immune System Discourse',[262] is the predominant orientation. The central position which Haraway accords to the immune system is, for Esposito, the expression of a historico-cultural transformation of the life sciences and their conception of the body. The transformation renders Foucault's biopolitics, and its distinction between body and technique, a historical phenomenon which has been superseded by a 'technicization of life'.[263] Within this framework, the subject becomes 'a functional construct'[264] through its relationship with the immune system. The immune system is a 'point of tangency – of connection and tension', which, in

257   Ibid., 146.
258   Esposito (2011): 16.
259   Ibid., 16.
260   Ibid., 16–17.
261   Haraway (1991a).
262   Haraway (1991c).
263   Esposito (2011): 149. See Haraway (1991b): 152, fn. 4, for the critique of Foucault.
264   Esposito (2011): 149.

turn, involves a broader conception of the 'interaction between species, or even between the organic world and the artificial world'.[265]

The notion of the technicisation of life is then re-thematised by reference to Jean-Luc Nancy's text, 'Intrus', contained in *Corpus*.[266] For Esposito, this text restores the original sense of Greek word *technē* as the essentially 'technical foundation of human nature'.[267] It indicates that the 'existent does not fully coincide within itself; neither does it imply any transcendental basis: this is the condition of *technē* . . . [T]he fact *that there is no nature*'.[268] Rather, there is exposure to 'what is not itself, and about "all bodies" because this place is precisely the broken contour through which each body comes into contact with the other'.[269]

The desubstantialisation of the body, by Haraway and Nancy, is then the basis on which Esposito proceeds to reflect upon the work of the historian and philosopher of biology and medicine, Alfred Tauber. Tauber's *The Immune Self, Theory or Metaphor?*[270] is situated as part of this constellation of thought of the body and its relation to the immune system. The life of the body, presented by *The Immune Self*, involves a relationship to the immune system as 'a process that always involves an open system of self-definition that consistently produces self and other'.[271] Within this process, the 'self is no longer a genetic constant or a pre-established repertoire, but rather a construct determined by a set of dynamic factors, compatible groupings, fortuitous encounters; nor is it a subject of an object, but rather a principle of action'.[272] The relationship between the body and the immune system entails that the body is

> never original, complete, intact, 'made' once and for all; rather, it constantly makes itself from one minute to the next, depending on the situation and encounters that determine its development. Its boundaries do not lock it up inside a closed world; on the contrary, they create its margin, a delicate and problematic one to be sure, but still permeable in its relationship with that which, while still located outside it, from the beginning traverses and alters it.[273]

The experience of this relationship – the notion of subjectivity which arises from this relationship – is one of 'the experience of its own original alteration'.[274] Hence, prior to 'any transformation, each body is already exposed to the need for its own

265   Ibid., 149.
266   Nancy (2008b).
267   Esposito (2011): 153.
268   Ibid., 150–1 (emphasis in original).
269   Ibid., 151.
270   Tauber (1997).
271   Esposito (2011): 169.
272   Ibid., 169.
273   Ibid., 169.
274   Ibid., 174.

140   Roberto Esposito: Law, Community and the Political

exposure. This is the condition common to all that is immune: the endless perception of its own finitude.'[275] Common immunity is, therefore, revealed to be intertwined with this experience of original alteration.

The thought of common immunity, on the biological plane of Tauber's theoretical framework, is predicated on the coincidence of the self 'with its alteration'.[276] The rejection of all thought of the subject as an 'uncontaminated genetic principle'[277] raises the question of whether one can still ascribe to this systemic process of internal differentiation and alteration of the body, by the immune system, the term 'self'. The relationship between the body and the immune system reproduces a fundamental negativity in which experience is confined to an 'absolutely indeterminate and indeterminable'[278] form of the subject. To conceive of an immunological self is to

> refer to a contradiction by which identity is simultaneously affirmed and altered at the same time: it is established in the form of its own alteration ... [T]he immunological self would thus be that which is more individual and that which is more shared. By overlaying these two divergent meanings onto one figure, what we get is the unique profile of shared individuality or a sharing of individuality.[279]

The separation of body and technique of Foucauldian biopolitics is overcome by its transformation into an originary bioethics.[280] The experience of embodiment, as the relationship between body and immune system, is the experience of the co-belonging of immunity and community – common immunity – within the immunological 'self'.

The originary bioethics with which *Immunitas* concludes is the culmination of a metacritique of the human sciences. The presence of the 'figure' of exclusionary inclusion in the disciplines of law, theology, philosophical anthropology and politics reveals a logic of self-dissolution which occludes the possibility of a thought beyond this immunitary paradigm. The metacritique indicates this possibility in the return to the biological plane and the presentation of a common immunity. This originary bioethics is the prolegomena to the further reworking of the notions of law, community and the political.

---

275   Ibid., 174.
276   Ibid., 168.
277   Ibid., 174.
278   Ibid., 168.
279   Ibid., 177.
280   This is to be contrasted with a 'traditional bioethics', which Mackenzie defines as 'the biomedical normalization of differences by trying to deal only with the moral rights of the rational self and by leaving the differing character of embodiment – a most profound aspect of the ethical habitat – aside' (Mackenzie (1996): 1).

Chapter 8

From *Immunitas* to *Bíos*

The outline of an affirmative biopolitics

The metacritique, which guides and orientates the structure of *Immunitas*, reveals merely the potential outlines of common immunity. The originary bioethics, as 'a shared individuality or a sharing of individuality',[1] with which *Immunitas* concludes, indicates the limit of the theoretical framework of *Immunitas* and a further task. The renewed reflection upon this enigmatic shape of common immunity becomes the path, for Esposito, beyond the limits of *Immunitas*.

The further task is undertaken in *Bíos: Biopolitics and Philosophy*,[2] and involves a reorientation of Esposito's theoretical framework. The theoretical acquisitions of *Immunitas* – the different philosophy of immunity as a common immunity – are preserved, rethought and, finally, transformed into the possibility of an affirmative biopolitics. In this reorientation, the previous metacritique of the human sciences is replaced with a sustained reconsideration of the notion of biopolitics. The reflection centres on the 'double tendency'[3] of biopolitics: 'a growing superimposition between the domain of power or of law and that of life', accompanied by 'an equally close implication that seems to have been derived from death'.[4]

It is from this perspective that a return to Foucauldian biopolitics is undertaken which concentrates explicitly upon Foucault's articulation of this double tendency as the paradoxical risk of the reversal of a politics of life into a 'work of death'.[5] The paradoxical form is, for Esposito, the expression of a hesitation or indecision in Foucault's thematisation of the notion of biopolitics. This 'epistemological uncertainty'[6] is itself the indication of a limit: the absence of a notion of immunisation and the relation it 'posits between biopolitics and modernity'.[7] The introduction of the notion of immunisation – the preservation of the preceding

---

1 Esposito (2011): 177.
2 Esposito (2008).
3 Ibid.
4 Ibid., 7–8.
5 Ibid., 8.
6 Ibid., 9.
7 Ibid., 9.

theoretical accomplishment of *Immunitas* – enables a rethinking of the notion of biopolitics. The 'specifically modern genesis' of biopolitics is located in 'individual self-preservation' as 'the presupposition of all other political categories, from sovereignty to liberty'.[8] From this genesis arises a 'self-preserving' paradigm of exclusionary inclusion, differentiated into 'earlier and later modernities', underlain by an immunitary logic which 'turns the protective apparatus against its own body'.[9] National Socialism, in its 'intrinsically biological characterization of life', is 'the culmination of biopolitics, at least in that qualified expression of being absolutely indistinct from its reversal into thanatopolitics'.[10]

The task for thought is initiated by the recognition that 'the antiphilosophical and biological philosophy of Hitlerism' introduces, rather than closes, the central question of the alteration of life 'by a part of politics identified with technology'.[11] Hence, the articulation of the 'relationship between philosophy and biopolitics *after Nazism*',[12] a philosophy of *bios*, commences beyond the framework of modern political and legal concepts which originate with the emergence of biopolitics.

Esposito, therefore, subjects the three predominant biopolitical notions of National Socialism – 'the absolute normativization of life, the double enclosure of the body, and the anticipatory suppression of birth'[13] – to a 'constructive deconstruction'.[14] From this process, the figures of 'flesh, norm, and birth' are derived, as the 'admittedly approximate and provisional contours of an affirmative biopolitics that is capable of overturning the Nazi politics of death in a politics that is no longer over life but *of* life'.[15] The co-implication or co-originary status of politics and life – a thought of 'politics within the same form of life' – becomes the basis for a philosophy of *bios* from within which the notions of law, community and the political are articulated.

The development of *Bíos* is both an explicit consideration of Foucault, Nietzsche, Merleau-Ponty, Simondon, Canguilheim and Deleuze and a response to the notion of biopolitics in Agamben. The philosophy of *bios*, and the affirmative biopolitics which it reveals, should be understood as a form of 'constructive deconstruction' of Agamben's *Homo Sacer: Sovereign Power and Bare Life*,[16] and, to a lesser extent, its later supplement, *The State of Exception*.[17] The point of convergence and divergence centres on the exclusively 'biopolitical horizon'

---

8   Ibid., 9.
9   Ibid., 11.
10   Ibid., 11.
11   Ibid., 11.
12   Ibid., 10 (emphasis in original).
13   Ibid., 10.
14   Ibid., 12.
15   Ibid., 12, 11 (emphasis in original).
16   Agamben (1998).
17   Agamben (2005a).

From *Immunitas* to *Bíos* 143

from which Agamben interrogates the foundational categories of modern politics in *Homo Sacer*.[18]

For Agamben, the biopolitical horizon is itself delineated through an emendation of the original, Foucauldian notion of biopolitics. It acknowledges the theoretical advances of the Foucauldian reorientation of the conceptualisation of 'the problem of power' from the traditional, 'juridico-institutional models (the definition of sovereignty, the theory of the State)' to 'the concrete ways in which power penetrates subjects' very bodies and forms of life'.[19] The 'two faces of power' – the knowledge and techniques of the State directed to 'the care of the natural life of individuals' and the 'processes of subjectivization' or 'technologies of the self' which simultaneously individuate and bind 'to an external power' – are described and differentiated, but remain without a clearly articulated 'point of intersection'.[20] The revelation of this point of intersection, and the concomitant re-thematisation of the original Foucauldian biopolitical horizon, constitute one of the central elements of Agamben's text.

In this reconstruction of the biopolitical horizon, the history of biopolitics ceases to emerge and be co-terminus with the modern or modernity. It is projected back to the very origin of Western politics in which 'the inclusion of bare life in the political realm constitutes the original – if concealed – nucleus of sovereign power'.[21] The Foucauldian history of biopolitics – the emergence of 'biological life at the centre of [the modern State's] calculations' – is simply the rendering visible of this 'secret tie uniting power and bare life' in which the modern is intertwined with the archaic.[22] The archaic is condensed, for Agamben, in archaic Roman law, in the definition of *homo sacer*: 'the first paradigm of the political realm of the West'.[23] This figure is exemplary, because it defines a human being as one who may be killed, and whose killing must exist outside a logic of religious sacrifice. *Homo sacer* is the origin of the human being as bare life – inclusion 'in the juridical order solely in the form of its exclusion (that is, of its capacity to be killed)'.[24] The biopolitical horizon then becomes constituted by a history of the movement of bare life from its marginal position, as *homo sacer*, to one of the coincidence of bare life and the political realm. This coincidence or 'zone of irreducible indistinction' is the decisive determinant of the parameters of modern politics as the 'bare life of the citizen, the new biopolitical body of humanity'.[25]

The history of the biopolitical horizon is marked by the separation of classical and modern democracy in the definitive collapse of the original, Aristotelian distinction between *zoē* ('simple, natural life') and *bios* ('the way or form of life

18 Agamben (1998): 4.
19 Ibid., 5.
20 Ibid., 5–6.
21 Ibid., 6.
22 Ibid., 6.
23 Ibid., 9.
24 Ibid., 8.
25 Ibid., 9.

144   Roberto Esposito: Law, Community and the Political

proper to an individual or a group').[26] Modern democracy emerges with the coincidence or indistinction of *zoē* and *bios*, and attempts to distinguish from within bare life 'a way of life and to find, so to speak, the *bios* of *zoē*'.[27] The attempt becomes, for Agamben, the experience and repetition of an aporia: 'it wants to put the freedom and happiness of men into play in the very place – "bare life" – that marked their subjection'.[28] This aporia also indicates, at a 'historico-philosophical level', the 'inner solidarity of democracy and totalitarianism'.[29] For the failure of modern democracy to differentiate a way of life from within bare life – the repetition of the aporia – is initially reflected in the ease of passage into the way of life installed by 'totalitarian states'.[30] The subsequent collapse of the totalitarian states is accompanied by the continued repetition of the aporia: the generalisation of the way of life of 'post-democratic spectacular societies (which comes to be evident in Alexis de Tocqueville and finds its final sanction in the analyses of Guy Debord)' combined with the continued emergence of the camp as a space of confinement.[31]

The retracing of the history of the biopolitical horizon leads Agamben to formulate its distinctive parameters in '[t]hree theses'.[32] These theses present bare life as the origin and untranscendable horizon from which 'a politics no longer founded on the exception of bare life' must commence.[33] This has to be undertaken through the acknowledgement that there is no return to the categories of classical political thought; and that the 'notions of the social sciences (from jurisprudence to anthropology)' be held capable of being 'revised without reserve'.[34] The aporia, formed and reproduced by the inclusion of bare life 'in politics in the form of an exception', is to be rendered inoperative by conceiving bare life as a 'form-of-life': 'this being that is only its own bare existence and to this life that, being its own form, remains inseparable from it'.[35]

The thought of bare life as a thought of immanence – the differentiation of bare life from within itself – is the initial horizon and task which Esposito shares with Agamben in *Bíos*. The initial convergence or sharing of horizons is one which becomes, through the development of the text of *Bíos*, a divergent accord concerning the conception of this thought of the immanence of bare life.

26   Ibid., 1.
27   Ibid., 9.
28   Ibid., 9–10.
29   Ibid., 10.
30   Ibid., 10.
31   Ibid., 11.
32   Ibid., 181. '1. The original political relation is the ban (the state of exception as zone of indistinction between outside and inside, exclusion and inclusion). 2. The fundamental activity of sovereign power is the production of bare life as originary political elements and as threshold of articulation between nature and culture, *zoē* and *bios*. 3. Today it is not the city but rather the camp that is the fundamental biopolitical paradigm of the West' (ibid.)
33   Ibid., 11.
34   Ibid., 12.
35   Ibid., 188.

From *Immunitas* to *Bíos*   145

The biopolitical horizon, as the interpretative background for the thought of the immanence of bare life, arises, for both Esposito and Agamben, in Foucault. The beginning of the divergence between Esposito and Agamben concerns the definition and determination of the incompleteness or uncertainty of the Foucauldian notion of biopolitics.

For Esposito, this incompleteness or uncertainty is the expression of the absence, within Foucauldian biopolitics, of an integral articulation of the elements of life and politics of which it is comprised. The biopolitical horizon and its history – the relationship between life and politics – are to be re-thematised by situating life and politics within the 'paradigm of "immunization"'.[36] The effect of this re-thematisation is to combine the integration and extension of the theoretical analyses of *Immunitas* with the detachment of the biopolitical from the history ascribed to it by Agamben. The central position of the figure of *homo sacer* is displaced by the presupposition of a 'first condition' for the self-preservation of society: a paradigm of exclusionary inclusion.[37] From this first condition, the history of the biopolitical horizon comes to focus on modernity, and its internal division between a first and second modernity. The central importance of modernity derives from its definition as the position in which the self-preservation of society and paradigm of immunisation 'constitutes its most intimate essence'.[38]

The biopolitical horizon rests upon its detachment from, rather than its insertion within, a philosophy of history generated by Agamben's analogy between bare life and pure Being in *Homo Sacer*. The analogy, based on the correspondence of 'bare' in the 'syntagm "bare life"' and pure Being to the ancient Greek word *haplōs*, indicates a fundamental commonality in the constitution of man 'as a thinking animal' and 'as a political animal'.[39] The fundamental commonality is the expression of affinity between 'the fundamental activity' of Western metaphysics and of Western politics.[40] The isolation of the 'proper element' of both Western metaphysics and Western politics is, simultaneously, the limit of both endeavours: the equally 'indeterminate and impenetrable' character of pure Being and bare life.[41] It is the very emptiness and indeterminacy of these two concepts, however, which, for Agamben, 'safeguard the keys to the historico-political destiny of the West'.[42] The thought of the immanence of bare life is, therefore, the attribution of a form to this empty and indeterminate concept. In this thought of immanence is the overcoming or resolution of both the 'subjection to political power' and the 'enigma of ontology'.

The notion of modernity, in *Bíos*, interrupts Agamben's analogy, because the central political categories of first modernity (sovereignty, property and liberty),

36   Esposito (2008): 45.
37   Ibid., 54.
38   Ibid., 55.
39   Agamben (1998): 182.
40   Ibid., 182.
41   Ibid., 182.
42   Ibid., 182.

146   Roberto Esposito: Law, Community and the Political

as expressions of the paradigm of immunity, ascribe a determinate intelligibility to bare life. The revelation of the aporia contained within these central categories – the preservation of life through 'the same powers that interdict its development'[43] – is the basis of their exhaustion, and the distinction between first and second modernity. The thought of Nietzsche, in contrast to Agamben in *Homo Sacer*, occupies a pivotal position in the emergence of the distinction between first and second modernity. For Nietzsche's thought exposes the underlying nihilism and, hence, exhaustion, of the aporetic character of the central categories of first modernity. From the exhaustion of these categories emerges the ambivalent 'new horizon of sense' of second modernity of which Nietzsche's thought is the essential prefiguration.[44] The passage to second modernity entails a new ascription of intelligibility to bare life, through the ambivalent notion of biological life. The periodisation of second modernity, for Esposito, results from the radicalisation of a particular connection between biological life and politics of National Socialism. The particular linkage of biological life and politics under National Socialism generates the three 'bio-thanatological principles' of 'the normativization of life, the double enclosure of the body, and the preemptive suppression of birth'.[45] It is these principles, rather than the central figure of the camp in Agamben's analysis, which become the horizon of biopolitics against which the thought of an affirmative biopolitics has to be reconstructed.

In this reconstruction, the overcoming of the thanatological potential of these principles, contained in each of their distinct linkages between bare life and politics, is substituted for Agamben's overcoming of the subjection to political power and the enigma of ontology. For Esposito, this involves commencing from:

> the same categories of 'life,' 'body,' and 'birth,' and then of converting their immunitary (which is to say self-negating) declension in a direction that is open to a more originary and intense sense of *communitas*. Only in this way – at the point of intersection and tension among contemporary reflections that have moved in such a direction – will it be possible to trace the initial features of a biopolitics that is finally affirmative.[46]

It is the thought of immanence, within this interpretative process, which facilitates the conceptual work of conversion of each of these bio-thanatological principles. The task of conversion, in response to the specificity of each bio-thanatological principle, renders the thought of immanence a complex theoretical framework from which the outlines of an affirmative biopolitics emerge.

The presence of a notion of law in the outlines of this affirmative biopolitics is revealed in the conversion of the bio-thanatological principle of the

43   Esposito (2008): 56.
44   Ibid., 78.
45   Ibid., 157.
46   Ibid., 157.

normativisation of life. The conceptual process of conversion is also the further displacement of Agamben's thought of immanence in *Homo Sacer*, and of the central position accorded to the paradigm of the state of exception in the *State of Exception*. For Esposito, in conformity with Agamben in the *State of Exception*,[47] the legal form of National Socialism is introduced by the suspension and not the abolition of the Weimar Constitution and, hence, exists, for the duration of the regime, as a state of exception. The divergence between Esposito and Agamben concerns the position to be accorded to the state of exception in the analysis of the specific character of National Socialism and its associated biopolitics. For Esposito, in contrast to Agamben, the state of exception is to be understood as the initial stage, in the form of a legal act, for the further development of the bio-thanatological principle of the normativisation of life. The coherence and consistency of this bio-thanatological principle is predicated upon 'a normative framework that was objective precisely because it originated from the vital necessities of the German people'.[48] The normative framework expresses an absolute and immediate identity between 'biology and law, and life and norm' in which the norm is an '*a posteriori* application of a present determination in nature: it is the racial connotation that attributes or removes the right to exist to or from individuals and peoples'.[49] From this link between the 'biologisation of life' and the 'juridicalisation of life', the normative framework produces the specific 'norm of life' of National Socialism which is characterised by its continuous reversal into a norm of death.[50]

This is the point at which Esposito's constructive deconstruction of Agamben's thought is marked by its clearest divergence. For the conversion of this bio-thanatological principle, through a thought of immanence, also distinguishes itself from Agamben's notion of immanence in *Homo Sacer*. Esposito commences directly from the 'norm of life' of National Socialism and, in converting it into 'logic of reciprocal immanence',[51] substitutes a thought of immanence, as a norm-of-life, for Agamben's thought of immanence as a 'form-of-life'. The norm-of-life which Esposito develops is the thought of an immanent relationship between law and life which retains the notion of law insofar as it is capable, as normativity, of expressing this immanent relationship.

The affirmative biopolitical horizon of *Bíos* proceeds beyond status of a prolegomena (the originary bio-ethics of *Immunitas*) to furnish the philosophical preconditions for the re-thematisation of law, community and the political. The enigma of common immunity has become the thought of immanence arising from the conversion of the three bio-thanatological principles of National Socialism.

---

47 Agamben (2005a): 2, 14–15.
48 Esposito (2008): 183.
49 Ibid., 182.
50 Ibid., 183–4.
51 Ibid., 185.

Chapter 9

Bíos I

Rethinking biopolitics – from Foucault to Nietzsche

The text of *Bíos* initially develops through a reconsideration of the theoretical framework of biopolitics. The constant possibility for a politics of life – biopolitics – to transform itself into a politics of death is, for Esposito, what remains unexplained in the most distinctive contemporary conception of biopolitics represented by the work of Michel Foucault. The limit of Foucauldian biopolitics is subject, in the first three chapters of *Bíos*, to a double gesture. Esposito preserves the theoretical advances contained in Foucauldian biopolitics, while reconfiguring the underlying parameters of its conceptual framework. The reconfiguration involves its redescription as paradigm of immunisation: a form of exclusionary inclusion in whose immunitary effect – the protection of life – inheres the potential for a politics of death.

The limits of Foucauldian biopolitics

The central importance of Foucault, for Esposito, relates to the articulation of an original conception of biopolitics which breaks with its preceding thematisation within organic, anthropological and naturalistic frameworks. The break flows from the underlying affinity of Foucault's thought with 'Nietzschean genealogy'.[1] The genealogical orientation of his thought is evident in 'the oblique capacity for disassembly and conceptual re-elaboration',[2] which, in turn, furnishes the distinctive presentation of the relationship between modernity and biopolitics.

The presentation finds its most concise, programmatic formulation in Foucault's essay 'What is Enlightenment?'.[3] The 'type of philosophical interrogation', which Foucault identifies as originating in Kant's 1784 essay of the same title, is of 'the outline of what one might call the attitude to modernity'.[4] The outline emerges from the character of the essay – 'at the crossroads of critical reflection and

---

1 Esposito (2008): 24. Here, Esposito considers Foucault's essay, 'Nietzsche, Genealogy, History' (Foucault (1980)) as a dominant, organising text for the further development of Foucault's thought from the middle of the 1970s.

2 Ibid., 24.

3 Foucault (2000).

4 Ibid., 309.

Bíos I: rethinking biopolitics   149

reflection on history' – which presents a 'reflection on "today" as difference in history and as motive for a particular philosophical task'.[5] The intersection between this approach to Kant's essay and Nietzschean genealogy becomes evident in the practice of this philosophical task as critique. The practice of critique can only be that of

> a historical investigation into events that have led us to constitute ourselves and to recognise ourselves as subjects of what we are doing, thinking, saying. In that sense, this criticism is not transcendental, and its goal is not that of making a metaphysics possible: it is genealogical in its design and archaeological in its method. Archaeological – and not transcendental – in the sense that it will not seek to identify the universal structures of all knowledge or of all possible moral action, but will seek to treat the instances of discourse that articulate what we think, say, and do as so many historical events. And this critique will be genealogical in the sense that it will not deduce from the form of what we are what it is impossible for us to do and to know; but it will separate out, from the contingency that has made us what we are, the possibility of no longer being, doing, or thinking what we are, do, or think.[6]

For Esposito, the relationship between critical reflection and reflection on history, which Foucault's own analysis develops, enables 'a different sort of gaze'.[7] It interrupts the solidity of predominant understandings of the connection between past and present.

An essential aspect of this interruption concerns the notion of sovereignty and its associated juridico-political framework. The interruption involves the dissolution of the connection between sovereignty and modernity and, in this dissolution, emerges the 'site' of biopolitics: 'the product of a series of causes, forces and tensions that themselves emerge as modified in an incessant game of action and reaction, of pushing and resisting'.[8] It is in relation to this 'site' – situated between life in the order of nature and life in the order of human history – that the Foucauldian genealogy of the modern political order is presented.

The dissolution of the connection between sovereignty and modernity is, for Esposito, a fundamental critique of 'all modern [political] philosophies'.[9] The juridico-political framework within which the notion of sovereignty inheres forms a 'triangular grid': 'the totality of individuals and power that at a certain point enters into relation between individuals in the modalities defined by a third element, which is constituted by law'.[10] The individual subjects exist prior to

5   Ibid., 309.
6   Ibid., 315.
7   Esposito (2008): 24.
8   Ibid., 30.
9   Ibid., 28.
10   Ibid., 25.

150   Roberto Esposito: Law, Community and the Political

sovereign power, and the law assigns rights to individual subjects which, as a 'counterweight', determine the degree of superiority of sovereign power over the totality of individual subjects.[11] The triangular grid is traversed by a 'topological alternative that sees politics and law, decision and the norm as situated in opposite poles of a dialectic that has as its object the relation between subjects and the sovereign'.[12] The 'entire modern philosophical-juridical debate' is the repetitive reproduction of these topological alternatives.[13]

The repetitive character of modern political philosophy, through the oppositions of 'law and power, legality and legitimacy, norm and exception', obscures a more fundamental question revealed in Foucault's conscious break with this juridico-political framework.[14] The question becomes apparent by concentrating on one of the basic attributes of 'the classical theory of sovereignty' – the right to life or death.[15] This right inserts life and death into the 'field of power' of the sovereign, and, in relation to it, the subject 'is neutral, and it is thanks to the sovereign that the subject has the right to be alive, or, possibly the right to be dead'.[16] The 'presumed conflict between sovereignty and law' obscures a more fundamental question or problematisation of life: the addition or supplementation of 'sovereignty's old right – to take life or let live' – by 'the right to make live and to let die':[17] 'relations of subjugation [which] manufacture subjects'.[18]

The addition to, or supplementation of, the previous juridical schema, by this new form of right, is the expression of the direct entry of life 'into the mechanisms and *dispositifs* of governing human beings'.[19] The genealogy of this supplementation, which Foucault presents in the *Lecture Courses* between 1974 and 1979, together with the book *Discipline and Punish*,[20] constitute, for Esposito, the corpus of work which dissolves the essential connection between the notion of sovereignty and modernity. In this dissolution, modernity becomes this process of supplementation, which reveals sovereignty as that which 'compresses or represses' this notion of life.[21] Modernity is, therefore, the passage to the governing of the life of human beings:

> On the one side, all political practices that governments put into action (or even those practices that oppose them) turn to life, to its processes, to its needs, to its fractures. On the other side, life enters into power relations not only on

11   Ibid., 25.
12   Ibid., 25.
13   Ibid., 25.
14   Ibid., 26.
15   Foucault (2004a): 240.
16   Ibid., 240.
17   Ibid., 241.
18   Ibid., 265.
19   Esposito (2008): 27.
20   Foucault (1991); (2003); (2004a); (2009); and (2010).
21   Esposito (2008): 25.

the side of its critical thresholds or its pathological exceptions, but in all its extension, articulation, and duration.[22]

The supplementation of sovereignty is reflected in the transposition of law from 'the transcendental level of codes and sanctions that essentially have to do with subjects of will to the immanent level of rules and norms that are addressed instead to bodies'.[23] The relationship between rules, norms and the body becomes the point of intersection of politics and life. The intersection is the site of biopolitics which is itself the expression of the relationship of 'bio-history' and 'bio-power'.[24]

For Esposito, the Foucauldian conception of biopolitics marks a profound shift in the 'field, logic and object of politics' within modernity.[25] It effectively introduces an untranscendable horizon in which '[n]o other politics is conceivable other than as a politics of life'.[26] However, it is in the conception of the parameters of this politics of life – the 'adequate categorical exactitude'[27] of biopolitics – that the limits of this Foucauldian conception become apparent. The concept of biopolitics – the relationship between politics and life – displaces the classical theory of sovereignty with the generalisation of a continuous struggle between politics and life which is punctuated by temporary or provisional periods of submission.

The dynamic schema which appears to underlie the relationship between politics and life creates an internal division within the concept of biopolitics between a politics of life and a politics over life. For Esposito, the internal division produces indeterminacy or indecisiveness between two mutually irreconcilable possibilities situated 'on the extremes of its semantic extension: these are subjectivization and death'.[28] They express the presence of two radically antagonistic *forms of life* within biopolitics, and reveal the underlying tendency of the Foucauldian concept of biopolitics to fold 'in upon itself' as it 'seems not to admit any mediation'.[29]

> Either life holds politics back, pinning it to its impassable natural limit or, on the contrary, it is life that is captured and prey to a politics that strains to imprison its innovative potential. Between the two possibilities there is a breach in signification, a blind spot that risks dragging the entire category into a vacuum of sense. It is as if biopolitics is missing something (an intermediary segment or a logical juncture) that is capable of unbinding the

22 Ibid., 28.
23 Ibid., 28.
24 Ibid., 29.
25 Ibid., 15.
26 Ibid., 15.
27 Ibid., 14.
28 Ibid., 31–2.
29 Ibid., 32.

absoluteness of irreconcilable perspectives in the elaboration of a more complex paradigm that, without losing the specificity of its elements seizes hold of the internal connection or indicates a common horizon.[30]

The limitation is revealed in the confinement of biopolitics to the generation of either a politics of life or a politics over life. In this position, the Foucauldian concept of biopolitics is, for Esposito, simply the formal, negative repository of these two antagonistic forms of life into which it constantly disappears.

The limits of the Foucauldian concept of biopolitics are reflected in the character of the genealogico-historical presentation of modernity. In a presentation of modernity as a form of life orientated by a politics of life, a genealogy of this particular relationship between power and life describes the distinctive modalities of:

> the disciplinary apparatus and *dispositifs* of control; the techniques put into action by power with regard first to individual bodies and then of populations as a whole; the sectors – schools, barracks, hospital, factory – in which they drill and the domains – birth, disease, mortality – that they affect.[31]

This framework of rules and norms intimately connected to the individual body and populations is combined with a broader genealogy which traces this distinctiveness to the combination of 'the three categories of *subjectivization, making immanent*, and *production*'.[32] These three categories are themselves the expression of three regimes of power – 'pastoral power, the art of government, and the police sciences' – which combine in the displacement of sovereignty to orientate the form of life of a politics of life.[33]

The combination of these three categories involves their mutual modification and intensification. The art of government generalises the function of pastoral power as 'a new distribution, a new organisation of this kind of individualizing power'.[34] The process of generalisation of pastoral power is accompanied by 'a change in objective' in which 'a series of "worldly" aims took the place of the religious aims of the traditional pastorate'.[35] The state is no longer distinguished by its separation and distance from the individual, 'but, on the contrary, [it becomes] a very sophisticated structure, in which individuals can be integrated, under one condition: that this individuality would be shaped in a new form and submitted to a set of very specific patterns'.[36] The rules and norms generated by

30 Ibid., 32.
31 Ibid., 35.
32 Ibid., 35 (emphasis in original).
33 Ibid., 35.
34 Foucault (2002b): 334.
35 Ibid., 334.
36 Ibid., 334.

Bíos I: rethinking biopolitics   153

this sophisticated structure involve the superimposition or co-presence of 'a pastoral power and a political power' orientated to 'an individualizing "tactic" which characterized a series of powers: those of the family, medicine, psychiatry, education and employers'.[37] The 'tactic' responds to an altered relationship of power to the life of individuals and populations.

The preceding juridical schema of sovereignty consists of the reproduction of a closed circuit of power centred on the maintenance of obedience through the relationship between sovereign power and individual rights. The art of government moves beyond this closed circuit, as it is 'addressed to subjects' lives, not only in the sense of their defence, but also with regard to how to deploy, strengthen and maximize life'.[38] The character of governmental power 'reinforces, augments, and stimulates' life in the form of the individual and of populations.[39] Governmental power, as the extension beyond obedience of the governed to the 'welfare of the governed', centres biopolitics on a politics of life.[40]

In this extension, the relationship between life, in the form of the individual and of populations, and governmental power is shaped by both a vertical and a horizontal movement. The vertical movement emerges from their 'continuous communication' reaching from 'population and families' to 'single individuals'.[41] The horizontal movement is initiated by the contact between 'the practices and languages of life in a form that amplifies the horizons, improves the services, and intensifies the performance'.[42]

The intensification of this relationship, and its associated vertical and horizontal movements of the art of government, is the effect of the regime of power of the 'science of the police'.[43] The exemplary text of this science, which, for Foucault, reaches its most advanced expression in the eighteenth century, is Johnan Heinrich Gottlob von Justi's *Elements of Police*.[44] The science founds and describes a political technology or 'productive modality' of government in which 'the positive reconversion of the ancient sovereign right of death reaches its zenith'.[45] The police, as the institutionalised body which applies this science to the life of individuals and populations, are actively engaged in the reproduction of *both* 'the vital development of individuals and the strengthening of the forces of the state'.[46]

The combination of these three regimes of power generates a politics of life in which the Foucauldian concept of biopolitics describes a relationship which:

37   Ibid., 335.
38   Esposito (2008): 36.
39   Ibid., 36.
40   Ibid., 36.
41   Ibid., 36.
42   Ibid., 36.
43   Ibid., 37.
44   Foucault (2002a); and Foucault (2002b).
45   Esposito (2008): 37. See, for an alternative perspective on von Justi as the origin of the modern science of political economy, Backhaus (2009).
46   Ibid., 37.

does not limit or coerce life, but expands it in a manner proportional to its development ... [A] singular expansive process in which power and life constitute the two opposing and complementary faces. To strengthen itself, power is forced at the same time into strengthening the object on which it discharges itself; not only, but ... it is also forced to render it subject to its own subjugation. Moreover, if it wants to stimulate the action of subjects, power must not only presuppose but also produce the conditions of freedom of the subjects to whom it addresses itself.[47]

The politics of life, as biopolitics, represents a particular understanding of the relationship between power, individuals and populations. Each element of the relationship is 'indispensible', and the essential form of their relationship is 'not violence; nor is it consent', but 'always a way of acting upon an acting subject or acting subjects by virtue of their acting or being capable of action. A set of actions upon other actions.'[48] The action of power upon life, as the acting upon the actions of individuals and of populations, produces a 'complicated interplay' between the elements of power and life.[49] For this acting upon is an attempt by power to 'conduct' life and, thereby, introduces 'conduct' as both an attempt to '"lead" others (according to mechanisms of coercion which are, to varying degrees, strict) and a way of behaving within a more or less open field of possibilities'.[50] Hence, the politics of life presents life as both 'free *for* power' and 'free *against* power':[51] 'an "agonism" – of a relationship which is at the same time reciprocal incitation and struggle, less of a face-to-face confrontation that paralyzes both sides than a permanent provocation'.[52]

For Esposito, the difficulty and limitation of this particular presentation of the relationship between power and life is its essentially self-contained character. The possibility of death – the transformation of a politics of life into a politics over life – seems absent from the agonistic relationship between power and life. This absence, and the corresponding concentration upon relations of power and strategy,[53] results from the genealogico-historical description of modernity, as the supplementation of sovereignty by biopolitics.[54] The co-presence of sovereignty and the three supplementary regimes of pastoral power, the art of government and the science of the police produce a 'mutual relation, [in which] different times are compressed within a singular epochal segment constituted and simultaneously altered by their reciprocal tension'.[55]

47 Ibid., 37–8.
48 Foucault (2002b): 340–1.
49 Ibid., 342.
50 Ibid., 341.
51 Esposito (2008): 38.
52 Foucault (2002b): 342.
53 Ibid., 346–8.
54 Esposito (2008): 39.
55 Ibid., 41.

The mutual relation effectively suppresses the question of transition as either one of 'contemporaneity or succession'.[56] Thus:

> What remains suspended here is not only the question of the relation of modernity to its 'pre', but also that of the relation with its 'post'. What was twentieth-century totalitarianism with respect to the society that preceded it? Was it a limit point, a tear, a surplus in which the mechanism of biopower broke free, got out of hand, or, on the contrary, was it society's sole and natural outcome? Did it interrupt or did it fulfil it? Once again the problem concerns the relation with the sovereign paradigm: does Nazism (but also true communism) stand on the outside or inside vis-à-vis it? Do they mark the end or the return? Do they reveal the most intimate linking or the ultimate disjunction between sovereignty and biopolitics?[57]

The Foucauldian concept of biopolitics can only offer, for Esposito, the paradoxical response of both continuity *and* discontinuity, of both distinction *and* indistinction.[58]

The initial appearance of the limitations of the Foucauldian approach as a theoretical paradox, contained in the genealogico-historical approach, is, for Esposito, revealed to be a more fundamental difficulty in the form of an antinomy. The transition from theoretical paradox to antinomy is evident, for Esposito, once the orientations of continuity and discontinuity can only be understood as opening towards 'two opposing possibilities'.[59] The divergence becomes evident in the comprehension of the connection 'between sovereignty, biopolitics, and totalitarianism'.[60]

From the perspective of an underlying continuity and indistinction, the comprehension is orientated by a 'continuist hypothesis'.[61] The connection between sovereignty, biopolitics and totalitarianism undergoes a simplification and reduction of 'historical distinctions', as it is definitively shaped, if not determined by, a trajectory which results in genocide.[62] This possibility – biopolitics as 'an absolute power over life' – exists in parallel with the perspective of an underlying discontinuity and distinction between sovereignty, biopolitics and totalitarianism. The divergent, 'discontinuist hypothesis'[63] is orientated by a trajectory which accords primacy to life as a biopolitics of 'an absolute power of life'.[64] The greater potential of this perspective to acknowledge historical distinctions and

56 Ibid., 40.
57 Ibid., 42–3.
58 Ibid., 43.
59 Ibid., 43.
60 Ibid., 43.
61 Ibid., 43.
62 Ibid., 43.
63 Ibid., 43.
64 Ibid., 43.

discontinuity is dependent on the presupposition of the inherent resistance of life to power. The presence of death 'inside the circle of life, not only during the first half of the 1900s, but also after', reveals the attendant simplification and reduction of complexity of this perspective.[65]

The passage from theoretical paradox to antinomy, for Esposito, describes and extends the 'hermeneutic impasse' of Foucauldian biopolitics,[66] beyond that of 'historical periodization or genealogical articulation', to encompass the notions of life and politics contained in the Foucauldian concept of biopolitics.[67] The limits of Foucauldian biopolitics 'demand a new horizon of meaning, a different interpretative key that is capable of linking the two polarities together in a way that is at the same time more limited and more complex'.[68]

Thinking with Foucault beyond Foucault: biopolitics and immunisation

The disjunction between the contemporary relevance of biopolitics and the lack of 'adequate categorical exactitude' revealed to underlie the Foucauldian conception leads Esposito to re-conceive biopolitics through the 'paradigm of "immunization"'.[69] The notion of immunisation enables the impasse of the Foucauldian conception – the reproduction of a ceaselessly antinomic relationship between power and life – to be overcome while preserving 'the two principal declinations of the [Foucauldian] biopolitical paradigm: one affirmative and productive and the other negative and lethal'.[70] The introduction of the paradigm of immunisation proceeds, in the process of re-conception, to delineate a 'structural connection between modernity and immunization',[71] which is itself differentiated into the phases of a first and a second modernity. The differentiation of modernity is traced through the predominant 'historical-political categories' of the first phase – sovereignty, property and liberty – as the 'linguistic and institutional forms adopted by immunitary logic in order to safeguard life from the risks that derive from its own collective configuration and conflagration'.[72]

The re-conception of biopolitics, through the paradigm of immunisation, replaces the external relationship between power and life – superimposition or juxtaposition – with 'a single, indivisible whole that assumes meaning from their interrelation'.[73] The interrelation between power and life becomes 'the intrinsically

---

65 Ibid., 43.
66 Ibid., 43.
67 Ibid., 43.
68 Ibid., 44.
69 Ibid., 14, 45.
70 Ibid., 46.
71 Ibid., 51.
72 Ibid., 56.
73 Ibid., 45.

Bíos I: rethinking biopolitics   157

antinomic mode by which life preserves itself through power'.[74] The paradigm of immunisation introduces the possibility of mediation between power and life, because it displaces the thought of negation as 'the violent subordination that power imposes on life from the outside', by a form which manifests a negative 'protection of life'.[75] Negation as immunisation

> saves, insures, and preserves the organism either individual or collective, to which it pertains, but it does not do so directly, immediately, or frontally; on the contrary, it subjects the organism to a condition that simultaneously negates or reduces its power to expand.[76]

The transformation of the thought of negation into negation as immunisation is then revealed to emerge from its 'contrastive symmetry with the concept of community – itself read in the light of its original meaning – and on the other by its specifically modern characterization'.[77] In this contrastive symmetry, the Foucauldian category of life is also transformed by the etymological origin of *communitas*, in which life is originally experienced as 'that relation, which in binding its members to an obligation of reciprocal donation, jeopardizes individual identity'.[78]

Bíos marks the intersection of Foucauldian biopolitics with Esposito's two preceding works of *Immunitas* and *Communitas*. At this intersection, Foucauldian biopolitics is rethought in a manner which also supplements the combined conceptual framework of these two preceding works. The turn, in *Immunitas*, from the critique, in *Communitas*, of modern political philosophy to the critique of a paradigm of immunity based on exclusionary inclusion, is now qualified by the reappearance of certain categories of modern political philosophy. Their reappearance flows, in *Bíos*, from the 'structural connection' between the paradigm of immunisation and 'the processes of modernisation',[79] which remains underdetermined in *Immunitas*.[80] This, in turn, expresses the passage from the 'bio'-ethics of *Immunitas* to the 'bio'-politics of *Bíos*.

Esposito seeks, with the presentation of this structural connection, to acknowledge the theories of modernity of Weber, Löwith and Blumenberg, while simultaneously revealing the more fundamental connection between modernisation and immunisation. The character of the theoretical relationship between immunity and community is one of *both* logical derivation and essential co-belonging: 'the negative of *immunitas* (which is another way of saying *communitas*) does not

74 Ibid., 46.
75 Ibid., 46.
76 Ibid., 46.
77 Ibid., 50.
78 Ibid., 50.
79 Ibid., 51.
80 Esposito (2011): 78.

158   Roberto Esposito: Law, Community and the Political

only disappear from its area of relevance, but constitutes simultaneously its object and motor'.[81] In contrast, the three preceding and predominant theories of modernity 'originate in a circumscribed thematic centre, or rather are situated on a unique sliding axis' in which each theory, while commencing with the presupposition of its alterity,[82] assumes that it is subject to disappearance 'or at least changes into something different'.[83]

The paradigm of immunisation, as the immunisation of community from the *munus* of the common, is the self-preservation of the community through an 'internal mechanism' of exclusionary inclusion: 'the negation of its original sense', which simultaneously preserves the community.[84] The more fundamental connection between modernisation and immunisation flows, for Esposito, from this philosophico-anthropological presupposition. The paradigm of immunisation becomes the philosophico-anthropological condition of the possibility of a community. For the process of self-preservation creates an internal border or boundary 'which separates community from itself, sheltering it from an unbearable excess'.[85] The existence of a community is, therefore, dependent upon its capacity for self-preservation. Hence, '*every* community, is forced to introject the negative modality of its opposite, even if the opposite remains precisely a lacking and contrastive mode of being of the community itself'.[86] The effect of this necessary introjection is to produce 'a substitution or an opposition of private or individualistic models with a form of community organisation'.[87] The self-preservation of the community is simultaneously the reshaping of the subject's relationship to the community and, in this process of reshaping, Esposito identifies the operation of the processes of modernisation within the paradigm of immunisation.

The paradigm of immunisation, as this philosophic-anthropological invariant of self-preservation, transforms the previous limitations and difficulties of periodisation of the Foucauldian concept of biopolitics. The hermeneutical impasse of the relationship described by Foucault between a politics of life and a politics over life is resolved, for Esposito, by commencing from an originary biopolitics of self-preservation: 'no society can exist without defensive apparatus'.[88] The paradigm of immunisation, through the necessity of self-preservation, contains

---

81   Esposito (2008): 52.
82   Here, Esposito establishes the difference of this position in relation to Weber's process of rationalisation (itself a not uncontested characterisation of Weber) as disenchantment; to Löwith's secularisation as the process affecting the presupposition of the alterity of the divine (Löwith (1957)) and in Blumenberg's question of legitimation affecting the presupposition of transcendence (Blumenberg (1999)).
83   Ibid., 51–2.
84   Ibid., 52.
85   Ibid., 52.
86   Ibid., 52. My emphasis.
87   Ibid., 51.
88   Ibid., 54.

both a politics of life and a politics over life, as two integral elements. Modernity, and its associated processes of modernisation, becomes an internal development of the paradigm of immunisation itself. In this internal development, the passage is from natural to artificial forms of immunisation which are marked by 'the tear that suddenly opens in the middle of the last millennium in that earlier immunitarian wrapping' of natural 'defences that had up to a certain point constituted the symbolic, protective shell of human experience', 'none more important than the transcendental order that was linked to the theological matrix'.[89]

Modernity originates in the space opened by this 'tear' and, for Esposito, the period of first modernity is one in which self-preservation is explicitly thematised as the question of '*conservatio vitae*'.[90] The response, articulated through the artificial forms of the categories of modern political philosophy, transforms the question of *conservatio vitae* into the question of order. The categories of sovereignty, property and liberty each express an essentially immunitarian logic: the configuration of a politics of life and a politics over life into a stable unity.

The period of first modernity, initiated through this artificial defensive apparatus of the categories of modern political philosophy, is from its inception accompanied by a process of self-dissolution. The critique of the categories of modern political philosophy, in contrast to the approach in *Communitas*, is the expression of the propensity of the categories of sovereignty, property and liberty to reduce the relationship between life and politics 'to the security of the subject'.[91] In this reduction, there is an intensification, rather than a mediation, of the negative effects of the immunitary logic of the paradigm of immunisation.

The constitution of these categories as artificial forms introduced between politics and life reflects a further rethinking of Foucauldian biopolitics. Esposito commences from a biopolitical interpretation of first modernity which is distinct from that of Foucault in its return to the modern categories of political philosophy which, for Foucault, are an interpretative obstacle to the comprehension of biopolitics.[92] For Esposito, the categories of modern political philosophy perform an essential role, once one understands biopolitics from within the paradigm of immunisation. The new art of governing, whose origins arise, for Foucault,[93] in the eighteenth century, is to be sought, for Esposito, in the artificial forms of the categories of modern political philosophy. The Foucauldian passage to the art of governing is simultaneously absorbed, and preserved by, a concentration upon the aporetic structure generated by these artificial forms in their application to the maintenance of life.

89   Ibid., 55.
90   Ibid., 56.
91   Ibid., 56.
92   See Foucault (2002a).
93   See Foucault (2002b).

The biopolitics of first modernity

The categories of sovereignty, property and liberty, as artificial forms of self-preservation, are each presented and analysed through the dynamics of their internal dissolution. This is combined within a broader framework which presents the passage from sovereignty to property to liberty, as the culmination of first modernity in the self-dissolution of liberalism. In relation to each of these categories, and their combined effect, the interpretation rests upon the presence of the paradigm of immunisation in modern political philosophy. Esposito presents not a history of modern political philosophy, but a history of the paradigm of immunisation insofar as it is reflected in these artificial forms of immunisation.

For Esposito, it is the category of sovereignty which emerges first, and finds its central expression in the work of Hobbes.[94] Sovereignty understands and responds to the question of *conservatio vitae* – the incapacity of human life to generate its own spontaneous self-limitation – as a question of politics. Politics 'is this interval or doubling of life with respect to itself' in which 'the move from nature to artifice is to be positioned'. [95] Human life is to be detached and preserved, by artifice, from an original state of nature where it is driven by its passions, predominant among which is 'the acquisitive desire for everything that places itself in the path of a deadly reprisal'.[96] The generalisation of acquisitive desire is the continuous 'possibility of internecine warfare'.[97]

Sovereignty introduces an artificial form – the political state – which detaches and preserves human life from the state of nature. The political state seeks, through the neutralisation of conflict, to provide the conditions for the self-preservation of human life. The process of detachment and preservation is created through a juridico-political framework centred on the fundamental, vertical relationship between sovereign and individual subjects.

The artificial form of the political state, created by the category of sovereignty, reproduces, rather than resolves, the potential for a politics of life to transform itself into a politics over life. The 'constitutively negative character of sovereign immunization' arises at the passage from the state of nature to the political state through the procedure of a voluntary agreement of a contract.[98] At the inception of the procedure of agreement, all individuals are equal and 'subjects of sovereignty', but once the agreement has been made, these individuals have become 'subjects to sovereignty'.[99] In this transition, the stage of voluntary agreement is 'requested only once, after which they can no longer take it back'.[100]

---

94 The primary text is *The Leviathan*, with additional reference to *De Cive* and *The Elements of Law*.
95 Esposito (2008): 58.
96 Ibid., 59.
97 Ibid., 61.
98 Ibid., 60.
99 Ibid., 59.
100 Ibid., 59.

The character of this transition is the corollary of the creation of a site of sovereignty in which the figure of the sovereign 'is simultaneously identical and different with respect to those that he represents'.[101] Sovereignty emerges 'as an immanent transcendence situated outside the control of those that also produced it as the expression of their own will'.[102]

The passage, by free contract, from the state of nature to the political state, is for Esposito the 'self-legitimating account of modern immunization' which creates the individual as the artificial form in which human life is protected.[103] The self-preservation of human life, within the political state governed by the sovereign, is the imposition of the essentially private character of each individual life.

> Individual literally means this: to make indivisible, united in oneself, by the same line that divides one from everyone else. The individual appears protected from the negative border that makes him himself and not other [sic] (more than from the positive power of the sovereign). One might come to affirm that sovereignty, in the final analysis, is nothing other than the artificial vacuum created around every individual – the negative of the relation or the negative relation that exists between unrelated entities.[104]

The neutralisation of conflict, as the creation of a private individual, is accompanied by the creation of an unlimited power – the sovereign – which expresses 'the independence of power from every external limit'.[105] This disparity contains the possibility for the transformation of sovereignty from a politics of life – the neutralisation of conflict – into a politics over life – the 'sovereign's capacity to put to death any individual'.[106] It is the 'remnant of violence that the immunitary apparatus cannot mediate because it has produced it itself':[107] 'the residue of transcendence that immanence cannot reabsorb ... as if the negative, keeping its immunitary function of protecting life, suddenly moves outside the frame and on its re-entry strikes life with uncontrollable force'.[108]

The 'structural antinomy' of the category of sovereignty is then complemented by the artificial form of the category of property. The political state, created by the category of sovereignty, produces a juridico-political framework orientated to security – the expectational certainty that acquisitive desire and deadly reprisal have been excluded from this framework. Property arises with the possibility of security, and 'marks a qualitative intensification of the entire immunitary logic'.[109]

---

101 Ibid., 60.
102 Ibid., 60.
103 Ibid., 60.
104 Ibid., 61.
105 Ibid., 61.
106 Ibid., 62.
107 Ibid., 62.
108 Ibid., 63.
109 Ibid., 63.

The process of intensification is accompanied by a shift from Hobbes to Locke as the origin of the artificial form of the category of property.[110] For Esposito, Locke displaces, through the category of property, the primacy of the Hobbesian immunitary framework between 'individuals and the sovereign'.[111] In this process, property 'precedes sovereignty, which instead is ordered to defend it',[112] because life and property are now situated at the origin of the preservation of life *as* self-preservation. The artificial form of property operates within 'the more complex relation that moves between subjectivity and property'.[113] The relation is that of their necessary co-implication: 'without a life in which to inhere, property would not be given; but without something of one's own – indeed, without prolonging itself in property – life would not be able to satisfy its primary demands and thus would be extinguished'.[114] This 'metaphysical proviso of bodily inclusion' marks the body as 'the primary site of property because it is the location of the first property, which is to say what each person holds over himself'.[115] It is in the internal differentiation 'between being (a body) and having one's own body that the Lockean individual finds its ontological and juridical, its onto-juridical foundation for every successive appropriation'.[116] From this onto-juridical foundation derives the 'private character of appropriation' through the essential interrelationship between the individual human body, work and property.[117]

The logic of immunisation in this artificial form of property is revealed in its contrast to a world subject to private appropriation. The world, which pre-exists the transformative labour of human individuals, only assumes a common or communal form through this transformative process. Hence, while it

> is not directly negated, [it] is incorporated and recut in a division that turns it inside out into its opposite, in a multiplicity of things that have in common only the fact of being all one's own to the degree that they have been appropriated by their respective owners.[118]

The self-preservation of life, through the artificial form of property, reveals the private character of appropriation as the negative effect of its immunitary logic. The experience of work and appropriation is of a 'reciprocal subjection' which expresses both the control of the object by the individual and the continued direction of individual by the object as 'the necessary objective of his acquisitive

---

110 Here, the reference is to the theory of property in the *Two Treatises on Government*.
111 Ibid., 67.
112 Ibid., 65.
113 Ibid., 67.
114 Ibid., 64.
115 Ibid., 65.
116 Ibid., 65.
117 Ibid., 67.
118 Ibid., 66.

desire'.[119] The generalisation of this process of appropriation transforms the world of things into a world of private property. In this transformation, the world of things available for future appropriation decreases, thereby solidifying a space of peaceful, private possession in contrast to a 'formless space of non-property' to which non-ownership and violence is confined.[120]

The Lockean attempt to regulate this immunitary logic occurs with the 'double limit' imposed upon individual acquisitive desire of 'an obligation to leave for others the things necessary for their maintenance', and a 'prohibition of appropriating for oneself what it is not possible to consume'.[121] The fragility of these limits is revealed to Locke himself 'when goods become commutable into money and therefore infinitely capable of being accumulated without fear of being lost'.[122] It is with the effect of monetary dissolution that Esposito considers the further modification of the artificial form of property in Hume[123] and Kant[124] as an attempt by modern political philosophy to restabilise self-preservation in the process of private appropriation.

The further modification involves a profound break with the original Lockean position of physical possession 'within an indissoluable link with the body that works'.[125] The artificiality of the category of property increases through its juridification: the capacity for property to be and remain privately appropriated in a form which 'is distant from the body of him who juridically possesses it'.[126] From the introduction of an essential distance between the body and private appropriation, there emerges a further element of the negative logic of this artificial form of immunisation. Beyond the Lockean 'appropriative procedure' which creates 'the reification of the person, disembodied of its subjective substance',[127] juridification 'inaugurates a path of inevitable desubjectification'.[128] The combination of private appropriation and juridicial separation from the object produces 'a subject who is isolated and absorbed by the autonomous power of the thing'.[129]

The immunitary mechanism of the artificial form of property reveals a 'movement of self-refutation' analogous to the category of sovereignty whose primacy it had displaced.[130] For the substitution of the institution of sovereign

119   Ibid., 67.
120   Ibid., 68.
121   Ibid., 68.
122   Ibid., 68. See, in contrast, Kramer (2004); and Waldron (2002). See Caffentzis (1990) for an alternative critique of Locke and money.
123   See, on Hume's political economy, Wennerlind and Schabas (2007).
124   The reference here is to the Doctrine of Right in the *Metaphysics of Morals*. However, see, in contrast, Byrd and Hruschka (2012) and Ripstein (2009).
125   Esposito (2008), 68–9.
126   Ibid., 68.
127   Ibid., 69.
128   Ibid., 69.
129   Ibid., 69.
130   Ibid., 69.

164   Roberto Esposito: Law, Community and the Political

power, by the appropriative power of individual subjects, initiates a negative logic of immunisation in which property 'is able to preserve life only by enclosing it in an orbit that is destined to drain it of its vital element'.[131]

The immunitary logic of the categories of sovereignty and of property is completed with the 'negative reconversion that the concept of liberty undergoes in its modern formulation'.[132] The process of negative reconversion originates in Hobbes and extends, through Locke and Bentham, to the conscious reflection upon the 'entropic result' of this further immunitary logic in Tocqueville.[133] The trajectory of this immunitary logic concludes with the 'immunitary loss of meaning' of the individualism and institutions of first modernity.

The process of negative reconversion of the category of liberty arises with the equivalence established by Hobbes between freedom and self-preservation: the passage from the state of nature to the installation of a sovereign who legitimately represents all free subjects equally. The institution of the sovereign constitutes these free subjects 'as equally sovereign within their own individuality – obliged to obey the sovereign because they are free to command themselves and vice versa'.[134] For Esposito, this marks the 'enclosing of liberty in the bounds of its own predetermination',[135] and represents the immunitary self-preservation of life flowing from the artificial form of the category of liberty. The effect of this artificial form is to transform immunity into a generalised framework of security within which community only arises subsequently in the experience of the possibility of 'the free appropriation of "one's own"'.[136] The category of liberty creates the distinctive individualism of first modernity, in which:

> modern liberty consists essentially in the right of every single subject to be defended from the arbiters that undermine autonomy and, even before that, life itself. In the most general terms, modern liberty is that which insures the individual against the interference of others through the voluntary subordination to a more powerful order that guarantees it.[137]

The self-preservation of life, in the artificial form of liberty, thereby inserts an essential, internal connection between liberty and this more powerful order. The connection becomes the experience of the co-belonging of liberty with 'its opposites of law, obligation and causality'.[138]

The passage from the artificial form of sovereignty to that of property modifies and extends the understanding of liberty to encompass 'the subjective right that

131   Ibid., 69.
132   Ibid., 69.
133   Ibid., 77. The reference is exclusively to Tocqueville's *Democracy in America*.
134   Ibid., 72.
135   Ibid., 73.
136   Ibid., 72.
137   Ibid., 72.
138   Ibid., 72.

Bíos I: rethinking biopolitics   165

corresponds to the biological-natural obligation to preserve oneself in life under the best possible conditions'.[139] In this extension, the boundary between category of liberty and security becomes narrower and, finally, 'coincides with it' in the work of Bentham.[140] The importance of Bentham is that this coincidence of liberty and security is to be the effect of a broader and explicit art of governing. The apparatus of government arises as a 'control mechanism' which constitutes the 'preliminary condition of liberty'.[141] This, in turn, marks the re-conception of the primary object of the immunitary orientation of the apparatus of government. For Esposito, the category of liberty in Bentham indicates the transition of the focus of self-preservation 'from the domain of individual preservation to that of the species'.[142] The negative reconversion of the category of liberty has, thereby, intensified to reveal an art of government – liberalism – which in its requirement 'to construct and channel liberty in a non-destructive direction for all society, ... continually risks destroying what it wants to create'.[143]

In this analysis, Esposito acknowledges that, in the presentation of the artificial form of liberty, he returns to Foucault's original analyses,[144] but in a manner where the 'tragic antinomy' revealed by these analyses is already more fully articulated in the work of Tocqueville. The self-dissolution of liberalism – the art of government of first modernity which combines the categories of sovereignty, property and liberty – is not to be sought in the continual violence of the inscription of the individual within the apparatus of government. Rather, it results from liberalism's creation of an 'intersection and friction between atomism and massification, solitude and conformity, and autonomy and heteronomy': 'the immunitary loss of meaning that afflicts modern politics'.[145] The logic of the immunitary paradigm of first modernity is the revelation of self-preservation as a politics over life. The apparatus of government is a protective preservation of life which can only deepen and intensify the process of the desubjectification of life.

---

139 Ibid., 73.
140 Ibid., 74. Here, the reference is exclusively to *The Rationale of Judicial Evidence* and the *Manuscripts* (in particular, Box. lxix, 56). This effectively leaves undiscussed, in Bentham, both the theory of fictions and the distinctive project of juridico-political reform derived from the underlying theory of utilitarianism (see Laval (1994), (2003); Ogden (2007); Rosen (1993); Schofield (2006); and Tusseau (2003)). This absence enables Bentham and Tocqueville to be situated on the common trajectory of the art of government of liberalism in first modernity.
141 Ibid., 74.
142 Ibid., 75.
143 Ibid., 74.
144 Here, in particular, Foucault (1988).
145 Ibid., 77. This leaves undiscussed both the relationship of Tocqueville to the other representatives of French liberalism (e.g. Constant and Guizot) and the enthusiasm of Tocqueville for the French colonial project in Algeria (see Tocqueville (2003)). In addition, the notion of equality, for Esposito, is not considered to be a central aspect of first modernity. See, in contrast, Balibar (1994) and (2014), and his insistence upon the notion of 'equaliberty' as the distinguishing feature of a modernity inaugurated by the French Revolution.

The return to Nietzsche

The acknowledgement of the definitive exhaustion of the categories of sovereignty, property and liberty and, beyond them, the disclosure of 'a new horizon of sense' arises, for Esposito, in the work of Nietzsche.[146] The presence of Nietzsche is itself the consequence of Esposito's return to Foucault's essay, 'Nietzsche, Genealogy, History', which is now interpreted as the prolegomena to a biopolitical thematisation of Nietzsche's thought. In this thematisation, the difficulty embedded in Foucauldian biopolitics is supplanted by the existence of an already distinctive biopolitics in which 'the immunitary paradigm . . . represents the peculiar figure of Nietzschean biopolitics'.[147] The turn to Nietzsche is a deliberate enrichment of Foucauldian biopolitics, by a more originary biopolitics, centred on a relationship between notions of life and power which has explicitly relinquished its connection to these categories of first modernity. The interpretative enrichment is accompanied by the underlying ambivalence of a biopolitics in which the intensification and deconstruction of an immunitary paradigm are equally present. The inherent ambivalence of Nietzschean biopolitics becomes the interpretative horizon in relation to which the possibilities of a politics over life and a politics of life find their further development in the period of second modernity.

The ascription, by Esposito, of the status of a prolegomena to Foucault's essay, 'Nietzsche, Genealogy, History', results from an understanding that the critique of origin, revealed in the essay's presentation of Nietzsche, is itself the expression of Nietzsche's distinctive conception of the connection between life and power. The Nietzschean critique of the notion of origin is thereby one which extends to 'the entire regulating form that European society has for centuries given itself'.[148] For the critique encompasses:

> not only the linearity of a history destined to substantiate the conformity of the origin to the end – the finality of the origin and the originality of the end – but also the entire conceptual foundation on which such a conception is based.[149]

The critique of the notion of origin, as a critique of the entirety of 'the regulating form of European society', reveals the essential falsity and ineffectiveness of the artificial forms of the categories of modern political philosophy, and their underlying immunitary logic. The regulatory form of European society expresses

---

146 Ibid., 78. Here, the concentration is on the corpus of texts formed by the presupposition of their biopolitical continuity: Nietzsche's *Beyond Good and Evil, Daybreak, Ecce Homo, Human, All Too Human, The Gay Science, The Genealogy of Morals, Thus Spoke Zarathustra, Twilight of the Idols, Posthumous Fragments* (there is no complete English translation of these Fragments).
147 Ibid., 86.
148 Ibid., 80.
149 Ibid., 79.

a flawed logic of mediation of 'the power which informs life from the beginning in all its extension, constitution, and intensity'.[150] The falsity of the regulatory form, reflected in its incapacity 'to restore the effective dynamics in operation behind their surface figures',[151] is intertwined with a progressive ineffectiveness. The inability of the form 'to hold or to strengthen a content that is in itself elusive of formal control'[152] culminates in the self-dissolution of the regulatory form itself. The critique is a critique of European society as an art of government through the artificial regulatory form of the institution: the application, at the societal level, of the immunitary logic of mediation. The institution seeks, through the interval created between itself and life, 'to assume, preserve, and develop' life through mediation – the direction of life towards its self-preservation.[153] The interval, orientated by the flawed logic of mediation, can only reproduce a distance between life and the institutions of liberalism: a 'constitutive antinomy' in which the preservation of life is also 'given to destroying the power of life'.[154]

The self-dissolution of the institutional apparatus of European society reorients the question of life to 'redefining the human species' and 'the mobile thresholds that define it, by contiguity or difference with respect to other living species'.[155] The logic of mediation is replaced with a different understanding of politics predicated on life as a 'vital element'. This understanding, as the immanent relationship between life and politics, emerges as 'an originary modality in which the living *is* or in which being *lives*'.[156] In this redefinition of the human species, by Nietzschean biopolitics, the immanent relationship between life and politics occurs in and through the body.[157] The body, as a 'form of life', expresses the replacement of the categories of modern political philosophy with a biopolitical interpretation of the categories of physiology and psychology.

The body enables the passage to an 'essentially political and hence biopolitical semantics' through Nietzsche's 'dual principle that the body is produced by determinate forces and that such forces are always in potential conflict among them'.[158] The 'form of life' represented by the body is merely the 'always provisional result of the conflict of forces that constitute it':[159] a particular configuration of the 'principle of struggle'.[160] Hence, for Nietzschean biopolitics, the human species is animated by 'a complex of forces counterpoised in conflict

---

150 Ibid., 81.
151 Ibid., 80–1.
152 Ibid., 81.
153 Ibid., 82.
154 Ibid., 82.
155 Ibid., 83.
156 Ibid., 81 (emphasis in original).
157 Ibid., 84. The reference here is to Nietzsche (1974): 34–5.
158 Ibid., 84. Esposito refers to the influence of the theories of Ribot and Roux on Nietzsche, following the work of Haaz (2002) and Müller-Lauter (1978).
159 Ibid., 84.
160 Ibid., 85.

168 Roberto Esposito: Law, Community and the Political

that never ends conclusively',[161] and 'no politics exists other than that *of* bodies, conducted *on* bodies, *through* bodies'.[162]

This represents the point of intersection and enrichment of Foucauldian biopolitics. For, while Foucault extends and refines certain elements of Nietzsche's biopolitical framework,[163] an integral aspect of Nietzschean biopolitics is the relationship between life and the immunitary paradigm. For Esposito, Nietzschean biopolitics explicitly reverses the position and primacy of the immunitary demand in its relationship to life. The reversal is the identification of life with an 'imperative of development' in relation to which the immunitary demand – the preservation of life – is not merely 'incidental and derivative', 'but in latent contradiction with it'.[164] The imperative of development – the perpetual 'strengthening of the vital organism' – causes life to be constantly 'projected beyond itself'.[165] Hence:

> Life does not evolve from an initial deficit but from an excess, which provides its double-edged impulse. On the one hand, it is dedicated to imposing itself over and incorporating everything that it meets. On the other hand, once it has been filled to the brim with its own acquisitive capacity, it is prone to tip over, dissipating its own surplus of goods, but also itself . . .[166]

The imperative of development, as life's evolution from an excess, contains an inherently destructive and self-destructive tendency as 'the constitutive character of life'.[167] This tendency, for Esposito, introduces the distinction, within Nietzschean biopolitics, between a notion of community and a 'general process of immunization'.[168]

The notion of community demonstrates an affinity to the etymological derivation of the earlier work *Communitas* – 'the common *munus* in all its semantic ambivalence'.[169] The negative potential of this common *munus* inheres in life's evolution from an excess. It is the continual projection towards a '[p]ure relation and therefore absence or implosion of subjects in relation to each other: a relation without subjects'.[170] The process of immunisation arises from this

---

161 Ibid., 86.
162 Ibid., 83.
163 Esposito indicates that this ranges 'from the centrality of the body as the genesis and termination of sociopolitical dynamics, to the founding role of struggle and also of war, to the configuration of the juridico-institutional orders, to finally the function of resistance as the necessary counterpoint to the deployment of power' (Ibid., 85).
164 Ibid., 87.
165 Ibid., 87.
166 Ibid., 88. The reference here is to Nietzsche (2001): 153, 154 and Nietzsche (1986): 376.
167 Ibid., 89.
168 Ibid., 89.
169 Ibid., 89.
170 Ibid., 89.

Bíos I: rethinking biopolitics 169

tendency towards the self-dissolution of life. The distinctiveness of Nietzschean biopolitics, for Esposito, is the combination of 'the return of the immunitary paradigm to its originary biological matrix, and ... the capacity to reconstruct critically the negative dialectic of the paradigm'.[171] The reconstruction presents the immunitary response as a generalised process of the preservation of life orientated to 'restabilizing meaning and redrawing lost boundaries'.[172] From the perspective of Nietzschean biopolitics, knowledge, power and 'the juridical and political institutions that flank moral and religious codes' are comprehended as equally directed towards the process of the preservation of life.[173]

In this explicitly biopolitical relationship, at the level of the species, between self-dissolution and the self-preservation of life, there emerges the intrinsic ambivalence of Nietzschean biopolitics.

> [A] contradiction that is as it were structural, according to which immunization, on the one hand, is necessary for the survival of any organism, but, on the other, is harmful, because, blocking the organism's transformation, it impedes biological expansion ... Development presupposes duration, but duration can delay or impede development. Preservation implies expansion, but expansion compromises and places preservation at risk ... [T]he survival of a force opposes the project of strengthening it.[174]

The structural contradiction raises the question of the 'biologism' in Nietzschean biopolitics. The presence and dynamics of this 'biologism' – the ambivalence of Nietzschean biopolitics – is determined by 'the [two] different semantics ... found in the perspective that Nietzsche assumes with regard to the process of biological decadence, which is defined in terms of degeneration or of passive nihilism'.[175] The question of 'biologism' is, therefore, intimately connected to the demarcation of the relationship between Nietzschean biopolitics and the theories of Darwin, and the broader theoretical framework of social Darwinism.

For Esposito, Nietzschean biopolitics contains both an affinity with, and a divergence from, Darwin and social Darwinism. Nietzschean biopolitics, shaped by the critique of 'the debilitating effects of modern immunization',[176] arises from a conception of life, as 'exuberance and prodigality', which indicates its initial detachment from any affinity with the Darwinian conception of life as natural

---

171 Ibid., 90.
172 Ibid., 90.
173 Ibid., 90. On the question of Nietzsche and law, see Balke (2003); Goodrich and Valverde (2005); and Rose (1984). Esposito's reading of Nietzsche, through the paradigm of immunisation, is distinct from both recent Anglo-American work (see Gemes and May (2011); Janaway and Robertson (2012); and Leiter and Sinhababu (2007)) and the work of Lemm (2009).
174 Ibid., 94.
175 Ibid., 101.
176 Ibid., 102. On Nietzsche and Darwin(ism), see Clark (2000), (2007); Johnson (2010); Moore (2006); Richardson (2008); and Stiegler (2001).

170   Roberto Esposito: Law, Community and the Political

selection.[177] The affinity emerges in the dynamics of struggle which Nietzsche traces from the projection of life's vital energy. The struggle concerns the relation of forces present in life subject to the immunitary apparatus of first modernity. The attribution of a logic of decadence and nihilism – immunisation as degeneration – to the analysis of these forces entails their comprehension through the diagnostic language of health and sickness.

The diagnostic language, overtly orientated to a critique of the 'process of immunitary degeneration', effectively intensifies this logic in a 'hyperimmunitary direction'.[178] The intensification arises from the designation of the process of degeneration 'as both the cause and the effect of the progressive contagion of the uncontaminated by the contaminated'.[179] The response to this progressive contagion – the regulatory apparatus of first modernity – is itself articulated in the form of an immunitary response.

> A stronger and more impenetrable barrier must be constructed, stronger than the one already in place. In doing so, the separation between the healthy and the sick parts will be rendered definitive, where the biological distinction, or opposition, between the physiological and the pathological has a transparent social meaning . . .[180]

Hence, the critique of the immunitary effect of first modernity upon life becomes a project for 'an artificial regeneration that is capable of restoring its [life's] original essence'.[181] The project of restoration remains fundamentally immunitary in its 'incorporation of the negative, both in the lethal sense of the annihilation of those that do not deserve to live, and in the sense of the crushing of the originary dimension of animality of those who remain'.[182]

The ambivalent position of the hyperimmunitary logic in Nietzschean biopolitics results from the equally prominent presence of a reconception of the relationship between health and illness. From this perspective, the hyper-immunitary logic becomes an initial 'degenerative hypothesis':[183] 'the first hyperimmunitary or thanatological stratum of the Nietzschean lexicon'.[184] The passage to the second stratum of Nietzschean biopolitics flows from the possibility of the reversal of the negative quality of the hyperimmunity logic into a poten-tially positive quality. The reversal proceeds from a distinct conception of the logic of force as a self-suppression: a logic of force which opens a 'field for new

---

177   Ibid., 95.
178   Ibid., 97.
179   Ibid., 96.
180   Ibid., 97. The reference here is to the *Posthumous Fragments* (1888–89) and Nietzsche (2001): 152.
181   Ibid., 99.
182   Ibid., 99.
183   Ibid., 103.
184   Ibid., 104.

affirmative powers' of life.[185] For Esposito, following Deleuze's *Nietzsche and Philosophy*,[186] all forces, in Nietzschean biopolitics, have an internal limit resulting from their full extension or realisation at the expense of other forces. Here, the fully realised force, having effectively negated all other forces, has only itself as its field for potential action and reaction and, in this situation, 'it can only recoil against itself . . . and reverse itself in the affirmative'.[187]

The reversal results from the force of the hyperimmunitary logic which, in the active preservation of health, through the imposition of forms of immunitary enclosure of life, dissolves the distinction between health and illness. For, in its attempt to distinguish and preserve a healthy life, it creates a space of exclusionary inclusion which cannot recognise health and illness as intrinsic elements of 'life's own propulsive force'.[188] The space of exclusionary inclusion is one in which life, in its 'preventive withdrawal from danger',[189] is preserved through its deprivation of force or devitalisation. Hence, the hyperimmunitary logic, through the process of forcibly distinguishing health from illness, intensifies the degeneration from which it sought to preserve life.

The reversal of the negative logic of generalised degeneration or decadence arises from its affirmation as the condition from which the further projection of life is possible.[190] For Esposito, the affirmative experience of degeneration entails the reconception of the immunitary relationship between health and illness through the notion of inoculation or vaccination. The comprehension of inoculation or vaccination, as 'innovation and alteration',[191] replaces self-preservation with metamorphosis in which life projects itself as both health and illness. The danger which the initial hyperimmunitary logic would situate as external to life now 'forms an essential part of life, even if, precisely because, it continually endangers it, pushing it on to a problematic fault line to which it is both reduced and strengthened'.[192]

This, for Esposito, marks the distinctive reversal of force in Nietzschean biopolitics: 'immunity's opening to its own communal reverse'.[193] The opening, as the reversal of the initial hyperimmunitary logic, is 'metamorphosis' – 'the inexhaustible power of transformation' beyond the logic of immunity.[194] Life is

---

185 Ibid., 102.
186 Deleuze (2006). Esposito relies on the final part of this text, 'The Overman: Against the Dialectic'. The final period of Deleuze's work will become an integral part of Esposito's exposition in the latter part of *Bíos*.
187 Ibid., 102.
188 Ibid., 104.
189 Ibid., 105.
190 The reference here is to Nietzsche (1998): 49.
191 Ibid., 105. The reference is to 'Enoblement through Degeneration', in Nietzsche's *Human, All Too Human*.
192 Ibid., 106.
193 Ibid., 105.
194 Ibid., 108.

172   Roberto Esposito: Law, Community and the Political

'a becoming that carries together within itself the traces of a different past and a prefiguration of a new future'.[195] At this 'threshold', Nietzschean biopolitics indicates the possibility for a fundamental reconception of both the logic of immunisation and the human species: 'a biopolitics potentially different from what we know because it is in relation not only to human life, but to what is outside life, to its other, to its after'.[196]

The threshold, as the indication by the second stratum of Nietzschean biopolitics of a 'horizon of a new politics of life',[197] is circumscribed by the first stratum. The hyperimmunitary logic and its affirmative reversal remain in a permanently ambivalent relationship in which they are 'perilously juxtaposed and superimposed'.[198] Nietzschean biopolitics is located at the boundary between the self-dissolution of the immunitary logic of first modernity and the possibility for a different politics of life. The horizon of the new politics of life, as the thought of life outside the paradigm of immunisation, cannot simply be that of the development of a Nietzschean biopolitics. For the boundary marked by Nietzschean biopolitics has already been crossed, for Esposito, by the biopolitics of National Socialism. The ambivalence of Nietzschean biopolitics is thereby provided with its initial 'resolution' which reduces its complexity, through the simple intensification of the force of the first stratum of Nietzschean biopolitics. The hyperimmunitary logic is unleashed from the limits of affirmative reversal in the second stratum of Nietzschean biopolitics, and the politics of life, beyond the self-dissolution of first modernity, becomes a politics of death.

195   Ibid., 107.
196   Ibid., 109.
197   Ibid., 109.
198   Ibid., 109. This marks the divergence between Esposito and Deleuze in relation to Nietzsche.

Chapter 10

Bíos II

Towards an affirmative biopolitics

National Socialism, in its interruption and displacement of the Nietzschean biopolitics, introduces the particular configuration of a second modernity. This forms the horizon for the further demarcation of Esposito's conception of biopolitics, as a philosophy of *bios*, from the biopolitics of both Foucault and Nietzsche. For Esposito, the biopolitics of National Socialism, in the formation of a conceptual connection between degeneration, eugenics and genocide, is the overt and transparent reversal of an immunitary apparatus into a politics of death. From within this framework of National Socialist biopolitics, Esposito identifies three mutually complementary immunitary paradigms. These paradigms – the absolute normativisation of life, the double enclosure of the body and the anticipatory suppression of birth – then constitute the final, fully negative horizon of immunisation as exclusionary inclusion.

This horizon endures, beyond the collapse of National Socialism, in the continued prominence of 'the direct relationship between life and death' in 'a tendency to flatten the political into the purely biological (if not the body itself) of those who are at the same time subjects and objects'.[1] This is accompanied, in a further periodisation of second modernity, after the collapse of National Socialism, and the later collapse of the Soviet Union and the group of associated regimes, by the generalisation of immunitary biopolitics to become a global phenomenon. In relation to the persistence of immunitary biopolitics, the categories of modern political philosophy have, for Esposito, ceased to provide the conceptual resources required for the elaboration of an affirmative biopolitics. The philosophy of *bios*, as the thought of an affirmative biopolitics, arises from the reversal, in thought, of the three immunitary paradigms of National Socialism. The reversal is undertaken through recourse to a corpus of theoretical work which furnishes the outlines of a biopolitics beyond its continued negative existence in the contemporary paradigm of immunitary biopolitics. Within this process of theoretical reflection, Esposito's philosophy of *bios* engages in the active reconstruction of the relationship between law, community and the political.

---

1 Esposito (2008): 146.

National Socialism: biopolitics as thanatopolitics

The specificity of National Socialism rests on the extension of certain tendencies of the paradigm of immunisation as a paradigm of exclusionary inclusion. This process of extension involves the radicalisation of the paradigm of immunisation, which supplants the preceding tendency, in first modernity, of self-dissolution with one of 'the figure of the autoimmune illness ... in which the protective apparatus becomes so aggressive that it turns against its own body (which it should protect), leading to its death'.[2] The passage to this paradigm of autoimmunisation entails that 'every division collapses between politics and biology', and, with this, 'that politics be identified directly with biology in a completely new form of biocracy'.[3]

The biopolitics of National Socialism, as a biocracy determined by the constitutive instability of a paradigm of autoimmunisation, assigns to the medical sciences 'the theoretical framework within which Nazi biopolitics develops its specificity'.[4] The initial stage in this development flows from the identification of 'the patient as the German people as a whole, rather than a single individual'.[5] The 'health of the German body' then becomes the exclusive and privileged living object to be protected.

The health of the German body – its continued preservation and reproduction – is conceived solely in response to 'a degenerative tendency that appears to undermine vital forces'.[6] The degenerative tendency is understood as 'a *process* of dissolution. Produced by the intake of toxic agents, it can lead in a few generations to sterility and therefore to the extinction of a specific line.'[7] This tendency, and its inevitable effect of dissolution, produces a form of diagnosis of society – the German body – in which 'biological abnormality is nothing but the sign of a more general abnormality that links the degenerate subject to a condition that is steadily differentiated with regard to other individuals of the same species'.[8]

From this diagnosis, the healthy human individual, distinguished from the animal, and attributed with a 'juridical subjectivity',[9] coexists with those who bear the sign of degeneration. The degenerate – the sign of 'an animal element that re-emerges in man in the form of an existence that is not properly animal or human, but exactly at their point of intersection' – then requires an explanation of the pathology of the process of degeneration.[10] The understanding of the pathology of degeneration involves:

2   Ibid., 116.
3   Ibid., 113.
4   Ibid., 113.
5   Ibid., 115–116.
6   Ibid., 117.
7   Ibid., 118.
8   Ibid., 119.
9   Ibid., 113.
10   Ibid., 119.

the idea of contagion: degenerative pathology does not only multiply metonymically within the same body as a series of interrelated diseases, but spreads irresistibly from one body to the next. We can say that degeneration is always degenerative. It reproduces itself intensely and extends from inside to outside and vice versa. This contaminating power of an internal transmutation and of an external transposition is in fact its most characteristic feature. For this to be so, it must follow that it is both hereditary and contagious, which is to say contagious on the vertical level of lineage as well as on the horizontal level of social communication.[11]

The theory of degeneration is the initial level, in the interweaving of the 'biological norm and the juridico-political norm',[12] in which the signs of degeneracy render the autonomy of the juridico-political norm and the individual, as a point of attribution of 'law and judgement',[13] unstable. These signs attest to the permanent fragility of the separation between the abnormal and the normal and, hence, of the health of the German body.

The essentially diagnostic stance of the theory of degeneration is modified with the introduction and development of a theory of eugenics. Once the theory of degeneration has revealed the perilous state of health of the German body, the response to this diagnosis becomes eugenics: 'a project and a program[me] of intervention'.[14] Eugenics represents the attempt to protect life – the life of the German body – from the threat of degeneration. The presence of the process of degeneration, manifestly visible in the signs of degeneracy, is the continuous possibility of the decline in the vitality and health of the German body. The process of degeneration arises spontaneously within the German body, and contains no internal limit or point of repose in its ineluctable movement of decline. Eugenics, therefore, can only be an external intervention in this spontaneous, 'natural phenomenon' of degeneration which 'intends precisely to modify [its] spontaneous development'.[15]

Eugenics, as a project of external modification, constitutes a paradigm of immunisation in relation to the threat of degeneration. This comprehension of eugenics, as a paradigm of immunisation, qualifies the exclusively positive self-understanding of this project, by the proponents of eugenics, centred on 'the idea of an artificial reconstruction of the natural order'.[16] For Esposito, this project, as a paradigm of immunisation – exclusionary inclusion – necessarily involves both a positive and a negative eugenics. The artificial, external intervention, as the

11   Ibid., 121–2.
12   Ibid., 119–20.
13   Ibid., 120.
14   Ibid., 127.
15   Ibid., 127.
16   Ibid., 127.

176 Roberto Esposito: Law, Community and the Political

restoration of 'a natural selection that has been weakened or nullified',[17] entails the rejection 'as unnatural [of] all that does not conform to the model'.[18]

> This is the reason that a positive eugenics (from the work of Francis Galton on) directed to improving the race, is always accompanied by a negative eugenics, one designed to impede the diffusion of dysgenic exemplars. And yet, where would the space for increasing the best exemplars be found if not in the space produced by the elimination of the worst?[19]

The notion which facilitates this passage between positive and negative eugenics is that of 'racial hygiene'. It is 'the immunitary therapy that aims at preventing or extirpating the pathological agents that jeopardize the biological quality of future generations'.[20] The implementation of this therapy marks the emergence of the biopolitics of second modernity: the national body is the therapeutic object whose treatment is 'derived rigidly from a calculation of the productivity of human life with regard to its costs'.[21]

National Socialist biopolitics is distinguished by a further reversal of the relationship between economic calculation and man. The central concern is 'the definition of the human generally and its internal thresholds'.[22] For it is the 'typology of human life' which is held to determine the level of 'economic productivity'.[23] The typology, based on blood groups, distinguishes between superior and inferior races. The human is, thus, traversed by 'radically diverse biotypologies';[24] and this 'first intraspecies *clivage*' is situated more broadly in relation to a set of 'diverse qualitative levels that include both plants and animals'.[25] The identification and comparative hierarchical ordering of these levels produces an effect of 'superimposition' in which 'one appears contemporaneously outside and inside the other'.[26] This is expressed in 'the projection of established human types in the botanical and zoological "catalogue"' which is combined with 'the incorporation of a particular animal and vegetable species within the human race'.[27] It is in relation to these thresholds within and between levels of life that eugenics intervenes both positively and negatively. The therapeutic intervention produces a paradigm of immunisation which is constantly alert 'to all the possible channels for degenerative contagion: from the area of

17   Ibid., 127.
18   Ibid., 127.
19   Ibid., 127–8.
20   Ibid., 128.
21   Ibid., 128.
22   Ibid., 129.
23   Ibid., 129.
24   Ibid., 129.
25   Ibid., 129.
26   Ibid., 129.
27   Ibid., 129.

Bíos II: towards an affirmative biopolitics   177

immigration to that of matrimony, which were regulated by ever more drastic norms of racial homogeneity'.[28]

The reproduction of norms of racial homogeneity, through a framework of legal norms, is accompanied, and supplemented by, other practices of eugenic intervention. For Esposito, it is the practices of sterilisation and euthanasia which exemplify the passage to the distinctively autoimmunitary character of the biopolitics of National Socialism. Sterilisation intervenes to prevent the further creation of life from a source which is defined as degenerate. It thereby seeks to isolate the sign of degeneration, and prevent its potential proliferation, by 'impeding its genesis, prohibiting life from giving life, devitalizing life in advance'.[29] The negative contagion, which the sign of degeneration represents, is rendered pre-emptively sterile, in the sense of non-contagious, deprived of its potential to contribute to the process of degeneration and sterility of the German body. The sterilised source or sign of degeneration remains alive, as the particular degenerative threat does not require physical elimination.

The relationship between positive and negative eugenics, as the relationship between life and death within a paradigm of immunity, is intensified with the practice of euthanasia.[30] The therapeutic response actively introduces death into the immunitary paradigm: the preservation of life is combined with the designation of those who are effectively dead. For those who are already effectively dead, the termination of life is, therefore, 'part of their lives – or, more precisely, of these existences because it is the term that follows from the subtraction of life itself. A life inhabited by death is simply flesh, an existence without life'.[31]

The fundamental distinction between existence and life orientates the intervention of National Socialist biopolitics, within the German body, to preserve it from 'something that does not belong to it and indeed essentially negates it'.[32] The fundamental distinction furnishes a diagnostic rationale for the radically different treatment of those designated as containing the sign of existence without life. The immunitary paradigm of National Socialism responds to this negative presence within the German body, through the initial practices of sterilisation and euthanasia. These practices preserve the life of the German body – its racial health and vitality – by their active intervention to create 'racial hygiene'.

The passage beyond sterilisation and euthanasia to a project of mass extermination – genocide – as an integral part of the specific trajectory of National Socialist biopolitics is, for Esposito, to be sought in the 'singular logical and

28   Ibid., 131–2.
29   Ibid., 132.
30   Esposito traces the genesis of this development from the initial concept of 'life without value' of Jost's 1895 text, *Das Recht auf den Tod*, to Binding and Koch's book of 1920, *Die Freigabe der Vernichtung lebensunwerten Leben*. On the National Socialist interventions of sterilisation and euthanasia, see Aly *et al.* (1994); Friedlander (1997); Burleigh (2002); and Kuntz and Bachrach (2004).
31   Ibid., 134.
32   Ibid., 134.

178   Roberto Esposito: Law, Community and the Political

semantic chain [that] links degeneration, regeneration and genocide: regeneration overcomes degeneration through genocide'.[33] The intensification of the auto-immunitary form of National Socialist biopolitics emerges from the increasing prominence of death within the space created by these practices of exclusionary inclusion. Death is here both the 'instrument of the cure, the sickness and its remedy', and the 'force to resist the mortal infection' which is transmitted by 'dead ancestors'.[34]

> A response was needed to the presence of death in life (this was degeneration) by tempering life on the sacred fire of death: giving death to a death that had assumed the form of life and in this way invaded life's every space. It was this insidious and creeping death that needed to be blocked with the aid of the saving Great Death bequeathed by the German heroes. Thus, the dead became both the infectious germs and the immunitary agents, the enemies to be extinguished and the protection to be activated. Confined to this double death and its infinite doubling, Nazism's immunitary machine wound up smashed. It strengthened its own immunitary apparatus to the point of remaining victim to it. The only way for an individual or collective organism to save itself definitively from the risk of death is to die. It was what Hitler asked the German people to do before he committed suicide.[35]

The increasing intensification of the paradigm of immunisation present in National Socialist biopolitics results in the self-destruction of the German body which it has dedicated itself to protect. For the acceleration of the project of the elimination of 'the contagion of the German people by a part of life inhabited and oppressed by death' leads to the generalisation of death: a thanatopolitics.[36]

The general, destructive, auto-immunitary logic of the biopolitics of National Socialism is then subject to further analytical consideration. Within this auto-immunitary logic, Esposito seeks to distinguish 'its decisive articulations and its principal immunitary *dispositifs*'.[37] This leads to the identification and examination of three central frameworks which, in combination, form the underlying impetus of the general auto-immunitary logic.

From the complete superimposition of 'the biological and the juridical', there emerges the framework of 'the absolute normativization of life'.[38] The fundamental

---

33 Ibid., 137. Esposito's presentation of the dynamics of National Socialist biopolitics does not ascribe central significance to the relationship between mass extermination and the National Socialist military campaign of the early years of World War II. On this see, in particular, Herbert (2000).

34 Ibid., 138.

35 Ibid., 138.

36 Ibid., 137.

37 Ibid., 138.

38 Ibid., 138.

Bíos II: towards an affirmative biopolitics   179

importance of life, in the form of the German body, is expressed in its total subordination to political control through the normative framework of the legal instruments of National Socialism. This is exemplified by the position and role that National Socialism accords to doctors whose professional autonomy is replaced with responsibility to the National Socialist state. The doctor becomes a 'symbolic functionary' whose official signature legitimates 'decisions . . . that had been made in the political sphere and translated into laws by the new legal codes of the Reich'.[39] Hence, 'a political judicialization of the biological sphere corresponded to the biologization of the space that before had been reserved for juridical science'.[40]

The position of the doctor under National Socialism is the precursor to the most extreme extension of this overlapping of the juridical and the biological in the concentration camps. This 'expression of the indistinction that emerges between the horizon of life and that of law that has been completely politicized'[41] situates the concentration camp as the dedicated repository for the detention of those whose existence represented a potential threat to the health of the German body. Their concentration within this space is merely the prelude to their inevitable elimination.

The overlapping of 'medical power and political-juridical power' is accompanied by the framework of the 'double enclosure of the body'.[42] The framework of enclosure is created by the reduction of the body to a 'biological given as the ultimate truth',[43] and becomes a double enclosure in which 'everyone's life is exposed to the ultimate alternative between continuation and interruption'.[44] The double enclosure body involves both 'an absolute materialism' and a 'spiritual racism',[45] and expresses more than a mere

> reduction of *bios* to *zōē* or to 'bare life' (which the Nazis always opposed to the fullness of 'life' understood in a spiritual sense as well), we need to speak of the spiritualization of *zōē* and the biologization of the spirit. The name assumed by such a superimposition is that of race, which constitutes both the spiritual character of the body and the biological character of the soul. It is what confers meaning on the identity of the body with itself, a meaning that exceeds the individual borders from birth to death.[46]

The enclosure is further reinforced by the incorporation of 'every corporeal member . . . into a larger body that constitutes the organic totality of the German

---

39 Ibid., 139.
40 Ibid., 139.
41 Ibid., 140.
42 Ibid., 140–1.
43 Ibid., 141.
44 Ibid., 141.
45 Ibid., 141.
46 Ibid., 142.

180   Roberto Esposito: Law, Community and the Political

people'.[47] It is, at this level, that the distinctively spiritual tonality of the biopolitics of National Socialism becomes evident. The process of incorporation of 'all the single bodies within the one body of the German community' is one deriving from 'hereditary patrimony': 'the incarnation of the racial substance from which life itself receives its essential form'.[48] Life depends on the continued vitality of this biological being which, in turn, requires that it contains 'the force to expel from itself all of that which does not belong to it (and for which reason hampers its expansive power). It is the lethal outcome that inevitably derives from the first part of the discourse.'[49] Hence, the integral connection with the immunitary practice of genocide, 'as the spiritual demand of the German people' to ensure the enclosure of the healthy German body.[50]

The lethal combination of absolute materialism and spiritual racism, in the double enclosure of the body, is extended by 'the *anticipatory suppression of birth*'[51] – the projection backwards to the genesis of birth – which accompanies the 'pro-natalist campaign intent on strengthening the German population quantitatively'.[52] The event of birth, within the biopolitics of National Socialism, rests on a 'political-racial calculation', in which each birth is accorded a 'pre-determined . . . value'.[53] Birth is unintelligible apart from 'the racial heredity that birth carries with it'.[54] Therefore, if the 'living being re-entered the biological enclosure dedicated to breeding, it was accepted or even encouraged; if it fell outside, it has to be suppressed even before it was announced'.[55] This, in turn, provides the distinctive character of the relationship between birth and nation under National Socialism. Birth 'appears to determine the level of citizenship in the Reich', and these levels are reproduced through the power to 'nullify [life] in advance'.[56]

The identification and analysis of these three biopolitical frameworks of National Socialism enables Esposito to distinguish between National Socialism, as a political regime, and the continued persistence of biopolitics beyond the collapse of National Socialism. For Esposito, the subsequent history of second modernity, after National Socialism, reflects the expansion, with particular moments of acceleration represented by the end of the Cold War and the emergence of the 'war on terror', of 'the absolute coincidence . . . between biopolitics and immunization'.[57] In this history, 'the politicization of the biological, which began in late modernity', is complimented by 'a similarly intense biologization

47   Ibid., 142.
48   Ibid., 142.
49   Ibid., 142–3.
50   Ibid., 143.
51   Ibid., 143 (emphasis in original).
52   Ibid., 144.
53   Ibid., 145.
54   Ibid., 145.
55   Ibid., 145.
56   Ibid., 145.
57   Ibid., 147.

Bíos II: towards an affirmative biopolitics 181

of the political which makes the preservation of life through reproduction the only project that enjoys universal legitimacy'.[58]

The distinctiveness of Esposito's approach is to confront this generalisation of the reduction of life to 'the sphere of *bíos*', and its associated paradigm of exclusionary inclusion, through the elaboration of a philosophy of *bíos*.[59] From this philosophy, there emerges an affirmative biopolitics: the possibility for the re-conception, beyond modern political philosophy and legal theory, of the notions of law, community and the political.

An affirmative biopolitics: the philosophy of *Bíos*

The development of a philosophy of *bíos* commences from the negative trajectory of the paradigm of immunisation from first to second modernity. A thought of an affirmative biopolitics situates itself within and against this trajectory of the paradigm of immunisation; and proceeds by the rejection of certain modes of thought which Esposito considers to be incapable of sufficient depth of critical engagement.

The preceding chapters of *Bíos*, in their presentation of the paradigm of immunisation in the categories of modern political philosophy and legal theory, prevent their simple reassertion, in relation to a biopolitics held to result from the relinquishing of these categories. For Esposito, the predominant assumption that these categories retain the theoretical resources to undertake the transformation of an essentially exceptional or 'aberrant' biopolitics is to engage in a mis-recognition of biopolitics. The return to, and reanimation of political philosophy and legal theory, irrespective of the particular combination or configuration of these categories, remains essentially incapable of grasping or critically transforming 'the biopolitical question'.[60]

Esposito considers that the work of Arendt and Heidegger contains certain, initial rudiments of a thematisation of the biopolitical question.[61] In Arendt, these rudiments emerge from the characterisation of modernity as a process of secularisation and depoliticisation which is itself prefigured by the displacement of 'the Greek conception of the world held in common' by the Christian 'concept of the sacredness of individual life'.[62] Modernity transposes the foundation of individual life 'from the celestial realm to that of the earth' and, thereby, ascribes to 'biological survival the highest good'.[63] The primacy accorded to biological

---

58 Ibid., 147.
59 Ibid., 146.
60 Ibid., 149.
61 Esposito refers here to Heidegger's *Phenomenological Interpretations of Aristotle: Initiation into Phenomenological Research, Being and Time, The Fundamental Concepts of Metaphysics: World, Finitude, Solitude, Contributions to Philosophy: From Enowning* and *The Letter on Humanism*; and to Arendt's *The Human Condition*.
62 Esposito (2008): 149.
63 Ibid., 149.

survival initiates the process of depoliticisation in the reduction of the relationship between individual life and that of the species to labour: 'work that satisfies material necessities became the prevalent form of human action'.[64] The presence of the notion of life, as biological life, arises from its essential separation from politics. Hence, the 'withdrawal of politics under the double pressure of work and production, [entails that] the term "biopolitics" emerges devoid of any sense'.[65]

The incapacity to proceed from a notion of life to the 'point of intersection' between politics and biological life is the expression, for Esposito, of the underlying presupposition that 'the only valid form of political activity is what is attributable to the experience of the Greek *polis*'.[66] This experience is predicated on the separation between 'the private sphere of the *idion* and the public sphere of the *koinon*'.[67] The recourse to the tradition of classical political philosophy produces the perpetual absence of biopolitics, as 'where there is authentic politics, a space for the meaning of life cannot be opened; and where the materiality of life unfolds, something like political action can no longer emerge'.[68]

The limitations of Arendt's approach extend to another notion of life within her work – natality – which exists outside the re-appropriation of the tradition of classical political philosophy. This notion situates birth as that moment 'in which life is given form in a modality that is drastically distant from its own biological bareness'.[69] A politics of life arises from the 'doubled point of divergence or noncoincidence of the individual life with respect to the species, as well as the single action vis-à-vis the repeated course of daily life (which is marked by natural needs)'.[70] The limits of this conception of life relate to its dependence on the distinction 'between life and the condition of existence'.[71] Natality, as the event of birth, remains unable, for Esposito, '(except in metaphoric and literary terms) to penetrate into the somatic network between politics and life'.[72]

The continued impenetrability of biopolitics revealed by the Arendtian notion of natality is the consequence of the continued dependence of Arendt's thought upon that of Heidegger.[73] For Esposito, this dependence derives from the conception of the event of birth as the introduction of a 'caesura between life and condition of existence'.[74] The caesura remains within the parameters of the more fundamental Heideggerian distinction between 'factical life' and 'biology'.[75]

64 Ibid., 149.
65 Ibid., 150.
66 Ibid., 150.
67 Ibid., 150.
68 Ibid., 150.
69 Ibid., 178.
70 Ibid., 176.
71 Ibid., 180.
72 Ibid., 179.
73 However, see Taminaux (1997), for whom *The Human Condition* is Arendt's detachment from Heidegger's thought.
74 Esposito (2008): 180.
75 Ibid., 153.

Bíos II: towards an affirmative biopolitics   183

While indicating the preparation for 'the philosophical confrontation with biopolitics',[76] this distinction is itself constrained by the separation that it installs 'between man and animal'.[77] For Esposito, this is Heidegger's 'point of greatest divergence from Nazi biopolitics' and the potential to relinquish '*bíos* to nonphilosophy, or better, to that antiphilosophy that was terrifyingly realized in the 1930s in its most direct politicization'.[78]

The critique of all forms of biologism – the reduction of life to biology – is embedded in the notion of *Dasein*, in *Being and Time*. For *Dasein* expresses both the deficient character of the biological definition of life and its 'different and incomparable dimension': it 'can only be deduced negatively from *Dasein* as this which is not it, precisely because it is "only life" (*Nur Lebenden*); as "something that only lives" (*etwas wie Nur-noch-leben*)'.[79] The distinction determines an intrinsically different experience of death in which 'death is the authentic mode of being of an existence distinct from bare life'.[80] Bare life 'dies too, but in a form lacking in meaning that, rather than a true dying, refers to a simple perishing, to a ceasing to live'.[81] It is from this distinction, and its differentiation of modes of experience of death, that the question of the definition of the animal is more specifically delineated in *The Fundamental Concepts of Metaphysics* and *Contributions to Philosophy*.

For Esposito, in Heidegger's path of questioning, the animal assumes the position of an unbridgeable 'distance in relation to human experience'.[82] The animal is not situated as 'a lesser level of participation in a common nature with all living beings, including man, but [as] an insurmountable barrier which excludes any conjugated form'.[83] Man and animal are installed as 'two universes [which] remain reciprocally incommunicable'.[84] This incommunicability attests to 'the progressive loss of contact with the theme of "factical life" in which the semantics of *bíos* seemed inevitably implicated'.[85] The essential distance between man and animal reflects the disappearance of 'the originary impulse to think life in the "end of philosophy" (or the end of philosophy in the facticity of life)': the increasingly overt and fundamental detachment of Heidegger's thought 'from the horizon of *bíos*'.[86]

The failure of both Arendt and Heidegger to fully comprehend and thematise 'the dimension of *bíos* that is in itself political' indicates, for Esposito, the

---

76 Ibid., 152.
77 Ibid., 156.
78 Ibid., 155–6.
79 Esposito (2008): 154. This is supported by reference to *Being and Time*, Division Two, §49.
80 Esposito (2008): 154.
81 Ibid., 154–5.
82 Ibid., 155.
83 Ibid., 155–6.
84 Ibid., 156.
85 Ibid., 156.
86 Ibid., 156.

184   Roberto Esposito: Law, Community and the Political

necessity to adopt a mode of thought which directly confronts the three central dispositifs of the biopolitics of National Socialism.[87] In this confrontation, the 'bio-thanatological principles' of '*the normativization of life, the double enclosure of the body*, and the *preemptive suppression of birth*' are surmounted as the passage to a philosophy of *bíos*.[88] The theoretical resources from which Esposito commences and develops the capacity to overturn the three bio-thanatological principles of National Socialist biopolitics are contained in the work of Merleau-Ponty, Simondon, Canguilhem and Deleuze.[89] The interpretative approach is one which establishes, beyond each of their distinct theoretical projects, a set of concepts capable of forming the framework for a philosophy of *bíos*. The process of confrontation and overturning is initiated with the dispositif of the double enclosure of the body, proceeds to the pre-emptive suppression of birth and concludes with the normativisation of life. The process of confrontation and overturning entails the re-emergence of the notions of the political, community and law as the fundamental prerequisites for an intrinsically affirmative conceptualisation of biopolitics: a philosophy of *bíos*.

The confrontation with the dispositif of the double enclosure of the body entails both an overturning of its specific bio-thanatological principles and the wider notion of the 'body politic'. The re-thematisation of the political arises from the comprehensive extrication of the relationship between politics and life from a necessary connection to the notion of the body. In this critique and reconstruction, Esposito proceeds, through a combination of theoretical reinterpretation and a history of the progressive weakening of the notion of the body, to situate the relationship between politics and life in the notion of the flesh. This notion grasps life without recourse to 'a semantics of the body',[90] and understands it as 'both singular and communal, generic and specific, and undifferentiated and different, not only devoid of spirit, but a flesh that does not even have a body'.[91]

The elaboration of this notion of the flesh commences from Merleau-Ponty's *The Visible and the Invisible*,[92] which, for Esposito, expresses the 'originary impulse to think life in the "end of philosophy" (or the end of philosophy in the facticity of life)', which Heidegger's thought only indicated in a limited and partial form.[93] The capacity to express this originary impulse is contained in the explicit

---

87 Ibid., 157.

88 Ibid., 157 (emphasis in original).

89 Esposito draws, in particular, on Merleau-Ponty's *The Visible and the Invisible*, Simondon's *L'individu et sa genèse physico-biologique* and *L'Individuation psychique et collective*, Canguilhem's *The Knowledge of Life* and *The Normal and the Pathological*, and Deleuze's *The Logic of Sense, Francis Bacon: The Logic of Sensation* and his final essay, 'Immanence: A Life'.

90 Esposito (2008): 166.

91 Ibid., 167.

92 This notion is contained in the final part of *The Visible and the Invisible*, entitled 'The Intertwining – the Chiasm'.

93 Ibid., 156, 160. On the development of Merleau-Ponty's relationship to Husserl, through the notion of naturalism in biology, see Moinat (2012). See, for a contrasting view of the relationship

thinking beyond, in *The Visible and the Invisible*, of the notion of the body which asserts its primacy over life in the form of 'the identity of a unitary figure'.[94] The notion of the body is situated as an essentially derivative category in relation to the notion of the flesh as a primordial 'horizon of meaning in which the body recognizes itself and which is traversed by the diversity that keeps it from being co-terminus with itself'.[95] The interruption of the primacy of the body, by the notion of the flesh, also entails the dissolution of the separation and hierarchical ordering of both the human and animal species and the living and the non-living.[96]

For Esposito, Merleau-Ponty undermines the specifically National Socialist 'biopolitics that had made man an animal and driven life into the arms of non-life'.[97] The overturning of the particular bio-thanatological principle of the double enclosure of the body is combined with the withdrawal of thought from its intertwining with all figures and forms of the installation of the individual body within the 'idea of the political body'.[98] The notion of the flesh 'that constitutes the tissue of relations between existence and world' is one which 'represents the end and reversal' of the double enclosure of the body 'in its modern as well as in its totalitarian declensions'.[99] In revealing this primordial relationship between existence and world, the notion of the body is reconfigured as an aspect of 'a vital reality that is extraneous to any kind of unitary organisation because it is naturally plural'.[100] The body has, thereby, become 'one with its outside': 'the enlargement of the body to the dimension of the world (or the configuration of the world as singular body)'.[101]

The political, as the primordial relationship between politics and life, articulated by the Merleau-Pontian notion of the flesh, is held, by Esposito, to be revealed by the history of the decline of the body as the primary apparatus of 'political identification'.[102] The decline is traced from the origin of the installation of the body, as this primary apparatus, in the 'theological-political mechanism' of incorporation of Christianity[103] to its subsequent transformation under the Roman Empire and 'the nascent nation-states'.[104] The further biopolitical transformation of the nation-states intensifies 'the semantics of the body inherited from medieval

> between Merleau-Ponty and Husserl, Rokstad (2013) and Toadvine and Embree (2010). On the relationship between Merleau-Ponty and Heidegger, see Dastur (2000). On the relationship between Merleau-Ponty and the question of anthropology, see Bimbenet (2004).

94 Esposito (2008): 161.
95 Ibid., 160.
96 Ibid., 161.
97 Ibid., 162.
98 Ibid., 161.
99 Ibid., 160–1.
100 Ibid., 164.
101 Ibid., 161.
102 Ibid., 166.
103 Ibid., 164.
104 Ibid., 165.

political theology'.[105] The notion of the body, 'in the individual and collective sense', is directed towards a particular 'reciprocal implication between politics and life' which is centred on 'the life of subjects in all their biological requirements for protection, reproduction and development'.[106] These requirements are predicated on the presupposition of bodily representation of legitimate citizenship, and this presupposition entails a complementary collective body: 'the presence of a transcendent principle that is capable of unifying the members according to a determined functional design'.[107] The specificity of National Socialist biopolitics becomes the transformation of this transcendent principle into the bio-spiritual preservation of the 'radical heredity' of a people. In this transformation, the 'purely biological' preservation of a people, which has 'the form and substance of a body', leads to the auto-immunitary dissolution of the body which it had sought to preserve.

National Socialism, as the dispositif of the double enclosure of the body, marks the final assertion of the reciprocal implication of politics and life through the notion of the body. The end of National Socialism marks not the end of the 'biopolitical paradigm', but the continued presence and insistence of the 'question of life'[108] detached from the notion of the body. It marks the period of a biopolitics which comes after the body. For Esposito, in this period of 'the eclipse of the political body',[109] there arises 'something like a "flesh" that precedes the body and all its successive incorporations. Precisely for this reason it appears again when the body is in decline'.[110]

The indication that the period of biopolitics after the body reveals the potential primacy of the notion of the flesh is not, however, to be understood as the simple confirmation of the theoretical framework of Merleau-Ponty. The notion of the flesh remains caught, in *The Visible and the Invisible*, in the continual possibility of a reversion to its original, Christian foundation in the idea of incarnation. The potential risk[111] of the re-presentation of an essentially spiritual understanding of the notion of the flesh requires that the notion be rendered absolutely and resolutely material. This additional transformation of the Merleau-Pontian notion leads Esposito to alter the manner of its representation. The original and exclusively philosophical mode of presentation of the Merleau-Pontian notion of the flesh is replaced with the mode of aesthetic representation of this notion in the work of Francis Bacon and its attendant philosophical thematisation in Deleuze's *Francis*

---

105 Ibid., 165.
106 Ibid., 165.
107 Ibid., 165.
108 Ibid., 166.
109 Ibid., 166.
110 Ibid., 166.
111 Esposito distinguishes his position from Lyotard's *Discourse, Figure*; Derrida's *On Touching – Jean-Luc Nancy* and Nancy's *The Sense of the World*, which view Merleau-Ponty's notion of the flesh as *essentially* undifferentiated from the Christian conception of the flesh.

Bacon: The Logic of Sensation.[112] The alteration attests to a notion of the flesh which, while retaining the indistinction between the human and the animal, subsists in a brute materiality: the negative representation of life as nothing more than flesh.

The pertinence of this representation corresponds to the relationship between politics and life in which the decline of the body is expressed by its incapacity to establish and maintain 'precise immunitary borders [which] will mark and circumscribe it'.[113] The thought of the political commences from the flesh as the primordial relationship between politics and life. The political, as the politics of the flesh, is the negative horizon from which the further delineation of the question of life is undertaken.

The confrontation with the National Socialist principle of the anticipatory suppression of birth leads Esposito, beyond the negative horizon of the flesh, to the history of the notion of the common as the relationship between birth and the nation. The position of the nation in this history is analogous to the initial position of the body in the preceding confrontation with the dispositif of the double enclosure of the body.[114] The nation is situated as 'the domain in which all births are connected to each other in a sort of parental identity that extends to the boundaries of the state'.[115] It is the nation which confers 'a political signification [upon] the biological phenomenon of birth (which is impolitical in itself)'.[116] The nation, as a concept, has a history in which its 'monarchical, popular ... voluntaristic and naturalistic' variations leave an essential invariance as the 'territorial, ethnic, linguistic complex whose spiritual identity resides in the relation of every part to the whole, which is included in it'.[117] The specificity of National Socialism is, for Esposito, 'a development and a variation' of this history of the concept of the nation and its relationship to birth.[118]

The nation, under National Socialism, no longer merely ensures the biological value of a distinctly German people, through the 'biological continuity of the people across generations',[119] but affirms this value as a 'living force of history': 'the spiritual material that destines the German people to dominate all other peoples (given its absolute purity of blood)'.[120] The National Socialist nation, as the Third Reich, renders birth immediately political. In this 'copresence between the biological sphere and the political horizon',[121] the event of birth is to be interpreted

---

112 Deleuze (2005).
113 Esposito (2008): 166.
114 Ibid., 170–1.
115 Ibid., 171.
116 Ibid., 170.
117 Ibid., 170.
118 Ibid., 171.
119 Ibid., 171.
120 Ibid., 171.
121 Ibid., 171.

188 Roberto Esposito: Law, Community and the Political

and responded to in accordance with its value for the Reich. This produces the particular configuration of the anticipatory suppression of birth through the operation of 'a sovereign decision'.[122] A birth is either subject to 'the preventive exaltation of a life that is racially perfect', or 'is assigned to death by the same statute of what is considered to be living'.[123]

The overturning of the anticipatory suppression of birth involves the interruption of the immunitary relationship between birth and nation – the imposition of the unity of the nation upon the initial plurality of birth. Under National Socialism, the constitution of birth as political arises from its continual potential to undermine 'the continuity of ethnic filiation'.[124] The biopolitics of an anticipatory suppression of birth is the corollary of the conception that:

> Birth is the first *munus* that opens it to that in which it does *not* recognise itself. Annihilating birth, the Nazis believed that they were filling up the original void, that they were destroying the *munus* and so definitively immunizing themselves from their traumas.[125]

The confrontation with this principle, and the wider history of the concept of the nation, prevents a return and reinvigoration of the modern political concept of fraternity. For fraternity is already an essentially biopolitical concept, embedded 'in the natural *bíos*',[126] revealed, for Esposito, in the trajectory of the French Revolution in which fraternity assumes an increasing predominance over the concepts of liberty and equality. Fraternity establishes itself as the sole concept capable of articulating 'the indivisible unity of the nation against its enemies'[127] which arises from the process of 'self-identification founded on the consanguinity of belonging to the same nation'.[128] The character of this belonging is inherently restrictive and exclusionary, because it presupposes a 'fatherland (*patria*)', and 'confirms the biological bond that joins in a direct and masculine lineage the brother to the father (the "motherland" has always had symbolic connotations of virility)'.[129] Hence, fraternity, as brotherhood, 'excludes all those who do not belong to the same blood as that of the common father'.[130]

The restrictive, exclusionary character of fraternity is a form of unity traversed by an internal instability. The unity created by its insistence upon the vertical origin of the common father leaves the horizontal relationship between the members of

---

122 Ibid., 171.
123 Ibid., 171.
124 Ibid., 176.
125 Ibid., 176 (emphasis in original).
126 Ibid., 172.
127 Ibid., 172. Here, Esposito draws upon Marcel David's *Fraternité et Révolution française: 1789–1799* and *Le Printemps de la Fraternité: Genèse et Vicissitudes, 1830–1851*.
128 Ibid., 173.
129 Ibid., 173.
130 Ibid., 173.

Bíos II: towards an affirmative biopolitics   189

the brotherhood itself undetermined. The modern political concept of fraternity thereby remains, for Esposito, connected to the more ancient or primordial figure of the brother as the repository of 'fratricide': 'identity through opposition' which can transform itself into 'absolute enmity'.[131]

The overturning of the relationship between birth and nation involves recourse to a notion of plurality. For Esposito, plurality cannot merely be the assertion of the primacy of the event of biological birth against the nation. The concept of birth, if confined to biological birth, is unable to fully thematise the relationship between politics and life. Birth has itself to be further differentiated from a notion of plurality in order to proceed to reconceptualise community as a relationship between plurality and singularity.

The re-conceptualisation differentiates birth from plurality through the comprehension of life as a process of individuation. In this re-conceptualisation, Esposito utilises the work of Simondon in order to elaborate 'a dynamic conception of being that identifies it with becoming and . . . an interpretation of this becoming as a process of successive individuations in diverse and concatenated domains'.[132] This, in turn, introduces a foundation which is prior to the individual, and from which the individual emerges, through a process of individuation. Individuation refers to an 'always incomplete movement', in each domain of an individual's existence, which 'actualizes the potentialities without ever arriving at a definitive form that is not in turn the occasion and material for further individuation'.[133] The movement of individuation 'is never separated from the living roots from which it originates in the form of a splitting between the somatic and psychic levels in which the first is never decided in favour of the second'.[134] The separation between the biological and the psychical becomes one of 'level and function', thereby rendering the distinction between man, animal, 'vegetal and natural object' a series of more open transitions.[135]

These transitions are characterised as thresholds, and the movement or passage between thresholds becomes, in place of a foundational event of biological birth, the notion of birth.

> Every step in each phase, and therefore every individuation, is a birth on a different level, from the moment that a new 'form of life' is disclosed . . .

---

131   Ibid., 173.
132   Ibid., 180. Esposito's discussion of Freud's *Totem and Taboo* and *Moses and Monotheism* is left aside here. For Esposito's argument accords Simondon's work a more central position in the elaboration of notion of community. However, Esposito leaves the relationship between Merleau-Ponty and Simondon unexamined. This arises explicitly in the brief, unpublished working notes of Merleau-Ponty, in Volume 8, in the Bibliothèque Nationale. On this, see de Saint Aubert (2005) and Garelli (2005). For Simondon's approach to Merleau-Ponty, see Guchet (2001/02).
133   Esposito (2008): 180.
134   Ibid., 180.
135   Ibid., 180. For Simondon's explicit discussion of the relationship between man and animal, see Simondon (2012).

life and birth are superimposed in an inextricable knot that makes one the margin of opening to the other.[136]

The process of individuation, as a continual series of movements towards and beyond thresholds, 'deconstructs the individual into something that was prior to, but also contemporaneously after, him'.[137] The relationship between the preindividual and the process of individuation is simultaneously the presence of the common – the community of those who 'share the same vital experience, but also with that collective, which far from being its simple contrary or the neutralization of individuality, is itself a form of more elaborate individuation'.[138] This is Simondon's level of the transindividual in which a single process of individuation, within the domain of psychic life, can only relate more fully to the preindividual by placing that which remains of it in common with others. The transindividual, for Esposito, is the affirmative relationship between politics and *bíos*, as the common thematisation of the remainder of the preindividual. While the 'subject is always thought through the form of *bíos*, this, in turn, is inscribed in the horizon of a *cum* that makes it one with the being of man'.[139]

The history of the concept of the nation and its relationship to birth, which finds its final and most extreme expression in the anticipatory suppression of birth in National Socialism, is overturned and displaced by Esposito's appropriation of these elements of Simondon's theoretical framework. From these elements, the notion of life, as differentiated internally between the preindividual and the process of individuation, generates a notion of community beyond the relationship between birth and nation. The preservation of life is detached from any necessary dependence on the creation and imposition of an immunitary framework of exclusionary inclusion. The notion of community arises, from within life, in a form which is predicated upon an essential process of differentiation, through the interconnection of singularity (the process of individuation) and plurality (the preindividual).

The confrontation with, and overturning of, the dispositif of the absolute normativisation of life leads to a further conceptual development of an affirmative biopolitics. In this process of confrontation and overturning, Esposito seeks to break with the two main approaches to the norm and normativity of the 'modern juridical tradition': normativism and juris-naturalism.[140] For Esposito, both approaches are superficial attempts to respond to the absolute normativisation of life through the re-introduction of a 'more precise separation between the two domains [of norm and nature]'.[141] These attempts are distinguished by the primacy accorded, in this separation, to either the domain of the norm (normativism) or

136 Ibid., 181.
137 Ibid., 181.
138 Ibid., 181–2.
139 Ibid., 182.
140 Ibid., 184.
141 Ibid., 184.

nature (juris-naturalism). Normativism introduces the separation between norm and nature by 'autonomizing and almost purifying the norm in an obligation always more separate from the facticity of life'.[142] Juris-naturalism produces this separation by 'deriving the norm from the eternal principles of nature that coincides with the divine will or, otherwise, with human reason'.[143]

These main approaches of the modern juridical tradition are revealed to be superficial and deficient in relation to the character of the absolute normativisation of life. For Esposito:

> neither the absoluteness of the norm nor the primacy of nature is to be considered external to the phenomenon of Nazism, which seems to be situated exactly at the point of intersection and tension of their opposing radicalizations. What else is the Nazi bio-law if not an explosive mixture between an excess of normativism and an excess of naturalism, if not a norm superimposed on nature and a nature that is presupposed in the norm? We can say that in these circumstances the 'norm of life' was the tragically paradoxical formula in which life and norm are held together in a knot that can be cut only by annihilating both.[144]

The confrontation with this dispositif has, therefore, to commence explicitly from the confluence, or 'knot', of nature and norm in the National Socialist 'norm of life'. The overturning proceeds from 'an attempt to vitalize the norm'.[145] In this approach, 'a logic of [mutual] presupposition' between life and law is relinquished for a logic of 'reciprocal immanence'.[146] The alternative relationship between life and law, nature and norm is held to originate in the thought of Spinoza, in particular, the first chapters of *The Political Treatise*,[147] in which Esposito recognises the presentation of a 'norm of life' which is shaped by the logic of reciprocal immanence.[148] Within this logic, the notion of the norm becomes 'the intrinsic modality that life assumes in the expression of its own unrestrainable power to exist'.[149] The norm is 'the immanent rule that life gives itself in order

---

142 Ibid., 184. Esposito's reference to the modern juridical theory of normativism is essentially to Kelsen; and exclusively to Kelsen's 1963 essay 'Die Grundlage der Naturrechtslehre', and the posthumous *General Theory of Norms*.

143 Ibid., 184. Esposito's sole reference to this tradition is the essay by Cassirer, 'Vom Wesen und Werden des Naturrechts' of 1932.

144 Ibid., 184.

145 Ibid., 184.

146 Ibid., 184.

147 Spinoza (2003). The central focus of Esposito's interpretation is Chapter 2, on natural right (ibid.: 682–9).

148 Here, Esposito draws upon the affirmative biopolitical interpretation of Spinoza, and its subsequent genealogy, in Ciccarelli (2003), which is further developed in Ciccarelli (2006) and (2008). See, however, Belaief (1971); Frydman (2003); Garrett (2003); and Pfersmann (2003). Also, the distinct interpretation of Negri (1999), (2004) and (2013) is absent.

149 Esposito (2008): 184, 185–6.

192   Roberto Esposito: Law, Community and the Political

to reach the maximum point of its expansion' and, therefore, 'the principle of unlimited equivalence for every single form of life'.[150]

The norm is conceived as an integral aspect of the 'constitution of the living organism': the thought of 'the norm together with life'.[151] Thus, the norm 'does not invest the subject from outside because it emerges from the same capacity for existence'.[152] The logic of reciprocal immanence of norm and life generates a concept of normativity as a process of normativisation. The process expresses the constant 'comparison and conflict between individual norms that are measured according to the different power that keeps them alive, without ever losing the measure of their reciprocal relation'.[153] From the generalisation of this process of normativisation, the juridical order emerges as 'the product of this plurality of norms and the provisional result of their mutable equilibrium'.[154] For Esposito, 'Spinoza configures the juridical order as a meta-stable system of reciprocal contaminations in which the juridical norm, rooted in the biological norm, reproduces the latter's mutations'.[155]

The Spinozan origin of a thought of a logic of reciprocal immanence enables Esposito to present the work of Simondon, Canguilhem and Deleuze as 'the heirs of Spinozan juridical naturalism (consciously or unconsciously)'.[156] The connection to this origin rests upon 'the object of their research [as] the development of individual and collective life. Or better: the moving line that runs from the first to the second, constantly translating the one into the other.'[157] The filiation of Simondon, Canguilhem and Deleuze to this Spinozan juridical naturalism is traced through the trajectory from Simondon's notion of the transindividual, through Canguilhem's category of the norm, to Deleuze's notion of the impersonal singularity.

The notion of the transindividual, with which Esposito had concluded the preceding confrontation and overturning of the dispositif of the anticipatory suppression of birth, becomes, through this Spinozian origin, the reflection of a logic of reciprocal immanence. Beyond the presence of community, as the relationship between plurality and singularity, it is to be comprehended as the expression of a theory of norms and normativity.[158]

The notion of the transindividual, as a theory of norms and normativity, and its filiation with the juridical naturalism of Spinoza, arises from Simondon's critique of the underlying presuppositions of the human sciences.[159] The central

150   Ibid., 186.
151   Ibid., 186.
152   Ibid., 187.
153   Ibid., 187.
154   Ibid., 187.
155   Ibid., 188.
156   Ibid., 186.
157   Ibid., 186–7.
158   For an alternative interpretation of Simondon's notion of the transindividual, see Virno (2009).
159   Simondon (2005): 531–51. On this question, see Guchet (2012).

Bíos II: towards an affirmative biopolitics **193**

presupposition is a division between an internal and an external human existence, and the constitution of this division into two separate fields of investigation by psychology (internal) and sociology (external). The human, in the field of internal life, is open to a multiplicity of sources of affectation and is essentially formless. The inherent absence of an intrinsic limit or norm of behaviour within the field of internal life constitutes the external life as the field of the origin and imposition of norms. Hence, the human sciences reproduce a variant of the separation between norm and nature, law and life, of the normativism of modern juridical philosophy. The variant is one which is constructed from the relationship between three elements: '[i]nfluenceable – modifiable – normative response'.[160]

The relationship between the preindividual and the process of individuation is both Simondon's response to the limitations of the human sciences and, with the notion of the transindividual, a thought of immanent normativity. For the transindividual expresses the underlying logic of the relationship between the pre-individual and the process of individuation as one of reciprocal immanence. The impasse of the rigid separation between internal and external life is dissolved by the notion of the transindividual. The internal and the external are now elements of a process of continual exchange and development between the preindividual and the process of individuation.[161] A norm is generated at a particular juncture of this wider process of exchange and development, and to formulate this as a theory of normativity is to reveal the outlines of a juridical naturalism.

From the notion of the transindividual, as a theory of norms and normativity, Esposito passes to the work of Canguilhem and the notion of the norm. The passage from Simondon to Canguilhem marks a more specific re-conception of the relationship between 'normality and normativity'.[162] The particular configuration of normality and abnormality Canguilhem attributes to the field of biology becomes the critique of the separation of norm and nature of modern juridical philosophy.[163] The norm of life, as organic life in its normality or state of complete health, 'cannot be prefixed or imposed on life, but only inferred from it'.[164] This inference cannot be generated positively, for it is abnormality or illness which furnishes this inference negatively, in the loss of health, as the absence of the full 'physiological potentiality of the organism'.[165]

The distinct character of the norm of life in the biological field enables the difference from the legal norm to be articulated as 'the constitutively affirmative nature of the biological'.[166]

---

160 Guchet (2012): 78.
161 Esposito (2008): 187.
162 Ibid., 191.
163 This critique extends, beyond the *Normal and the Pathological*, to Canguilhem (2008); (2011).
164 Esposito (2008): 190.
165 Ibid., 190.
166 Ibid., 190.

194   Roberto Esposito: Law, Community and the Political

> While [the legal norm], which establishes a code of behaviour that is anterior to its actuation, necessarily needs to foresee the possibility of the deviation of life (and therefore of sanctions with respect to it), the biological norm coincides with the vital condition in which it is manifested . . . [R]ather than circumscribing life within the limits of the norm, [it] opens the norm to the infinite predictability of life.[167]

The biological field becomes the norm of life contained in the existence of the organism. The organism is the origin of its own norm of life, and, from this origin, emerges not an internal order of constraint and determinacy, but an intrinsic source of dynamism, creativity and variation.

The notion of the norm, as a norm of life, becomes the passage to the more explicit philosophy of immanence in Deleuze. The filiation to the Spinozan origin of a juridical naturalism becomes more complex, as it has to be traced through the conception of a 'transcendental field [which] would be defined as a plane of pure immanence, because it eludes all transcendence of the subject and the object'.[168] The thought of a plane of pure immanence produces 'the connecting and diverging point between *the* life and precisely *a* life'.[169] This point is both the reflection of life as a logic of reciprocal immanence and the presentation of the 'category of *bios*'.[170] The logic of reciprocal immanence detaches 'the dimension of life [from] that of individual consciousness'.[171] For the category of *bios* 'cannot be inscribed within the borders of the conscious subject, and therefore is not attributable to the form of the individual or of the person'.[172] The lack of inscription 'is the mark not of an empirical indetermination, but of a determination by immanence or a transcendental determinability'.[173]

A life, 'the singularity of *a* life', 'is not ascribable to an individual', but to the differentiation of the plane of immanence: its own differentiation.[174] The differentiation generates singularities from which the individual or person is only subsequently actualised. The individual or person is the derivative and always imperfect expression of an 'impersonal singularity' which is never coextensive with the individual.[175] The distinction between singularity and the individual or person represents the Deleuzian notion of a norm of life and, thereby, reveals the particular filiation with Spinozan juridical naturalism.

---

167   Ibid., 190.
168   Deleuze (2001): 26.
169   Esposito (2008): 192 (emphasis in original).
170   Ibid., 192.
171   Ibid., 192.
172   Ibid., 192.
173   Deleuze (2001): 30.
174   Esposito (2008): 193 (emphasis in original).
175   Ibid., 194.

For Esposito, it indicates:

> 'a norm of life' that does not subject life to the transcendence of a norm, but makes the norm an immanent impulse of life. The appeal to the impersonal as the only vital and singular mode is not unrelated to the going beyond a semantics of a person that has been represented from the origin of our culture in its juridical status (at least insofar as the law was and continues to function in relation to the intangible individuality of the person). It is this biojuridical node between life and norm that Deleuze invites us to untie in a form that, rather than separating them, recognizes the one in the other, and discovers in life its immanent norm, giving to the norm the potentiality of life's becoming.[176]

The Deleuzian notion of a norm of life, as the final aspect of the inheritance of Spinozan juridical naturalism, provides the philosophy of *bíos* with its basic theoretical presupposition.[177] The definition of the 'transcendental field . . . by a plane of immanence, and the plane of immanence by a life',[178] entails that the norm, as the potentiality of life's becoming, creates an originary, impersonal equality between all forms of life. Any form of life 'is a form of life and every form refers to life': 'no part of it can be destroyed in favour of another'.[179] The philosophy of *bíos* becomes the affirmation of life as the essential precondition for an affirmative biopolitics.

The confrontation with, and overturning of, the three dispositifs of National Socialist biopolitics is the concluding stage of the critique of a biopolitics shaped by the paradigm of immunisation. The impasse of a thought of life, orientated by its preservation within an immunitary framework of exclusionary inclusion, is traced from its origin in the first modernity of the concepts of modern political philosophy to its extreme installation in the second modernity of the regime of National Socialism. The history of this thought of biopolitics, as the genealogy of the modern paradigm of immunisation, presents its internal modification from immunity to auto-immunity. The immunitary paradigm, as the external re-imposition of an element of life's original negative or self-destructive potential, is revealed to be incapable of undertaking the preservation of life. The incapacity is initially indicated in the self-dissolution of the framework of the immunitary paradigm constituted by the concepts of modern political philosophy. The installation of the immunitary biopolitics of National Socialism is the trans-formation of the paradigm into one of auto-immunity. This immunitary paradigm intensifies and radicalises the intervention in life by the protective, external framework. The protective framework shifts from the negative protection of life

176 Ibid., 194.
177 Ibid., 194.
178 Deleuze (2001): 28.
179 Esposito (2008): 194.

to an 'excessive defence that ruinously turns on the same body that continues to activate and strengthen it'.[180]

For Esposito, the collapse of National Socialism, as a political regime, marks the continued presence and extension of the auto-immunitary or thanatological potential of the immunitary paradigm beyond its configuration in the specific political form of National Socialism. The collapse of the USSR and its allied regimes in the Warsaw Pact, and the emergence of the 'war on terror', enables the expansion of the auto-immunitary paradigm, and the generation of a politics over life which is essentially negative: 'an absolute identification of opposites: between peace and war, defence and attack, and life and death, they consume themselves without any differential remainder'.[181]

This phenomenon of planetary or global nihilism becomes the horizon against which Esposito calls for a philosophy of *bíos* as the responsibility of thought towards life. The recognition of this horizon – the assumption of the negativity of global nihilism – requires the reconstruction of a philosophy of *bíos* which consciously detaches itself from the concepts of modern political and juridical philosophy. The reconstruction, therefore, reveals the notions of the political, community and law to arise from a distinct tradition of the thought of life, acknowledging its filiation to Spinoza, in Merleau-Ponty, Simondon, Canguilhem and Deleuze. In their underlying commonality, for Esposito, is a thought of life as a thought of a logic of reciprocal immanence. This logic furnishes thought with an understanding of life as an affirmative biopolitics from which the notions of the political, community and law are themselves to be generated and determined.

180 Ibid., 148.
181 Ibid., 148.

Conclusion

Bíos, in the direct confrontation and overturning of National Socialist biopolitics, removed the thanatopolitical orientation of the relationship between life and politics. In this confrontation, there emerges the prefiguration of an affirmative biopolitics in which the overturning of National Socialist biopolitics cannot reveal a pristine, positive origin or foundation.[1] For the project of an affirmative biopolitics requires the reconfiguration of community (*communitas*) and immunity (*immunitas*) as partial aspects of a conception of life of which neither is alone the adequate expression.

An affirmative biopolitics is related to a tradition of Italian philosophy in which detachment from the nation – the location 'outside the boundaries of the nation state'[2] – is also a different orientation to the question of modernity. Modernity becomes the modern comprehended as the relationship between 'the form and sense of its own actuality' and 'the origin'.[3] The origin, distinguished from one created by processes of break or rupture, is itself inherently or 'structurally absent'.[4] The absence entails that the relation to the origin can never be 'the restoration of a past experience': there is no 'originary moment that is identifiable as such, and from which history (or a certain kind of history) is supposed to have started or to which it could return'.[5] The impossibility of the 'restoration of a past experience',[6] in which reflection is based on a movement of commencement and return, is the counterpart of a different process of reflection, in which the 'origin is always latently coeval with each historical moment'.[7] This 'actuality of the originary' is, for Esposito, the continual possibility for the reactivation of the origin in the present and, in this reactivation, the potential for that presence to be distinct and of varying intensity in each moment of the future.[8]

1   Esposito (2012c): 270.
2   Ibid., 21.
3   Ibid., 23.
4   Ibid., 23.
5   Ibid., 23.
6   Ibid., 23.
7   Ibid., 23.
8   Ibid., 23.

198   Roberto Esposito: Law, Community and the Political

The 'actuality of the originary' shapes an affirmative biopolitics through the intersection of the notion of life with three predominant strands of Italian philosophy. These strands each situate life as a notion traversed by a particular internal, immanent distinction. The forms of life which arise remain conditioned by this immanence, and are incapable of overturning or transcending these internal distinctions.

A politics of life intersects with the 'immanentization of antagonism',[9] in which the question of 'political conflict is life itself'.[10] Hence, 'conflict is constitutive of order ... The origin cannot be eliminated by an order that, in its factual concreteness, derives from conflict and that, indeed, continues incessantly to reproduce it'.[11] In an affirmative biopolitics, the *immanentisation of antagonism* is the relationship between community (*communitas*) and immunity (*immunitas*). Community, as the structurally absent origin of life in common, relates to the immunitary paradigm which seeks to preserve life by excluding it from the negative effects of life in common. The notion of life, constituted by the relationship between community and immunity, is one in which its 'reproduction, and enhancement ... [is one of] perennial tension'.[12] An affirmative biopolitics re-conceives immunity as both 'a process of differential transformation of the very subjects it identifies' and 'a filter for contact and communication with the surrounding environment'.[13] The rethinking or 'internal rotation' of immunity establishes the tension between community and immunity as a 'line of tangency that simultaneously separates and connects them, making one the irreducible content of the other'.[14]

The line of tangency introduces the further internal distinction between the historical and the non-historical. For while '[a]long that tangent, perilously "in time", is where human history runs',[15] the development of life confronts the 'actuality of the originary' in the form of the tension 'between ontology and history'.[16] The tension expresses itself, within the notion of life, as one between 'an absolute naturalization' and 'an absolute historicization'.[17] An affirmative biopolitics assumes and maintains this tension against the thanatopolitical temptation to dissolve it into an exclusive process of naturalisation or historicisation: the absolutisation of life as either nature or history.[18] This tension is reconceived 'as the relationship of two superimposed planes resting on top of each other but also, to some extent, lodged inside each other: the one above,

9   Ibid., 24.
10   Ibid., 25.
11   Ibid., 24.
12   Ibid., 261.
13   Ibid., 261.
14   Ibid., 260, 83.
15   Ibid., 83.
16   Ibid., 269.
17   Ibid., 269.
18   Ibid., 269.

Conclusion 199

historical in nature, and the other below, indescribable in historical terms'.[19] The tension becomes an 'internal movement' whereby 'the lower level comes to surface whenever an opening or fracture appears in the upper level'.[20] An affirmative biopolitics becomes the insistence on the positive expression of this internal tension and movement, and the opening or fracture is the gap through which the common, non-historical origin appears: 'the *munus* that the common origin bears within [it]'.[21] The presence of this internal distinction – the historicisation of the non-historical – within an affirmative biopolitics situates the notions of the political and community as integral aspects of the notion of life.

The immanence of the political and community in this notion of life are the preparation for the final internal distinction related to the conception of the subject within the thought of an affirmative biopolitics. The internal distinction expresses the 'mundanization of the subject' as the 'intersection' between life and 'the constitution of knowledge'.[22] The notion of the subject is 'deconstructed and reconstructed as a category of life',[23] and becomes a category merely differentiated 'from the collective dynamics out of which [it arises] on each occasion'.[24] In this process, a form of subjectivity is articulated from a 'critique of the logic of presupposition as a constitutive structure of subjectivity'.[25] The subject is no longer to be constituted by its strict separation from life and the creation of 'a set of unrelated individuals who are owners of themselves'.[26]

The critique identifies the logic of presupposition as inherently aporetic, and passes from aporia to a genealogical retrieval of this 'origin', in the 'actuality of the originary', through recourse to the Roman and Christian conceptions of the person. The presence of law emerges in this critique, as the Roman and Christian conceptions are held to introduce the hierarchical division, within 'the living being', between the domain of the personal and the domain of the animal.[27] This division inaugurates a particular configuration of the person as a legal subject: 'The original legal definition of *persona*, . . . is someone who is subject to objectivization by himself or herself or by others'.[28]

The division introduced by *persona* is 'quite different from a simple conceptual category'.[29] It enables the simultaneous production of separation and unity in which unity is achieved through 'an ordering . . . that layers or superimposes one [separated element] under the other'.[30] The effect of this 'absent' origin is to have

19 Ibid., 267.
20 Ibid., 267.
21 Ibid., 268.
22 Ibid., 28.
23 Ibid., 31.
24 Ibid., 29.
25 Ibid., 29.
26 Ibid., 30.
27 Ibid., 30.
28 Ibid., 30.
29 Esposito (2012a): 20.
30 Ibid., 20–1.

200 Roberto Esposito: Law, Community and the Political

produced a primordial valuation of 'the category of person'.[31] It installs the 'superiority of the personal over the impersonal: only a life that can provide the credentials of personhood can be considered saved or qualitatively significant'.[32]

The intertwining of the Christian and Roman conceptions of the person is exemplified in the Emperor Justinian's *Corpus juris civilis* and, in particular, the *Institutiones*. For Esposito, the importance of Roman codification is the creation of a framework – *ius* – which defines 'the category of the person and the subject of law, tying them together in such a way as to make the former a condition for conceiving of the latter and vice versa'.[33] Personhood enables a spectrum of positions or statuses with regard to the degree of personhood attributed to a particular individual life.[34] The logic, centred on 'the notion of person',[35] generates both 'differential thresholds within mankind' and 'the continual movement between them'.[36] The logic of the notion operates through universalisation *and* separation, which produces both personalisation *and* depersonalisation.

The perpetual movement between person, human and thing reflects a legal order predicated on 'the subjection to a complex of objective rules and regulations'.[37] The category of the person, as 'a general category', is a repository into which, in conformity with this perpetual movement, an individual could be either transferred or removed.

Eposito then initiates a genealogical re-description of the transformation effected by European natural law jurists upon the categories of Roman law:[38] the transition 'from the objectivist formalism of Roman law to the individualistic subjectivism of modern rights'.[39] In this transition, the category of the person, detached from its position in an objective web of legal relations, is re-situated within a theory of the subject. The subject becomes the site of 'sentient, functional activity', from which a 'rational will' arises, and legal personality becomes the 'power any subject has over itself and the things that belong to it'.[40] The category of the person is, thus, 'a quality implicit in every human being, ... different and

---

31 Esposito (2012b): 1.
32 Ibid., 2.
33 Ibid., 2.
34 Esposito (2012a): 22.
35 Ibid., 22.
36 Ibid., 22.
37 Esposito (2012b): 82.
38 In Esposito's genealogy, the history of legal thought is the conceptual history of the category of the person and its associated aporias or limitations. Hence, for example, the importance that Esposito accords to Hugo Donellus (1527–91) and Hermann Vultejus (1555–1634), in 're-elaborating the Roman formulation of person' (Esposito (2012a): 25), contrasts with their characterisation, by Decock (2012), as having a position of 'relative insignificance [. . .] in the development of early modern scholastic contract law' (Decock (2012): 119). For Decock, their reformulation of Roman law derives from their Calvinist opposition to Papal law, and the Canonists conception of contract (ibid., 134–5).
39 Esposito (2012b): 11.
40 Ibid., 82.

superimposed on the natural substrate it was implanted in'.[41] From this superimposition, there then arises the reciprocal association of 'the category of the person and the subject of law'.[42]

The French Revolution marks the culmination and realisation of the logic of individual, subjective rights, and the aporia or splitting inherent in the theory of the subject. The legal person and the physical person are superimposed or juxtaposed in the form of 'a biological body and a site of legal imputation, the first being subject to the discretionary control of the second'.[43] The French Revolution establishes the initial parameters of the modern legal person to whom rights are attributed.

The genealogy indicates both continuity and discontinuity between the modern, subjectivist logic of the legal person and the archaic, objectivist logic of Roman law. The discontinuity, as the very possibility to distinguish a modern, subjectivist logic, is the reinterpretation of the archaic vocabulary of Roman law through a theory of the subject. The continuity with this archaic horizon arises through its retention, within the subject, of a 'continuously shifting and oscillating distinction between a type of human being who is completely human, and another bordering on the regime of things'.[44] The theory of the subject generates an essentially aporetic structure in which its unity is 'based on a prior division'.[45] This division is 'the founding structure of subjectivity': 'the subject must presuppose itself – to rest on itself and, at the same time, be the support on which it rests'.[46] The modern, subjectivist logic of the legal person 'presupposes the separation from itself', and the subordination of 'the role of one part to the mastery of the other'.[47] The legal person, as the separation within the subject, 'cannot join together the epochal hiatus between life and rights . . . since it is the notion of person itself which produces it'.[48]

41 Ibid., 82.
42 Ibid., 2.
43 Ibid., 83. See, in contrast, the interpretation of the French Revolution, centred on natural law, in Gauchet (1989) and Gauthier (1992/2014). See also the formulation of these natural rights in a Declaration, and the wider question of a Constitution, in Jaume and Troper (1998), Jaume (1991) and Jaume (1993).
44 Esposito (2012c): 273.
45 Ibid., 272.
46 Ibid., 272.
47 Ibid., 272–3.
48 Esposito (2012a): 19. Esposito acknowledges Kelsen's work as the radicalisation of the distinction between legal person and human person (Esposito (2012b): 83), in which the legal person occupies the site of imputation in a theory of positive or pure law. However, the division of the theory of legal imputation, in the *Pure Theory of Law*, between central and peripheral imputation, is not a significant aspect of Esposito's analysis. As a result, the re-interpretation of Roman civil law, which initially distinguishes between a legal person and a human person, in Savigny (1779–1861), and which is subsequently rethought by Carl Friedrich von Gerber (1823–1891) and Julius Binder (1870–1939), is absent from this analysis. It is against this body of work that Kelsen develops his theory of imputation, and the definition of legal and human person. On this, see Paulson (2001).

The genealogy furnishes a response to the depersonalisation effected by National Socialist biopolitics – the unification of the 'person and the body by crushing the former into the biological matter of the latter'[49] – which is other than the restoration of legal personality and the re-establishment of this 'separation between personal subject and human being'.[50] The logic of subjective rights installs a hierarchy in which the upper part, 'which is rational or spiritual in nature',[51] is superior to that of 'the remaining area, which is devoid of these characteristics and therefore thrust into the regime of objecthood'.[52] The attribution or possession of rights, resulting from the logic of subjective rights, is a process of 'being subjected to one's own objectification'.[53]

The genealogical presentation of the logic of the category of the person also distinguishes Esposito's project from contemporary Anglo-American moral philosophy or meta-ethics.[54] This becomes evident through the comparison with its main currents in Scanlon's *Being Realistic about Reasons*.[55] Contemporary meta-ethics, for Scanlon, arises with the shift from morality and motivation by moral judgments to the wider question of 'normativity in general, treating morality as a special case' of motivation by reasons.[56] In this shift, the question centres on the determination of the character of motivation by reasons. Motivation relates to 'claims about reasons for action',[57] and the capacity to act, through motivation by reasons, entails the presence of a subject to whom these motivations can be attributed and evaluated.

The common question of the determination of the character of motivation by reasons also differentiates particular meta-ethical theories depending upon the specific basis of the relationship between the reasons for action and the subject of attribution and evaluation. The difference regarding the basis of the relationship is the site for meta-ethical disagreement in which differing conceptions of motivations by reasons are also differing conceptions of the theory of the subject of action. Hence, these differing conceptions are accompanied by the question of the necessity to introduce an internal division, within the subject of action, depending upon the source of the relationship between the reasons for action and the subject of action.

The pertinence of Esposito's genealogy of the category of the person becomes apparent once the conflicts between these meta-ethical positions are understood

---

49   Esposito (2012b): 11.
50   Ibid., 11.
51   Ibid., 11.
52   Ibid., 11.
53   Ibid., 12.
54   The *Third Person* concentrates solely on the personalism of Jacques Maritain and the liberal bioethics of Engelhardt and Singer as the exemplars of the aporetic logic of the person. However, the distinctiveness of Esposito's project is further emphasised if one passes beyond these strictly textual limits to the broader tradition of Anglo-American moral philosophy or meta-ethics.
55   Scanlon (2014).
56   Ibid., 2.
57   Ibid., 2.

as conflicts regarding the degree of internal division of the subject whose actions are to be motivated by reasons. Scanlon's middle position is one which locates a motivational source beyond the exclusive alternatives of either desire or rational agency. It derives, for Scanlon, from the difficulties of the competing meta-ethical theories which offer, in the form of desire or rational agency, an insufficient motivational source.

The definition of reasons for action as the effect of desires, in which reasons for action are simply the function of natural facts about an individual's desires, finds its exemplary exponent, for Scanlon, in Schroeder's *Slaves of the Passions*.[58] The insufficiency of this position is its lack of significant distinction between desire and reason and, therefore, the lack of sufficient internal division within the subject between reason and desire. The reduction of reasons for action to desire, and of the evaluation of these reasons by the particular strength of a desire which 'reasons "come with"',[59] renders this theory 'entirely psychological and explanatory rather than normative'.[60] It is the reduction of the source of motivation to the subject as desiring, natural substance, and hence, of the inability to distinguish, within the subject, a site of intrinsic normative motivation. The category of the person is unable to appear fully as the source of motivation, as the undifferentiated, natural fact of desire is unable to impose itself as a distinctive, normative domain upon the subject.

The rejection of normative desire theory is then the passage to the conflict over the site and definition of motivation by 'an idea of rationality'.[61] The conception of rationality introduces a distinction within the subject, as it is elaborated independently of 'a substantive conception of the reasons people have' for action.[62] The conflict centres on the determination of normative authority, namely, the necessity that a subject must be motivated by the particular normative force of a reason for action. Scanlon develops his position against the equation of normative force with 'a kind of normativity – some grounding for a "must" – that does not start from a claim about which things are reasons'.[63] The equation of normative force with this type of normativity finds its exemplary exponent, for Scanlon, in the work of Korsgaard.[64] From Korsgaard's position, '[c]laims about moral requirements are grounded in things that an agent must accept insofar as she sees herself as acting at all'.[65] Normativity is the practical identity of a rational agent,

---

58 Schroeder (2007). The question of the plausibility of Scanlon's critique of Schroeder, and the further development of Schroeder's position in Schroeder (2010) and (2014) is not considered here.

59 Ibid., 7.

60 Ibid., 89.

61 Ibid., 7.

62 Ibid., 8.

63 Ibid., 10.

64 Scanlon refers here to Korsgaard (1996, 2008 and 2009).The question of the plausibility of Scanlon's critique of Korsgaard is not considered here.

65 Schroeder (2007): 10–11.

and this involves the application of a test for the 'moral acceptability' of reasons for action. The determination of normative authority requires a clear division within the subject between its natural substance – the site of desire – and its identity as a rational agent from which the standard and test for the 'moral acceptability' of reasons for action are derived. The division enables the 'reflective "stepping back"' to 'an unconditioned starting point for reasoning about what reasons one has'.[66]

The insufficiency of this position, for Scanlon, relates to the lack of necessity to establish this distinct, unconditioned starting point. The challenge is not to the process of a reflective 'stepping back', but to the degree of its autonomy from the reasons which it seeks to test. The conception of rational agency, and the accompanying division which this creates within the subject, is displaced by a process of reflective equilibrium. This process is orientated towards 'clarifying what particular judgment we in fact accept, rather than a matter of finding a separate principle that "explains" this judgment'.[67] The displacement asserts that the division within the subject, generated through the process of reflective equilibrium, arises as the subject engages in the specific assessment of its own reasons for action.[68]

Esposito's genealogy reveals the contemporary Anglo-American tradition of meta-ethics to be orientated by the continued embeddedness of the 'logic of the person'. The positions within the field of meta-ethics each adhere to the logic of the person, through the 'subjection of the subject, before others, to itself, submitting it to, or superimposing it onto, its selfsame subjective substance'.[69] Hence, the project of an affirmative biopolitics adopts a position which is external to the logic of the person, and reorientates reflection from the theory of the subject to a theory of life and the category of the impersonal.

The reorientation proceeds from the association of the impersonal with a theory of life which commences otherwise than through reference to either 'a rational subject' or 'a bare material substrate', and its concomitant 'hierarchical division between these two entities within the separating dispositif of the person'.[70] The theory of life entails a re-conception of the relationship between life and knowledge as a reciprocal relationship involving a process of differentiation of the singularity of an individual life from the life of the species. The primacy accorded to differentiation denotes that this process, by which the singularity of an individual life is distinguished, retains an essential connection to the life of the species. The difference between the two terms or notions is understood to subsist in a productive unity which is maintained by their equal coexistence.

66 Ibid., 13–14.
67 Ibid., 102. This aspect of Scanlon's position is fully developed in Scanlon (2011).
68 Ibid., 104.
69 Esposito (2012c): 272.
70 Esposito (2012b): 147.

Conclusion 205

The equal coexistence of the singularity of an individual life and the life of the species enables singularity to be conceived as 'a life that coincides to the very last with its simple mode of being, with its being such as it is, a life that is precisely, "a life", singular and impersonal'.[71] This re-conception of singularity prevents the passage from singularity to a division 'into two reciprocally subordinated zones' of a theory of the subject,[72] and the associated category of the person. This, in turn, enables the theory of life to be conceived as a theory of community, as it is '[o]nly the community – conceived of in its most radical signification – [that] can rebuild the connection between rights and human beings that was severed by the ancient blade of the person'.[73]

In place of a 'philosophy of life', as 'an undifferentiated or independent mode of a biological or metaphysical type',[74] the necessary interconnection and differentiation between community, singularity and impersonality orientates Esposito's project towards an ontology. The central concern of an affirmative biopolitics, therefore, becomes the determination of the mode of being of life.

Thus, the ontology accords the notion of law its own particular mode of being, which, beyond Esposito's genealogical presentations of *Third Person* and *Living Thought*, is comprehensible through a return to a form of Roman law.[75] In its original Roman definition, and the later natural law tradition, commencing from the seventeenth century, this form of law is respectively marginalised or rejected as a source or notion of law. This form of law, as the first type or level of law distinguished by the *Institutes* and *Digest*, is the law of nature, a natural law common to man and animals: 'a law not peculiar to the human race'.[76] In this lack of peculiarity, it is set apart from the specifically human law constituted by the *ius gentium* and the civil law. This non-human law would then be the negative presence, within Roman law, of a form of law which would not be distinct from life and imposed upon life.

This negative presence, as the mode of being of law within a theory of life, in accordance with Esposito's theoretical framework, cannot be rendered positive, as a thought of origin, in which nature is a personified law giver and law is the expression of mere instinct. Rather, what remains is the presence of a thought of impersonality and singularity within this non-human law which is 'not peculiar to the human race'. The retrieval and re-conceptualisation of this negative presence in Roman law provides an alternative path which, in turn, confers a different locus

---

71   Ibid., 147.
72   Ibid., 147.
73   Ibid., 103.
74   Esposito (2012c): 31.
75   For *Third Person* and *Living Thought* propose distinct genealogies for a theory of life external to the tradition of Roman law. The genealogy of *Third Person* is formed from Benveniste, Kojève, Jankélévitch, Levinas, Blanchot, Foucault and Deleuze. The genealogy of *Living Thought* is the distinctive theory of life that Esposito traces within Italian thought.
76   Justinian (2013): 1.2pr. On the relationship between Roman Law and the jurists of the seventeenth century, see Watson (1992).

for the notion of the 'becoming-animal' which Esposito, in *Third Person*, appropriates from Deleuze.[77] The law of nature, in the *Institutes* and the *Digest*, would be the 'becoming-animal' in the specific sense, for Esposito, of 'our most tangible reality', namely, 'the process of mutation that our nature has always undergone . . . humankind brought back to its natural alteration'.[78] The law of nature would then become intelligible, against the privileging of the human particular to Roman law, and the subsequent tradition constituted by its interpretation. The reconfiguration of the relationship between human and animal would reorientate the law of nature towards a theory of life in which 'the living person' is 'coextensive with' life.[79] The living person would be 'this being that is both singular and plural . . . the non-person inscribed in the person, to the person open to what has never been before'.[80]

The openness created in the initial determination of the mode of being of law emphasises that this ontology is also an ethics. The co-extensiveness of the living person and life is the 'singular plural finiteness of an existence', encompassed by this theory of life, which installs an 'ontological ethics' as that which the mode of being of law is to express.[81] The reflection upon law thus becomes the question of the form that this ontological ethics is to take as a mode of being of law. The determination of the form of connection between ethics and law represents an 'internal critique' of law which furnishes the basis for a different characterisation of the concept and nature of law. The outlines of this different characterisation reside, at the level of singular life, in the assertion of the primacy of obligations over rights and, at the level of life as a whole, in the 'deformalisation' of law.[82]

At the level of singular life, the primacy of obligations over rights creates a duty or obligation towards other forms of singular life.[83] The further differentiation or specification of this duty or obligation would then delineate a distinct set or 'system' of obligations from the contemporary Anglo-American schema of defined rights claims and abstract rights claims.[84] Under this schema, obligations, as duties, are intimately related to rights, and the distinction between defined and abstract rights claims relates to the degree to which the right imposes a specific obligation upon an individual as the corollary of that right. Defined rights claims are, in contrast to abstract rights claims, those which delineate a specific duty which,

---

77 The reference is to Deleuze and Guattari (2013), Plateau ('Chapter') 10, *1730: Becoming Intense, Becoming-Animal, Becoming-Imperceptible* . . . Esposito, however, detaches the notion of becoming-animal from the subsequent discussion, in this Plateau, of the pack and the loner, pure multiplicity and the exceptional individual, and beyond this, the phenomenon of bordering.

78 Esposito (2012b): 150.

79 Ibid., 151.

80 Ibid., 151.

81 Esposito (2010): 75, 82.

82 Ibid., 75, 82.

83 This is drawn from Esposito's identification of the primacy of obligation in Weil, as the positive content of her critique of law and rights. See Esposito (2011): 23–7; (2012a): 28–30; and (2012b): 100–3.

84 This general schema is present, for example, in Scanlon (1998); (2008); and Sen (2000); (2004).

Conclusion   207

in turn, imposes a direct or 'perfect' obligation upon the individual to whom it is addressed. Abstract rights claims are those which remain without the degree of specificity of defined rights claims and, therefore, impose only indirect or 'imperfect' obligations upon the individual to whom it is addressed. The 'imperfect' character of these obligations is demonstrated by the lack of a clearly and immediately identifiable individual right-holder whose right would be affected by any breach of this obligation.

The primacy accorded to obligation in relation to rights, by Esposito, would entail that the necessary connection between rights and obligations of this schema be relinquished. The schema is predicated on the prior division of the subject, and the attribution of personhood, through which it creates a determinate right-holder whose individual values or interests are the foundation for rights claims. The primacy of obligation establishes the absolute character of obligation, as it expresses the connection between the ontological and ethical aspects of the theory of life. The enclosure and division of the subject as right-holder is replaced with the exposure of an impersonal, singular life to the multiplicity or plurality of life with which it is co-extensive. This turning away from rights, through the primacy accorded to obligation, prevents the transposition or transformation of the mode of being of law into a theory of the subject and its compliment in the category of the person.

However, without further elaboration, this remains a preliminary critique of law, as the place of a set or system of obligations remains undetermined. The lack of further elaboration is the counterpart of a concern that the primacy of obligation to the multiplicity and singularity of life can become a resignation to the existing configuration of life: 'a simple function of keeping the world as it is'.[85] Here, the primacy of obligation confronts the preceding acknowledgement of the 'immanentization of antagonism', and the question of the place, within the impersonality of a singular life, for a conception of the self which owes obligations to itself.

The internal critique of law, at the level of life as a whole, also indicates its preliminary character in the presentation of the deformalisation of law. The critique of the strict separation of norm and life involves the consideration of the phenomenon of international law as global law: the pertinence and capacity of global law to regulate life. The parameters of this question are redefined as the question of 'how to think biopolitics and globalization within the other'. [86] International law becomes a particular immunitary instrument, and deformalisation of law is, in contrast, a specific instance of the construction of 'a reciprocal relation' between 'community and immunity'.[87] Deformalised law would be a specific mode of 'immunitary tolerance'.[88]

---

85   Esposito (2010): 82.
86   Esposito (2013b): 133.
87   Ibid., 134.
88   Ibid., 134.

208 Roberto Esposito: Law, Community and the Political

The distinctive conception of deformalised law in Esposito's theory of life is revealed in relation to the contemporary debate regarding the definition and status of international law, as soft law, between theorists of international law.[89] The primacy of this definitional question concerns the determination of the parameters of international law. It focuses, through a distinction between law and non-law, on a reordering or re-categorisation of the multiplicity of forms of international agreement. Deformalisation is recognised as a process which shapes the content of an international agreement, and encompasses those forms of international agreement which do not conform to the totality of elements contained in the definition of international law. The international agreement, created by the process of deformalisation, becomes soft law to the extent that the absence of the totality of these elements marks not non-law, but a different type of international law, which exists in contrast to a type of international law in which all these elements are present – hard law.

The primacy accorded to the question of the definition of international law reflects the effect of the proliferation of forms of international agreement, and the extent to which definitions of international law, when confronted with these agreements, furnish a narrow or broad conception of global law. The character of this definition is connected to the question of whether the authority to create, and the obligations that arise from, international agreements are to remain exclusively legal. This, in turn, involves the consideration of the position of the state and non-state actors in relation to a reflection on 'the relative functions and merits of law and politics and about the interaction of the two'.[90]

The question of deformalisation and soft law, for Esposito, is not the question of 'a legal conceptualization of international public authority',[91] but the relation between law and life. Deformalisation arises from the re-conception of the relationship between law and life, as the relationship between unity and difference. In this theoretical trajectory, although not explicitly present in *Third Person*,[92] it would entail the critique of the notion of legal personality underlying the notion of international public authority.

The further development of this level of internal critique of law remains in a preliminary form, because a concern has subsequently emerged, in *Due. La macchina della teologia politica e il posto del pensiero*[93] and 'Politica e Metafisica',[94] of the continued obstruction and occlusion of a thought of unity and

---

89 The deformalisation debate is extensive, with a very significant body of academic material concerning both the general conception of soft law and the character of its presence in particular fields of international law. For example, see Bogdandy *et al.* (2008); d'Aspremont (2008); Ellis (2012); Goldmann (2012); Günther (2008); and Robilant (2006).

90 Ellis (2012): 334.

91 Goldmann (2012): 366.

92 Apart from the brief examination of the connection between the 'juridical category of the person' and the 'political category of sovereignty' in Esposito (2012b): 83–7.

93 Esposito (2013d). An English translation, entitled, *Two: The Machine of Political Theology and the Place of Thought* is forthcoming from Fordham University Press in Autumn 2015.

94 Esposito (2013c).

difference by political theology. The effect is of the continued repetition of a thought of unity as the separation from, and exclusion of, difference. In order to break with this perpetual repetition, a position for thought outside the parameters of political theology becomes the question which precedes the internal critique of law. This 'return' to political theology, and the critical path on which Esposito has now commenced, will determine the further elaboration and development of the notions of law, community and the political within this theoretical project.

Bibliography

Agamben, G. (1998) *Homo Sacer: Sovereign Power and Bare Life*, Heller-Roazen, D. (trans.), Stanford: Stanford University Press.

Agamben, G. (2005a) *The State of Exception*, Attell, K. (trans.), Chicago: Chicago University Press.

Agamben, G. (2005b) *The Time That Remains: A Commentary on the Letter to the Romans*, Dailey, P. (trans.), Stanford: Stanford University Press.

Alexy, R. (2008) 'On the Concept and the Nature of Law', *Ratio Juris*, 21, 3, 281–299.

Aly, G., Chroust, P. and Pross, C. (1994) *Cleansing the Fatherland. Nazi Medicine and Racial Hygiene*, Cooper, B. (trans.), Baltimore: John Hopkins University Press.

Amendola, A. (2012) 'The Law of the Living: Material for Hypothesizing the Biojuridical', *Law, Culture and the Humanities*, 8, 1, 102–118.

Arendt, H. (1953) 'The Origins of Totalitarianism: A Reply', *Review of Politics*, 53, 1, 76–84.

Arendt, H. (1958) *The Human Condition*, Chicago: Chicago University Press.

Arendt, H. (1963) 'What is Freedom?' in *Between Past and Future. Six Exercises in Political Thought*, New York: World Publishing Company, 143–171.

Arendt, H. (1972a) 'Civil Disobedience' in *Crises of the Republic*, New York: Harcourt, Inc., 51–102.

Arendt, H. (1972b) 'On Violence' in *Crises of the Republic*, New York: Harcourt, Inc., 105–198.

Arendt, H. (1978) *The Life of the Mind*, New York: Harcourt, Inc.

Arendt, H. (1982) *Lectures on Kant's Political Philosophy*, Beiner, R. (ed.), Chicago: Chicago University Press.

Arendt, H. (1988) *On Revolution*, London: Penguin Books. Original published in 1963.

Arendt, H. (1995) 'Hermann Broch' in *Men in Dark Times*, New York: Harcourt, Inc, 111–151. Original published in 1968.

Arendt, H. (2007a) 'No Longer and Not Yet', Young-ah Gottlieb, S. (ed. and introduction) in *Reflections on Literature and Culture*, Stanford: Stanford University Press, 121–125. Original published in 1946.

Arendt, H. (2007b) 'The Achievement of Hermann Broch', Young-ah Gottlieb, S. (ed. and introduction) in *Reflections on Literature and Culture*, Stanford: Stanford University Press, 148–155. Original published in 1949.

Augustine, St. (1998) *The City of God against the Pagans*, Dyson, R. W. (trans.), Cambridge: Cambridge University Press.

Backhaus, J. G. (ed.) (2009) *The Beginnings of Political Economy: Johann Heinrich Gottlob von Justi*, Dordrecht: Springer.

Badiou, A. (2003) *Saint Paul: The Foundation of Universalism*, Brassier, R. (trans.), Stanford: Stanford University Press.

Balibar, E. (1994) *Masses, Classes, Ideas: Studies on Politics and Philosophy before and after Marx*, Swenson, J. (trans.), London: Routledge.

Balibar, E. (2014) *Equaliberty: Political Essays*, Ingram, J. (trans.), Durham, NC: Duke University Press.

Balke, F. (2003) 'From a Biopolitical Point of View: Nietzsche's Philosophy of Crime', *Cardozo Law Review*, 24, 2, 705–722.

Bataille, G. (1970a) 'Materialisme' in *Oeuvres Complètes*, t.1, Paris: Gallimard, 179–180.

Bataille, G. (1970b) 'L'Informe' in *Oeuvres Complètes*, t.1, Paris: Gallimard, 215.

Bataille, G. (1970c) 'La Base Materalisme et la Gnose' in *Oeuvres Complètes*, t.1, Paris: Gallimard, 220–226.

Bataille, G. (1970d) 'Propositions sur le fascisme' in *Oeuvres Complètes*, t.1, Paris: Gallimard, 339–371. Original published in 1933 and 1934, in the revue *La Critique sociale*.

Bataille, G. (1970e) 'Nietzsche et les Fascistes' in *Oeuvres Complètes*, t.1, Paris: Gallimard, 447–465. Original published in 1937, in the revue *Acéphale*.

Bataille, G. (1970f) 'Jaspers' in *Oeuvres Complètes*, t.1, Paris: Gallimard, 474–476. Original published in 1937, in the revue *Acéphale*.

Bataille, G. (1970g) 'Chronique nietzschéenne' in *Oeuvres Complètes*, t.1, Paris: Gallimard, 477–490. Original published in 1937, in the revue *Acéphale*.

Bataille, G. (1973) 'Lettre à X., chargé d'un cours sur Hegel . . .' in *Oeuvres Complètes*, t.V, Paris: Gallimard, 369–371. Written in 1937, but published posthumously.

Bataille, G. (1979a) 'L'apprenti sorcier' in Hollier, D. (ed.), *Le Collège de Sociologie (1937–1939)*, Paris: Gallimard, 36–59.

Bataille, G. (1979b) 'Attraction et répulsion II' in Hollier, D. (ed.), *Le Collège de Sociologie (1937–1939)*, Paris: Gallimard, 208–231.

Bataille, G. (1979c) 'Le Pouvoir' in Hollier, D. (ed.), *Le Collège de Sociologie (1937–1939)*, Paris: Gallimard, 232–254.

Bataille, G. (1979d) 'Le Collège de Sociologie' in Hollier, D. (ed.), *Le Collège de Sociologie (1937–1939)*, Paris: Gallimard, 522–536.

Bataille, G. (1986) 'Sacrifice', *October*, 36, 61–74.

Bataille, G. (1988a) 'La victoire militaire et la banqueroute de la morale qui maudit' in *Oeuvres Complètes*, t. XI, Paris: Gallimard, 532–549. Original published in 1949.

Bataille, G. (1988b) 'Hegel, la mort et le sacrifice' in *Oeuvres Complètes*, t. XII, Paris: Gallimard, 326–345. Original published in 1955.

Bataille, G. (1988c) 'Hegel, l'homme et l'histoire' in *Oeuvres Complètes*, t. XII, Paris: Gallimard, 349–369. Original published in 1956.

Bataille, G. (1988d) *Inner Experience*, Boldt, L. A. (trans. and introduction), Albany, NY: State University of New York Press. Original published in 1943, with a subsequent revised, corrected and extended version in 1954.

Bataille, G. (1991) *The Accursed Share*, Vol. 1, Hurley, R. (trans.), New York: Zone Books. Original published in 1949.

Bataille, G. (1993) *The Accursed Share*, Vols. II and III, Hurley, R. (trans.), New York: Zone Books. Original published posthumously in 1976.

Bataille, G. (1994) *On Nietzsche*, Boone, B. (trans.), Lotringer, S. (introduction), St. Paul: Paragon House. Original published in 1945.

212 Bibliography

Bataille, G. (2005a) *The Cradle of Humanity: Prehistoric Art and Culture*, Kendall, M. and Kendall, S. (trans.), New York: Zone Books.

Bataille, G. (2005b) 'The Passage from Animal to Man and the Birth of Art' in Bataille, G., *The Cradle of Humanity: Prehistoric Art and Culture*, Kendall, M. and Kendall, S. (trans.), New York: Zone Books, 57–80. Original published in 1953.

Bataille, G. (2011) *Guilty*, Kendall, S. (trans.), New York: State University of New York Press. Original published in 1944, and with subsequent additions in 1961.

Bataille, G. (2012) *Theory of Religion*, Hurley, R. (trans.), New York: Zone Books. Original published posthumously in 1973.

Bataille, G. and Caillois, R. (1979) 'La sociologie sacrée du monde contemporain' in Hollier, D. (ed.), *Le Collège de Sociologie (1937–1939)*, Paris: Gallimard, 291–293.

Belaief, G. (1971) *Spinoza's Philosophy of Law*, The Hague: Mouton.

Benjamin, W. (1989) 'The Critique of Violence' in Jephcott, E. (trans.), Demetz, P. (introduction), *Reflections. Essays, Aphorisms, Autobiographical Writings*, New York: Schocken Books, 277–300. Original published in 1921.

Benveniste, E. (1973) *Indo-European Languages and Society*, Palmer, E. (trans.), London: Faber and Faber. Original published in 1969.

Berger, P. L. and Kellner, H. (1965) 'Arnold Gehlen and the Theory of Institutions', *Social Research*, 32, 1, 110–116.

Bimbenet, E. (2004) *Nature Et Humanite: Le Probleme Anthropologique Dans L'Oeuvre de Merleau-Ponty*, Paris: Vrin.

Blondel, E. (1991) *Nietzsche: The Body and Culture. Philosophy as a Philological Genealogy*, Hand, S. (trans.), London: Athlone Press.

Blumenberg, H. (1999) *The Legitimacy of the Modern Age*, Wallace, R. M. (trans.), Cambridge: MIT Press. Original published in 1966.

Bogdandy, A. V., Dann, P. and Goldmann, M. (2008) 'Developing the Publicness of International Public Law: Towards a Legal Framework for Global Governance Activities', *German Law Journal*, 9, 11, 1375–1400.

Bondy, M. (1921) 'Jugendbewegung und Katholizismus', *Die Schildgenossen*, 1, 44–56.

Bourreau, A. (2000) *Le simple corps du roi. L'impossible sacralité des souverains français – XVe–XVIIIe siècle*, Paris: Editions de Paris.

Bourreau, A. (2006) *La religion de l'Etat: La construction de la République étatique dans le discours théologiques de l'Occident médiéval (1250–1350)*, Paris: Belles Lettres.

Bourreau, A. and Claudio Sergio Ingerflom, C. S. (eds.) (1992) *La royauté sacrée dans le monde chrétien*, Paris: Editions de l'EHESS.

Bredekamp, H. (1999) 'From Walter Benjamin to Carl Schmitt, via Thomas Hobbes', *Critical Inquiry*, 25, 2, 247–266.

Bridet, G. (2007) 'Roger Callois dans les Impasses du Collège de Sociologie', *Littérature*, 146, 2, 90–103.

Broch, H. (1977) 'Die erkenntnistheoretische Bedeutung des Begriffes "Revolution" und die Wiederbelebung der Hegelschen Dialektik. Zu den Büchern Arthur Lieberts: A.L., Vom Geist der Revolutionen, Wie ist kritische Philosophie überhaupt möglich?' in Broch, H., *Philosophische Schriften 1 Kritik* Frankfurt am Main: Suhrkamp, 257–263. Original published in 1922 in *Prager Presse* (Beilage 'Dichtung und Welt'), 2, Jg., Nr.206 (30.7.1922), S.III–IV.

Broch, H. (1986) *The Sleepwalkers*, Muir, W. and Muir, E. (trans.), London: Quartet Books. German original 1931.

Bibliography   213

Broch, H. (1995a) *The Death of Virgil*, Untermeyer, J. S. (trans.), New York: Vintage Books. German original 1945.

Broch, H. (1995b) *Massenwahntheorie. Beiträge zu einer Psychologie der Politik*, Berlin: Suhrkamp.

Broch, H. (2008) *Théorie de la folie des masses*, Renault, D. and Rusch, P. (trans.), Paris: Editions de l'éclat. Original posthumous publication in 1995.

Bröckling, U. (1993) *Katholische Intellektuelle in der Weimarer Republik. Zeitkritik und Gesellschaftstheorie bei Walter Dirks, Romano Guardini, Carl Schmitt, Ernst Michel und Heinrich Mertens*, Munich: Wilhelm Fink Verlag.

Burleigh, M. (2002) *Death and Deliverance. Euthanasia in Germany 1900–1945*, London: Pan Books.

Byrd, S. B. and Hruschka, J. (2012) *Kant's Doctrine of Right. A Commentary*, Cambridge: Cambridge University Press.

Cacciari, M. (2009a) 'Nietzsche and the Unpolitical', Carrera, A (ed.), Verdicchio, M. (trans.) in *The Unpolitical: On The Radical Critique of Political Reason*, New York: Fordham University Press, 92–103.

Cacciari, M. (2009b) 'The Language of Power in Canetti: A Scrutiny', Carrera, A. (ed.), Verdicchio, M. (trans.) in *The Unpolitical: On The Radical Critique of Political Reason*, New York: Fordham University Press, 159–172.

Caffentzis, C. G. (1990) *Clipped Coins, Abused Words and Civil Government: John Locke's Philosophy of Money*, New York: Autonomedia.

Caillois, R. (1979) 'Le Vent d'Hiver' in Hollier, D. (ed.), *Le Collège de Sociologie* (1937–1939), Paris: Gallimard, 75–97.

Calabrò, D. (2012) *Les Detours d'une Pensée Vivante. Transitions et Changements de Paradigme dans la Réflexion de Roberto Esposito*, Paris: Editions Mimesis.

Campbell, T. (2011) *Improper Life: Technology and Biopolitics from Heidegger to Agamben*, Minneapolis, MN: University of Minnesota Press.

Canetti, E. (1981) *Crowds and Power*, Stewart, C. (trans.), London: Penguin Books.

Canetti, E. (1986a) *The Human Province*, Neugroschel, J. (trans.), London: Picador.

Canetti, E. (1986b) *The Wedding*, Honneger, G. (trans.), London: PAJ Publications. Originally published in German in 1932.

Canetti, E. (1989) *The Torch in My Ear*, Neugroschel, J. (trans.), London: André Deutsch.

Canetti, E. (1991a) *The Play of the Eyes*, London: Picador.

Canetti, E. (1991b) *The Secret Heart of the Clock. Notes, Aphorisms, Fragments 1973–1985*, Agee, J. (trans.), London: André Deutsch.

Canetti, E. (1996) 'Discussion with Theodor W. Adorno', *Thesis Eleven*, 45, 1, 1–15. Original published in 1972 in *Elias Canetti: Die gespaltene Zukunft, Aufsätze und Gespräche*, Munich: Hanser Verlag, 66–92.

Canetti, E. (2005) *Auto da Fé*, Wedgwood, C. V. (trans.), London: The Harvill Press. Original published in 1935, as *Die Blendung*, Zürich: Herbert Reichner.

Canetti, E. (2012) *Kafka's Other Trial: The Letters to Felice*, Middleton, C. (trans.), London: Penguin Books. Original published in 1969.

Canguilhem, G. (2007) *The Normal and the Pathological*, Fawcett, C.R. (trans.), New York: Zone Books. Original published in 1943.

Canguilhem, G. (2008) *The Knowledge of Life*, Geroulanos, S. and Ginsburg, D. (trans.), New York: Fordham University Press. Original published in 1965.

Canguilhem, G. (2011) *Writings on Medicine*, Geroulanos, S. (trans.), New York: Columbia University Press.

214 Bibliography

Carrino, A. (1999) 'Carl Schmitt and European Juridical Science' in Mouffe, C. (ed.), *The Challenge of Carl Schmitt*, London: Verso, 180–194.

Cassier, S. (1960) 'Hermann Broch's Early Writings', *PMLA*, 75, 4, 453–462.

Cassirer, E. (1932) 'Vom Wesen und Werden des Naturrechts', *Zeitschrift für Rechtsphilosophie in Lehre und Praxis*, 6, 1, 1–27.

Cassirer, E. (1953) *Substance and Function*, Swabey, W. C. (trans.), New York: Dover Publications. Original published in 1910.

Chestov, L. (1925) *L'ideé de bien chez Tolstoï et Nietzsche*, Paris: Editions du Siècle.

Chestov, L. (1926) *La Philosophie de la tragédie. Nietzsche et Dostoïevski*, Paris: Gallimard.

Chignola, S. (2001) 'The Experience of Limitation: Political Form and Science of Law in the Early Writings of Eric Voegelin', Murphy, F. (trans.), in Hughes, G., McKnight, S. and Price, G. (eds.), *Politics, Order, and History: Essays on the Work of Eric Voegelin*, Sheffield: Sheffield Academic Press, 61–84.

Ciccarelli, R. (2003) *Potenza e beatitudine. Il diritto nel pensiero di Baruch Spinoza*, Rome: Carocci.

Ciccarelli, R. (2006) *Immanenza e politica in Spinoza*, Ariccia: Aracne.

Ciccarelli, R. (2008) *Immanenza. Filosofia, diritto e politica della vita dal XIX al XX secolo*, Bologna: Il Mulino.

Clark, E. A. (1992) *The Origenist Controversy: The Cultural Construction of an Early Christian Debate*, Princeton, NJ: Princeton University Press.

Clark, M. (2000) 'Nietzsche's Doctrine of the Will to Power: Neither Ontological nor Biological', *International Studies in Philosophy*, 32, 3, 119–135.

Clark, M. (2007) 'On Nietzsche's Darwinism', *International Studies in Philosophy*, 39, 3, 117–134.

Cohen, H. (1978) 'Logik der reinen Erkenntnis' in Cohen, H., *Werke*, Bd. 6, Hildesheim: Olms Verlag. Original published in 1902.

Colliot-Thélène, C. (1999) 'Carl Schmitt versus Max Weber: Juridical Rationality and Economic Rationality' in Mouffe, C. (ed.), *The Challenge of Carl Schmitt*, London: Verso, 138–154.

Crignon, P. (2007) 'L'altération du christianisme. Hobbes et la trinité', *Les Etudes Philosophiques*, 81, 2, 235–263.

Dastur, F. (1992) *Hölderlin. Tragédie et Modernité*, Paris: Encre Marine.

Dastur, F. (2000) 'La lecture merleau-pontienne de Heidegger dans les notes du Visible et l'invisible et les cours du Collège de France (1957–1958)', *Chiasmi International*, 2, 373–387.

David, C. (2011) 'Fidélité de Günther Anders à l'anthropologie philosophique: de l'anthropologie négative de la fin des années 1920 à *L'obsolescence de l'homme*', *L'Homme et la société*, 181, 3, 165–180.

David, M. (1992a) *Fraternité et Révolution française: 1789–1799*, Paris: Aubier.

David, M. (1992b) *Le Printemps de la Fraternité: Genèse et Vicissitudes, 1830–1851*, Paris: Aubier.

D'Agostino, F. (2005) 'Nihilism in Italy', *Philosophy Today*, 49, 4, 342–354.

D'Agostino, F. (2009) *The Last Fumes: Nihilism and the Nature of Philosophical Concepts*, Colorado: The Davies Group.

D'Aspremont, J. (2008) 'Softness in International Law: A Self-Serving Quest for New Legal Materials', *European Journal of International Law*, 19, 5, 1075–1093.

Decock, W. (2012) *Theologians and Contract Law: The Moral Transformation of the 'Ius Commune' (ca.1500–1650)*, Leiden: Brill/Nijhoff.

Bibliography 215

Deleuze, G. (2001) 'Immanence: A Life' in Deleuze, G., Boyman, A. (trans.), *Pure Immanence. Essays on Life*, New York: Zone Books, 25–33. Original published in 1995.

Deleuze, G. (2004) *The Logic of Sense*, London: Continuum. Original published in 1969.

Deleuze, G. (2005) *Francis Bacon: The Logic of Sensation*, Smith, D.W. (trans.), London: Continuum. Original published in 1981.

Deleuze, G. (2006) *Nietzsche and Philosophy*, Tomlinson, H. (trans.), London: Continuum Publishing. Original published in 1962.

Deleuze, G. and Guttari, F. (2013) *A Thousand Plateaus. Capitalism and Schizophrenia*, London: Bloomsbury. Original published in 1980.

De Baecque, A. (1997) *The Body Politic: Corporeal Metaphor in Revolutionary France, 1770–1800*, Mandell, S. (trans.), Stanford: Stanford University Press.

De Lubac, H. (2006) *Corpus Mysticum: The Eucharist and the Church in the Middle Ages: A Historical Survey*, Simmonds, G. (trans.), Norwich: SCM Press. Original published in 1949.

De Saint Aubert, E. (2005) 'From Brute Being to Man. A Contextualization of Two Unpublished Merleau-Ponty Notes', *Chiasmi International*, 7, 31–34.

Derman, J. (2011) 'Carl Schmitt on Land and Sea', *History of European Ideas*, 37, 2, 181–189.

Derrida, J. (1998) 'Faith and Knowledge: The Two Sources of "Religion" at the Limits of Reason Alone' in Derrida, J. and Vattimo, G. (eds.), *Religion*, Cambridge: Polity Press, 1–78.

Derrida, J. (2005) *On Touching: Jean-Luc Nancy*, Stanford: Stanford University Press. Original published in 2000.

Dobson, M. J. (2007) *The Army of the Roman Republic: The Second Century BC, Polybius and the Camps at Numantia, Spain*, Oxford: Oxbow Books.

Doremus, A. (2004) 'La théologie politique de Carl Schmitt', *Les études philosophiques*, 68, 1, 65–104.

Eiden, P. (2006) '*Translatio Imperii Ad Americam*. Working through the Poetics and Politics of Empire in Hermann Broch's *The Death of Virgil*', *Literary Imagination*, 8, 3, 441–466.

Elbaz, R. (2003) 'On Canetti's Social Theory', *Heohelicon*, 30, 2, 133–144.

Ellis, J. (2012) 'Shades of Grey: Soft Law and the Validity of Public International Law', *Leiden Journal of International Law*, 25, 2, 313–334.

Esposito, R. (1995) 'Donner la technique', *Revue du MAUSS*, 6, 2, 190–206.

Esposito, R. (1996a) *L'origine della politica: Hannah Arendt o Simone Weil?*, Rome: Donzelli.

Esposito, R. (1996b) 'Réflexions sur l'impolitique', *Philosophie*, 51, 69–87.

Esposito, R. (2005) *Catégories de l'Impolitique*, Le Lirzin, N. (trans.), Paris: Editions du Seuil.

Esposito, R. (2008) *Bíos: Biopolitics and Philosophy*, Campbell, T. C. (trans.), Minneapolis, MN: University of Minnesota Press.

Esposito, R. (2009) 'Preface to Categories of the Impolitical', *Diacritics*, 39, 2, 99–115.

Esposito, R. (2010) *Communitas. The Origin and Destiny of Community*, Campbell, T. C. (trans.), Stanford: Stanford University Press.

Esposito, R. (2011) *Immunitas. The Protection and Negation of Life*, Hanafi, Z. (trans.), Cambridge: Polity Press.

Esposito, R. (2012a) 'The Dispositif of the Person', *Law, Culture and the Humanities*, 8, 1, 17–30.

216 Bibliography

Esposito, R. (2012b) *Third Person,* Hanafi, Z. (trans.), Cambridge: Polity Press.

Esposito, R. (2012c) *Living Thought: The Origins and Actuality of Italian Philosophy,* Hanafi, Z. (trans.), Stanford: Stanford University Press.

Esposito, R. (2013a) 'Totalitarianism or Biopolitics: Toward a Philosophical Interpretation of the Twentieth Century', Welch, R. (trans.), in Esposito, R., *Terms of the Political: Community, Immunity, Biopolitics,* New York: Fordham University Press, 100–111.

Esposito, R. (2013b) 'Community and Violence', Welch, R. (trans.), in Esposito, R., *Terms of the Political: Community, Immunity, Biopolitics,* New York: Fordham University Press, 123–134.

Esposito, R. (2013c) 'Politica e Metafisica', *Filosofia Politica,* 3, December, 465–476.

Esposito, R. (2013d) *Due. La macchina della teologia politica e il posto del pensiero,* Turin: Einaudi.

Ferri, L. and Gauthier, C. (eds.) (2006) *L'Histoire-Bataille: l'écriture de l'histoire dans l'œuvre de Georges Bataille,* Paris: Ecole Nationale Des Chartes.

Fischer, J. (2009) 'Exploring the Core Identity of Philosophical Anthropology through the Works of Max Scheler, Helmuth Plessner, and Arnold Gehlen', *Iris,* 1, 153–170. Online, available at http://www.fupress.net/index.php/iris/article/view/2860/2992 (accessed December 2014).

Foucault, M. (1980) 'Nietzsche, Genealogy, History' in Bouchard, D. F. (trans. and ed.), *Language, Counter-Memory, Practice: Selected Essays and Interviews by Michel Foucault,* Ithaca: Cornell University Press, 139–164.

Foucault, M. (1988) *Technologies of the Self: A Seminar with Michel Foucault,* Martin, L. M. (ed.), Cambridge MA: MIT Press.

Foucault, M. (1991) *Discipline and Punish: The Birth of the Prison,* Sheridan, A. (trans.), London: Penguin.

Foucault, M. (2000) 'What Is Enlightenment?' in Foucault, M., *The Essential Works of Foucault 1954–1984,* Vol. 1, *Ethics,* London: Penguin, 303–320.

Foucault, M. (2002a) '"Omnes et Singulatim": Toward a Critique of Political Reason' in Foucault, M., *The Essential Works of Foucault 1954–1984,* Vol. 3, *Power,* London: Penguin Books, 298–325.

Foucault, M. (2002b) 'The Subject and Power' in Foucault, M., *The Essential Works of Foucault 1954–1984,* Vol. 3, *Power,* London: Penguin Books, 326–348.

Foucault, M. (2003) *The Birth of the Clinic. An Archaeology of Medical Perception,* Sheridan, A. M. (trans.), London: Routledge. French original 1963.

Foucault, M. (2004a) *Society Must be Defended: Lectures at the Collège de France, 1975–76,* Macey, D. (trans.), London: Penguin Books.

Foucault, M. (2004b) 'The Crisis of Medicine or the Crisis of Anti-medicine?' *Foucault Studies,* 1, 5–19. Online, available at http://rauli.cbs.dk/index.php/foucault-studies/issue/view/68/showToc (accessed December 2014).

Foucault, M. (2009) *Security, Territory, Population: Lectures at the Collège de France, 1977–1978,* Burchill, G. (trans.), London: Palgrave.

Foucault, M. (2010) *The Birth of Biopolitics: Lectures at the Collège de France, 1978–1979,* Burchill, G. (trans.), London: Palgrave.

Freud, S. (1955) 'Totem and Taboo' in Strachey, J. (ed.), *The Standard Edition of the Complete Psychological Works of Sigmund Freud,* Vol. XIII (1913–1914), London: The Hogarth Press and the Institute of Psycho-analysis, 1–163.

Freud, S. (1961a) 'Civilization and Its Discontents' in Strachey, J. (ed.), *The Standard Edition of the Complete Psychological Works of Sigmund Freud,* Vol. XXI (1927–1931), London: The Hogarth Press and the Institute of Psychoanalysis, 57–146.

Freud, S. (1961b) 'Dostoevsky and Parricide' in Strachey, J. (ed.), *The Standard Edition of the Complete Psychological Works of Sigmund Freud*, Vol. XXI (1927–1931): The Future of an Illusion, Civilization and Its Discontents, and Other Works, London: The Hogarth Press and the Institute of Psychoanalysis, 173–194.

Freud, S. (1964) 'Moses and Monotheism' in Strachey, J. (ed.), *The Standard Edition of the Complete Psychological Works of Sigmund Freud*, Vol. XXIII (1937–1939), London: The Hogarth Press and the Institute of Psychoanalysis, 3–140.

Friedlander, H. (1997) *The Origins of Nazi Genocide. From Euthanasia to the Final Solution*, Chapel Hill, NC: University of North Carolina Press.

Frydman, B. (2003) 'Divorcing Power and Reason: Spinoza and the Founding of Modern Law', *Cardozo Law Review*, 25, 2, 607–626.

Garelli, J. (2005) 'La Remise en Cause de l'Inconscient Freudien par Merleau-Ponty et Simodon, Selon Deux Notes Inédites de Merleau-Ponty', *Chiasmi International*, 7, 75–89.

Garrett, A. (2003) 'Spinoza as a Natural Lawyer', *Cardozo Law Review*, 25, 2, 627–642.

Gauchet, M. (1989) *La Révolution des droits de l'homme*, Paris: Editions Gallimard.

Gauthier, F. (1992/2014) *Triomphe et mort de la révolution des droits de l'homme et du citoyen: 1789–1795–1802*, Paris: Editions Syllepse.

Gehlen, A. (1957) *Urmensch und Spätkultur*, Frankfurt-Bonn: Athenäum.

Gehlen, A. (1961a) *Anthropologische Forschung. Zur Selbstbegegnung und Selbstentdeckung des Menschen*, Hamburg: Rowoholt.

Gehlen, A. (1961b) *Über kulturelle Kristallisation*, Bremen: Angelsachsen-Verlag.

Gehlen, A. (1969) *Moral und Hypermoral. Eine pluralistische Ethik*, Frankfurt-Bonn: Athenäum.

Gehlen, A. (1980) *Man in the Age of Technology*, Lipscomb, P. (trans.), New York: Columbia University Press. Original published in 1957.

Gehlen, A. (1988) *Man, His Nature and Place in the World*, McMillan, C. and Pillemer, K. (trans.), New York: Columbia University Press. Original published in 1940.

Gehlen, A. (1993) *Der Mensch. Seine Natur und seine Stellung in der Welt (textkritische Edition unter Einbeziehung des gesamten Textes der 1. Auflage von 1940), Gesamtausgabe Bd. 3*, Frankfurt: Vittorio Klostermann.

Gemes, K. and May, S. (eds.) (2011) *Nietzsche on Freedom and Autonomy*, Oxford: Oxford University Press.

Geroulanos, S. (2011) 'Heterogeneities, Slave-Princes, and Marshall Plans: Schmitt's Reception in Hegel's France', *Modern Intellectual History*, 8, 3, 532–560.

Gibbs, R. (2005) 'Jurisprudence is the Organon of Ethics: Kant and Cohen on Ethics, Law, and Religion' in Munk, R. (ed.), *Hermann Cohen's Critical Idealism*, Dordrecht: Springer, 193–230.

Gilman, S. L. (1995) *Franz Kafka, the Jewish Patient*, London: Routledge.

Girard, R. (2001) *I see Satan Fall Like Lightening*, New York: Orbis Books.

Girard, R. (2005) *Violence and the Sacred*, Gregory, P. (trans.), London: Continuum. Original published in 1972.

Girard, R. (2008) *Evolution and Conversion. Dialogues on the Origins of Culture*, London: Continuum.

Girard, R. (2010) *Battling to the End: Conversations with Benoît Chantre*, Walker, M. (trans.), East Lansing, MI: Michigan State University Press.

Goddard, J.-C. (2010) 'Absence de Dieu et Anthropologie de la Peur chez Georges Bataille', *Revue Philosophique de la France et de l'étranger*, 135, 3, 371–380.

218   Bibliography

Goldmann, M. (2012) 'We Need to Cut Off the Head of the King: Past, Present, and Future Approaches to International Soft Law', *Leiden Journal of International Law*, 25, 2, 335–368.

Goodrich, P. and Valverde, M. (eds.) (2005) *Nietzsche and Legal Theory: Half-Written Laws*, London: Routledge.

Gordon, P. E. (2010) *The Continental Divide. Heidegger-Cassirer-Davos*, Cambridge, MA: Harvard University Press.

Guardini, R. (1922) 'Katholische Religion und Jugendbewegung', *Die Schildgenossen*, 2, 2, 96–110.

Guardini, R. (1946) *Der Heilbringer in Mythos, Offenbarung und Politik*, Zurich: Thomas.

Guardini, R. (1954) *La Puissance*, Ancelet-Hustache, J. (trans.), Paris: Editions du Seuil. Original published in 1951 as *Die Macht*, Würzburg: Werkbund.

Guardini, R. (1957) *Sorge um den Menschen*, Vol. I, Würzburg: Werkbund.

Guardini, R. (1996a) *Letters from Lake Como. Explorations in Technology and the Human Race*, Grand Rapids: William B. Eerdmans Publishing Co. Original published in 1927 as *Briefer vom Comer See. Gedanken über die Technik*, Mayence: Matthias Grünwald.

Guardini, R. (1996b) *The Lord*, Washington, DC: Regnery Publishing, Inc. Original published in 1937 as *Der Herr. Betrachtungen über die Person und das Leben Jesu Christi*, Würzburg: Werkbund.

Guardini, R. (1998) *The End of the Modern World*, Wilmington, DE: ISI Books. Original published in 1950 as *Das Ende der Neuzeit*, Basle: Hess.

Guardini, R. (2010) *La polarité: Essai d'un philosophie du vivant concret*, Greisch, J. and Todorovitch, F. B. (trans.), Paris: Editions du Cerf. Original published in 1925 as *Der Gegensatz. Versuche zu einer Philosophie des Lebendig-Konkreten*, Mayence: Matthias Grünwald.

Guchet, X. (2001/02) 'Théorie du lien social, technologie et philosophie: Simondon lecteur de Merleau-Ponty', *Les Etudes Philosophiques*, 57, 2, 219–237.

Guchet, X. (2012) 'Technology, Sociology, Humanism: Simondon and the Problem of the Human Sciences', *Substance: A Review of Theory & Literary Criticism*, 41, 3, 76–92.

Günther, K. (2008) 'Legal Pluralism or Uniform Concept of Law? Globalisation as a Problem of Legal Theory', *No Foundations: Journal of Extreme Legal Positivism*, 5, 5–21.

Haaz, I. (2002) *Les conceptions de corps chez Ribot et Nietzsche*, Paris: L'Harmattan.

Habermas, J. (1990) 'Philosophy as Stand-In and Interpreter' in Habermas, J., Lenhardt, C. and Nicholsen, S. W. (trans.), *Moral Consciousness and Communicative Action*, Cambridge: MIT Press, 1–20.

Haraway, D. (1991a) *Simians, Cyborgs and Women: The Reinvention of Nature*, London: Free Association Books.

Haraway, D. (1991b) 'A Cyborg Manifesto: Science, Technology, and Socialist-Feminism in the Late Twentieth Century' in Haraway, D., *Simians, Cyborgs and Women: The Reinvention of Nature*, London: Free Association Books, 149–182.

Haraway, D. (1991c) 'The Biopolitics of Postmodern Bodies: Constitutions of Self in Immune System Discourse' in Haraway, D., *Simians, Cyborgs and Women: The Reinvention of Nature*, London: Free Association Books, 203–230.

Harnack, A. von (1996) *Marcion: Das Evangelium vom Fremden Gott. Eine Monographie zur Geschichte der Grundlegung der katholischen Kirche*, Darmstadt: Wissenschaftliche Buchgesellschaft. Original published in 1921.

Bibliography   219

Harrington, A. (2006) 'Hermann Broch as a Reader of Max Weber: Protestantism, Rationalization and the "Disintegration of Values"', *History of the Human Sciences*, 19, 4, 1–18.

Heidegger, M. (1962) *Being and Time*, Macquarrie, J. and Robinson, E. (trans.), New York: Harper & Row.

Heidegger, M. (1988) *Les hymnes de Hölderlin: La Germanie et Le Rhin*, Fédier, F. and Hervier, J. (trans.), Paris: Editions Gallimard. Lecture Course of 1934–35.

Heidegger, M. (1997a) *Phenomenological Interpretation of Kant's Critique of Pure Reason*, Emad, P. and Maly, K. (trans.), Bloomington, IN: Indiana University Press.

Heidegger, M. (1997b) *Kant and the Problem of Metaphysics*, Taft, R. (trans.), Bloomington, IN: Indiana University Press.

Heidegger, M. (2000a) *Introduction to Metaphysics*, Fried, G. and Polt, R. (trans.), New Haven, CT: Yale University Press. Original published in 1935.

Heidegger, M. (2000b) *Contributions to Philosophy (from Enowing)*, Emad, P. and Maly, K. (trans.), Bloomington, IN: Indiana University Press. Written in 1936–38, but published posthumously in 1989.

Heidegger, M. (2000c) *Elucidations of Hölderlin's Poetry*, Hoeller, K. (trans.), New York: Humanity Books. Original published in 1944.

Heidegger, M. (2001) *Phenomenological Interpretations of Aristotle: Initiation into Phenomenological Research*, Rojcewicz, R. (trans.), Bloomington, IN: Indiana University Press. Original Lecture Course of 1921–22, and originally published in 1985.

Heidegger, M. (2008a) *The Concept of Time: Prolegomena*, Kisiel, T. (trans.), Bloomington, IN: Indiana University Press.

Heidegger, M. (2008b) *The Fundamental Concepts of Metaphysics: World, Finitude, Solitude*, McNeill, W. and Walker, N. (trans.), Bloomington, IN: Indiana University Press.

Heidegger, M. (2010) 'On the Question Concerning the Determination of the Matter of Thinking', *Epoché*, 14, 2, 213–223.

Heidegger, M. (2011) *Introduction to Philosophy – Thinking and Poetizing*, Braunstein, P. J. (trans.), Bloomington, IN: Indiana University Press.

Herbert, U. (ed.) (2000) *National Socialist Extermination Policies: Contemporary German Perspectives and Controversies*, Oxford: Berghahn Books.

Hobbes, T. (1991) 'De Cive' in Hobbes, T., *Man and Citizen*, Gert, B. (ed.), Indianapolis: Hackett Publishing, 87–386. Original 1642, with Hobbes's translation in 1651.

Hobbes, T. (1998) *The Leviathan*, Gaskin, J. C. A. (ed.), Oxford: Oxford University Press. Original published in 1651.

Hobbes, T. (1999) *The Elements of Law, Natural and Politic*, Gaskin, J. C. A. (ed.), Oxford: Oxford University Press. Original published in 1640.

Hohendahl, P. U. (2008) 'Political Theology Revisited: Carl Schmitt's Postwar Reassessment', *Konturen*, 1, 1–14. Online, available at http://journals:oregondigital.org/konturen/article/view/1266 (accessed December 2014).

Hölderlin, F. (1988) *Friedrich Hölderlin. Essays and Letters on Theory*, Pfau, T. (trans. and ed.), New York: State University of New York Press.

Hölderlin, F. (1998) 'Rousseau' in Hamburger, M. (trans.), *Friedrich Hölderlin. Selected Poems and Fragments*, London: Penguin Books, 49–51.

Hollier, D. (1979) *Le Collège de Sociologie (1937–1939)*, Paris: Gallimard.

Hollier, D. (1990) 'The Dualist Materialism of Georges Bataille', *Yale French Studies*, 78, 124–139.

220 Bibliography

Honneth, A. (2009) 'Problems of Ethical Pluralism: Arnold Gehlen's Anthropological Ethics', *Iris*, 1, 1, 187–194. Online, available at http://www.fupress.net/index.php/iris/article/view/2862 (accessed December 2014).

Ifegan, P. (2010) 'Cutting to the Chase: Carl Schmitt and Hans Blumenberg on Political Theology and Secularization', *New German Critique*, 37, 3, 149–170.

Janaway, C. and Robertson, S. (eds.) (2012) *Nietzsche, Naturalism, and Normativity*, Oxford: Oxford University Press.

Jardine, M. (1995) 'Eric Voegelin's Interpretation(s) of Modernity: A Reconsideration of the Spiritual and Political Implications of Voegelin's Therapeutic Analysis', *Review of Politics*, 57, 4, 581–604.

Jaspers, K. (1997) *Nietzsche: An Introduction to the Understanding of His Philosophical Activity*, Walruff, C. F. and Schmitz, F. J. (trans.), Baltimore, MD: John Hopkins University Press. Original published in 1936.

Jaume, L. (1991) *Echec au libéralisme, les Jacobins et l'État*, Paris: Editions Kimé.

Jaume, L. (1993) *Les Déclarations des droits de l'homme: Du Débat 1789–1793 au Préambule de 1946*, Paris: Editions Flammarion.

Jaume, L. and Troper, M. (eds.) (1998) *1789 et l'Invention de la Constitution*, Paris: LDGJ.

Jhering, R. von (1993) *Geist des römischen Rechts auf den verschiedenen Stufen seiner Entwicklung*, Bd. 1, Aalen: Scientia Verlag. Original published in 1866.

Johnson, D. J. (2010) *Nietzsche's Anti-Darwinism*, Cambridge: Cambridge University Press.

Justinian (2013) *Justinian's Institutes*, Birks, P. and McLeod, G. (trans. and Intro.), Bristol: Bristol Classical Press.

Kant, I. (1996) *The Metaphysics of Morals*, Gregor, M. (trans. and ed.), Cambridge: Cambridge University Press. Original published in 1797.

Kant, I. (1997) *Critique of Practical Reason*, Gregor, M. (trans. and ed.), Cambridge: Cambridge University Press. Original published in 1788.

Kant, I. (1998) *Groundwork of the Metaphysics of Morals*, Gregor, M. (trans. and ed.), Cambridge: Cambridge University Press. Original published in 1785.

Kant, I. (2001) 'On the Miscarriage of All Philosophical Trials in Theodicy' in Wood, A. and Di Giovanni, G. (trans. and eds.), *Religion and Rational Theology*, Cambridge: Cambridge University Press, 19–38. Original published in 1791.

Kant, I. (2003) 'Conjectures on the Beginning of Human History' in Nisbet, H. B. (trans.), *Kant: Political Writings*, Cambridge: Cambridge University Press, 221–233. Original published in 1786.

Kant, I. (2004) 'Religion within the Boundaries of Mere Reason' in Wood, A. and Di Giovanni, G. (trans.), *Religion within the Boundaries of Mere Reason and Other Writings*, Cambridge: Cambridge University Press, 31–191. Original published in 1793.

Kant, I. (2007) *The Critique of Judgment*, Walker, N. and Meredith, J. C. (trans.), Oxford: Oxford University Press. Original published in 1790/1793.

Kantorowicz, E. (1997) *The King's Two Bodies: A Study in Medieval Political Theology*, Princeton, NJ: Princeton University Press. Original published in 1957.

Keech, D. (2012) *The Anti-Pelagian Christology of Augustine of Hippo, 396–430*, Oxford: Oxford University Press.

Kelsen, H. (1963) 'Die Grundlage der Naturrechtslehre', *Osterreichische Zeitschrift für Öffentliches Recht*, 13, 1–37 ('Foundation of the Natural Law Doctrine', *Anglo-American Law Review* (1973), 83, 83–111).

Kelsen, H. (1973) 'God and State' in Kelsen, H., *Essays in Legal and Moral Philosophy*, Weinberger, O. (ed.) and Heath, P. (trans.), Dordrecht: D. Reidel Publishing Co, 61–82. Original published in 1922/23.

Bibliography 221

Kelsen, H. (1991) *General Theory of Norms*, Hartney, M. (trans.), Oxford: Oxford University Press. Original published posthumously in 1979.

Kelsen, H. (1997) *Introduction to the Problems of Legal Theory: A Translation of the First Edition of the Reine Rechtslehre or Pure Theory of Law*, Paulson, S. L. and Paulson, B. L. (trans.), Oxford: Oxford University Press. Original published in 1934.

Kervégan, J.-F. (2007) 'Les amgiguïtés de la théorème. La sécularization, de Schmitt à Löwith et retour' in Foessel, M., Kervégan, J.-F. and Revault d'Allonnes, M. (eds.), *Modernité et sécularisation. Hans Blumenberg, Karl Löwith, Carl Schmitt, Leo Strauss*, Paris: CNRS Editions, 107–117.

Kiss, E. (2004) 'Does Mass Psychology Renaturalize Political Theory? On the Methodological Originality of "Crowds and Power"', *European Legacy*, 9, 6, 725–738.

Kojève, A. (1980) *Introduction to the Reading of Hegel: Lectures on the Phenomenology of Spirit*, Bloom, A. (ed.) and Nichols, H. J. (trans.), New York: Cornell University Press. Originally published in 1947, from a set of lectures given at the Ecole des Haut Etudes between 1933 and 1939, as *Introduction à la Lecture de Hegel*, Paris: Gallimard.

Korsgaard, C. (1996) *The Sources Normativity*, Cambridge: Cambridge University Press.

Korsgaard, C. (2008) *The Constitution of Agency*, Oxford: Oxford University Press.

Korsgaard, C. (2009) *Self-Constitution: Agency, Identity and Integrity*, Oxford: Oxford University Press.

Kramer, M. H. (2004) *John Locke and the Origins of Private Property: Philosophical Explorations of Individualism, Community, and Equality*, Cambridge: Cambridge University Press.

Krieg, R. A. (2004) *Catholic Theologians in Nazi Germany*, London: Athlone Press.

Krüger, H.-P. (2010) 'Persons and Their Bodies: The *Körper/Leib* Distinction and Helmuth Plessner's Theories of Ex-centric Positionality and *Homo absconditus*', *Journal of Speculative Philosophy*, 24, 3, 256–274.

Kuntz, D. and Bachrach, S. D. (2004) *Deadly Medicine. Creating the Master Race*, Chapel Hill, NC: University of North Carolina Press.

Lacoue-Labarthe, P. (2007) *Heidegger and the Politics of Poetry*, Fort, J. (trans.), Chicago, IL: University of Illinois Press.

Laval, C. (1994) *Jeremy Bentham: Le pouvoir des fictions*, Paris: Presses Universitaires de France.

Laval, C. (2003) *Jeremy Bentham: Les artifices du capitalisme*, Paris: Presses Universitaires de France.

Leibniz, G. W. (1990) *Theodicy: Essays on the Goodness of God, the Freedom of Man, and the Origin of Evil*, Huggard, E. M. (trans.), Chicago, IL: Open Court Publishing. Original published in 1710.

Leiris, M. (1979) 'Lettre à Georges Bataille' in Hollier, D. (ed.), *Le Collège de Sociologie (1937–1939)*, Paris: Gallimard, 548–550.

Leiter, B. and Sinhababu, N. (eds.) (2007) *Nietzsche and Morality*, Oxford: Oxford University Press.

Lemm, V. (2009) *Nietzsche's Animal Philosophy: Culture, Politics, and the Animality of the Human Being*, New York: Fordham University Press.

Leroi-Gourhan, A. (1993) *Gesture and Speech*, Berger, A. B. (trans.), Cambridge, MA: MIT Press. Originally published, in French, in 1964, as *Le geste et la parole*, Editions Albin Michel.

Link, J. (1995) *Hölderlin et Rousseau: Retour inventif*, Paris: Presses Universitaires de Vincennes.

222 Bibliography

Locke, J. (1988) *Two Treatises on Government*, Laslett, P. (ed.), Cambridge: Cambridge University Press. Original published in 1689.

Louette, J.-F. (2008) 'Informitas de l'univers et figures humaines. Bataille entre Queneau et Leiris', *Littérature*, 152, 4, 119–133.

Löwith, K. (1957) *Meaning in History: The Theological Implications of the Philosophy of History*, Chicago, IL: University of Chicago Press.

Löwith, K. (1993) *Max Weber and Karl Marx*, Fantel, H. (trans.), London: Routledge. Original published 1960.

Luhmann, N. (1995a) *Social Systems*, Bednarz, J. and Baecker, D. (trans.), Stanford: Stanford University Press.

Luhmann, N. (1995b) 'Legal Argumentation: An Analysis of Its Form', *Modern Law Review*, 58, 3, 285–298.

Luhmann, N. (2008) *Law as a Social System*, Zeigert, K. A. (trans.), Oxford: Oxford University Press.

Luhmann, N. (2013) *Introduction to Systems Theory*, Gilgen, P. (trans.), Cambridge: Polity Press.

Lyotard, F. (2011) *Discourse, Figure*, Hudek, A. (trans.), Minneapolis, MN: University of Minnesota Press. Original published in 1971.

Mackenzie, A. (1996) '"God has No Allergies": Immanent Ethics and the Simulacra of the Immune System', *Postmodern Culture*, 6, 2, available at http://pmc.iath.virginia.edu/text-only/issue.196/mackenzie.196 (accessed December 2014).

Marquard, O. (1984) 'Das gnostische Rezidiv als Gegenneuzeit. Ultrakurztheorem in lockerem Anschluß an Blumenberg' in Taubes, J. (ed.), *Gnosis und Politik*, Munich: Paderborn, 31–36.

Marquard, O. (1989) *Farewell to Matters of Principle: Philosophical Studies*, Wallace, R. M. (trans.), Oxford: Oxford University Press.

Marquard, O. (1991) 'Unburdenings: Theodicy Motives in Modern Philosophy' in Marquard, O. (1991) *In Defense of the Accidental: Philosophical Studies*, Wallace, R. M. (trans.), Oxford: Oxford University Press, 8–28.

Marramao, G. (2000) 'The Exile of the *Nomos*: For a Critical Profile of Carl Schmitt', *Cardozo Law Review*, 21, 1567–1587.

Meaney, M. C. (2007) *Simone Weil's Apologetic Use of Literature. Her Christological Interpretations of Ancient Greek Texts*, Oxford: Oxford University Press.

Merleau-Ponty, M. (1968) *The Visible and the Invisible*, Lingis, A. (trans.), Evanston, IL: Northwestern University Press. Original published posthumously in 1962.

Moinat, F. (2012) *Le vivant et sa naturalisation: Le problème du naturalisme en biologie chez Husserl et le jeune Merleau-Ponty*, Dordrecht: Springer.

Moll, S. (2009) *The Arch-Heretic Marcion*, Tübigen: Mohr Siebeck.

Moore, G. (2006) *Nietzsche, Biology and Metaphor*, Cambridge: Cambridge University Press.

Mouffe, C. (ed.) (1999) *The Challenge of Carl Schmitt*, London: Verso.

Müller-Lauter, W. (1978) 'Der Organismus als innere Kampf: Der Einfluss von Wilhelm Roux und Friedrich Nietzsche', *Nietzsche Studien*, 7, 89–223. English translation in Chapter 6 of Müller-Lauter, W. (1999) *Nietzsche: His Philosophy of Contradictions and the Contradictions of His Philosophy*, Parent, D. J. (trans.), Champaign, IL: University of Illinois Press.

Nadler, S. (2010) *The Best of All Possible Worlds: A Story of Philosophers, God, and Evil in the Age of Reason*, Princeton, NJ: Princeton University Press.

Nancy, J.-L. (1991) *The Inoperative Community*, Connor, P. (ed.), Connor, P., Garbus, L, Holland, M. and Sawhney, S. (trans.), Minneapolis, MN: University of Minnesota Press.

Nancy, J.-L. (1992) 'La Comparution/The Compearance: From the Existence of "Communism" to the Community of "Existence"', *Political Theory*, 20, 3, 371–398.

Nancy, J.-L. (1998) *The Sense of the World*, Librett, J. S. (trans.), Minneapolis, MN: University of Minnesota Press.

Nancy, J.-L. (2003) 'The Unsacrificable' in Nancy, J.-L., *A Finite Thinking*, Stanford: Stanford University Press, 51–77.

Nancy, J.-L. (2008a) 'The Being-with of Being-there', *Continental Philosophy Review*, 41, 1, 1–15.

Nancy, J.-L. (2008b) 'The Intruder' in Nancy, J.-L., *Corpus*, Rand, R. A. (trans.), New York: Fordham University Press, 161–170.

Negri, A. (1999) *The Savage Anomaly: The Power of Spinoza's Metaphysics and Politics*, Hardt, M. (trans.), Minneapolis, MN: University of Minnesota Press.

Negri, A. (2004) *Subversive Spinoza: (Un) Contemporary Variations*, Manchester: Manchester University Press.

Negri, A. (2013) *Spinoza for Our Time: Politics and Postmodernity*, McCuaig, W. (trans.), New York: Columbia University Press.

Nietzsche, F. (1967) *Ecce Homo*, Kaufmann, W. (trans.), New York: Vintage Books. Original written in 1888.

Nietzsche, F. (1974) *The Gay Science*, Kaufmann, W. (trans.), New York: Vintage Books. Original written in 1882.

Nietzsche, F. (1982) *Daybreak: Thoughts on the Prejudices of Morality*, Hollingdale, R. J. (trans.), Cambridge: Cambridge University Press. Original written in 1881.

Nietzsche, F. (1986) *Human, All Too Human: A Book for Free Spirits*, Hollingdale, R. J. (trans.), Cambridge: Cambridge University Press. Original written in 1878.

Nietzsche, F. (1998) *Twilight of the Idols, or How to Philosophize with a Hammer*, Large, D. (trans.), Oxford: Oxford University Press. Original written in 1888.

Nietzsche, F. (2001) *Beyond Good and Evil: Prelude to a Philosophy of the Future*, Norman, J. (trans.), Cambridge: Cambridge University Press. Original written in 1886.

Nietzsche, F. (2003) *Thus Spoke Zarathustra*, Hollingdale, R. J. (trans.), London: Penguin Books. Original written in 1883–1885.

Nietzsche, F. (2006a) *On the Genealogy of Morality*, Cambridge: Cambridge University Press. Original published in 1887.

Nietzsche, F. (2006b) 'Truth and Lies in a Non-Moral Sense' in Ansell-Pearson, K. and Large, D. (eds.), *The Nietzsche Reader*, Oxford: Blackwell Publishing, 114–123. Published posthumously.

Nigro, R. (2012/13) 'Le grondement de la critique du sujet fondateur dans le réveil du sommeil anthropologique', *Rue Descartes*, 75, 3, 60–71.

Nordgaard, S. (2012) 'Body, Sin and Society in Origen of Alexandria', *Studia Theologica – Nordic Journal of Theology*, 66, 1, 20–40.

Ogden, C. K. (2007) *Bentham's Theory of Fictions*, London: Routledge.

Paulson, S. L. (2001) 'Hans Kelsen's Doctrine of Imputation', *Ratio Juris*, 14, 1, 41–63.

Peerbolte, L. J. (1997) 'The *Katechon/Katech_n* of 2. Thess. 2: 6–7', *New Testament* 39, 2, 138–150.

Pfersmann, O. (2003) 'Law's Normativity in Spinoza's Naturalism', *Cardozo Law Review*, 25, 2, 643–656.

224 Bibliography

Plato. (2000) *The Statesman*, Waterfield, R. (trans.), Cambridge: Cambridge University Press.

Plessner, H. (1966) *Diesseits der Utopie*, Diederichs: Düsseldorf-Köln.

Plessner, H. (1975) *Die Stufen des Organischen und der Mensch: Einleitung in die philosophische Anthropologie*, Berlin: Walter de Gruyter.

Plessner, H. (1999) *The Limits of Community: A Critique of Social Radicalism*, Wallace, A. (trans.), New York: Humanity Books. Original published in 1924.

Plessner, H. (2003a) *Gesammelte Schriften*, Bd. 1, *Frühe philosophische Schriften* 1, Frankfurt: Suhrkamp.

Plessner, H. (2003b) *Gesammelte Schriften*, Bd. 3, *Anthropologie der Sinne*, Frankfurt: Suhrkamp.

Plessner, H. (2003c) *Gesammelte Schriften*, Bd. 5, *Macht und menschliche Natur*, Frankfurt: Suhrkamp.

Plessner, H. (2003d) *Gesammelte Schriften*, Bd. 8, *Conditio Humana*, Frankfurt: Suhrkamp.

Poirier, N. (1999) 'Le problème de l'être et la question de l'homme sur la polémique Cassirer – Heidegger', *Le Philosophoire*, 9, 3, 139–149.

Poma, A. (2012) *The Impossibility and Necessity of Theodicy: The 'Essais' of Leibniz*, Dordrecht: Springer.

Quiviger, P.-Y. (2008) *Le principe d'immanence: Métaphysique et droit administratif chez Sieyès*, Paris: Honoré Champion.

Rateau, P. (ed.) (2012) *Lectures et Interpretations des Essais de Theodicee de G. W. Leibniz*, Stuttgart: Franz Steiner Verlag.

Richardson, J. (2008) *Nietzsche's New Darwinism*, Oxford: Oxford University Press.

Ripstein, A. (2009) *Force and Freedom. Kant's Legal and Political Philosophy*, Cambridge, MA: Harvard University Press.

Robilant, A. di (2006) 'Genealogies of Soft Law', *American Journal of Comparative Law*, 54, 3, 499–554.

Rokstad, K. (2013) *Husserl and Merleau-Ponty Inquired into the Historicity of Human Existence*, Berlin: Logos Verlag.

Rorty, A. O. (1991) 'Rousseau's Therapeutic Experiments', *Philosophy*, 66, 258, 413–434.

Rose, G. (1984) *Dialectic of Nihilism: Post-structuralism and Law*, Oxford: Wiley-Blackwell.

Rosen, F. S. (1993) *Jeremy Bentham and Representative Democracy: A Study of the Constitutional Code*, Oxford: Oxford University Press.

Rousseau, J.-J. (1979) *Emile: or, on Education*, Bloom, A. (trans.), New York: Basic Books. Original published in 1762.

Rousseau, J.-J. (1992) *Discourse on the Origin of Inequality*, Cress, D. A. (trans.), Indianapolis, IN: Hackett Publishing. Original published in 1755.

Rupp, E. G. and Watson, P. S. (eds.) (1999) *Luther and Erasmus: Free Will and Salvation*, Philadelphia, PA: Fortress Press.

Scanlon, T. M. (1998) *What We Owe to Each Other*, Cambridge, MA: Harvard University Press.

Scanlon, T. M. (2008) 'Rights and Interests' in Basu, B. and Kanbar, R. (eds.), *Arguments for a Better World: Essays in Honor of Amartya Sen Volume I: Ethics, Welfare, and Measurement*, Oxford: Oxford University Press, 68–79.

Scanlon, T. M. (2011) 'How I Am Not a Kantian' in Parfit, D. (ed.), *On What Matters*, Vol. 2, Oxford: Oxford University Press, 116–139.

Scanlon, T. M. (2014) *Being Realistic About Reasons*, Oxford: Oxford University Press.

Scheler, M. (1958a) 'Philosopher's Outlook' in Scheler, M., *Philosophical Perspectives*, Haac, O. A. (trans.), Boston, MA: Beacon Press, 1–12. Original published in 1928.

Scheler, M. (1958b) 'Man and History' in Scheler, M., *Philosophical Perspectives*, Haac, O. A. (trans.), Boston, MA: Beacon Press, 65–93. Original published in 1926.

Scheler, M. (2009) *The Human Place in the Cosmos*, Frings, M. S. (trans.) Evanston, IL: Northwestern University Press. Original published in 1927.

Schiavone, A. (2012) *The Invention of Law in the West*, Shuggar, A. (trans.), Cambridge, MA: Havard University Press.

Schluchter, W. (2002) 'The Sociology of Law as an Empirical Theory of Validity', *Journal of Classical Sociology*, 2, 3, 257–280.

Schmitt, C. (1965) 'Die vollendete Reformation', *Der Staat*, 4, 51–65.

Schmitt, C. (1986) *Political Romanticism*, Oakes, G. (trans.), Cambridge, MA: MIT Press. Original published in 1919.

Schmitt, C. (1990) 'The Plight of European Jurisprudence', *Telos,* 83, 35–70.

Schmitt, C. (1993) 'The Age of Neutralizations and Depoliticizations', *Telos,* 96, 130–142. Originally delivered as a lecture in 1929, and subsequently published, in 1932, as 'Das Zeitalter der Neutralisierung und Entpolitisierung', in the third edition of *Der Begriff des Politischen*, Munich: Duncker und Humblot.

Schmitt, C. (1996a) *Roman Catholicism and Political Form*, Ulmen, G. L. (ed. and trans.), Westport, CT: Greenwood Press. Original published in 1923.

Schmitt, C. (1996b) *The Leviathan in the State Theory of Thomas Hobbes: Meaning and Failure of a Symbol*, Schwab, G. and Hilfstein, E. (trans.), Westport, CT: Greenwood Press. Original published 1938.

Schmitt, C. (2003) *The Nomos of the Earth in the International Law of the Jus Publicum Europeaum*, Ulmen, G. L. (trans.), New York: Telos Press. Original published in 1950.

Schmitt, C. (2006) *Political Theology. Four Chapters on the Concept of Sovereignty*, Schwab, G. (trans.), Chicago, IL: Chicago University Press. Original published in 1922.

Schmitt, C. (2007) *The Concept of the Political*, Schwab, G. (ed. and trans.), Chicago, IL: Chicago University Press. Original published in 1932.

Schmitt, C. (2008a) *Constitutional Theory*, Seitzer, J. (ed. and trans.), Durham, NC/London: Duke University Press. Original published in 1928.

Schmitt, C. (2008b) *Political Theology II: The Myth of Closure of Any Political Theology*, Hoezel, M. and Ward, G. (ed. and trans.), Cambridge, MA: Polity Press. Original published in 1970.

Schmitt, C. (2009) 'Three Possibilities for a Christian Conception of History', *Telos*, 147, 167–170. Original published in 1950.

Schofield, P. (2006) *Utility and Democracy: The Political Thought of Jeremy Bentham*, Oxford: Oxford University Press.

Schroeder, M. (2007) *Slaves of the Passions*, Oxford: Oxford University Press.

Schroeder, M. (2010) *Noncognitivism in Ethics*, London: Routledge.

Schroeder, M. (2014) *Explaining the Reasons We Share: Explanation and Expression in Ethics*, Vol. 1, Oxford: Oxford University Press.

Sen, A. (2000) 'Consequential Evaluation and Practical Reason', *Journal of Philosophy*, 97, 9, 477–502.

Sen, A. (2004) 'Elements of a Theory of Human Rights', *Philosophy & Public Affairs*, 32, 4, 315–356.

Sigwart, H.-J. (2006) 'Modes of Experience – On Eric Voegelin's *Theory of Governance*', *Review of Politics*, 68, 2, 259–286.

226 Bibliography

Simón, F. M. (2008) 'Images of Transition: The Ways of Death in Celtic Hispania', *Proceedings of the Prehistoric Society*, 74, 53–68.

Simondon, G. (1986) *L'individu et sa genèse physico-biologique*, Grenoble: Editions Jérôme Millon. Original published in 1964.

Simondon, G. (2005) *L'Individu à la lumière des notions de forme et d'information*, Grenoble: Jérôme Millon.

Simondon, G. (2007) *L'individuation psychique et collective: A la lumière des notions de Forme, Information, Potentiel et Métastabilité*, Paris: Editions Aubier. Original written in 1958, but only published in 1986.

Simondon, G. (2012) *Two Lessons on Man and Animal*, Burk, D. S. (trans.), Minneapolis, MN: Univocal Publishing.

Spinoza, B. (2003) 'Political Treatise' in Shirely, S. (trans.), *Spinoza. Complete Works*, Cambridge, MA: Hackett Publishing, 676–754. Original published posthumously, and uncompleted, in 1677.

Stegmaier, W. (2006) 'Nietzsche's Doctrines, Nietzsche's Signs', *Journal of Nietzsche Studies*, 31, 20–41.

Steinbrecher, T. (2007) 'La Théodicée réhabilitée ou Kant versus Elihu', *Archives de Philosophie*, 70, 2, 201–226.

Stiegler, B. (1998) *Technics and Time, 1: The Fault of Epimetheus*, Beardsworth, A. and Collins, G. (trans.), Stanford: Stanford University Press. Original published in 1994.

Stiegler, B. (2001) *Nietzsche et la biologie*, Paris: Presses Universitaires de France.

Surya, M. (1995) 'L'Arbitraire. Après Tout' in Hollier, D. (ed.), *Georges Bataille Après Tout*, Paris: Belin, 213–232.

Taminaux, J. (1997) *The Thracian Maid and the Professional Thinker: Arendt and Heidegger*, Gendre, M. (trans.), Albany, NY: State University of New York Press.

Tassin, E. (2007) '"... sed victa Catoni": The Defeated Cause of Revolutions', *Social Research*, 74, 4, 1109–1126.

Tauber, A. (1997) *The Immune Self, Theory or Metaphor?*, Cambridge: Cambridge University Press.

Taylor, D. (2001) 'Hannah Arendt on Judgment: Thinking for Politics', *International Journal of Philosophical Studies*, 10, 2, 151–169.

Toadvine, T. and Embree, L. (eds.) (2010) *Merleau-Ponty's Reading of Husserl*, Dordrecht: Springer.

Tocqueville, A. (2003) *Writings on Empire and Slavery*, Pitts, J. (trans. and ed.), Baltimore, MD: John Hopkins University Press.

Tocqueville, A. (2004) *Democracy in America*, Goldhammer, A. (trans.), New York: The Library of America. Original published in two volumes, in 1835 and 1840 respectively.

Tönnies, F. (2001) *Community and Civil Society*, Hollis, M. (trans.), Cambridge: Cambridge University Press. Original published in 1887.

Tusseau, G. (2003) *Jeremy Bentham et le droit constitutionnel. Une approche de l'utilisarisme*, Paris: L'Harmattan.

Tyson, J. B. (2006) *Marcion and Luke-Acts. A Defining Struggle*, Columbia, SC: University of South Carolina Press.

Tzamalikos, P. (2007) *Origen: Philosophy of History & Eschatology*, Leiden: Brill.

Ungar, S. (1990) 'Phantom Lascaux: The Origin of the Work of Art', *Yale French Studies*, 78, 246–262.

Vattimo, G. (1988) *The End of Modernity. Nihilism and Hermeneutics in Post-modern culture*, Oxford: Polity Press.

Bibliography   227

Vattimo, G. (2002) *Nietzsche: An Introduction*, Martin, N. (trans.), Stanford: Stanford University Press. Original published in 1985.

Vetö, M. (1997) *La Métaphysique Religieuse De Simone Weil*, Paris: Harmattan.

Virno, P. (2009) 'Angels and the General Intellect: Individuation in Duns Scotus and Gilbert Simondon', *Parrhesia*, 7, 58–67. Online, available at: http://www.parrhesiajournal.org/parrhesia07/parrhesia07_virno.pdf (accessed July 2014).

Voegelin, E. (1953a) 'The Origins of Totalitarianism', *Review of Politics*, 53, 1, 68–76.

Voegelin, E (1953b) 'The Origins of Totalitarianism: A Concluding Remark', 53, 1: *Review of Politics*, 84–85.

Voegelin, E. (1987) *The New Science of Politics. An Introduction*, Chicago, IL: Chicago University Press. Original published in 1952.

Voegelin, E. (2001) 'Review Essay of *Verfassungslehre*, by Carl Schmitt (Munich: Dunker und Humbolt, 1928)' in Voegelin, E., *Collected Works*, Vol. 13, *Selected Book Reviews*, Cockerill, J. and Cooper, B. (eds. and trans.), Columbia, MO/London: University of Missouri Press. Original published in 1931.

Voegelin, E. (2007) *Collected Works*, Vol. 30, *Selected Correspondence 1950–1984*, Hollweck, T. A. (ed.), Alder, S., Hollweck, T. A. and Petropulos, W. (trans.), Columbia, MO/London: University of Missouri Press.

Volpi, F. (2001) 'Heidegger et la romanité philosophique', *Revue de métaphysique et de morale*, 31, 3, 287–300.

Waldron, J. (2002) *God, Locke, and Equality: Christian Foundations in Locke's Political Thought*, Cambridge: Cambridge University Press.

Waterlot, G. (2010) 'Expérience spirituelle et loi naturelle: une approache de Simone Weil', *Revue d'éthique et de théologie morale*, Hors-série 7, 185–200.

Watson, A. (1992) 'Seventeenth-century Jurists, Roman Law, and the Law of Slavery', *Chicago-Kent Law Review*, 68, 3, 1343–1354.

Weber, D. (2009) *Hobbes et le corps de Dieu*, Paris: Vrin.

Weber, M. (1978) *Economy and Society. An Outline of an Interpretative Sociology*, Roth, G. and Wittich, C. (eds.), Berkeley, CA: University of California Press.

Weil, S. (1987a) 'Reflections on War' in McFarland, D. T. and Ness, W. van (trans. and eds.), *Formative Writings 1929–1941*, London: Routledge. Original published in 1933.

Weil, S. (1987b) *Intimations of Christianity amongst the Greeks*, Geissbuhler, E. C. (ed. and trans.), London: Routledge.

Weil, S. (1994)*, Cahier III*, Oeuvres complètes, t.VI, vol. 1, Paris: Editions Gallimard.

Weil, S. (1997) *Cahier VII*, Oeuvres complètes, t.VI, vol. 2, Paris: Editions Gallimard.

Weil, S. (1999) 'L'Allemagne en Attente' in de Lussy, F. (ed.), *Oeuvres*, Paris: Gallimard, 221–238.

Weil, S. (2001a) 'Prospects: Are We Heading for the Proletarian Revolution?' in Weil, S., *Oppression and Liberty*, Wills, A. and Petrie, J. (trans.), London: Routledge, 1–23. Original published in *Revolution prolétarienne*, No. 158, 25 August 1933.

Weil, S. (2001b) 'Reflections Concerning the Causes of Oppression and Liberty' in Weil, S., *Oppression and Liberty*, Wills, A. and Petrie, J. (trans.), London: Routledge, 36–117. Originally published, posthumously, in 1955, as *Oppresssion et liberté*, Paris: Gallimard.

Weil, S. (2002) *Cahier XI*, Oeuvres complètes, t.VI, vol. 3, Paris: Editions Gallimard.

Weil, S. (2002a) *Gravity and Grace*, Crawford, E. and von der Ruhr, M. (trans.), London: Routledge. Originally published, posthumously, in 1947, as *La Pesanteur et la grâce*, Paris: Librarie PLON.

228 Bibliography

Weil, S. (2002b) *Letter to a Priest*, Wills, A. (trans.), London: Routledge. Originally published, posthumously, in 1951, as *Lettre à un religieux*, Paris: Gallimard.

Weil, S. (2002c) *The Need for Roots. Prelude to a Declaration of Duties towards Mankind*, Wills, A. (trans.), London: Routledge. Originally published, posthumously, in 1949, as *L'Enracinement*, Paris: Gallimard.

Weil, S. (2005a) *War and the Illiad*, McCarthy, M. (trans.), New York: New York Review of Books. Original published in 1940.

Weil, S. (2005b) 'Human Personality' in Miles, S. (ed.), *Simone Weil: An Anthology*, London: Penguin Books, 69–98. Original published posthumously, in 1957.

Weir, L. (2013) 'Roberto Esposito's Political Philosophy of the Gift', *Angelaki*, 18, 3, 155–167.

Wennerlind, C. and Schabas, M. (eds.) (2007) *David Hume's Political Economy*, London: Routledge.

Wiser, L. (1980) 'From Cultural Analysis to Philosophical Anthropology: An Examination of Voegelin's Concept of Gnosticism', *Review of Politics*, 42, 1, 92–104.

Worms, F. (2007) 'Les effets de la nécessité sur l'âme humaine: Simone Weil et le moment philosophique de la seconde guerre mondiale', *Les Etudes Philosophiques*, 82, 3, 223–237.

Yar, M. (2000) 'From Actor to Spectator: Hannah Arendt's "Two Theories" of Political Judgment', *Philosophy & Social Criticism*, 26, 1, 1–27.

Zarka, Y.-C. (1987) *La décision métaphysique de Hobbes: Conditions de la politique*, Paris: Vrin.

Zarka, Y.-C. (2001) *Hobbes et la pensée politique moderne*, Paris: Presses Universitaires de France.

Zerilli, L. (2005) '"We Feel Our Freedom". Imagination and Judgment in the Thought of Hannah Arendt', *Political Theory*, 33, 2, 158–188.

Index

A Living Thought. Esposito, Roberto 1, 9, 205
Abel 72
absolutism 86–7
Accursed Share. Bataille, Georges 76
action, notion of 15, 31, 48–9, 58–9, 202–4
Adam 71–2
The Aeneid 39–42
affirmative biopolitics 141–7, 173–96, 205–6
Agamben, Giorgio 125, 142–7
American Revolution 31–3
Ancient Greece 31, 54, 69, 76, 97–9, 181–2
Anglo-American communitarianism 3–4
Anglo-American moral philosophy 202, 204, 206
animals 86, 102, 127, 174, 176, 183, 187, 199, 206
anthropology 5, 45–56, 126–33: negativism 21, 43–5, 46–56; nihilism 125; philosophico-anthropological presupposition 158; political 21, 52, 83–4; unpolitical 21, 28, 30
Apel, Karl-Otto 3–4
aporias 31, 33–7, 199: anthropology 45; biopolitics 144, 146, 159; *communitas* 70, 76, 85, 89, 91, 105–6; constitution 35–7; democracy 144; exclusionary inclusion 106, 113; experience 21, 70, 76; historical transition and development 15; hyper-political 16–19; *immunitas* 105–6, 146; legal aporias

35–7; new aporias 35–6; revealability 119–20; subject, theory of the 201; unpolitical 18, 21, 31, 34–7, 69–70
L'apprenti sorcier. Bataille, Georges 63
Arendt, Hannah 20–1, 31–8: biopolitics 181–4; *Civil Disobedience* 35–6; *The Human Condition* 30–1; *Lectures on Kant's Political Philosophy* 20, 34; *The Life of the Mind* 20, 31–2, 34; *On Revolution* 20, 31–2; *On Violence* 35–6; *The Origins of Totalitarianism* 29–30; unpolitical 20–1, 37–8
Aristotle 143–4
art and culture 76–7, 101
atheism 22, 58–9
Augustine of Hippo, saint 71–2, 121, 123
Augustus, Roman emperor 39–42
authenticity and inauthenticity 95–6
Auto da Fé. Canetti, Elias 43–4
autopoeisis 116–17

Bacon, Francis 186–7
bare life 143–6, 179, 183
Bataille, Georges 11, 46, 56–67, 74–7, 79: *Accursed Share* 76; *L'apprenti sorcier* 63; *Chronique nietzschéenne* 3, 64–5; *communitas* 2–3, 5, 19, 56–67, 71, 75, 99–104, 107–9; *L'Expérience intérieur* 60, 63; *Nietzsche et les Fascistes* 65; non-knowledge 99–102; *La Part Maudite* 65; *Propositions sur le fascime* 64–5; *Sur Nietzsche* 60, 63; *Theory of Religion* 76–7, 101
Being and Time. Heidegger, Martin 94, 96–7, 183

230 Index

being-in-common: *communitas* 2–3, 78–81, 84, 86–7, 91–2, 95, 107; *Dasein* 75; finitude and death 69; *munus* 5, 111; state of nature 83
being-in-the-world 75, 95
Being Realistic about Reasons. Scanlon, Thomas M. 202
Benjamin, Walter 111, 113–14, 118
Bentham, Jeremy 8, 164–5
Benveniste, Émile 119–20
Bichat, Xavier 135
biocracy 174
bioethics 7–8, 110, 140–1, 147
bio-history 151
biologism 169–70, 183
biology: biocracy 174; exclusionary inclusion 5–6, 105; factical life and biology 182–3; final figure of biology 6; law 147; normality and abnormality 193
biomedicine 5, 7, 104–8, 119
biopolitics 148–72; affirmative 141–7, 173–96, 205–6; Arendt 181–4; bio-history 151; biologism 169–70, 183; birth 180–2, 187–90; *communitas* 7, 77, 157–8, 168–9, 174, 184, 197–8; death 8, 148, 150–1, 153–6, 161, 172–4, 177–9; deconstruction and reconstruction 133–4; Deleuze 142, 171, 184, 186–7, 192, 194–6, 206; exclusionary inclusion 7, 110; Foucault 148–59, 165–6, 168, 173; globalization 207; Heidegger 181–4; Hobbes 134, 160, 162, 164; immunisation 7–8, 133, 141–8, 156–78, 181, 187–8, 195, 197–8; *immunitas* 7, 77, 133–8, 157, 197–8; Kant 148–9, 163; life 8, 148, 150, 154–6, 159–68, 171–2; limits of Foucauldian biopolitics 148–56; modernity 143–52, 155, 158–66, 170, 174, 181, 197; *munus* 199; Nietzsche 142, 148–9, 166–72, 173; person, notion of the 199–200; site of biopolitics 149; sovereignty 7, 149–51, 153–5, 159–66; thanatopolitics 174–81, 184, 196, 197–8 *see also* biopolitics and immunisation; National Socialism and biopolitics

biopolitics and immunisation 156–77; hyperimmunitary logic 170–2; life, politics of 198; modernity 158, 170; origin, notion of 166–7; paradigm 148, 158, 181, 195; self-preservation 158–9, 165
bíos see biopolitics
Bíos: Biopolitics and Philosophy. Esposito, Roberto 1, 7–9, 77, 141–96, 197
bio-thanatological principle 146–7
birth 180–3, 187–90, 192
The Birth of the Clinic. Foucault, Michel 135
Blumenberg, Hans 157
body: biopolitics 179, 184–6; desubstantialisation of the body 139; lived body (*Leib*) and physical body (*Körper*) 129; politic, metaphor of 7; primacy of body 185
Böhlendorff, Casimir Ulrich. *Fernando* 98
Broch, Hermann 21, 37–43, 46
bureaucracy 50–2

caesura 97–8, 182
Caillois, Roger 61–3
Cain 71–2
Canetti, Elias 21, 43–56: *Auto da Fé* 43–4; *Crowds and Power* 44; *The Human Province* 44, 47; *Kafka's Other Trial: The Letters to Felice* 47; negative anthropology 46–56; *The Play of the Eyes* 43, 47–8; *The Wedding Party* 43
Canguilheim, Georges 142, 184, 192–3, 196
capitalism 50–1
caring-in-common 95
Cassirer, Ernst 93, 106
categorical imperative 74, 91–2, 93
Catégories de l'Impolitique. Esposito, Roberto 1–3, 10–12, 14, 18–68, 71, 73–6, 100
Chestov, Leon 58–9
Christianity: Christian Monarch and Christian Church, division of competences between 122; de-formalisation 13; evil 120–4; Gnosticism 28; heterodoxy 53;

idolatry 54; *immunitas* 120–4; modernity 12–13; person, notion of the 199–200; political theology 20; polytheism 28; Reformation 123; *res publica christiana* 71; Roman Catholic Church 20–4, 54; Roman Empire 185; salvation 23, 121, 123; secularisation 13, 20, 54; state of nature 72; transcendence 28–30; victims, identification with 62 *see also* Jesus Christ

Chronique nietzschéenne. Bataille, Georges 3, 64–5

civil disobedience 36–7

Civil Disobedience. Arendt, Hannah 35–6

Civilization and Its Discontents. Freud, Sigmund 83

classical Marxism 50–2

co-existence 5, 49, 72, 75, 93–9, 174, 204–5

Cohen, Hermann 106

Cold War 180

Collège de Sociologie 60–3

common non-belonging 3, 70, 78

communication and immunisation 6–7, 117–18

communitarianism 3–4, 65, 94

communitas 1–5, 78–102; aporias 70, 76, 85, 89, 91; Bataille 2–3, 5, 19, 56–67, 71, 75, 99–104, 107–9; being-in-common 2–3, 78–81, 84, 86–7, 91–2, 95, 107; biopolitics 7, 77, 157–8, 168–9, 174, 184, 197–8; death 19, 62–3, 68–72, 77–81, 84, 100–1, 107; etymology 3–4, 69–70, 78–9; exclusionary inclusion 130; finitude 2, 63–4, 68–70, 76–9, 91–4, 98–101, 107; genealogy 10–19, 71, 74–7; Heidegger 69, 71, 74–6, 79, 93–9, 102, 104, 107–9; Hobbes 4, 72–4, 88, 107, 111; *immunitas* 8, 76, 79, 83–7, 104, 138–41, 146; Kant 4, 74–5, 79, 87–95, 97, 107, 109; law 10–19, 66–7, 74, 87–93, 97, 109, 111; *munus* 70–3, 76, 78–80, 88–9, 106–7; negativity 46–57, 75; nihilism 3–4, 73, 100, 102; 'own', community as which is most properly our 78; Rousseau 4, 73–4, 79, 84–9,

107; self-preservation 158; unpolitical 2–3, 10–19, 46–7, 68–77; Weil 2–3, 46–59, 69 *see also Communitas* to *Immunitas*, from

Communitas to *Immunitas*, from 5–6, 103–9: aporias 105–6; bioethics 140; biomedical discourse 105–7; biopolitics 7, 77, 157, 197–8; common immunity 138, 141, 147; etymological approach to *Immunitas* 103, 108; etymological derivation of *communitas* 103; exclusionary inclusion 5, 105–9; immunisation 8, 79, 107–9, 129–31, 158; interpretative category, *immunitas* as 104; law 109, 111; *munus* 5, 103–4, 107–8; negation of life 76; sacrifice 83

Communitas: The Origin and Destiny of Community. Esposito, Roberto 1, 3, 5, 67–109

community *see communitas*

The Concept of the Political. Schmitt, Carl 14, 66

Conjectures on the Beginning of Human History. Kant, Immanuel 89

conservatio vitae 159–60

constitution and legal norms of constitutional law, distinction between 27

constitutions 35–7

Contributions to Philosophy (from Enowing). Heidegger, Martin 97, 183

Corpus juris civilis 200

Corpus. Nancy, Jean-Luc 139

crime 62, 81, 83–5, 112

critical legal studies 1–2

The Critique of Judgment. Kant, Immanuel 34, 92

The Critique of Practical Reason. Kant, Immanuel 90–1

The Critique of Violence. Benjamin, Walter 113–14

Crowds and Power. Canetti, Elias 44

crucifixion 22–3, 62

culture and art 76–7, 101

Darwin, Charles 169–70

Dasein 75, 93–8, 183

Davos Lecture Series of 1929 93

232 Index

death: aporias 120; biologism 183; biopolitics 8, 148, 150–1, 153–6, 161, 172–4, 177–9; bio-thanatological principle 146–7; *communitas* 19, 62–3, 68–72, 77–81, 84, 100–1, 107; destiny 22, 63; eugenics 177; euthanasia 177–8; exclusionary inclusion 105; fear of death 100–1; finitude 63, 68–9, 77; gift of death 81–2; God 59; Great Death 178; *immunitas* 120, 123, 135, 141, 177; Monarch, of the 122; National Socialism 142, 147, 173–9, 188, 196; negation of nature 57–9; politics of death 8, 142, 148, 150, 172, 173; power 114, 154, 156; right to death 150; sacrifice 5, 76, 83–4, 101, 120; sovereignty 150, 153, 161; state of nature 72, 100–1; unpolitical 5, 65, 68

The Death of Virgil. Broch, Hermann 38–42

Debord, Guy 144

deconstruction and reconstruction 133–4

deformalisation of law 207–8

degeneration 170–1, 173–8

Deleuze, Gilles: biopolitics 142, 171, 184, 186–7, 192, 194–6, 206; *Francis Bacon: the Logic of Sensation* 186–7; *Nietzsche and Philosophy* 171

democracy 27, 38, 42, 54, 143–4

Derrida, Jacques 119–20, 125

desire 54–5, 99–100, 114, 160, 203–4

destiny 3, 22, 63, 75–6, 96

destitution 78–9

desubstantialisation of the body 139

Digest 205–6

Discipline and Punish. Foucault, Michel 150

donum 3, 70

double enclosure of the body 179, 184–5

drives and instincts 11–12

Due. La macchina della teologia politica e il posto del pensiero. Esposito, Roberto 208–9

Durkheim, Emile 61

Elements of Police. Justi, Johann Heinrich Gottlob von 153

end of history 58–60

End of the Modern World. Guardini, Romano 25

Erasmus, Desiderius 123

eschatology of redemption 123

eternal return, notion of 60

ethics: bioethics 110, 140, 147; historical becoming 38; meta-ethics 202–4; non-positivism (morality) 2; positivism (law) 2, 18; purpose 57

eugenics 175–7

euthanasia 177–8

evil 40, 72, 74, 89–90, 114, 120–4

exclusionary inclusion 5–9: *communitas* 5, 105–9, 130; *immunitas* 5, 7, 105–16, 118–19, 125–36, 140, 145;immunisation 8, 107–8, 110, 129, 158, 171, 173–5, 181, 195

existential-anthropological condition 21

L'Expérience intérieur. Bataille, Georges 60, 63

Fascism 64–5

factory, organisation of the 50–1

fear 80, 100–1

Fernando. Böhlendorff, Casimir Ulrich 98

finitude 2–3, 99: biopolitics 133; *communitas* 2, 63–4, 68–70, 76–9, 91–4, 98–101, 107; death 63, 68–9, 77; *immunitas* 140; theodicy 125

force 52–3, 56, 112, 131

Foucault, Michel 7–8, 133–8, 140, 141–3, 145: biopolitics 148–59, 165–6, 168, 173; *The Birth of the Clinic* 135; *Discipline and Punish* 150; *Lecture Courses* 150

France: French Revolution 31–3, 134–5, 188, 201; sociology 61

Francis Bacon: the Logic of Sensation. Deleuze, Gilles 186–7

fraternity 188–9

freedom 31–5, 49, 89–90, 164–6

French Revolution 31–3, 134–5, 188, 201

Freud, Sigmund 83–4

friend/enemy distinction 59, 66

The Fundamental Concepts of Metaphysics. Heidegger, Martin 94, 183

Galton, Francis 176
Gehlen, Arnold 125–6, 131–3
Geist des römischen Rechts. Jhering,
  Rudolf von 112
genealogy: *communitas* 10–19, 71, 74–7;
  genealogico-historical presentation
  152; immunisation 110, 195; law
  10–19; Nietzschean genealogy 148;
  person, notion of the 201–3; teleology
  96; unpolitical 11–12, 73; will, theory
  of the 33
Der Gegensatz. Guardini, Romano 24
genocide 155, 173, 177–80
Germany *see* National Socialism
Gewalt 113
gift, notion of the 69, 71–2, 80–2, 106–7
  see also munus
Girard, René 111, 114–16, 118
Girardian scapegoat 114
globalization 207
Gnosticism 28
God: absence of God 54; creation 55–6,
  72, 89, 121, 123–4; death 59; evil
  123–4; experience of God 53–4; God-
  in-becoming 128–9; humans, boundary
  between gods and 114; idolatry 55; law
  as God's will 22; polytheism 28, 39;
  reality 56; secularisation 25; Spirit, as
  55, 128–9; transcendence 28–9, 114;
  unity and separation 71–2
governance 7, 24, 135–6
government, vertical and horizontal
  movement of 153
Groundwork of the Metaphysics of Morals.
  Kant, Immanuel 90
Guardini, Romano 14, 20, 22–6
guilt 4, 73, 83–7, 114

Habermas, Jürgen 3–4, 106
Haraway, Donna 138–9
Hegel, G.W.F. 58–60, 97
Heidegger, Martin: *Being and Time* 94,
  96–7, 183; biopolitics 181–4;
  coexistence 5; *communitas* 69, 71,
  74–6, 79, 93–9, 102, 104, 107–9;
  *Contributions to Philosophy (from
  Enowing)* 97, 183; *The Fundamental
  Concepts of Metaphysics* 94, 183;

*History of the Concept of Time:
  Prolegomena* 94; *immunitas* 119;
  Introduction to Metaphysics 97; *Kant
  and the Problem of Metaphysics* 75, 93;
  *Phenomenological Interpretation of
  Kant's Critique of Pure Reason* 75, 93
heterodoxy 46, 48–56, 101
history: becoming 38–9; bio-history 151;
  end of history 58–60; genealogico-
  historical presentation 152; negativity
  85; secularisation 11, 15; socio-
  historical development, law of 62–3;
  thinking and reflection, relationship
  between 2; transition and development
  15
*History of the Concept of Time:
  Prolegomena*. Heidegger, Martin 94
Hitler, Adolf 142, 178
Hobbes, Thomas: absolutism 87;
  biopolitics 134, 160, 162, 164;
  communitas 4, 72–4, 88, 107, 111;
  Hobbesian moment 101, 111; hyper-
  political 18; *Immunitas* 79–86, 107,
  111, 118, 162, 164; individualism 86;
  Leviathan 13–14, 15, 72–3, 79, 81–3;
  paradigm of order 17; sacrifice 100–1;
  sovereignty 8, 160, 162; state of nature
  4, 72–3, 80, 83–5, 100, 160, 164
Hölderlin, Friedrich 5, 76, 97–9
Homo Sacer, definition of 143
*Homo Sacer: Sovereign Power and Bare
  Life*. Agamben, Giorgio 142–3, 145–7
homogeneity 59, 177
The Human Condition. Arendt, Hannah
  30–1
The Human Province. Canetti, Elias 44, 47
Hume, David 163
hyper-political 16–19, 33

ideals and values 11–12, 20, 38–9
idion 182
idolatry 54–5
immanence: antagonism 198, 207; bare life
  144–6; biopolitics 161, 192–6, 198–9;
  communitas 58, 198; form-of-life 147;
  life 147, 167; reciprocity 192–6; sacred
  and profane, relationship between 61;
  subjectivity 152; totalitarianism 29–30;
  transcendence 27–8, 60, 194–6, 198

234 Index

The Immune Self. Tauber, Alfred 139
immunisation 8, 108–9, 110: artificial
forms 160, 162–3; autoimmunisation
174; communication 6–7, 117–18;
communitas 8, 79, 107–9, 129–31, 146,
158; eugenics 175–7; exclusionary
inclusion 8, 107–8, 110, 129, 158, 171,
173–5, 181, 195; hyperimmunitary
logic 170–2; legal immunisation 6, 111,
118; life 133–4, 156–7, 168–9, 177;
logic of immunisation 8, 113, 118,
162–7, 170–2; modernity 8, 17, 141–2,
157–8, 160, 170; National Socialism
142, 146–7, 174–80, 188, 195; origin,
notion of 166–7; paradigm 107–9, 145,
148, 156–60, 172, 174–6, 178, 181,
185; political immunisation 134;
preventive immunisation 109, 130–1;
social immunisation 117–18;
sovereignty 160, 164 *see also*
biopolitics and immunisation
immunitas 110–40; biopolitics 133–8,
141–7; common immunity 138–40,
141; *communitas* 8, 76, 79, 83–7, 104,
138–41, 146; death 120, 123, 135, 141,
177; etymology 103, 108; exclusionary
inclusion 110–16, 118–19, 125–36,
140, 145; finitude 2, 63–4, 68–70,
76–8, 91–4, 98–101, 107, 125, 133,
140; Hobbes 79–86, 107, 111, 118,
162, 164; immanence 198; law 6,
110–18; legal immunisation 111; life,
relationship with 133–8; modernity
145–6; philosophical anthropology
126–33; preventative immunization
130–1; self-dissolution 7, 110–11, 118,
138, 140, 160, 172, 174, 195; social
immunisation 117–18; theology
118–25; violence 6, 111, 113–18, 131
see also Communitas to *Immunitas*,
from; immunisation
*Immunitas: The Protection and Negation
of Life.* Esposito, Roberto 1, 5, 7–8, 67,
77, 103–9, 111, 138, 140–7, 157
impersonal singularity 192, 194, 205
impolitical *see* unpolitical
inclusion *see* exclusionary inclusion
individualism 3–4, 86, 201–2

individuation 189–90, 193
Indo-European Languages and Society.
Benveniste, Émile 119
inoculation or vaccination 171
The Inoperative Community. Nancy, Jean-
Luc 64
Institutes 200, 205
institutions 15, 120, 131–3
international agreements, forms of 208
international law 207–8
Introduction to Metaphysics. Heidegger,
Martin 97

Jaspers, Karl 58–60
Jesus Christ: absolute decision, as point of
25; Christian Monarch 122–3;
crucifixion 22–3, 62; decision, as 24–5;
incarnation 22, 120–2, 186;
resurrection 71, 120, 122–3; sacrifice
71; second coming 121; transcendence
122
Jhering, Rudolf von. *Geist des römischen
Rechts* 112
judgment, faculty of reflective 34–5, 91–2
juridical space of Europe 26
juris-naturalism 190–1
Justi, Johann Heinrich Gottlob von.
Elements of Police 153
justice 46, 49, 55–6
Justinian, Roman emperor 200

Kafka, Franz 47–8
Kafka's Other Trial: The Letters to Felice.
Canetti, Elias 47
Kant and the Problem of Metaphysics.
Heidegger, Martin 75, 93
Kant, Immanuel: biopolitics 148–9, 163;
communitas 4, 74–5, 79, 87–95, 97,
107, 109; *Conjectures on the Beginning
of Human History* 89; *The Critique of
Judgment* 34, 92; *The Critique of
Practical Reason* 90–1; finitude 125,
133; *Groundwork of the Metaphysics of
Morals* 90; guilt 4, 73; law 87–95; neo-
Kantianism 27, 106; post-Kantianism
124–5; *Religion within the Boundaries
of Mere Reason* 89–90; theodicy 124,
128

Index   235

katechon 123
Kelsen, Hans 23, 112
koinonia 71, 182
Kojève, Alexandre 58–60
Korsgaard, Christine M. 203
Kraus, Karl 48

language: action 48; *communitas* 74;
  development of language 85; health
  and sickness, diagnostic language of
  170; *immunitas* 120; Latin 3, 5, 69–70,
  78, 103, 108, 119; metaphor, as 12;
  obligations, of 55; political language
  37; power, of 44; representation, of 10,
  19; theory of language 12
Latin 3, 5, 69–70, 78, 103, 108, 119
law: *communitas* 10–19, 66–7, 74, 87–93,
  97, 109, 111; constitutional law 27;
  deformalisation of law 207–8;
  disappearance of law 69; ethics 2;
  freedom and the law 89–90; genealogy
  10–19; God's will 22; *immunitas* 6,
  109, 110–18; international law 207–8;
  Kant 87–95; meta-law and law,
  divergence between 52; place of law
  17–18; positive law 17–18, 20–2, 42,
  55; power 114; revenge, monopoly on
  means of 115; socio-historical
  development, law of 62–3;
  thematisation of law 4; theology
  118–19; unpolitical 10–19; violence 6,
  35–6, 111, 113–18; Weil 69, 74,
  111–12 *see also* Roman law
Lecture Courses. Foucault, Michel 150
Lectures on Kant's Political Philosophy.
  Arendt, Hannah 20, 34
legal persons 111–12, 201
Leibniz, Gottfried Wilhelm 123–4
Leiris, Michel 61
Leviathan. Hobbes, Thomas 13–14, 15,
  72–3, 79, 81–3
Leviathan-State 79, 81–3
liberalism 29–30, 160, 165, 167
life: absolutisation 198; bare life 143–6,
  179, 183 ; biopolitics 8, 148, 150,
  154–6, 159–68, 171–2; deformalisation
  of law 207–8; desire 99–100;
  differentiation from life of species

204–5; eugenics 175; factical life and
  biology 182–3; form-of-life 147;
  horizon of life 114; immunisation
  133–4, 156–7, 168–9, 177; *immunitas*
  133–8; negation of life 76;
  normativization 178–9, 192; norm-of-
  life 147, 190–5; phenomenon of life
  103; politics of life 173; power 154–6;
  preservation of life 72, 120; primacy of
  body 185; right to life 150; sacredness
  181; singularity 204–5, 207
The Life of the Mind. Arendt, Hannah 20,
  31–2, 34
literary communism, notion of 65
Locke, John 8, 36, 162–4
Löwith, Karl 157
Luhmann, Niklas 6, 109, 116–17
Luther, Martin 123

management and ownership, separation
  between 50–1
Marburg school of Neo-Kantianism 106
Marcionism 121, 123
Marquard, Odo 121, 123–5
Marxism 50–2
materialism 101, 179–80, 182, 187
Merleau-Ponty, Maurice 142, 184–6, 196
meta-ethics 202–4
meta-law and law, divergence between 42
metaphor 7, 12, 40–2, 120, 134–5
metaphysics 48, 53, 61, 112, 127–8, 145,
  205
mimetic desire and rivalry, theory of 114
Mitsein 96
modernity: biopolitics 143–52, 155,
  158–66, 170, 174, 181, 197;
  Christianity 12–13; first modernity,
  biopolitics of 160–5; first to second
  modernity, transition from 8;
  immunisation 8, 141–2, 157–8, 160,
  170; *immunitas* 106, 145–6;
  individualistic-universalistic model
  3–4; National Socialism 173, 180;
  origin, reactivation of 197; paradigm of
  order 17; political categories 8, 10–11,
  17; rationality 15; secularisation 14, 17;
  self-preservation 145, 159–60;
  sovereignty 149–50, 160, 165;

236 Index

technology 24–5; unpolitical 10–19, 24–6; values 38
Montesquieu, Charles de 36
morality *see* ethics
Moses 97
Moses and Monotheism. Freud, Sigmund 83
motivation 41, 60, 202–3
munus: absolute obligation, as 3; being-in-common 3, 111; biopolitics 199; *communitas* 5, 70–3, 76, 78–80, 88–9, 103–4, 106–8; *donum* 3, 70; *immunitas* 5, 103–4, 107–8, 111; immunisation 158
Musil, Robert 10
mysticism 57, 122
myths 5, 73, 75, 83, 86, 88, 113–14

Nancy, Jean-Luc 64–5, 101, 139
natality 182–3
nation states 135, 185–9, 197
National Socialism: collapse 8, 173, 180, 196; destiny 75–6, 96; economic situation in Germany 50; pseudo-revolutionary, as 50 *see also* National Socialism and biopolitics
National Socialism and biopolitics 172–81; bio-thanatological principles 147; birth, anticipatory suppression of 180, 187–8, 192; concentration camps 179; death 142, 147, 173–9, 188, 196; degeneration 173, 174–8; doctor, position of the 179; double enclosure of the body 8, 142, 146, 173, 179–80, 184–7; eugenics 173, 175–8; genealogy 202; genocide 173, 177–9; German body, health of 174; Great Death 178; immunisation 174–80, 188, 195; *immunitas* 142, 146–7; Marxism 50–1; Nietzsche 65; norm of life 191–2; self-destruction of German body 178; sovereignty 155; thanatopolitics 147, 174–81, 196, 197
natural law 22, 55, 112, 193–5, 200, 205–6
Nazism *see* National Socialism
The Need for Roots. Weil, Simone 56–8
negativity: anthropology 21, 43–5, 46–67; biopolitics 8; *communitas* 56–67, 75;

containment of the negative 7, 118–19; ethics 70; exclusionary inclusion 114; heterodox theology 48–56; history 85; *immunitas* 113; natural law 205–6; self-representation 68–9; transcendence 85; unpolitical 43, 68–9
neutralisation 15–19, 26, 59, 105, 123, 160–1, 190
The New Science of Politics. Voegelin, Eric 28
Nietzsche: An Introduction to the Understanding of his Philosophical Activity. Jaspers, Karl 59
Nietzsche and Philosophy. Deleuze, Gilles 171
Nietzsche et les Fascistes. Bataille, Georges 65
Nietzsche, Friedrich 58–60, 97, 100: biopolitics 142, 148–9, 166–72, 173; Fascists 65; genealogy 148; ideals and values 12; modernity 8, 146; National Socialists 65; *On the Genealogy of Morality* 11–13; secularisation 11; *Truth and Lies in a Non-Moral Sense* 12
nihilism: anthropology 125–8; being-in-common 3; biopolitics 196; *communitas* 3–4, 73, 100, 102; finitude 76–7; genealogy 12–13; *immunitas* 79; modernity 146; passive nihilism 169; secularisation 13
Niobe, myth of 114
Nomos of the Earth in the International Law of the Jus Publicum Europaeum. Schmitt, Carl 25–6
non-knowledge 99–102
non-place, determination of 1–3
nothing-in-common 88–9
nothingness 73–4, 95, 100, 105, 127–9
Numantines, tragedy of the 3, 65–6, 76–7, 100

obligation, notion of 55, 57–8, 206–7
Offenbarkeit (revealability) and *Offerbarung* (revelation) 119
On Revolution. Arendt, Hannah 20, 31–2
On the Genealogy of Morality. Nietzsche, Friedrich 11–13

On Violence. Arendt, Hannah 35–6
ontology 5, 72, 75, 129, 138, 145–6, 198, 205–7
opinion, plurality of 35
oppression 50–3, 128, 178
Oppression and Liberty. Weil, Simone 49, 52–3
order, restoration of 39–40
Origen 121, 123
originary splitting or *'Ur-Teilung'* 97–8
original sin 71–2, 121
The Origins of Totalitarianism. Arendt, Hannah 29–30
ownership 112–13; management and ownership, separation between 50–1; plundering 112

La Part Maudite. Bataille, Georges 65
Patristic literature 71, 122
Paul the Apostle, saint 71, 120–3
perpetual peace, project of 90–1
persecution 82–3
persons: genealogy 201–3; legal persons 111–12, 201; notion of the person 199–203; Roman law 199–201
Phenomenological Interpretation of Kant's Critique of Pure Reason. Heidegger, Martin 75, 93
Phenomenology of Spirit. Hegel, G.W.F. 58
philosophico-anthropological presupposition 158
pity, sense of 87
Plato. *The Statesman* 31
The Play of the Eyes. Canetti, Elias 43, 47–8
Plessner, Helmuth 125–6, 128–31
poetry 39–42, 76, 97, 99
police, science of the 152–4
political anthropology 21, 52, 83–4
Political Romanticism. Schmitt, Carl 14
political theology 14–15, 17, 20–46, 54, 125, 208–9
Political Theology. Four Chapters on the Concept of Sovereignty. Schmitt, Carl 14
The Political Treatise. Spinoza, Baruch 191

polytheism 28, 39
positive law 17–18, 20–2, 42, 55
power: being-in-common 80; biopolitics 152–7, 166; bio-power 151; death 114, 154, 156; freedom 32; government 153; law 114; life 154–6; mediation 20–1; necessity 53; oppression 52–3; pastoral power 152–3; sacredness 62; science of the police 152–4; sovereignty 153; technology 25; unity 83; violence 35–6; will to power 60
Power. Guardini, Romano 25
presupposition, logic of 199
private Roman physicians, immunity of 104–5
proletarian revolution 50–2
property, category of 161–3, 166
Propositions sur le fascisme. Bataille, Georges 64–5
proprium, semantics of 78
punishment 82

race: homogeneity 177; hygiene 176–7
realism and utopianism, oscillation between 26
reality 2, 24–8, 30, 40–1, 49, 53, 56–7, 206
redemption 121, 123
Reformation 123
religion: atheism 22, 58–9; legal system, transfer to 115; neutralisation of religious conflict in Europe 26 *see also* Christianity; God; Jesus Christ; secularisation; theology
Religion within the Boundaries of Mere Reason. Kant, Immanuel 89–90
remembrance 66–7
representation: language 12; metaphor 12, 40–1; modernity 11; representation-image, regime of 13, 40–2, 54, 66; representation-mandate, regime of 13, 16–17, 66; self-representation 68–9; subjectivity 18; unpolitical 10–11, 19, 21, 68–9
res publica christiana 71
resurrection 71, 120, 122–3
revealability 119–20

238 Index

revolution: American Revolution 31–3; foundation 31; French Revolution 31–3, 134–5, 188, 201; historical becoming 38–9; modernity 38; National Socialism as pseudo-revolutionary movement 50; plurality 31–2; potential for revolution 49–52; proletarian revolution 50–2; will, theory of the 32–3

rights: abstract claims 206–7; justice 55–6; obligations, primacy of 206–7; subjectivity 201–2

Roman Catholic Church 20–4, 54

Roman Catholicism and Political Form. Schmitt, Carl 14–15, 23–4

Roman Empire 185–6; Numantines, tragedy of the 3, 65–6, 76–7, 100; private Roman physicians, immunity of 104–5; representation-image, regime of 40–2

Roman law: codification 200, 205; *communitas* 104; *Digest* 205; *homer sacer*, definition of 143; *immunitas* 104; *Institutes* 200, 205; *ius,* property and violence 112; natural law 22, 112, 200, 205–6; objectivism 201; person, notion of the 199–201; political theology 22, 24, 26; secularisation 24; unpolitical 22, 24, 26, 54

Rousseau, Jean-Jacques 4, 73–4, 79, 84–9, 134

sacredness 55, 60–3, 100–1, 120, 181

sacrifice: death 5, 76, 83–4, 101, 120; exclusionary inclusion 114–15; finitude 76–7, 101; God 71; guilt 85; Hobbes 100–1; Jesus Christ 71; law 115, 118; sacredness 100–1; unpolitical 5, 100; violence 114–15

salvation 23, 57, 119, 121, 123

Scanlon, Thomas M. 202–4

Scheler, Max 125–8, 133

Schmitt, Carl: *The Concept of the Political* 14, 66; neutralisation 59; *Nomos of the Earth in the International Law of the Jus Publicum Europaeum* 25–6; *Political Romanticism* 14; political theology 14–15, 17, 20, 22–8, 125;

Political Theology. Four Chapters on the Concept of Sovereignty 14; *Roman Catholicism and Political Form* 14–15, 23–4; *Verfassungslehre* 20, 26–7

Scholastic tradition 122

Schroeder, Mark. *Slaves of Passions* 203

science: biomedicine 5, 7, 25, 104–8, 119; history 53; human sciences 140–1, 192–3; juridical science 179; law, of 112; life sciences 138; National Socialism 174; natural sciences 104, 133; police, of the 152–4; relationship with philosophy 106; social sciences 109, 133, 144; subordination to science 100; transcendence 63

Second Letter to the Thessalonians 121–2

secularisation: aporias 16–17; biopolitics 181; de-formalisation of Christianity 13; genealogy 11–13; God 25; irreversibility 24; juridification of war in Europe 25; modernity 14, 17; neutralisation of religious conflict in Europe 25; neutralisation-secularisation 15–19; place of law 17–18; political theology 14, 22, 24–6, 30; process 11, 20–1, 54; technology 24; totalitarianism 29; unpolitical 11, 22, 24–6, 30

security 28, 131, 159, 161, 164–5

self-destruction 133, 168, 178, 195

self-dissolution: *communitas* 6; exclusionary inclusion 7, 111, 132–3; *immunitas* 7, 110–11, 118, 138, 140, 160, 172, 174, 195; institutions 167; liberalism 165; life 169; modernity 159–60, 172; political and politics, separation between 19; regulatory form 167; theology 119–21

self-preservation 11–12, 81, 142, 145, 158–62, 165, 169

sensus communis 34–5, 91–2

Sièyes, Emmanuel Joseph 134

Simians, Cyborgs, and Women. The Reinvention of Nature. Haraway, Donna 138

Simondon, Gilbert 142, 184, 189–90, 192–3, 196

sin 71–2, 121

Index 239

Slaves of Passion. Schroeder, Mark 203
The Sleepwalkers. Broch, Hermann 38–9, 43
social contract 14, 16, 36, 81, 90–1, 196
social Darwinism 169–70
social sciences 109, 133, 144
socio-historical development, law of 62–3
sociology 15, 17, 61, 193
soft law 208
sovereignty: authority 14, 72, 122; biopolitics 7, 149–51, 153–5, 159–66; death 150, 153, 161; Hobbes 8, 160, 162; modernity 24–5, 149–50, 160, 165; obedience 153; power 25, 153; punishment 82; social contract 14, 81–2; unpolitical 25–6
Soviet Union 50–1, 173, 196
Spinoza, Baruch 191–6
splitting 97–8, 130, 189, 201
state of exception 147
State of Exception. Agamben, Giorgio 142, 147
state of nature: Christianity 72; civil state, transition to 80–4; *communitas* 4, 72–3; death 72, 100–1; desire 160; fear of death 101; Hobbes 4, 72–3, 80, 83–5, 100, 160, 164
The Statesman. Plato 31
sterilisation 177–8
subject, question of the 18–19, 201
subjectivity: *communitas* 4; finitude 64; French Revolution 201; human personality 54–5; hyper-political 18–19; immanence 152; immunisation 108; *immunitas* 138–40; individual rights 201–2; *munus* 107; non-knowledge, experience of 99; sacred and profane, relationship between 61–2; sacrifice 76–7
supernatural 54–7
Sur Nietzsche. Bataille, Georges 60, 63
systems theory 6–7, 109, 118

tangency, idea of 198
taste, reflexive judgment of 91–2
Tauber, Alfred. *The Immune Self* 139
technology 4, 15, 22, 24–5, 110, 137, 139, 142–3, 153

teleology 74, 96
thanatopolitics 174–81, 184, 196, 197–8
theodicy 88–90, 109, 123–5, 128
theology: Christianity 119–24; *communitas* 71; *corpus mysticum* 122; eschatology of redemption 123; heterodoxy 48–56; heresy 121; *immunitas* 118–25; law 118–19; political theology 14–15, 17, 20–46, 54, 125, 208–9; re-theologisation 23–4; self-dissolution 119–21; theio-logy 119; theodicy 88–90, 109, 123–5, 128; unpolitical 20–46
Theory of Religion. Bataille, Georges 76–7, 101
Third Person. Esposito, Roberto 1, 9, 205–6, 208
Tocqueville, Alexis de 144, 164–5
Tönnies, Ferdinand 129
totalitarianism 29–30, 144, 155 *see also* Fascism, National Socialism
Totem and Taboo. Freud, Sigmund 83
trade unions 51
tragedy, will to 60
transcendence: Christianity 28–30, 122; God 28–9, 114; gods and humans, boundary between 114; immanence 27–8, 60, 194–5, 198; law, notion of 74; negativity 85; self-transcendence 114; sovereignty 161; violence 114–15
truth 2, 11–12, 20, 35, 70, 86, 99, 179
Truth and Lies in a Non-Moral Sense. Nietzsche, Friedrich 12

United States Constitution 36–7
unity: civil society 16–17; difference 209; fraternity 188–9; God 71–2; plurality 32; political theology 208–9; power 83; real unity 27; state, of the 27–8; transcendence 27–8; will, theory of the 32, 34–5
universalistic–individualistic model 3–4
unpolitical: anthropology 28, 30, 46–67; aporias 18, 21, 31, 34–7, 69–70; Arendt 20–1, 37–8; Bataille 46, 56–8; boundaries between political and unpolitical 10–11, 16–19, 69; categories 46–7, 65; Christianity 20–3;

communitas 2–3, 10–19, 46–7, 68–77; death 5, 65, 68; formlessness 64–5; genealogy 10–19, 73; interwar Europe 21–2; law 10–19; mode of critique 10–19; modernity 10–19, 24–6; negativity 43, 46–67; non-place, determination of 1–3; order, restoration of 39–40; political, separation from 38–45, 46–7, 54–60; political theology 14, 20–46, 54; representation 10–11, 19, 21, 68–9; sacrifice 5, 100; secularisation 11, 22, 24–6, 30; technology 22, 24–5

Ur-Teilung 97–8

utopianism and realism, oscillation between 26

Valsalva, Antonio Maria 135

values 11–12, 20, 38–9, 207

Le Vent d'Hiver. Caillois, Roger 63

Verfassungslehre. Schmitt, Carl 20, 26–7

violence: *immunitas* 6, 111, 113–18, 131; *ius,* property and violence 112; law 6, 35–6, 111, 113–18; mediation 20–1; power 35–6; sacrifice 114–15; transcendence 114–15

Virgil 39–42

The Visible and the Invisible. Merleau-Ponty, Maurice 184–6

Voegelin, Eric 20, 26–31

voluntarism 36–7, 49, 187

Wall Street Crash of 1929 51

war: bureaucracy 51–2; juridification of war in Europe 25; preparation for war 51; 'war on terror' 180, 196; World War I 26; World War II 24, 26

War and the Illiad. Weil, Simone 53

Warsaw Pact 196

Weber, Max 14–15, 17–18, 157

The Wedding Party. Canetti, Elias 43

Weil, Simone: *communitas* 2–3, 46–59, 69; exclusionary inclusion 111; law 69, 74, 111–12; *The Need for Roots* 56–8; *Oppression and Liberty* 49, 52–3; *War and the Illiad* 53

Weimar Constitution 147

Western metaphysics 145

will: law, will and the 89–90; power, will to 60; theology 123; theory of the will 32–5, 49; tragedy, will to 60

World War I 26

World War II 24, 26